STONES
AND
STORIES

STONES AND STORIES

An Introduction to Archaeology and the Bible

Don C. Benjamin

Fortress Press

Minneapolis

STONES AND STORIES
An Introduction to Archaeology and the Bible

Excerpts from *Old Testament Parallels*, by Victor H. Matthews and Don C. Benjamin, Copyright © 2006 by Victor H. Matthews and Don C. Benjamin. Paulist Press, Inc., New York/Mahwah, N.J. Reprinted by permission of Paulist Press, Inc. www.paulistpress.com.

Artwork on pp. 34, 48, 61, 65, 90, 97, 106, 107, 115, 116, 146, 159, 160, 161, 163, 205, 254, 264 by Joe Vaughan; illustrations on pp. 23, 79, 164, 166, 167, 173, 174, 175, 180, 188, 190, 210, 231, 233, 257 by Luigi Galante.

Cover image: Phoenician model of a baker. Clay (900–800 B.C.E.) Israel Museum, Jerusalem. Photo: Erich Lessing/ArtResource, N.Y. Stone relief: © Clark Dunbar/Corbis
Cover design: brad norr design
Book design: HK Scriptorium, Inc.

Additional student and instructor resources for this textbook can be found at fortresspress.com/benjamin.

Library of Congress Cataloging-in-Publication Data

Benjamin, Don C.
    Stones and stories : an introduction to archaeology and the Bible / Don C. Benjamin. — 1st ed.
      p. cm.
    Includes bibliographical references and index.
    ISBN 978-0-8006-2357-9 (alk. paper)
    1. Bible. O.T.—Antiquities. I. Title.
  BS621.B46 2009
  220.9'3—dc22

              2009010353

The paper used in this publication meets the minimum requirements of American National Standard for Information Sciences—Permanence of Paper for Printed Library Materials, ANSI Z329.48-1984.

Manufactured in Canada

14 13 12 11 10 1 2 3 4 5 6 7 8 9 10

Brief Contents

Contents

Contents

Contents

Contents

Preface

Studying and writing are solitary, but not lonely, crafts. My studying and writing days are full of quiet conversations with colleagues from whose writings I learn, and with past and present students to whose questions I listen.

Stones and Stories is dedicated to all my students—graduates and undergraduates at universities, seminarians at divinity schools, adult learners in religious congregations—and general readers. Thank you for motivation, for your inspiration, and for your companionship on the journey of learning.

In the bibliography of *Stones and Stories* I acknowledge my colleagues who have taught me about archaeology and the Bible. I also want to thank those who made time to talk with me, in passing or at length, about this project: Kelley Hays-Gilpin (Northern Arizona University), Shelley Wachsman (Texas A&M University), Elizabeth Bloch-Smith (St. Joseph's University, Philadelphia), Oded Borowski (Emory University), Victor H. Matthews (Missouri State University), Douglas R. Clark (La Sierra University), Carol Meyers (Duke University), Leslie Hoppe (Catholic Theological Union), Steve Falconer (Arizona State University), Beth A. Nikhai (University of Arizona), Brian B. Schmidt (University of Michigan), William H. Krieger (University of Rhode Island), Miguel A. Aguilera (Arizona State University), John W. Baker (Houston, Texas), William G. Dever (University of Arizona), P. M. Michele Davaiu (University of Toronto), James K. Hoffmeier (Trinity International University),

David Noel Freedman, Eric H. Cline (George Washington University), and John Kaltner (Rhodes College).

The generous gift of time that colleagues gave to me is a wonderful example of the rich collegiality that can take place in the world of academics. They do not need to agree with me to spend time with me. They do not need to endorse *Stones and Stories* to take an interest in it.

Nor could I have completed *Stones and Stories* if the Hayden Interlibrary Loan Librarians (Arizona State University) had not kept the books coming, and if my friend Burak Kayhan had not kept my computer running.

Finally, I am grateful to my editors at Augsburg Fortress Publishers: Michael West, Neil Elliott, and Joshua Messner. Their engagement with me during the process of writing and rewriting *Stones and Stories* has made it a better book.

Stones and Stories began as a conversation with Niels C. Nielsen Jr., who founded and chaired the Department of Religious Studies at Rice University, where I got my first real teaching job. He was one of those remarkable colleagues who enriched my life as a scholar and teacher in many ways. One day, during a discussion of the program in biblical and Near Eastern studies I was creating for the department, Nielsen asked me: "Don, have you ever been to the Holy Land?" He was a firm believer in travel as learning.

"No, Niels," I answered, "I haven't."

"You need to go!" he told me.

"I know."

A couple of semesters passed, and I still had no plans to travel. "What are you doing about getting to the Holy Land?" Niels asked.

"Niels," I confessed, "when I was a student, I was too poor to travel, now that I am teaching I am too busy."

The third time we had a conversation about going to the world of the Bible, Niels called me into his office and announced, "Don, I have a grant of $10,000 for you. Do you think you could spend it in the Holy Land?"

I was off to travel in Egypt, Jordan, and Israel. With the grant money I was able to design a travel study program called *The Bible: On Location,* and a classroom course called "Archaeology and the Bible," which I taught and continue to teach. My travel, research, and teaching are the foundation of *Stones and Stories.*

BIBLE, OLD TESTAMENT, NEW TESTAMENT

Many Christians use the word *Bible* to refer to the Old Testament and the New Testament. In *Stones and Stories: An Introduction to Archaeology and the Bible* I use *Bible* as a synonym for Old Testament. Therefore this introduction to archaeology and the Bible focuses primarily on the excavation of Old Testament sites, not New Testament locations.

Stones and Stories explains the different schools or theories of how to excavate. It is not a survey of sites. Sites such as Gezer, Arad, and Qumran are described to demonstrate various theories of excavation. I hope instructors will choose other sites as well from both the Common Era and before the Common Era to show their students how to apply these theories.

DATES AND SPELLINGS

Spellings for the names of rulers of Egypt and dates for their reigns in *Stones and Stories* follow John Baines and Jaromír Málek, *Atlas of Ancient Egypt* (New York: Facts on File, 1980).

Dates before the Common Era are marked B.C.E. and during the Common Era, C.E. So, for example, the Dead Sea Scrolls were copied between 200 B.C.E. and 68 C.E.

Spellings for the names of rulers of Mesopotamia and dates for their reigns follow Michael Roaf, *Cultural Atlas of Mesopotamia and the Ancient Near East* (New York: Facts on File, 1990).

Spellings for the names of the rulers of Israel and Judah and dates for their reigns follow J. Maxwell Miller and John H. Hayes, *A History of Ancient Israel and Judah,* 2d ed. (Louisville: Westminster John Knox, 2006).

A *tell* (Hebrew: *tel*; Arabic: *tell, tall*) is an artificial hill or mound formed by the eroded debris from an ancient settlement. Spellings for sites follow Anson F. Rainey and R. Steven Notley, *The Sacred Bridge: Carta's Atlas of the Biblical World* (Jerusalem: Carta, 2006). If Rainey and Notley give both spellings, for example, *Tell Arad* and *Tel Arad,* or do not list the site in their index, I use *Tell* or *Tall* if the site is in an Arabic-speaking country, *Tel* if the site is in Israel.

Archaeologists working in the world of the Bible created a calendar using the raw materials used for tools and weapons, for example, *Stone Age, Chalcolithic* (Greek: *chalco* = copper; *lithic* = stone) *Age, Bronze Age, Iron Age.* The dates for these periods reflect the consensus of early archaeologists on when these materials first came into use. Subsequent research has made modifications in these dates, but the calendar dates have not been changed. Dates for the Archaeological Calendar in *Stones and Stories* follow *The Anchor*

Bible Dictionary, edited by David Noel Freedman (New York: Doubleday, 1992). See p. 3.

TRANSLATIONS

Citations from the Bible in *Stones and Stories* follow the numbering of the New Revised Standard Version (1989). The translations are mine. There are two kinds of translations. One tries to produce a faithful picture—a literal or functional equivalent—of the original language in a new language. The NRSV, for example, is such a translation. These translations emphasize the text. My translations are dynamic equivalents. I focus on the audience and try and use language that will help them better understand what they are reading.

The titles for the various traditions from the Bible that appear in *Stones and Stories* and the text divisions are my own, not those of the NRSV. For example, I identify a "Trial of Nineveh" and the text division as Nah 3:1-7. The NRSV titles the passage "Oracles against Nineveh" and identifies the text division as Nah 2:1—3:19. Likewise, I identify a hero story that I title "A Woman Delivers Thebez from Abimelech" and identify the text division as Judg 9:50–57. The NRSV titles the passage "The Downfall of Abimelech" and identifies the text division as Judg 9:22–57. My titles and text divisions are based on the form of the tradition and the intention of the genre to which it belongs, rather than on the content of the passage. The intention of the genre *hero story* is to describe divine deliverance, so I always use the verb *deliver* in the title. I also identify the hero, here *a woman*; the enemy, here *Abimelech*; and the victim, here *Thebez*.

During the Late Bronze Age (1500-1200 B.C.E.), the Hebrews were displaced households (Akkadian: *'apiru*) whose common bond was not ethnic but social. War and famine were common causes of their social dislocation. These Hebrews often fought as mercenaries or supported their household by raiding.

The Hebrews who founded the villages in the hills west of the Jordan River Valley and north of Jerusalem at the beginning of the Iron Age (1200–1100 B.C.E.) were from cities along the coast, not nomads from the desert. What these villagers had in common was that they were social survivors who fled the famine, plague, and war that brought the Bronze Age to an end. They were not warriors; they were farmers and herders. They left centralized, surplus states and created a decentralized, subsistence village federation called *Israel*. Politically these villagers were *Israelites;* culturally they were *Hebrews*.

The Hebrews' name for their divine patron is written with the four consonants: *yod he waw he* (YHWH; Exod 2:23–4:23). Scholars label this name the *Tetragrammaton* (Greek: *tetra* = four; *gramma* = letter). Originally, Hebrews probably pronounced the Tetragrammaton as *Yahweh*. Eventually, observant Jews stopped pronouncing or writing the name. This ritual of silence reminded them that the name of their divine patron was too holy for them to speak or write (Exod 20:7; Ps 68:4).

As a substitute, Jews refer to *Yahweh* simply as *Lord* (Hebrew: *'Adonai*) or as *The Name* (Hebrew: *HaShem*). When scribes began to punctuate or point biblical scrolls, they wrote the vowels above and below the lines of consonants to help cantors sing the words correctly. The Tetragrammaton (the consonants YHWH) was punctuated with the vowels for *'Adonai*, not the vowels for *Yahweh*.

Preface

Christian scribes unfamiliar with the Jewish convention of punctuating YHWH with the vowels from 'Adonai (AOAI) wrote out the name as Y-A-H-O-W-AI or *Jehovah*. *Jehovah* appears as the divine name in the King James Version of the Bible and is used as the name for God by the Jehovah's Witnesses tradition of Christianity (http://www.watchtower.org/e/na/article_01.htm). Most English translations of the Bible today, however, use *LORD* rather than *Yahweh*. Similarly, some Jewish and Christian scholars substitute the consonants—YHWH—for the divine name (Henry O. Thompson 1992; Ringgren, Freedman, O'Connor 1986).

Like the majority of scholars, I write *Yahweh* when I use the proper name for the divine patron of ancient Israel in *Stones and Stories* (Mark S. Smith 1990: 1–40; 2001: 67–82). One practical reason for this convention is that when I ask students to read aloud, they can pronounce *Yahweh*; they cannot pronounce *YHWH*. In my experience, observant Jewish students comfortably substitute *the Name, Lord,* or *HaShem* for *Yahweh* when they read aloud in class.

GLOSSARY

The glossary defines common technical terms used in *Stones and Stories*. Each term is also defined when it is first used in the book itself. *The Concise Oxford Dictionary of Archaeology* by Timothy Darvill (2nd ed.; New York: Oxford University Press, 2008) is a good general reference for terms not covered in the glossary here.

Compound technical terms in *Stones and Stories*—for example, *guffa*, bucket—are made up of two words with the same meaning. One word is English, the other is not. For example, *guffa* is the Arabic word for *bucket*. These compounds are a tool for learning the vocabulary of archaeology. Archaeologists would simply say: *Be sure the tag on every guffa (not guffa bucket) of pottery is filled out completely and correctly before sending it to the ceramicist to be read.*

Enjoy using *Stones and Stories* in your adventure to understand better and to appreciate the world of the Bible as much as I have enjoyed writing it! Your time and your effort will bring your Bible to life.

Additional student and instructor resources
for this textbook can be found at fortresspress.com/benjamin.

List of Illustrations

List of Illustrations

PREVIEW: INTRODUCTION

- The Task of Introductions
- Types of Introductions: Organized around
    - Archaeological Calendar
    - The Canon of the Bible
    - Daily Life
    - Archaeological Sites
    - Travel
    - History of Archaeology
    - Popular Interest
- Organization of This Introduction
    - Popular Archaeology
    - Cultural History
    - Annales Archaeology
    - Processual Archaeology
    - Post-Processual Archaeology

Introduction

THE TASK OF INTRODUCTIONS TO ARCHAEOLOGY AND THE BIBLE

The three Rs of archaeology are to recover, to read, and to reconstruct the cultural property of now-extinct cultures (Magness 2002, 4–13; Darvill 2002). Archaeologists listen to the stories that stones—like architecture, art, pottery, jewelry, weapons, and tools—have to tell. *Stones and Stories: An Introduction to Archaeology and the Bible* describes how archaeologists listen, what they are hearing, and what a difference it makes for understanding the Bible.

Archaeology is not the plunder of the treasures of ancient cultures, nor proving that the Bible's descriptions of people and events are historically accurate, nor a legal remedy for determining which people today have a legal right to the land.

Until the eighteenth century, the Bible was the primary source for understanding the worlds—and the worldviews—of ancient Israel. Both archaeologists and biblical scholars treated the Bible as history and worked to demonstrate that the history in the stories was reliable. Then the stones began to tell stories that were different from the Bible. There were stories in the stones that were not in the Bible; and there were stories in the Bible that were not in the stones (Finkelstein and Silberman 2001, 2006; Dave Davies 2006).

Despite the perception of conflict between archaeology and the Bible that so often captures public attention, archaeologists and biblical scholars have learned a great deal together about the world of the Bible—and about the Bible itself. Together archaeology and the Bible unlock the most profound responses to the challenges that confront humans who want not only to make a living but also to make a difference in the world that is their home.

> **Archaeology** *is the recovery, interpretation, and reconstruction of the cultural property of now-extinct cultures.*

Archaeology in the world of the Bible does not prove the Bible wrong, any more than biblical archaeology proves the Bible right. Archaeology offers new ways of defining the Bible in relation to its own world, and of using it more effectively in the world today. Archaeology provides different perspectives on the way the people of ancient Israel responded to their experiences, and consequently archaeology provides models for responding differently to experience today.

Culture is the tool that humans use to understand and respond to their experiences—good and bad. Every stone tells a story about how a now-gone people looked at their world and responded to their experiences. Archaeologists are the curators of this amazing legacy.

Archaeologists today have recovered more artifacts from the world of the Bible than were available since the great cultures that produced them vanished. Yet, although there are introductions to Bible, and there are introductions to

> **Biblical archaeology** *is a subdis-cipline of cultural history. William Foxwell Albright launched the biblical archaeology movement to demon-strate that the Bible was histori-cally accurate. For example, in 1922 Leonard Woolley was directing an excavation of the royal tombs at Ur (Arabic: Tell al Muqayyar) north of Basra (Iraq), when he uncovered an eight-foot-thick layer of clean clay. He considered this layer unmistakable evidence that the flood stories in the book of Genesis (Gen 6:1—11:26) are historically accurate.*

archaeology, there is still a need for a readable, affordable, and portable introduction to archaeol-ogy and the Bible.

There is also a need for an introduction to archaeology and the Bible that celebrates what biblical archaeologists have accomplished and continue to accomplish. Popular controversies like the minimalist-maximalist debate often make it seem as if archaeologists working in the world of the Bible have learned nothing of value for understanding the Bible.

Admittedly, biblical archaeologists have not definitively demonstrated that the biblical tra-ditions about Israel's ancestors—the patriarchs and matriarchs in Genesis—and the biblical tra-ditions about the appearance of the Hebrews in Syria-Palestine—are history. Nonetheless, archae-ologists have learned a great deal.

Maximalist scholars—such as William G. Dever—regard the Bible as the heritage of a Hebrew culture that first appeared in the hills north of Jerusalem after 1200 B.C.E. Minimalist scholars—such as Niels Peter Lemche—regard the Bible as the ingenious strategy of an elite

community of Jews who were trying to prevent the assimilation of Judaism into the dominant Greco-Roman culture after 333 B.C.E.

WAYS TO ORGANIZE INTRODUCTIONS TO ARCHAEOLOGY AND THE BIBLE

The need for a good book is clear; how to write that book is not (Dessel 2003, 67–98). There are introductions to archaeology organized around the archaeological calendar, the canon of the Bible, daily life in the world of the Bible, archaeo-logical sites, travel, the history of archaeology, and popular interest.

Introductions organized around the archaeo-logical calendar include *Archaeology of the Land of the Bible, 10,000–586 B.C.E.* (1992) by Amihay Mazar and *Archaeology of the Land of the Bible: The Assyrian, Babylonian, and Persian Periods, 732–332 B.C.E.* (2001) by Ephraim Stern. Mazar's work is part of the Anchor Bible Reference Library and is a commonly used textbook for introductory courses in archaeology and the Bible. Mazar chooses one or more sites to describe the cultures of each archae-ological period. The Carmel caves and the city of Jericho, for example, are exhibits for the Neolithic period (10,000–4,000 B.C.E.). Chapter outlines, however, are thematic. Mazar summarizes what material remains reveal about settlement planning, domestic and monumental architecture, farming

> The **"maximalist"** *approach to the Bible accepts much of the basic outline of history and culture as presented in the biblical books. The* **"minimalist"** *approach is skeptical of the historical value of the biblical material and relies on other written sources and archaeology to recon-struct the history of Israel.*

and herding, trade, pottery, tools and weapons, liturgical art, and burials.

The Archaeology of Ancient Israel (1992), edited by Amnon Ben-Tor, also uses the archaeological calendar as an overall outline for the book, which covers the Neolithic period to Iron Age III. Some chapters also follow the archaeological calendar. Other chapters, however, are outlined thematically.

The Archaeology of Society in the Holy Land (1995–1998), edited by Thomas E. Levy, combines themes with the archaeological calendar as an outline for this anthology from thirty contributors, all of whom follow some form of the Annales School of Archaeology.

A History of Ancient Israel and Judah (2006), by J. Maxwell Miller and John H. Hayes, also uses the archaeological calendar as an outline. Hayes and Miller make careful use of archaeology to assess and revise the history that William Foxwell Albright (1891–1971) proposed and which is reflected in works such as *A History of Israel* (1959–2000) by John Bright (1908–1995). Albright's and Bright's histories of Israel used archaeology to demonstrate the historical reliability of the Bible. Hayes and Miller, in contrast, use archaeology to evaluate and to interpret the biblical traditions.

Kathleen M. Kenyon (1906–1978) published *The Bible and Recent Archaeology* (1978) shortly

ARCHAEOLOGICAL CALENDAR	
Paleolithic	25,000–10,000 B.C.E.
Mesolithic	10,000–8000 B.C.E.
Pre-Pottery Neolithic A (PPNA)	8000–7000 B.C.E.
Pre-Pottery Neolithic B (PPNB)	7000–6000 B.C.E.
Pottery Neolithic A (PNA)	6000–5000 B.C.E.
Pottery Neolithic B (PNB or Early Chalcolithic)	5000–3800 B.C.E.
Chalcolithic (or Late Chalcolithic)	3800–3400 B.C.E.
Early Bronze I	3400–3100 B.C.E.
Early Bronze II	3100–2650 B.C.E.
Early Bronze III	2650–2350 B.C.E.
Early Bronze IV	2350–2000 B.C.E.
Middle Bronze I	2000–1800 B.C.E.
Middle Bronze II	1800–1650 B.C.E.
Middle Bronze III	1650–1550/1500 B.C.E.
Late Bronze IA	1500–1450 B.C.E.
Late Bronze IB	1450–1400 B.C.E.
Late Bronze IIA	1400–1300 B.C.E.
Late Bronze IIB	1300–1200 B.C.E.
Iron Age IA	1200–1100 B.C.E.
Iron Age IB	1100–1000 B.C.E.
Iron Age IC	1000–900 B.C.E.
Iron Age IIA	900–800 B.C.E.
Iron Age IIB	800–722 B.C.E.
Iron Age IIC	722–586 B.C.E.
Iron Age III	586–539/500 B.C.E.
Persian Period	539/500–323 B.C.E.
Hellenistic Period	323–37 B.C.E.
Roman Period	37 B.C.E.–324 C.E.
Byzantine Period	324–640 C.E.

before her death. P. Roger Moorey (1937–2004), director of the Ashmolean Museum at Oxford, issued a revised edition of these short essays in 1987. The book follows the archaeological calendar from the Bronze Age (3500 B.C.E.) to the Roman period.

Other introductions are organized around the canon of the Bible. The Anchor Bible Commentary Series, launched in 1956 by William Foxwell Albright and David Noel Freedman (1922–2008), promised to make available all the significant advances in languages, literatures, and archaeology that bear on the interpretation of the Bible. Their goal was to create a common body of knowledge for understanding the Bible to be shared by scholars and the general public.

Philip J. King also published two volumes using a canonical outline: *Amos, Hosea, Micah: An Archaeological Commentary* (1988) and *Jeremiah: An Archaeological Companion* (1993). The chapters of both volumes, however, are arranged thematically. After an introductory essay on the relationship of archaeology and biblical studies, for example, King provides a biography of Jeremiah and an outline of the contents of the book of Jeremiah. Then there are chapters demonstrating what archaeologists have learned about the history and the geography of the period, the political relationship of Edom and Judah, writing, worship, burials, farming, and crafts. Both works use archaeology for a better understanding of the social world of the Bible.

> The **canon of the Bible** is the list of books that are accepted as authoritative scripture. The enumeration of books included in the canon differs somewhat according to different traditions.

Yet other archaeological introductions are organized around daily life in the world of the Bible. In *Life in Biblical Israel* (2001), Philip J. King and Lawrence E. Stager use the kind of thematic outline of the social world of ancient Israel that King used in his archaeological commentaries. This well-illustrated book is a careful description of daily life based on the post-processual archaeology of the family carried out by Stager (1985: 1–35). After introducing the archaeology of daily life, they discuss the household, farming, herding, the state, clothing, music, writing, and worship. The book is a careful description of daily life based on the post-processual archaeology of the family done by Stager (1985).

The Religions of Ancient Israel: A Synthesis of Parallactic Approaches (2001), by Ziony Zevit, is an anthology of essays using archaeology to reconstruct Hebrew faith practice. The outline of the book is thematic. Essays reconstruct places of worship and liturgical furniture. They also describe the significance of inscriptions at sanctuaries, how the Hebrews describe their own worship, how outsiders describe Hebrew worship, and the names used by Hebrews for their divine patron.

The four volumes of *Civilizations of the Ancient Near East* (1995), edited by Jack M. Sasson, also follow a thematic outline using anthropology. The first volume begins with an essay on the discipline of Near Eastern studies as well as essays on the environment and population in the world of the Bible. Sasson groups the essays around ten themes. There are sections, for example, reconstructing social institutions such as the economy, trade, technology, art, science, and writing. Among the concluding essays is "Assessing the Past through Anthropological Archaeology" by Frank Hole.

Other resources are organized around archaeological sites. Encyclopedias like *The New Encyclopedia of Archaeological Excavations in the Holy Land* (1993), edited by Ephraim Stern, are site specific. They describe a single site, stratum by stratum, using material remains to reconstruct the cultures of each archaeological period. The profile of Bab edh-Dhra by R. Thomas Schaub, for example, identifies the site geographically on the eastern shore of the Dead Sea in Jordan today (see http://www.nd.edu/~edsp/personnel.html) and a brief history of excavations there. He then describes the material remains from the Paleolithic period, the Neolithic period, the Chalcolithic period, the Early Bronze Age IA, Early Bronze Age IB, Early

Bronze Age IC, Early Bronze Age II, Early Bronze Age III, and Late Early Bronze Age II or Early Bronze Age IV (Stern 1993, 1:130–36).

Originally, the five-volume *Oxford Encyclopedia of Archaeology in the Near East* (1997), edited by Eric M. Meyers with 560 contributors, was to be a one-volume introduction to archaeology and the Bible modeled on the *Biblisches Reallexikon* (1937–1977) by Kurt Galling. Four hundred fifty of the 1,125 entries are site reports from Syria-Palestine to Iran, Anatolia to Arabia, including Egypt, Ethiopia, Cyprus, North Africa, Morocco, Malta, and Sardinia. These reports are the basis for an additional 650 articles on geography (Ethiopia, Nubia, North Africa) and everyday life (farming, herding, households, medicine, clothing, and diet). There are also entries on the environment, the economies of the peoples of the world of the Bible—glass making, shipbuilding, and metalworking. Finally, there are entries on archaeological theory, methods, and practice: new archaeology, underwater archaeology, survey archaeology, salvage archaeology, development and archaeology, museums, ethics and archaeology, ideology and archaeology, nationalism and archaeology, tourism and archae-

A model of brickmakers, ca. 1900 B.C.E. Found at Beni Hassan. Brooklyn Museum.

ology. Biblical archaeology is described in the larger context of archaeology in the Near East.

Geography is the focus for introductions to archaeology and the Bible such as *The Traveler's Key to Ancient Egypt, Revised: A Guide to the Sacred Places of Ancient Egypt* (1995) by John West. West begins with a discussion of the history of ancient Egypt and the history of archaeology in Egypt, and then moves from north to south along the Nile River describing, for example, the antiquities on the Giza Plain, at Saqqara, Memphis, Beni Hassan, Luxor, Abydos, Dendera, Edfu, Aswan, and Abu Simbel.

In *The Holy Land: An Archaeological Guide from Earliest Times to 1700* (1980; 3rd rev. ed., 1992) Jerome Murphy-O'Connor also follows a geographical outline. He begins with a description of sites related to the Bible in Jerusalem and then alphabetically covers sites throughout Israel.

Journalist Bruce Feiler used a geographical outline to chart his reverse pilgrimage through the world of the Bible. *Walking the Bible: A Journey by Land through the Five Books of Moses* (2001) was inspired not by his faith but rather by a search for his faith. With archaeologist Avner Goren, Feiler traveled Israel, Jordan, Turkey, Egypt, and the Palestinian territories, retracing the steps of Abraham, Moses, Aaron, and Jacob in the Torah.

Some introductions are organized around the history of archaeology. *Benchmarks in Time and Culture: An Introduction to Palestinian Archaeology* (1988) edited by Joel F. Drinkard Jr., Gerald L. Mattingly, and Miller is an anthology of twenty-three essays dedicated to Joseph A. Callaway. Part 1 presents histories of the major national schools of archaeology in Syria-Palestine. Part 2 outlines the methods and techniques used in archaeology today. Part 3 discusses selected areas where archaeology has been integrated in order to bring about historical-cultural syntheses.

Neil A. Silberman uses a political outline in *Digging for God and Country* (1982). He reports, for example, on how archaeology became a tool for empire building. Napoleon used archaeology in Egypt to define his empire as the direct descendant of the empire of Alexander and the empires of the pharaohs (Silberman 1982, 10–17). Similarly, Wilhelm II (1888–1918) challenged British supremacy in the Middle East by offering the Ottoman Empire of Abdul Hamid (1842–1918) technical and financial support to build a railway from Constantinople to Palestine, to build a German Lutheran Church of the Redeemer adjacent to the Holy Sepulchre, and a German Catholic Monastery and Church of the Dormition of Mary. In return, the Deutscher Palästina Verein was given permission to conduct inaugural excavations at the coveted sites of Megiddo, Jericho, Jerusalem, the Roman Baalbek in Lebanon, and Galilean synagogues from the first century of the Common Era and to finish mapping the land east of the Jordan River. Consequently, archaeological, and therefore political, supremacy in the world of the Bible passed from Britain to Germany (Silberman 1982, 161–70).

Rachel Hallote combines both politics and biography to outline *Bible, Map and Spade: The American Palestine Exploration Society, Frederick Jones Bliss and the Forgotten Story of Early American Biblical Archaeology* (2006). Hallote studies the American Palestine Exploration Society sponsored by Syrian Protestant College, now the American University of Beirut, and the work of Frederick J. Bliss (1859–1937) and other pioneering American archaeologists and their political agendas during the years 1850–1900. Because Bliss worked for the British Palestine Exploration Fund for a decade, many scholars downplayed his American nationality and sensibilities, as well as his achievements as an archaeologist.

In *American Archaeology in the Mideast: A History of the American Schools of Oriental Research* (1983) Philip J. King anchors his story of the American Schools of Oriental Research in the biographies of Edward Robinson (1794–1863), Charles Clermont-Ganneau (1846–1923), William Foxwell Albright (1891–1971), James H. Breasted (1865–1935), Nelson Glueck (1900–1971), G. Ernest Wright (1909–1974), Millar Burrows (1889–1980), G. Lankester Harding, Roland de Vaux (1903–1971), Carl H. Kraeling (1897–1966), Kathleen M. Kenyon (1906–1978), Yigael Yadin (1917–1984), A. Henry Detweiler (1906–1970), James B. Pritchard (1909–1997), Callaway, Paul W. Lapp (1930–1970), William G. Dever, H. Dunscombe Colt, Frank Moore Cross, and other notable excavators who worked in the world of the Bible before 1980.

Finally, some introductions are organized around popular interest. The ongoing *Mysteries of Bible* series on the History Channel uses a hot-topics outline. This *what you always wanted to know about archaeology and the Bible but were afraid to ask* approach starts with the inquiring minds of the television-watching public and uses archaeology to both answer and intrigue. The producers promise to reveal to the audience the secrets that the guardians of religious traditions do not want their followers to know.

Digging Up the Bible: The Stories Behind the Great Archaeological Discoveries in the Holy Land (1980) by Moshe Pearlman also uses the hot-topics outline. Its strategy is kiss-and-tell. Sometimes, in almost tabloid fashion, Pearlman tells readers the story behind the story of de Vaux, Robinson, William Matthew Flinders Petrie, Jean F. Champollion, Henry Creswicke Rawlinson, Paul E. Botta, and Austen H. Layard—ending eventually with Kathleen Kenyon in Jerusalem and Yigael Yadin at Masada.

From Eden to Exile: Unraveling Mysteries of the Bible (2007) by Eric H. Cline is a print companion to the National Geographic television series *Science of the Bible*. Jesus is the focus of *Sci-*

ence of the Bible; the focus of *From Eden to Exile* is ancient Israel. Hot topics create the book's outline: the Garden of Eden, Noah's ark, Sodom and Gomorrah, Moses and the exodus, Joshua and the battle of Jericho, the ark of the covenant, and the ten lost tribes of Israel.

In addition, each chapter is outlined by hot topics. "Moses and the Exodus," for example, asks: *Did the exodus take place? When did the exodus take place? Was the exodus a single event or a gradual process? Who was the pharaoh of the exodus? How many Hebrews made the exodus? What kinds of disasters were the plagues? What caused the plagues? How was the Red Sea divided? What were the Ten Commandments?*

The book is Cline's effort to insert archaeologists and biblical scholars into the media market. If archaeologists ignore the notorious claims made by a growing number of unqualified individuals, Cline argues, these pundits will enjoy unchallenged influence over the public understanding of the relationship of archaeology and the Bible.

This book, *Stones and Stories: An Introduction to Archaeology and the Bible*, is a companion volume to *Old Testament Parallels: Laws and Stories from the Ancient Near East*, which Victor H. Matthews and I authored (now in its third revised and enlarged edition, 2006). *Old Testament Parallels* deals with verbal art—the languages and literatures of the world of the Bible; *Stones and Stories* deals with the other fascinating artifacts recovered from that same world. As William Foxwell Albright, the father of biblical archaeology, wrote, *"writing without artifacts is like flesh without a skeleton, and artifacts without writing are a skeleton without flesh"* (Albright 1969, 2).

For a long time biblical archaeologists were more committed to the practice of fieldwork than

Letter from Megiddo, ca. 1400 B.C.E. Brooklyn Museum.

to the theory of archaeology. The two most significant accomplishments of biblical archaeologists are the development of a ceramic calendar and the development of a scientific method of excavating and recording material remains one layer of settlement at a time (Dever 1988, 339).

Nonetheless, biblical archaeology still needs *"a deliberate and profound intellectual reorientation—the development of a systematic body of theory as this was understood in other branches of archaeology or in the social sciences generally"* (Dever 1997a, 1:316). Theory determines practice, and there really is no such thing as just digging and letting "the pots speak" (Hodder and Hutson 2003, 16). Artifacts speak only when they are questioned (Stager 1985, 1; Ricoeur 1980, 17). The answers that archaeologists get are shaped by the questions they ask. Biblical archaeologists all make assumptions about their sites and have implicit research designs for their excavations. The task today is to organize clearly what is taken for granted into a theory of biblical archaeology that can be easily understood and applied consistently to the material remains. Therefore, *Stones and Stories* is outlined by the theories of archaeology that developed during the nineteenth and twentieth centuries: Popular archaeology (part 1), cultural history (part 2), Annales archaeology (part 3), processual archaeology (part 4) and post-processual archaeology (part 5). This schools-of-archaeology approach parallels the outline of the widely used general introduction to archaeology: *Reading the Past: Current Approaches to Interpretation in Archaeology* (2003) by Hodder and Hutson.

Schools of archaeology are created by the questions that archaeologists ask to interpret the significance of the artifacts they recover (Hodder and Hutson 2003: 20). Each school is a blend of

Scribe reviewing an inventory, relief from the tomb of Kanofer, pharaoh's minister for foreign lands. Limestone; Giza; 2630–2524 B.C.E. Museum of Fine Arts, Boston.

material and ideal questions. Material questions are about the ritual of making things—about what the peoples of the past did with their raw materials. Ideal questions are about the worldviews of the people who make things—about how the peoples of the past explained their experiences in their artifacts.

For a long time biblical archaeologists built too few networks with their colleagues excavating other cultures in other parts of the world. Therefore *Stones and Stories* also emphasizes the importance of integrating archaeology throughout the world into the world of the Bible. The work of Fernand Braudel (1902–1985), Lewis R. Binford, and Ian Hodder needs to be as familiar to students of archaeology and the Bible as the work of Albright, Kenyon, and Dever.

Academic disciplines like archaeology are paradigms based on research that both solves problems and raises new problems and proposes new theories (Kuhn 1970). Paradigms are not only theories but also a consensus about what works among those in any discipline. When paradigms no longer evaluate evidence accurately or produce effective solutions, they shift. Each of the five parts

of *Stones and Stories* represents a paradigm shift in how and why to excavate the world of the Bible.

Part 1: School of Popular Archaeology

The School of Popular Archaeology identifies a diverse family of pilgrims, emperors, travelers, antiquities dealers, and missionaries who left their homes for the world of the Bible. They were inspired more by passion than by science. Yet, despite what were certainly undisciplined approaches by today's standards, their legacy to archaeology and the Bible remains significant.

The archaeology of antiquities dealers, for example, discusses the adventures of Giovanni B. Belzoni (1778–1823) in the Valley of the Pharaohs—the Valley of the Kings—and what these excavations revealed about the complex and sophisticated understanding of the afterlife in Egypt, in stark contrast to the minimalist view of afterlife in the Bible. It also reviews the ethical issues raised by the lifetime of collecting by Moshe Dayan (1915–1981). Should scholars, universities, and museums buy or accept artifacts of unknown origin from collectors regardless of their value for better understanding the world of the Bible? The chapter concludes with a discussion of the proposal by Roderick McIntosh and Susan McIntosh, the excavators of Jenne-jeno in Mali (Africa), that archaeologists seriously consider negotiating with *good collectors*—antiquities dealers who promote scholarship and national pride by acquiring and selling cultural legacies.

Part 2: School of Cultural History

The School of Cultural History chronicles the ideas and events of the rich and famous men reflected in unique political, diplomatic, or military events. It aims to reconstruct what happened and why it happened. Biblical archaeologists are, by and large, cultural historians. They want to reconstruct the significant events that took place at a site and to identify the causes of those events. The chapter on Gezer, for example, looks at the cultural-historical question, *Do the material remains support the biblical tradition that Gezer was part of the state structure of Solomon's Israel during 1000–900 B.C.E.?*

> The **Annales school of archaeology** takes its name from the French journal Annales: économies, sociétés, civilisations. *Its approach to history is to study structures, including climate, agriculture, commerce, social groups, and the like.*

Part 3: School of Annales Archaeology

The School of Annales Archaeology was founded by Marc Bloch (1886–1944) and Lucien Febvre (1878–1956) to study slowly developing and long-lasting social institutions (French: *la longue durée)* such as farming, herding, pottery making, and architecture. The school uses a wide variety of social sciences to reconstruct the daily life of everyday people. The chapter on architecture, for example, describes how Lawrence Stager applied Annales Archaeology to the study of early Israel (Stager 1985).

Part 4: School of Processual Archaeology

The School of Processual Archaeology is shaped by the Enlightenment and by modernism. Processual archaeologists are confident that the human mind, properly disciplined, can accurately reconstruct the past. They also assume that the world of the Bible was a single worldview or metahistory that explains how great men helped their cultures adapt to the changes in environment. Processual archaeologists are positivists who follow the scientific method. Nothing can be taken for granted. Everything must be supported by evidence and experiment. In the chapter on Tel Miqne, for example, Trude Dothan and Seymour Gitin apply the scientific method by testing the hypothesis *The transition from the Late Bronze period (1500–1200 B.C.E.) to the Iron IA period (1200–1100 B.C.E.) in Syria-Palestine was uniform and spontaneous.*

Despite the importance of processual archaeology for excavators working in other parts of the world, archaeologists working in Syria-Palestine in the 1960s were not struggling with whether they were processual archaeologists or cultural historians. They were trying to decide whether they were biblical archaeologists or Syro-Palestinian archaeologists. The close relationship that had existed between archaeology and biblical studies in the

> **Processual archaeology** *is tied to anthropology in that it examines human processes and systems. It applies the scientific method to archaeological data.*

United States since the time of Albright (Albright 1942) was repeatedly challenged by Dever (Dever 1973; 1985; 1992). He argued that the Albright school of biblical archaeology was so committed to proving that the Bible was historically accurate that it completely ignored the developments in theory and method that processual archaeology brought to the discipline. Dever also alleged that the Albright school ignored processual archaeology because it assumed that ancient Israel did not evolve like other cultures in Syria-Palestine and that it was unique and could not be studied using scientific method.

Part 5: School of Post-Processual Archaeology

By the 1980s Dever had prevailed. Archaeology in Syria-Palestine was no longer an amateur enterprise but a separate and professional and processual discipline (Dever 2005, 80). Curiously, however, just as biblical archaeologists began using processual archaeology, processual archaeologists working in other parts of the world began to reevaluate their method. This ongoing critique is called *post-processual archaeology* by Hodder. The School of Post-Processual Archaeology applies the principles of postmodernism and studies the world of the Bible by reconstructing the lives of ordinary men and women (Ackerman 2003, 173–84; C. L. Meyers 2003, 185–97). A chapter on how to use the archaeology of households to understand better a remarkable-hero story in the book of Judges introduces post-processual archaeology. The story of a woman who delivers Thebez from Abimelech (Judg 9:22-57) celebrates an unnamed woman for delivering her city from its enemy with an extraordinary weapon. The mill she uses to feed her household becomes the weapon she uses to defend it.

> **Post-processual archaeology** *is an umbrella term applied to a range of archaeological theories. What these schools have in common is their objection to the assumption of processual archaeology that cultural changes are always adaptations to changes in the human or natural environment.*

Biblical archaeology today provides an enriched understanding not only of the world of the Bible but of the Bible itself. *Stones and Stories* is a standing invitation to teachers, students, and the reading public to put archaeology and biblical studies back to work as partners in the exciting task of understanding these ancient peoples and their remarkable ways of looking at their lives, using the earth, and thinking about God.

STUDY QUESTIONS

1. Describe what is meant by the maximalist and minimalist approaches to the history of ancient Israel.
2. What approach to an introduction to archaeology appeals to you and why?
3. Describe the approaches to archaeology of the five "schools" of archaeology presented here.

Part 1

Popular Archaeology

Part 1 introduces the *School of Popular Archaeology*, a diverse family of pilgrims, emperors, travelers, antiquities dealers, and missionaries who left their homes for the world of the Bible. They were inspired more by passion than by science. Yet, despite what were certainly undisciplined approaches by today's standards, their legacy to archaeology and the Bible remains significant.

PREVIEW: ARCHAEOLOGY OF PILGRIMS

- Why Pilgrims Return to Their Homelands
- What Pilgrims Have Contributed to the Understanding of the Bible
  - Moses Basola
  - Abu Ibn Battuta
  - Helena
  - Eusebius
  - Egeria
- What Geographers Contribute to the Understanding of the Bible
  - Caesarea Maritima (Israel)
  - Annals of Merneptah

Chapter 1 describes why pilgrims in every culture return to their homelands and how they contribute to the understanding of the Bible. The chapter also describes what geographers who study the land and artifacts like the Annals of Merneptah contribute to the understanding of the Bible, and what they and pilgrims have in common.

1

Archaeology of Pilgrims

WHY PILGIMS IN EVERY CULTURE RETURN
TO THEIR HOMELANDS

Long before archaeology became an academic discipline, material remains in the world of the Bible caught the interest of pilgrims, emperors, travelers, antiquities dealers, and missionaries (Hobson 1987, 1–47). Each asked different questions about the artifacts they saw.

Pilgrimage is an ancient ritual for refreshing the connection between a household and the sacred center (Greek: *omphalos*) in its land. When the life of any household in the culture is at risk, pilgrims make their way to the sacred center to restore the flow of life from there to their households.

Symptoms that the life of a household is at risk are war, famine, plague, or the inability of the women to conceive or to carry their children to term. These crises occur because something is blocking the flow of life from the sacred center to the household. That life channel is like a garden hose. Turn on the water, and run the hose out into the yard. If there is no water at the nozzle, then follow the hose back toward the hose bib and find the kink. Clear the kink and the water is on its way.

> **Pilgrimage.** *A pilgrimage is a journey to a sacred site. It may be undertaken to fulfill an obligation, for adventure, or out of personal devotion.*

Similarly, when something is blocking the flow of life to a household, pilgrims make their way back along the route connecting the land of the household to the sacred center to find the kink that is blocking the flow of life and putting the household at risk. When the pilgrimage is complete, the flow of life is restored, and the connection between the land of the household and its sacred center is refreshed.

Jewish, Christian, and Muslim pilgrims were first-wave archaeologists. They were not content simply to walk their faith in their own lands. They wanted to walk in the lands where that faith was born. The material remains from the days when their teachers lived offered a privileged

THE SACRED CENTER

In *The Sacred and the Profane: The Nature of Religion* (1959) the anthropologist Mircea Eliade (1907–1986) describes how traditional cultures create sacred space. To take profane space and make it sacred these cultures locate the sacred center of the land. At this spot the umbilical cord of the culture's Godmother is connected to the land, and through this sacred center life continues to flow into their land. For example, in shamanic cultures a totem animal is a godparent who teaches its people a signature skill that they will need to survive.

Sometimes the sacred center is revealed by a sign. For example in 1345 the Mexica people arrived at Tenochtitlan—the place of the cactus—which is Mexico City today. The Mexicas saw an island in the middle of the lake, and an eagle sitting on a cactus eating a snake—the sign that identified the sacred center in their land.

Sometimes the totem animal of a people identifies the sacred center of their land. They hunt their totem and the place at which they make the kill identifies the sacred center of their land.

Sometimes a domestic animal identifies the sacred center. People release one of their herd animals, and wherever it stops to graze is the sacred center of their land.

Once people identify the sacred center, then all the roads and buildings in their land are aligned with it. Every household and every structure has a designated link to its sacred center. Life flows along that route from the sacred center into every household in the land. ∎

———————————

The earliest surviving journal of a pilgrimage to Syria-Palestine was written by a pilgrim from France during 332–333. This anonymous pilgrim traveled to Italy, to Serbia, to Constantinople, and to Jerusalem. Like a Roman itinerary, the journal lists places and their distances from one another. This *Itinerary from Bordeaux to Jerusalem* (Latin: *Itinerarium Burdigalense*) is the earliest record of the stories about the world of the Bible; it was to have an enduring legacy in Christian piety, preaching, and teaching (C. W. Wilson 1971). ∎

window into what it meant to be a Jew, a Christian, or a Muslim. If believers could walk, then the stones could teach.

To excavate the geography of the Bible and develop a comprehensive road map of the world of the Bible is a journey of a thousand miles. Pilgrims took the first step.

Pilgrim journals are not only geographies; they are also ethnographies. Pilgrim journals not only describe places; they also describe people. Pilgrims recorded the condition of the artifacts they saw. Their descriptions are sometimes the only records of certain material remains that vandalism and nature have now destroyed.

WHAT PILGRIMS HAVE CONTRIBUTED TO THE UNDERSTANDING OF THE BIBLE

Many of the people who over time have contributed to our knowledge of the biblical world have been Christian pilgrims—but Jewish and Muslim pilgrims have made contributions, too.

Moses Basola (1480–1560)

Moses Basola (1480–1560) was a Jewish pilgrim from Soncino (Italy), where his father was a proofreader in a Hebrew-language publishing house (Basola 1999). Basola made a pilgrimage from Fano (Italy) to the world of the Bible in 1521–23. He sailed from Italy to Greece, Cyprus, Libya, Lebanon, and Syria.

Basola begins his journal by describing his voyage from Italy to Libya. He describes the weather, the geography, and the Jewish communities at each port. In Cyprus, he notes that meat is cheap, eggs and birds are plentiful, and bread is expensive. He finds few Jews in Cyprus, and he does not like those he meets.

In Libya, Basola hired a camel driver and a bodyguard and continued his pilgrimage on land. He made Safed (Israel) his base. He describes this center of Jewish spirituality as a city full of good things, especially good food. From Safed he visited the graves of twenty-four biblical prophets and teachers.

Jerusalem was a high point of Basola's pilgrimage. He writes about Jewish life in the city, especially about synagogue rituals. He also describes the two prayers he recited at graves and offers travel advice.

After his pilgrimage Basola went on to lead a full and diverse life. In 1535, he was ordained a rabbi and became an expert in Jewish Law (Hebrew: *halakah*) and spirituality (Hebrew: *kabbalah*). He became the headmaster of a Hebrew school for boys (Hebrew: *yeshiva*), and in 1540 he and his son founded a bank.

At the end of his life Basola once again left Soncino for the world of the Bible. He was convinced that the Messiah was about to come and that he should await his arrival in Safed. Basola made it safely back to Safed, where he died at the age of eighty.

Abu Ibn Battuta (1304–1369)

Muslims made pilgrimages not only to biblical sites such as Jerusalem but also to sites associated with the life of Muhammad (570–632) and with the Qu'ran. Pilgrimage to Mecca is one of the five essential rituals or "pillars" of Muslim life. The first pillar is the profession of faith (Arabic: *Shahadah*): "Allah alone is God! Muhammad is the final prophet." The second pillar is generosity to the poor (Arabic: *Zakat*). The third pillar is to pray five times each day (Arabic: *Salat*). The fourth pillar is fasting (Arabic: *Siyam*) during the month of Ramadan to remember the giving of the Qu'ran to Muhammad. The fifth pillar reminds Muslims to pilgrimage (Arabic: *Hajj*) to Mecca once in their lifetime. They are to make the journey during *Zul Hijjah, the month for pilgrimage,* and the twelfth and last month in the Muslim calendar. Mecca (Saudi Arabia) is the site of Muhammad's birth and, for Muslims, also the birthplace of the human race.

In 1325, Abu Ibn Battuta (1304–1369), a Muslim attorney from Morocco, set out along the North African coast for Mecca. Along the way he visited Cairo and Damascus (Bullis 2000a, b, c). When he completed his pilgrimage, he did not go home but continued to travel for thirty years and eventually covered some seventy-five thousand miles.

In his journal, *Travels in Asia and Africa 1325–1345* (Arabic: *Rihla*), Ibn Battuta profiles more than two thousand people whom he met or whose tombs he visited. He made four pilgrimages to Mecca and visited more than forty countries. He met some sixty rulers, served as an advisor to two dozen of them. His descriptions of life in Turkey, Asia, Africa, the Maldives (southwest of Sri Lanka in the Indian Ocean), the Malay peninsula (Myanmar, Thailand, Malaysia) and India are still an important source for the anthropology of these once faraway places. His verbal portraits depict the lives of the rich and the powerful in these lands.

For Muslims the Qu'ran ("the *recitation*") is the word of Allah—Islam's unique name for God. It describes what Muslims believe and how Muslims are expected to behave. In Muslim tradition the angel Gabriel recited the Qu'ran to Muhammad during the last twenty-three years of his life. For Muslims, Muhammad is the last of the prophets and his Qu'ran is the last revelation of Allah, completing the teachings in the Torah, the Psalms, and the Gospels. ∎

Rome remained part of the Byzantine Empire until 476, when Odacer, ruler of the Scirian tribes from eastern Europe (Poland), conquered the city. Constantinople, the capital of the Byzantine Empire, survived until May 29, 1453. Mehmed II, sultan of the Ottoman Empire, conquered the city on the feast day of St. Theodosia. Theodosia was martyred in 717 while defending an icon of Jesus hanging over the Bronze Gate into the emperor's palace from Christians who considered icons to be idols. Constantine XI, the last Byzantine emperor, died in the battle. Ordinary Byzantines were at the Church of St. Theodosia celebrating her feast day when the city fell. Constantinople then became the capital of the Ottoman Empire. In 1922 the Ottoman Empire became the Republic of Turkey. In 1930 Constantinople was renamed *Istanbul* (http://www.fordham.edu/halsall/byzantium). ∎

Martin Luther (1483–1546) and other leaders of the Christian Reformation challenged the importance of visiting the lands of the Bible. They taught that the only pilgrimage that enriched the lives of Christians was the pilgrimage of the soul (Davis 2004, 3–4). John Bunyan (1628–1688) created a detailed guide for this devotion of spiritual pilgrimage in *Pilgrim's Progress* (1678). Nonetheless, pilgrims from every tradition of Christianity continue to make their way to the world of the Bible today. ∎

Fresco of Saint Helena. Location: S. Giovanni Decollato, Venice, Italy Photo Credit: Cameraphoto Arte, Venice / Art Resource, NY

Helena (250–330)

Christian pilgrims continued the Jewish tradition of walking the world of the Bible. They left their homelands to . . . *walk in the footsteps of their Master* as the teacher Origen (185–254) defined the ritual ("In Joannem" VI, no. 24).

In the closing months of a prolonged civil war, the Roman emperor Constantine (272–337) converted to Christianity. Subsequently in 313, Constantine issued the Edict of Milan, which established Christianity as the new official Roman worldview.

Although Roman bureaucrats rushed to embrace Christianity, few understood what it meant to be a Christian. Constantine delegated his mother, Helena, to reeducate these government Christians. Helena used the devotion of pilgrimage as a travel study, a kind of civics course in the new official religion of the empire. In 330, Constantine moved the capital of the Christian Roman Empire from Rome (Italy) to Byzantium (Turkey). Byzantium was founded by Byzantias in 667 B.C.E. Constantine renamed the city *Constantinople*. Thus the *Roman* Empire became the *Byzantine* or *Christian* Empire.

Well financed and highly motivated, Helena set out to design a grand tour of the world of the Bible. To encourage Roman Christians to make pilgrimages to the places mentioned in the Bible she interviewed Christian communities to learn how they were connected with the Bible. Then she built churches, monasteries, and convents with guest houses to provide for the pilgrims.

Pilgrimage became a popular sacrament of Christian renewal. Christians made pilgrimages to learn how to be better Christians. The devotion became so important that even when it was physically impossible for Christians to make the actual pilgrimage, they walked a virtual pilgrimage in their local churches. These *Stations of the Cross*, as they were called, were marked on the walls of churches throughout Europe. At each station Christians paused to remember some aspect of Jesus' passion and death.

Eusebius

Like Helena, early Christian pilgrims used the Bible as a map. Gradually other guides began to develop. The most significant was published by Eusebius (275–339), a bishop of Caesarea Maritima (Israel). The outline for Eusebius's *Onomasticon* (Greek: *onomastica* = lists of names) was a Jewish list of sites. This Jewish geography originated in Jerusalem and identified sites mentioned in the sections of the Bible known as the Torah and the Prophets. Eusebius and his students added place-names from the Gospels and other Roman itineraries as well as notes on geography and tombs. Origen and his students added Greek place-names from the Hexapla Bibles to the Jewish geography.

To identify sites in the Syria-Palestine of his day Eusebius matched the sound of the place-name in his day with the sound of the place-name in biblical Hebrew. His method is still used by archaeologists to identify sites (Elitzur 2004).

Edward Robinson (1794–1863), who traveled in the world of the Bible in 1837, rediscovered the technique of using popular place-names to identify sites named in the Bible (Robinson 1841, 1:376). Like Eusebius, Robinson believed that the ancient Semitic place-names were accurately reflected in the contemporary place-names, which in his day were in Arabic (Davis 2004, 6).

Although parallels in pronunciation can be helpful in excavating the geography of the Bible, comparisons between the names of sites today and biblical sites are not always reliable. For example, in June 1949 the Committee for Assigning Hebrew Names in the Negev established by David Ben Gurion (1886–1973) changed the Arabic names for mountains, valleys, springs, and wells into *Ivrit* or the Hebrew spoken in the state of Israel today.

Sometimes the committee matched the sound of the Arabic and Hebrew place-names, and sometimes it changed the place-names to associate them with a biblical tradition or with some natural characteristic of

---

The Hexapla was a six-column version of the Bible. The Hebrew Bible and its Greek translations were copied side by side. The Bible in Hebrew was in the first column; the Hebrew transliterated into Greek characters was in the second, the Greek translation of Aquila, the Greek translation of Symmachus, the Septuagint Greek translation, and the Greek translation of Theodotion were in the third, fourth, fifth and sixth columns (http://rosetta.reltech.org/TC/extras/Hexapla.html). ∎

The name *Syria-Palestine*, like *Levant* (Arabic: *esh-Sham*) or *Greater Syria*, is a geographical, not a political, term. Herodotus (484–425 B.C.E.) identified *Palestine* as the part of *Syria* between Lebanon and Egypt (*History* 1:105; 2:104; 3:5, 91; 4:39; 7:89). The term *Greater Syria* was used by the Ottoman rulers of Turkey to designate the land in Lebanon, Syria, Jordan, and Israel today. William Foxwell Albright also considered Syria-Palestine to be a single cultural region (Davis 2004, 64). Consequently, *The Oxford Encyclopedia of Archaeology in the Near East* (1997), edited by Eric M. Meyers, adopted this geographical convention as well. ∎

the site. *Seil Imran* (Aqueduct of the Wool-Makers), for example, became *Nahal Amram* (Valley of Amran, the father of Moses and Aaron). *Jabal Haruf* (Mountain of the Ewe) became *Har Harif* (Sharp Mountain). *Jabal Ideid* (Sprawling Mountain) was renamed *Har Karkom* (Mount Crocus), because crocuses grow there. Consequently, the Ivrit place-names in Israel today are seldom helpful in understanding the geography of the Bible.

Egeria

From 381 to 384 a woman named *Egeria* wrote letters describing the places she visited (Wilkinson 1999). These *Travels of Egeria* (Latin: *Itinerarium Egeriae*) joined the Bible and the *Onomasticon* of Eusebius as archaeological resources that Europeans could use better to understand the world of the Bible (http://www.christusrex.org/www1/jhs/TSspegria.html).

In 1884 Gian-Francesco Gamurrini (1835–1923) found some of Egeria's letters in the library of a monastery of the Brotherhood of St. Mary in Italy. The eleventh-century manuscript—the Codex Aretinus—had

Mount Sinai and Monastery of Saint Catherine, Egypt. Byzantine 15th c.e. Location: St. Catherine Monastery, Mount Sinai, Sinai Desert, Egypt. Photo Credit: Erich Lessing / Art Resource, NY.

been copied by monks at the Monastery of Monte Cassino. Only about four months of letters had survived. Nonetheless, Valerius, a Spanish monk who lived around 650, had described the contents of the missing letters. The surviving letters were all written after Egeria arrived in Jerusalem. Besides describing her pilgrimage to Sinai, she also describes the differences between the celebration of the Eucharist by Christians in Jerusalem and in Europe.

Egeria never introduces herself in her letters. She was certainly courageous to travel to this remote area of the empire, and apparently had enough time and money to spend three years away from home. To travel the twelve hundred miles between Constantinople and Jerusalem would have taken eight weeks if she covered twenty miles a day. Egeria spent three years in Jerusalem and then returned to Constantinople.

The letters of Egeria were written to women back home. Although she addresses the women as "my sisters," it is unlikely that Egeria was a nun. She never asks for money or complains about not being able to meet her expenses. Traveling monks and nuns in her day were almost always poorly funded by their monasteries and convents. Moreover, few nuns in her day would receive permission to stay out of the convent for three full years.

The language in Egeria's letters is colloquial. On the one hand, she may have deliberately written simply, avoiding references to classical Greek and Roman literature, because the letter-writing style of her day favored popular, not academic, language. On the other hand, she may have written simply because the women to whom she was writing were not educated. Thus, Egeria's writing style is not a clear indication of her education. Egeria wanted her sisters to see exactly what she had seen. Her letters are full of enthusiastic comments on ordinary things and people, on buildings and mountains—but what interested her most was how the sites she visited were connected with her understanding of the Bible.

The monks' trail that pilgrims followed to the top of Mt. Sinai (Arabic: *Jebel Musa*) was a physical initiation to biblical spirituality. The trail was punctuated with viewpoints and wayside shrines linked to the Bible. There was the Valley of the Golden Calf; the site where Moses herded the livestock of Jethro; the cave where Moses stayed; the cave where Elijah stayed; the site where Aaron and the seventy elders witnessed the covenant between Yahweh and Israel; the site of the Israelites' camp; and the rock where Moses broke the first set of tablets (Coleman and Elsner 1994, 86). ■

TRAVELS OF EGERIA

*Egeria's description of her visit to the Mountain of God in the Sinai Desert (*Travels of Egeria *3–7) is a good example of pilgrim archaeology.*

We reached the mountains late on Saturday. The monks who lived there were very hospitable. There is also a church and a priest there.

Early on Sunday we began our climb with the priest and the monks. It is hard work to climb these mountains. You cannot go up gently on a switchback trail; you climb straight up the whole way, as if up a wall. Then you must come straight down each mountain until you reach the very foot of the middle mountain which is called *Sinai*. Nonetheless—thanks be to Christ—and helped by the prayers of the holy men who accompanied us, we arrived on the summit of the Mountain of God in the morning. Here is where the covenant was given. Here is where the Glory of the Lord descended and set the mountain on fire [Exod 19:18].

The climb was difficult. I had to climb on foot. It would have been impossible in the saddle. Yet I did not feel the toil, because I realized that the desire which I had was being fulfilled at God's bidding.

On the Mountain of God there is now a church, not great in size. The summit of the mountain itself is not very great. Nevertheless, the church itself is great in grace.

When—thanks be to God—we arrived at the summit, and reached the door of the church, the priest came from his cell and met us. He was a healthy old man, a monk all his life. When the passage from the book of Exodus had been read, we celebrated the Eucharist and received communion.

As we were coming out of the church, the priests of the place gave us *eulogiae*,—the first fruits harvested on the mountain and specially blessed. Although Mt. Sinai is rocky—there are no bushes on it—yet down below, near the foot of the mountain there are little plots of soil where the monks diligently plant trees and orchards, and set up chapels with cells near to them, so that they may gather fruits which they have cultivated with their own hands.

I asked the monks to show us other sites mentioned in the Bible, so they showed us the cave where Moses stayed when he had climbed the Mountain of God for the second time in order to get another set of tablets after he had broken the first set when the people sinned [Exod 34:4]. They also showed us the other sites which we desired to see, and those which they themselves well knew.

From the place where we were standing, my sisters, outside the walls of the church on the summit of the Mountain of God, those mountains that we could scarcely climb at first seemed to be so far below us when compared with the Mountain of God where we were standing. They appeared to be little hills, although they were so very great, that I thought that I had never seen higher, except that the Mountain of God excelled them by far. From there we could see Egypt and Palestine, and the Red Sea and the eastern end of the Mediterranean Sea, which leads to Alexandria and the endless lands of the Saracen tribes, all so far below us as to be scarcely credible, but the monks pointed out each one of them to us.

The Sinai range, in its prime, was home to some one thousand monks. The mountains rise to 7,500 feet and receive two and one-half to three inches of rain each year—a climate that allowed monks to grow fruit and vegetables around their cells. Their gardens and orchards were small, some twenty feet by twenty feet, but sufficient. ∎

Mountains are sacred sites in many cultures (T. J. Wilkinson 2003, 206–9). Even when the cultures around mountains change, reverence for the mountains remains (Bradley 2000). Among the holy mountains in the world of the Bible are Nemrud Dagi (Turkey), Mt. Casios (Turkey), Mt. Sinai (Egypt), Mt. Hermon (Israel, Syria, Lebanon), and Jebel Sheikh Barakat (Syria). ∎

Having then fulfilled the desire with which we had hastened to ascend, we began our descent from the summit of the Mountain of God. We climbed down to another mountain joined to the Mountain of God, which is called *Horeb*. Mt. Horeb is where Elijah the prophet fled from Ahab, ruler of Israel, and where God spoke to him: "What are you doing here, Elijah?" [1 Kgs 19:9].

The cave where Elijah hid is near the door of the church on the mountain. A stone altar also is shown which Elijah built to offer sacrifice to God. We celebrated the Eucharist there, and also read the passage from the book of Kings. It was our custom that, when we had arrived at those places which I wanted to visit, the appropriate passage from the Bible should always be read....

Although it was already afternoon, there were still three miles left before we could get out of the mountains. We wanted to reach the entrance to the valley because there were many monks' cells there and a church near the burning bush. So after we climbed down from the Mountain of God we arrived at the burning bush in the middle of the afternoon. There is a very pleasant garden in front of the church, containing excellent and abundant water. Near there is where Moses stood when God said to him: "Take off your sandals" [Exod 3:5].

It was too late in the day to celebrate the Eucharist, so we simply prayed in the church and also at the bush in the garden, and read the passage from the book of Exodus. Then, we ate with the monks in the garden before the bush. We also spent the night there, and next day, rising very early, we asked the priests to celebrate the Eucharist for us.

See http://www.ccel.org/m/mcclure/etheria/etheria.htm. For a good, readable English translation see John Wilkinson, *Egeria's Travels to the Holy Land: Newly Translated with Supporting Documents* (Warminster: Aris & Phillips, 1999).

Today, the church next to the burning bush where Egeria prayed is the chapel of the Monastery of St. Catherine of Alexandria founded in 527. Emperor Justinian (483–565) fortified the monastery, and its walls were subsequently repaired by Napoleon Bonaparte (1769–1821). The architecture at the Mountain of God has changed, but pilgrims continue to gather at the same places described by Egeria. ■

WHAT GEOGRAPHERS WHO STUDY THE LAND CONTRIBUTE TO THE UNDERSTANDING OF THE BIBLE

Geographers like Edward Robinson and Eli Smith (1801–1857) inherited the work pioneered by pilgrims in the world of the Bible. Robinson was the first American to do archaeological work in Syria-Palestine. Like most biblical archaeologists, Robinson combined his scientific skills as an archaeologist with a profound personal faith. These early scholars were also pilgrims. In 1838 he identified many biblical sites in Syria-Palestine. This geographical work was an important impetus to biblical studies in

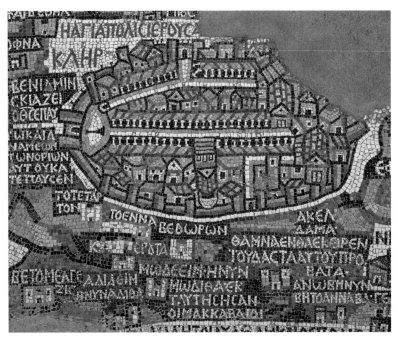

Jerusalem with Emperor Constantine's buildings rising above Calvary and the Holy Sepulchre. Detail of the "Map of Madaba," a mosaic floor of an early Christian church. Sixth century C.E. Location: St. George's Church, Madaba, Jordan, Kingdom. Photo Credit: Erich Lessing / Art Resource, NY.

the United States. He made a second trip in 1852. After his death, Robinson's writings and maps were preserved at Hamilton College (Clinton, New York) and at Union Theological Seminary (New York City) where he taught.

Caesarea Maritima (Israel)

About 470 the Christians of Caesarea Maritima, a Roman city on the eastern coast of the Mediterranean Sea, built a large octagonal *martyrion* shrine on the platform where Herod (73–74 B.C.E.) had constructed a temple to Roma and Augustus in 22 B.C.E. Eight-sided buildings mark sites of significance in a faith tradition and were pilgrimage destinations. The bones of a saint were buried directly under the dome at the center of the *martyrion* in Caesarea Maritima. Pilgrim Christians came to the tomb to pray for protection and healing.

Since 1989 Kenneth G. Holum has directed the Combined Caesarea Expeditions. This international archaeological project has ongoing land and underwater excavations. Holum used the New Testament and the journals of three pilgrim archaeologists to identify the saint buried in the *martyrion* at Caesarea Maritima as Cornelius, a Roman centurion and the first non-Jew to become a Christian (Holum 2004, 184–99).

The Acts of the Apostles (Acts 10:1-33) describes Cornelius welcoming Peter into his house at Caesarea Maritima. The journal of one pilgrim describes how Christians at Caesarea Maritima took pilgrims to the place where Cornelius was baptized. The journal of another pilgrim from 385 describes attending mass in the Church of St. Cornelius, which was built over the house of Cornelius. The Christians of Caesarea Maritima were now honoring Cornelius as a martyr and as one of their first bishops. The journal of a third pilgrim from about 570 describes taking a small stone relic as a souvenir of the *martyrion* of St. Cornelius.

Annals of Merneptah

During the twentieth century, geographers Yohanan Aharoni (1919–1976), Michael Avi-Yonah (1904–1974), and Anson F. Rainey continued to work with the geography of land itself, the geography described in the Bible, and the geography in parallel Near Eastern traditions, for example, the Annals, or Stela, of Merneptah (ruled 1224–1214 B.C.E.).

Annals were published by monarchs as yearly reports of their stewardship to their divine patrons. The two subjects commonly covered in annals are the monarchs' domestic policy and their foreign policy. They describe how they have fed the people and protected the land that their divine patrons placed in their care.

Merneptah was not a pilgrim; he was a pharaoh. He did not make a pilgrimage through Syria-Palestine; he invaded it. He did not write a journal describing his travels, but in his annals he published the names of his enemies in Syria-Palestine. One of those enemies was Israel.

William F. Petrie excavated Merneptah's funeral chapel in the Valley of the Pharaohs during 1896 and recovered his annals inscribed on a granite stela ten feet high and five feet wide. The stela is preserved today in the Egyptian Museum in Cairo. It was originally inscribed by Amenhotep III, but was recycled by Merneptah to celebrate his military campaigns. The stela was erected during year 5 of his reign (1219 B.C.E.).

The annals primarily commemorate Merneptah's victory over the Labu and Meshwesh peoples in Libya and the Aqawasa, Turusa, Luku, Sardana, and Sklusa Sea Peoples who fought with them against Egypt. The final lines of the annals, however, celebrate an earlier military campaign in Syria-Palestine. Here Merneptah celebrates his defeat of the cities of Ashkelon, Gezer, and Yanoam and of the people of

> A **martyrion** is a shrine, usually octagonal, erected to contain the remains of a **martyr**, someone who "gives witness." The octagonal architectural style was used for other sacred sites as well: for example, the Dome of the Rock on the Haram esh Sharif ("Noble Sanctuary") in Jerusalem was erected to mark the site where Muhammad ascended from earth into heaven. It was intentionally built to rival Christian sites in Jerusalem like the Church of the Holy Sepulchre.

In hieroglyphics a throw stick or Egyptian boomerang and three mountains identify Ashkelon, Gezer, and Yanoam as foreign cities. Israel, however, is identified as a foreign people by the hieroglyphics of a throw stick, a man, a woman and three vertical lines. ■

"The People of Israel"—
from Merneptah Stela

The section of the annals where Israel appears uses a literary device called *chiasmus* after the Greek letter *chi*, which is printed *X* (Ahlström and Edelman 1985; Rainey and Notley 2006, 99-100). The shape of the top of the Greek letter is mirrored by its base, just as "I plundered the land of Canaan from one end to the other" mirrors "I left the land of Hurru a widow." ■

Tyre (Lebanon) was a significant economic power in Syria-Palestine from 3000 B.C.E. until 640. It is about thirty miles north of the city of Acre (Israel) and the Carmel Mountains. Cloth dyed deep purple was a major trade commodity for Tyre. Piles of murex snail shells, from which the dye was harvested, and a dye factory have been excavated just outside the city walls. The murex shell also represents Tyre on its coins, and the pungent smell of dye manufacturing became the city's characteristic aroma. Originally, the word *Canaan* was used for the purple dye; then the word was applied to cloth dyed purple; then to the merchants who sold the cloth; and eventually to the region where the cloth was sold. The Egyptians called the peoples who lived in the land of purple cloth *Canaanites*. ■

THE TEXT OF THE STELA OF MERNEPTAH

The rulers of my enemies now prostrate before me begging for peace;
    Not one of my enemies raises a head in revolt.

I devastated Tehenu [Libya] in the west;
    I made peace with the land of Hatti [Turkey] in the north.
I plundered Canaan [Syria-Palestine] from one end to the other.
    I took slaves from the city of Ashkelon;
    I conquered the city of Gezer.
    I razed the city of Yanoam to the ground;
I slaughtered the people of Israel and burned their grain.
    I left the land of Hurru [Syria-Palestine] a widow.
All lands have been pacified;
    Every rebel is now prostrate before Merneptah.
      (Translation from Matthews and Benjamin 2006, 97–98)

Israel. One of the important features of the stela is that it preserves the name "Israel."

Anson Rainey's interpretation of the geography depicted on the stela places the homeland of early Israel east of the Jordan River, where he locates the city of Yanoam (Rainey and Notley 2006, 99–100). He argues that the order of the four names follows Merneptah's march into Syria-Palestine, referred to in the inscription as "Canaan," north along the coast where he conquers Ashkelon and Gezer, and then east across the Jordan River, where he conquers Yanoam and Israel. For Rainey, the annals emphasize that Merneptah conquered the peoples both west and east of the Jordan River. Only at a later period do the people of Israel conquered by Merneptah cross the Jordan River to the west and settle in the hills there, adopting the farming, herding, building, and pottery making of the indigenous peoples of Syria-Palestine.

Gösta W. Ahlström (1918–1992), Diana Edelman, Michael G. Hasel, and William G. Dever interpret the geography in the annals differently. They locate early Israel in the mountains west of the Jordan River (Hasel 1994, 52–54). For them, the annals emphasize that Merneptah conquered both the peoples on the plains (Ashkelon, Gezer, and Yanoam) and the people in the hills (Israel) (Ahlström and Edelman 1985, 61).

On either interpretation, the three cities (Ashkelon, Gezer, and Yanoam) and the one people (Israel) in the annals are natives of Syria-Palestine, and all are significant military threats to Egypt (Hasel 1994, 45–61). The material remains recovered from the villages in the hills west of the river are virtually identical with the cultures throughout Syria-

Palestine. These artifacts are neither foreign, nor military. These early Hebrews were not strangers from across the river. The Hebrews were social survivors who fled the famine, plague, and war that brought the Bronze Age to an end. These Hebrews did not wage war; they survived war. They fled the centralized, surplus economies of the great cities of Syria-Palestine and founded a decentralized subsistence economy of some three hundred villages in the hills along the Jordan River. The hills themselves were of no economic interest to Egypt, but the Hebrews threatened the economy of Egypt by raiding its caravans, plundering harvests and rustling cattle from nearby villages.

CONCLUSION

Archaeology is an academic discipline; pilgrimage is a devotion. The standards that pilgrims and archaeologists use to identify sites are different. Archaeologists want to know: *What happened here?* Pilgrims want to know: *Is this where we tell the story?* A pilgrim's experience of the land is not intellectual; it is physical (Coleman and Elsner 1994, 73–89). Pilgrims make the journey, tell the story, and say the prayer to join the present to the past and create a community of faith across time (R. S. Nelson 2006, 8).

Nonetheless, pilgrims and archaeologists both bring the Bible down to earth. They assume that the peoples in the Bible were real people and that biblical place-names are real places, not like Atlantis, Shangri La, the Land of Oz, Mordor, or the Shire. Both pilgrims and archaeologists believe that the land can teach them how these ancient people lived, and how the land taught these ancient people to think about life.

The Amarna Letters (clay tablets inscribed in Akkadian) written to Amenhotep III and Akhenaton (1352–1335 B.C.E.) by their governors in Syria-Palestine are full of complaints about ⁽apiru raiders.

The story of Abraham's negotiations with Lot (Gen 13:5—14:24) describes Abraham as something akin to an ⁽apiru raider when he delivers Sodom and Melchizedek from Elam. After being driven away by the father of the household of Gilead, Jephthah joins a tribe that might be described in Akkadian as ⁽apiru raiders and supports himself plundering caravans (Judg 11:1-40). In the covenant between Abigail and David (1 Sam 25:2-43) Nabal, Abigail's husband, accuses David of being a raider who extorts households to protect their herds, like the ⁽apiru raiders in the Amarna Letters. The ⁽apiru raiders in the Amarna correspondence are not identical with the Hebrews in the Bible, but the social unrest that the Amarna tablets describe is comparable to the social unrest in Syria-Palestine described in the Bible. ∎

STUDY QUESTIONS

1. What do pilgrims and archaeologists have in common, and how are their goals different?
2. What motivated a person in ancient times to undertake a pilgrimage? Do people have the same motivations today?
3. What types of information have we learned from pilgrims' journals?
4. What is the importance of the Annals of Merneptah?
5. What are the sources of information about the geography of ancient Syria-Palestine?

PREVIEW: ARCHAEOLOGY OF EMPERORS

- Museums
  - Nebuchadnezzar II
  - Napoleon
  - Egyptian Collections in Museums
  - Legacy of the Emperors
- Languages of the Biblical World
  - Semitic and Indo-European Language Families
  - Hieroglyphics
  - Greek and Coptic
  - Semitic and Indo-European Language Families
  - Hieroglyphics and Coptic
  - Cuneiform
- Modern Translation Projects
  - Chicago Assyrian Dictionary
  - Pennsylvania Sumerian Dictionary
- Understanding the Bible
  - Nabu-sharrusu-ukin and Jeremiah 39:13
  - Legal Systems in the Near East

Chapter 2 describes why emperors included archaeologists and other scholars in their armies, and how these imperial archaeologists contributed to the understanding of the world of the Bible. The chapter also explains who first translated hieroglyphics, and how he did it; who first translated cuneiform, and how they did it. Finally, it shows where the work of these early archaeologists of language is continued today and how that work contributes to understanding the world of the Bible.

2

Archaeology of Emperors

When emperors came to power in France, Britain, and Germany (1700–1918), they identified themselves as the heirs of the pharaohs of ancient Egypt and the great kings of Mesopotamia. To endorse their claims they dispatched archaeologists to study their imperial ancestors and to collect artifacts for their imperial museums. In the stones and stories of these ancient peoples, Europeans found vivid illustrations of their national character that explained and justified the unique position of their culture in the world (Silberman 1982). Despite the competition, intrigue, and conspiracy that characterized the archaeology of emperors, it inspired two important legacies for archaeology and the Bible: museums and the understanding of ancient languages.

MUSEUMS

Nebuchadnezzar II

Archaeologists may have found a precedent for the imperial museums of Europe in the ancient city of Babylon. Nebuchadnezzar II (604–562 B.C.E.), Great King of Babylon, may have been the first emperor to use archaeology to justify his authority (Casson 1974, 53–57).

The Euphrates River ran through the middle of the city of Babylon. The five hundred acres of the old city were on the east bank; a much smaller new city was on the west bank. Both the old city and the new city were fortified by two walls some twenty-four feet apart. The inner wall was twenty-one feet thick; the outer wall was twelve feet thick. Both walls were reinforced with towers every sixty feet. The river Euphrates was diverted into a forty-foot-wide moat around the outer wall. Nebuchadnezzar's antiquities museum, filled with monuments and trophies, was in his Northern Palace outside the double city wall (http://proteus .brown.edu/mesopotamianarchaeology/1310).

Nebuchadnezzar may also have built the Hanging Gardens at the Northern Palace. The artificial mountain that was the base for the park was almost seventy-five feet high. Seven vaulted chambers with thick walls created a foundation for the gardens. Pumps raised water from the Euphrates River to irrigate the gardens.

Nebuchadnezzar used the slaves, gold, silver, lead, and wood from his wars in Mesopotamia, Syria-Palestine, and Egypt to restore and enlarge Babylon and other cities. Members of the household of David, who were deported from Judah between 597 and 586 B.C.E., for example, were assigned to restore a section of Nippur on the Chebar canal (Ezek 1:1-3). More than fifteen million bricks, thirteen inches square and three inches thick, were used in the restoration of Babylon (Roaf 1990, 199). Nebuchadnezzar lavishly redecorated the Esagila sanctuary and the Etemenanki ziggurat, both dedicated to Marduk, divine patron of Babylon.

The Etemenanki was seven stories high—six platforms supporting a sanctuary on the seventh. The first story was about three hundred square feet. The sacred space surrounding the Etemenanki was bordered by a *temenos* wall warning pilgrims to enter only if their households were in good standing. Behind the wall there was housing for the priests who served at the sanctuary and administered the treasury of Babylon.

Nebuchadnezzar had several palaces in Babylon. The Southern Palace was at the corner of the old city just inside the double city wall. Nebuchadnezzar added five courtyards to this palace, quarters for his body guards, housing for administrators, a formal throne room and a residence for himself and his diplomatic wives. The architectural features of the palace were luxurious: kiln-fired brick, cedar beams, ceramic tile walls, gold, silver, and precious stones.

Napoleon

In 1798 Napoleon Bonaparte (1769–1821) launched an invasion of Egypt (Cole 2007; Strathern 2007). Like Alexander of Macedonia, who made Hellenistic culture an international culture, Napoleon wanted to make French culture an international culture. Therefore, he brought not only soldiers to conquer Egypt, but also artists, scientists, engineers, naturalists, and archaeologists to study Egypt and to integrate the culture of ancient Egypt into French culture.

In his campaign through Italy in 1797 Napoleon had sent back crate after crate of confiscated paintings and artworks to the Louvre Museum in Paris. The painting of the Mona Lisa by Leonardo da Vinci (1452–1519) was one of his war prizes. In Egypt he found even greater treasures. The

Napoleon's invasion of Egypt in 1798—part of his ongoing campaign challenging the British Empire—was a military disaster. Almost immediately after French troops disembarked, the British fleet sank much of the French fleet, stranding the French in Egypt. The French troops force-marched from Alexandria to Cairo in sweltering desert heat wearing alpine wool uniforms and without canteens. Hundreds died. Egyptians rioting in Cairo killed more French soldiers, which subsequently led to the looting and desecration of Al-Azhar mosque by French troops. Napoleon returned to France just one year after the invasion, leaving his generals to deal with both the increasingly hostile Egyptians and the oncoming British forces (Burleigh 2007). ∎

A. Vol. V. PYRAMIDES DE MEMPHIS. Pl. II.

VUE DU SPHINX ET DE LA GRANDE PYRAMIDE, PRISE DU SUD-EST.

The Sphinx at Giza. From "La Description de l'Egypte," published by the order of Napoleon Bonaparte during the Egyptian campaign. Engraving. Paris, 1809-1822. Edition in 30 volumes. Location: Private Collection, Cairo, Egypt. Photo Credit: © François Guenet / Art Resource, NY

lure of the past and the new science of archaeology fascinated Napoleon, and he wanted to reap the rich harvest of Egypt's antiquities. To this end he formed the Scientific and Artistic Commission to excavate ancient Egypt.

The French artist Dominique-Vivant Denon, for example, accompanied the army of General Desaix south along the Nile River. With remarkable accuracy Denon made sketches—often drawing while battles raged around him—of the great temples at Karnak and Luxor. Meanwhile other scholars moved north along the Nile River to excavate temples and palaces, draw maps, and collect artifacts.

The Scientific and Artistic Commission published its findings as *La Description de L'Egypte* (1809). This comprehensive, ten-volume work laid the foundations for Egyptology and kindled a new interest at European universities in the study of the world of the Bible (Gillispie and Dewachter 1987). Long after Napoleon's armies surrendered to the British and withdrew from the Near East, students of archaeology and the

> ## U.S. AND CANADIAN MUSEUMS
> ## WITH EGYPTIAN COLLECTIONS
>
> Kelsey Museum of Archaeology, University of Michigan, Ann Arbor, Michigan
> Michael C. Carlos Museum, Emory University, Atlanta, Georgia
> Phoebe A. Hearst Museum of Anthropology, University of California at Berkeley, Berkeley, California
> Museum of Fine Arts, Boston, Massachusetts
> Brooklyn Museum of Art, Brooklyn, New York
> Oriental Institute, University of Chicago, Chicago, Illinois
> Detroit Institute of Arts, Detroit, Michigan
> Nelson-Atkins Museum of Art, Kansas City, Missouri
> Metropolitan Museum of Art, New York, New York
> University of Pennsylvania Museum of Archaeology and Anthropology, Philadelphia, Pennsylvania
> Rosicrucian Egyptian Museum and Planetarium, San Jose, California
> Royal Ontario Museum, Toronto, Ontario

THOMAS MUNROE DAVIS

The United States was not yet an empire during the eighteenth and nineteenth centuries. Emperors did not fill its museums, but wealthy business people did. From 1903 to 1912, for example, Thomas Munroe Davis financed and participated in excavations that explored the Valley of the Pharaohs and identified the tombs of Hatshepsut (1473–1458 B.C.E.), Thutmosis IV (1401–1391 B.C.E.), Haremhab (1319–1307 B.C.E.), and the parents of Queen Tiye (1398–1338 B.C.E.). Their artifacts are now in the Museum of Fine Arts (Boston), the Metropolitan Museum of Art (New York), and the Cairo Museum (Egypt). Davis was one of the first Westerners voluntarily to leave Egypt's antiquities in their country of origin. The interest and financial investment of business people like Davis allowed

Bible would continue to benefit from the work of these French scholars and artists.

The Legacy of the Emperors

Today the Near Eastern collection of antiquities in the Louvre is joined by the collections in the British Museum (London), in the Pergamon Museum (Berlin), and in the Vatican Museums (Rome). These museums are, in some way, all the legacy of the archaeology of emperors.

Although European flagship museums began as imperial treasure chests, they evolved into irreplaceable archives of the life and times in the world of the Bible. Museum collections in Europe and the United States were responsible for creating an ongoing fascination with the world of the Bible among ordinary people, who came to admire their artifacts; among students and their teachers, who dedicated their lives to studying these material remains; and among wealthy patrons, who contributed the money to preserve and display them. The museum collections created an intense interest in the world of the Bible and its cultural legacy. Without these museums the world of the Bible would have been familiar only to a dedicated community of hearty pilgrims and a wealthy network of intrepid travelers.

The moral questions of who owns the artifacts in museums today and what should be done with them are far from answered. Yet many of the countries whose cultural legacies are on view in these museums survive on money that tourists and scholars spend to visit them, and the money that the museums continue to spend for ongoing exhibitions of artifacts from the world of the Bible. Like foreign workers who faithfully send home a portion of their pay to their families, antiquities in museums faithfully send home visitors and students to spend the money that their countries of origin need to survive.

the Near Eastern collections at the Metropolitan Museum of Art (New York), the Brooklyn Museum of Art (Brooklyn), and the Smart Museum of Art and the Oriental Institute (University of Chicago) to rival those of Europe (Thomas 1995). ∎

LANGUAGES OF THE BIBLICAL WORLD

Just as pilgrims brought the attention of archaeologists to the importance of the land in understanding the world of the Bible, emperors brought the attention of archaeologists to the importance of understanding the hieroglyphic and cuneiform languages of the world of the Bible.

The Ishtar Gate, Babylon, built during the reign of Nebuchadnezzar II (605–562 B.C.E.). Colored glazed terracotta tiles, 14.73 x 15.70 x 4.36 m. Inv. VAMF 94. Location: Vorderasiatisches Museum, Staatliche Museen zu Berlin, Berlin, Germany. Photo Credit: Bildarchiv Preussischer Kulturbesitz / Art Resource, NY. There is also a full-scale replica in Iraq.

Languages themselves are artifacts, no less than pottery, architecture, tools, and jewelry. Languages reflect worldviews, ways of understanding and processing human experience.

Semitic and Indo-European Language Families

Two important language families appear in the world of the Bible. One is Indo-European and the other is Semitic. Hittite and Persian are the only Indo-European languages in the world of the Bible. They are related to the languages of India to the east, and of the European language families, including Romance, Germanic, Slavic, Celtic, Hellenic, and so on.

The Rosetta Stone. EA 24. Location: British Museum, London, Great Britain. Photo Credit: Erich Lessing / Art Resource, NY

Semitic languages generally are divided into East Semitic, South Semitic, and Northwest Semitic. The East Semitic and Northwest Semitic languages are important in the study of the biblical world. (The category of South Semitic includes Ethiopic and the Arabic languages and dialects.) The East Semitic division includes Eblaite and Akkadian. Eblaite is the language of the ancient city of Ebla. In the 1970s about seventeen thousand tablets written in this language were discovered in the ruins of the city. Akkadian was named for Akkad in southern Mesopotamia, where the first inscriptions in this language were recovered by archaeologists. Babylonian and Assyrian are dialects of Akkadian. Babylonia was the cultural heartland of Mesopotamia, where the art and literature characteristic of all Mesopotamian cultures developed. Assyria (1000–614 B.C.E.) was a culture that developed the technologies of government and military science, but borrowed heavily from Babylonia for its art and literature. Mari, north of Babylon on the Euphrates River near Deir-ez-Zor in Iraq today, served as a gateway for Babylonian culture to enter Syria-Palestine during the Middle Bronze Period (2000–1550 B.C.E.).

The category of Northwest Semitic includes the languages that are most directly related to the world of the Bible, especially Ugaritic, Hebrew, Phoenician, and Aramaic. The most widespread Northwest Semitic language was Aramaic. It was written with an alphabet of just twenty-two letters instead of the hundreds of Akkadian symbols. Aramaic replaced Akkadian as the language of diplomacy after 1000 B.C.E. Arameans were associated with Aram (Syria), and particularly with Damascus, but they appeared throughout Mesopotamia and Syria-Palestine. Most of the Bible was written in Hebrew, although part of the book of Daniel (Dan 2:4—7:28) and a few other biblical passages were written in Aramaic (Gen 31:47; Jer 10:11; Ezra 4:8—6:18; 7:12-26).

Hieroglyphics

The most important artifact recovered by Napoleon's Scientific and Artistic Commission was the Rosetta Stone. While they were repairing the fortifications at Fort Julien near the Egyptian port city of Rosetta (Arabic: *Rashid),* French military engineers under the command of Captain Pierre-François Bouchard discovered the stone on July 15, 1799. It is dark grey and pink granodiorite. It weighs sixteen-hundred pounds and is forty-five inches high, twenty-eight inches wide, and ten inches thick.

The Rosetta Stone was originally erected to call on Egyptians to worship their thirteen-year-old pharaoh, Ptolemy V Epiphanes (204–181 B.C.E.) on the first anniversary of his coronation in 196 B.C.E. The priests ordered the inscription to be written three times; once in classic Egyptian hieroglyphics, once in Demotic Egyptian longhand, and once in Greek.

Egyptians used a hieroglyphic form of writing that underwent several stages of development (Bakir 1978; Gardiner 1957; Davies 1958; Budge 1978). Hieroglyphic Egyptian characters were carved or painted on stone. This system evolved into a cursive or longhand writing known as *Demotic* Egyptian. Demotic appeared about 650 B.C.E. and was used for business, legal, scientific, literary, and religious documents written on papyrus. Although the use of Demotic Egyptian in wood and stone inscriptions is not unknown, its use on the Rosetta Stone is exceptional.

In the days of the Rosetta Stone Egyptian hieroglyphics were used primarily in inscriptions on temple walls and tombs. Sometimes the glyphs or word-pictures are very detailed and painted in color; sometimes they are simple outlines. When Theodosius I (347–395) decreed that Christianity was the only religion that could be practiced in the Byzantine Empire, pre-Christian sanctuaries such as the temples in Egypt were closed, and knowledge of Egyptian hieroglyphics was lost.

Greek was the language of the rulers of Egypt after 331 B.C.E. when Greek-speaking Alexander of Macedonia—Alexander the Great—conquered Egypt from the Persians, who had ruled there for some two hundred years (525–331 B.C.E.). Like Nebuchadnezzar II before him, Alexander carved his own annals into the walls of the sanctuaries at Luxor to create a living museum identifying his empire with the empire of ancient Egypt.

Ptolemy, one of Alexander's generals, became governor of Egypt after Alexander's death in 323 B.C.E. In 305 B.C.E. Ptolemy declared himself Pharaoh Ptolemy I Soter. The Greek-speaking Ptolemies ruled Egypt for three hundred years (305–30 B.C.E.). Ptolemy V Epiphanes, honored by the Rosetta Stone, is one of Ptolemy I Soter's successors.

COPTIC ALPHABET			
ⲁ	ⲃ	ⲅ	ⲗ
alpha	beta	gamma	dalda
ⲉ	ⲋ	ⲍ	ⲏ
ei	sou	zeta	eta
ⲑ	ⲓ	ⲕ	ⲗ
theta	iota	kappa	laula
ⲙ	ⲛ	ⳅ	ⲟ
me	ne	ksi	ou
ⲡ	ⲣ	ⲥ	ⲧ
pi	ro	semma	tau
ⲩ	ⲫ	ⲭ	ⲯ
he	phi	khi	psi
ⲱ	ⲱ	ϥ	ⳃ
o	šai	fai	hai
ϩ	ϭ	ϯ	ⳉ
hori	čima	ti	dandia

GREEK ALPHABET			
αA	βB	γΓ	δΔ
alpha	beta	gamma	delta
εE	ζZ	ηH	θΘ
epsilon	zeta	eta	theta
ιI	κK	λΛ	μM
iota	kappa	lamda	mu
νN	ξΞ	oO	πΠ
nu	xi	omicron	pi
ρP	σΣ	τT	υΥ
rho	sigma	tau	upsilon
φΦ	χX	ψΨ	ωΩ
phi	chi	psi	omega

Jean F. Champollion

After Napoleon's defeat, the Treaty of Alexandria (1801) required the French to surrender the Rosetta Stone and other Egyptian artifacts to the British. These antiquities then became part of the Egyptian Collection at the British Museum.

In 1822 French linguist Jean F. Champollion (1790–1832) used the Demotic Egyptian inscription on the Rosetta Stone to decipher its hieroglyphic Egyptian inscription.

Champollion was a prodigy. He taught himself Hebrew, Arabic, Syriac, Chaldean (Iraq), and Chinese. When he was ten, he began his formal education and the study of Coptic (Egypt), Ethiopic (Ethiopia), Sanskrit (India), Zend (Iran), Pahlevi (Iran), and Persian (Iran). When he was sixteen, he read a research report to the Grenoble Academy proposing that Coptic was the same language that was spoken by the ancient Egyptians. At the age of eighteen, he was appointed to teach history and politics at Grenoble. He completed his Ph.D. and began publishing when he was twenty years old. *Introduction to Egypt under the Pharaohs* (1811) and *Egypt of the Pharaohs: Geography, Religion, Language and History of the Egyptians before the Invasion of Cambyses* (1814) were among his most important works.

As Champollion had argued at the Grenoble Academy, Coptic is the direct descendant of Egyptian hieroglyphics. The Coptic alphabet is a slightly modified form of the Greek alphabet, with some additional letters. As a living language, Coptic flourished throughout Egypt from 400 to 1700. During the European Renaissance, scholars traveled to Egypt to learn Coptic from native speakers. Coptic survives today as the liturgical language of the Coptic Orthodox Church.

Champollion matched seven Demotic Egyptian words on the Rosetta Stone with their Coptic equivalents. Then he matched the Coptic words with their hieroglyphic Egyptian equivalents. For the first time, inscriptions from the days of the pharaohs could be translated by Europeans. Champollion became the *Father of Egyptology.*

After Champollion had translated the Rosetta Stone, the French government hired him to visit the museums in Turin, Livorno, Rome, Naples, and Florence (Italy) to study how they preserved and exhibited their antiquities. The government then appointed him curator of the Egyptian Collection at the Louvre.

During the years 1828–1829, Champollion and his student from Pisa (Italy), Ippolito Rosellini (1800–1843), conducted a survey of Egypt. Champollion took detailed notes and made sketches that Rosellini later converted into engravings. Their fieldwork updated and enlarged the *Description d'Égypte* published by Napoleon's Scientific and Artistic Commission.

The Egyptian language deciphered by Champollion is an Afro-Asiatic language related to Berber and Semitic languages such as Hebrew, Amharic, and Arabic. Egyptian developed in Africa as early as 3200 B.C.E.

Cuneiform

France anchored its claim to the imperial heritage in the world of the Bible by colonizing Egypt, and Britain colonized Mesopotamia. Like the empires of Egypt and Mesopotamia before them, France and Britain divided Syria-Palestine, the homeland of ancient Israel. Once the colonization of these ancient lands was complete, the work of scholars began. Champollion's success in reading the language of ancient Egypt for France was paralleled by the work of Georg Friedrich Grotefend (Germany), Henry Rawlinson (Britain), Edward Hincks (Ireland), and Jules Oppert (German), who deciphered the Mesopotamian writing system of cuneiform.

The earliest cuneiform inscriptions were pictographs or icons. These pictographs evolved into signs or patterns created by wedges. Most of the cuneiform signs were so stylized that they bore little resemblance to the original pictographs. Originally, each cuneiform sign stood for one or more related words whose correct meaning was determined by their context. For example, a cuneiform star stood for both "a star in the night sky" and "a member of the divine assembly." Likewise, a cuneiform foot stood for both the verbs "to stand" and "to go." Cuneiform developed some six hundred signs. Eventually signs came to represent either words or syllables. A few signs could also indicate that the sign following it referred to a particular category such as *a city* or *a people*. The remarkable thing about the cuneiform system is that, for all its complexity, it had sufficient flexibility to permit its adaptation to a large number of extremely different languages (Daniels 1996; Rogers 1915, 1:1–273).

Georg F. Grotefend (1775–1853), a language teacher, was the first European who tried to decipher cuneiform writing. To translate Egyptian hieroglyphics Champollion used one inscription written three times in two different languages. In his attempt to translate cuneiform, Grotefend also used one inscription written in three different languages all using cuneiform. The inscription Grotefend chose was on a trade route through the Zagros Mountains between Babylon (Iraq) and Ecbatana (Iran). These annals for the year 519 B.C.E. were carved by Darius I (ruled 521–486 B.C.E.), Great King of Persia, high up on the face of Mount Behistun. The visual effect is as imposing as the faces of the four American presidents carved on Mount Rushmore in South Dakota.

The annals describe how Darius successfully preserved the unity of the Persian Empire by defeating his enemies and becoming Great King after the death of Cambyses (530–521 B.C.E.). Darius promulgated his annals throughout the empire, even as far south as the Island of Elephantine in Egypt. Persia had stationed a detachment of soldiers from Judah to guard Egypt's southern border against Nubia (Sudan). Among the official documents of the detachment was a copy of these annals of Darius written in the Aramaic language on papyrus.

Grotefend correctly identified the languages on Mount Behistun as Persian (Iran), Babylonian (Iraq), and Elamite (Iran). He was also able to identify some personal names that appeared in the inscription. Nonetheless, he was ultimately unsuccessful in translating the inscription and learning how to read cuneiform itself.

In 1846 **Henry Rawlinson** (1810–1895) finally learned how to read cuneiform. Rawlinson was a British army intelligence officer serving in the Middle East. While stationed in Persia (Iran), he learned Persian and took a great interest in the archaeological ruins at Persepolis and other ancient

Rock relief of Darius the Great in the act of chaining up the imposter kings and with inscriptions in three languages. Hovering above the scene is the official Persian divinity, Ahura Mazda, who is rendered in a winged sun-like disk. Location: Behistun, Iran.
Photo Credit: Alinari / Art Resource, NY.

sites. Rawlinson was a cryptographer, a specialist in breaking military codes. He decided to use his skills to decipher the cuneiform code. Learning to read an ancient language, like learning to decipher a military code, requires both intelligence and instinct. These he applied to the Annals of Darius, discerning that there were three different languages using the same script and that the content was the same in each language.

Rawlinson went to Mount Behistun to make his own copy of the annals. He balanced a home-made ladder on a twelve-inch ledge. Behind him was a sheer drop of several hundred feet. Although Rawlinson was not initially able to copy the entire inscription, he did copy enough to use as the basis for a presentation to the Royal Asiatic Society of London in 1839 (Rawlinson 1852).

Working independently of Rawlinson, **Edward Hincks** (1792–1866) argued correctly that cuneiform writing had been invented by the Sumerians but was then used for writing Babylonian, Assyrian, and Elamite (Larson 1997). He also discovered that each cuneiform symbol represented a syllable or sound, not a word, and that cuneiform symbols were polyphonic—they could have more than one meaning. He determined the sound value of the vowels by studying Persian written in cuneiform, and he identified the meaning of determinatives (e.g., name of a city, name of a people) used in cuneiform. His greatest achievement, however, was translating cuneiform when it was used to write Akkadian.

To prove whether the work of Hincks, Rawlinson, and Oppert was reliable, William Henry Fox Talbot suggested that the four of them simultaneously and independently translate a recently discovered annal of Tiglath-Pileser I (1114–1076 B.C.E.). The contest took place in London in 1857. The translations of Hincks and Rawlinson were almost identical, which satisfied other Assyriologists that cuneiform could be accurately translated.

MODERN TRANSLATION PROJECTS

The work of deciphering ancient languages by intrepid archaeologists of language like Grotefend, Hincks, Rawlinson, and Oppert still continues. Today, however, the patrons of these translation projects are no longer emperors but museums. The Oriental Institute at the University of Chicago began work on the *Assyrian Dictionary* (CAD) in 1921 (http://oi.uchicago.edu). The University of Pennsylvania Museum of Archaeology and Anthropology began work on *The Sumerian Dictionary of the University Museum of the University of Pennsylvania* (PSD) in 1974.

Chicago Assyrian Dictionary

William Rainey Harper (1856–1906), a professor of Semitic languages, not only founded the University of Chicago and served as its first president but also created a Semitics department that would become an international center of excellence in Near Eastern studies. Harper had been president of the Chautauqua Institution (New York), where he met John D. Rockefeller, the owner of Standard Oil Company. Rockefeller convinced him to start a university in the Midwest that could rival schools such as Yale University (Connecticut) on the East Coast. With Rockefeller's financial help, Harper founded the University of Chicago in 1891. During his tenure, the university attracted some 120 distinguished faculty to the growing ten-building campus.

One promising young scholar hired by Harper was James H. Breasted. He was the first scholar in the United States to earn an advanced degree in Egyptology. Breasted championed the study of the impact of the Near East on Western cultures. In 1919, he established the Oriental Institute to reconstruct the connections between the eastern Mediterranean cultures—Egypt, Mesopotamia and Syria-Palestine—and the western Mediterranean cultures—Greece and Rome. In 1921, he launched the *Chicago Assyrian Dictionary* as a comprehensive resource for the various dialects of Akkadian, the earliest known Semitic language recorded in cuneiform on tablets between 2400 B.C.E. and 100 C.E.

Today the Oriental Institute is a complex of laboratories, museum galleries, libraries, and offices. Visitors to the museum each year number in the thousands; scholars using its collections, in the hundreds. By compiling dictionaries and developing special techniques for copying ancient texts, the Oriental Institute continues to be at the forefront of epigraphy—the copying and interpreting of inscriptions and associated pictures. Since 1924, the Epigraphic Survey has been located at Chicago House in Luxor (Egypt), where its staff of Egyptologists and artists record the rapidly eroding inscriptions carved on the monuments of ancient Egypt.

Pennsylvania Sumerian Dictionary

The *Sumerian Dictionary* project was begun in 1974 by Åke Sjöberg and Erle Leichty. Using thousands of note cards each containing a single, hand-copied Sumerian sign, Sjöberg and Leichty began reconstructing the uses and meanings of the signs. Initially the *Sumerian Dictionary* was to be hardcopy volumes like the *Assyrian Dictionary* at the University of Chicago. It took until 1998 to produce four volumes, which covered only a small portion of the Sumerian signs catalogue. Today the dictionary is primarily digital and published online (http://psd.museum.upenn.edu). Steve Tinney is now the director of a seven-member team responsible for the project. This electronic dictionary is an updatable collection of signs with their definitions. Each entry is linked by a search engine to scanned images of the tablets where the sign appears.

Sumerian does not belong to either the Semitic or Indo-European language families common in the ancient Near East. It is unique. Therefore, the *Sumerian Dictionary* is more than just a translation tool. To understand each word requires a detailed encyclopedia-style entry explaining how each word was used and its shades of meaning.

The Sumerians settled and farmed in Mesopotamia between the Tigris and Euphrates Rivers as early as 3200 B.C.E. This talented people invented the cuneiform writing system (Glassner 2003). Sumerian cuneiform or "wedge writing" is a way of carving wedge-shapes (Latin *cuneus*) into clay, wax, stone, or metal tablets (Kramer 1956).

Some thirty thousand Sumerian cuneiform tablets and fragments are now at the University of Pennsylvania Museum of Archaeology and Anthropology. Most were copied not for the royal library at Nippur (Iraq), as excavators first thought, but for use as home school texts for the children of Nippur's elite. It is surprising that these tablets survived. Typically school texts were recycled at the end of each class; the soft clay tablets were collected, rolled into balls and then left soaking in water until the next class.

There are tablets as small as 2 x 4 inches and as large as 8 x 12 inches. Initially Sumerian merchants recorded transactions by using soft clay tablets impressed with symbols representing the goods they were selling or transporting. Eventually the contents of tablets dealt with every aspect of Sumerian life—finance, medicine, herding, childbearing, mathematics, astronomy, and politics. Merchants, teachers, priests, and politicians throughout the world of the Bible would eventually use cuneiform, and thousands of their clay tablets would survive. Most surviving Sumerian tablets were written between 3000 and 2000 B.C.E.

Sumerian culture was preserved by the Semitic peoples of Babylon and Assyria who followed the Sumerians in Mesopotamia. Because Sumerian is an *isolate* language—without language relatives, living or dead—scholars translate Sumerian using tablets written in both Sumerian and Akkadian, a better-known Semitic language. Like hieroglyphics, cuneiform writing remained in use for almost four thousand years and was used to write a whole range of different languages: Akkadian (Iraq), Babylonian (Iraq), Assyrian (Iraq), Hurrian (Iraq), Eblaite (Syria), Ugaritic (Syria), Hittite (Turkey), Luwian (Turkey), Palaic (Turkey), Urartian (Armenia), Elamite (Iran), and Persian (Iran). Ugaritic (Syria) was written in a cuneiform writing system that developed independently from the cuneiform writing system developed by the Sumerians.

UNDERSTANDING THE BIBLE

Nabu-sharrusu-ukin and Jeremiah 39:13

Ongoing work on cuneiform languages like the Chicago *Assyrian Dictionary* and the Pennsylvania *Sumerian Dictionary* continues to enrich the understanding of the world of the Bible in many ways. Some ways are quite simple, others are more complicated.

There are some 130,000 cuneiform tablets in the British Museum. In 2007 Michael Jursa was studying a group of tablets containing receipts for business transactions. Among them was a receipt for a deposit of gold on a tablet just over two inches wide.

Nabu-sharrusu-ukin, the prime minister, gave twenty-six ounces of gold to Arad-Banitu, the minister of finance, to deposit at the Temple of Esagila—dedicated to Marduk, the divine patron of Babylon. In the presence of Bel-usat, son of Alpaya, a royal bodyguard, and in the presence of Nadin, son of Marduk-zer-ibni, Arad-Banitu deposited the gold at the Temple of Esagila on Month Eleven, Day Eighteen, Year Ten of the reign of Nebuchadnezzar, Great King of Babylon (595 B.C.E.).

In the book of Jeremiah (Jer 39:13) the same Nebuchadnezzar II appoints Nebu-shazban to negotiate the surrender of Jerusalem with Zedekiah, king of Judah, in 587 B.C.E. On the cuneiform tablet, the official's name is spelled: *Nabu-sharrusu-ukin*; in the Hebrew Bible his name is spelled: *Nebu-shazban*. The differences in spelling are somewhat parallel to *Guillermo* in Spanish being spelled *William* in English. For biblical archaeologists, who are maximalists, the parallel is one small part in their larger argument that the Bible reliably reflects real people and real events. Teachers composing stories to help Jews preserve their identity in a Hellenistic world would probably not have known the name of the Babylonian official who negotiated the surrender of Jerusalem some three hundred years earlier. This is a example of the simple contributions that archaeologists of language make to the understanding of the world of the Bible.

Legal Systems in the Ancient Near East

Work on cuneiform languages has had a more profound impact on understanding the subtlety and complexities of the legal systems in the Near East. These legal systems had a marked influence on the legal traditions in the biblical books of Deuteronomy and Leviticus, and on the Qur'an and *Shari'a* (Westbrook 1985).

Shari'a

Shari'a is a way of life that developed during the first two hundred years of Islam (600–800). *Shari'a* is an important influence in Muslim morality, but it is the official legal system only in Nigeria, Sudan, Iran, Libya, and Saudi Arabia. Rooted in the Qur'an, *Shari'a* has also been

THE RIGHT WAY

Qur'an 45:18-20 (Ali 1993, 428)

"We have put you on the right way (Arabic: *Shari'a*) in the matter of divine law. So follow it, and do not follow the wishes of those who are ignorant. They will not avail you in the least against God. Surely the wicked are each other's friends, but God befriends those who fear and follow the right path. These are precepts of wisdom for men, and guidance and grace for people who believe with certainty." ∎

influenced by legal traditions in the Bible; by Bedouin traditions; by commercial regulations from Mecca and Medina, which were early Islamic communities; by Roman law, which governed the Byzantine Empire to which Arabia belonged; and by legal systems in the countries conquered by Muslims. Although *Shari'a* covers many aspects of Muslim private and public life, it has become notorious for the use of stoning as a punishment for women who commit adultery. The sentence of stoning cannot be imposed unless either the defendant confesses, or four men (or eight women) testify that they witnessed the adultery (Qur'an 24:13). The large number of witnesses required was meant to make enforcing the sentence of stoning almost impossible.

After a woman named Suriya confessed to committing adultery with Abdul Jabbar, Taliban leaders stoned her to death on May 1, 2000. The stoning was carried out at Mazar-e-Sharif sports stadium in Kabul (Afghanistan) before several thousand spectators. Abdul Jabbar was not punished.

Shari'a was enforced again in March 2002, when Amina Lawal was sentenced to death by stoning for committing adultery and having a child with her partner. On September 23, 2003, however, an Islamic court of five judges in Katsina (Nigeria) overturned the sentence. The right of appeal varies from place to place throughout the Islamic world but is not uncommon.

Reading the Bible or the Qur'an without archaeology can create serious misunderstandings of their legal traditions that lead to the imposing of cruel, unusual, or excessive punishments. Before the work of archaeologists of language, it was generally assumed that legal teachings in the Bible described the only possible punishment for the crime in the indictment. Hence, the instruction "If the father of a household is convicted of adultery with the mother of another household, both of them shall be put to death" (Deut 22:22) was assumed to mean that the only sentence that an assembly could impose for adultery was death. The archaeology of language is now beginning to show that these legal teachings stipulate the maximum sentence for a crime, not the only sentence.

The Trial of the Slandered Bride

During the spring of 1737 B.C.E. in Nippur (Iraq), a marriage covenant was negotiated between a man named Enlil-issu and a woman named Ama-sukkal. The covenant stipulated that the household of Ama-sukkal would pay Enlil-issu a dowry of nine ounces of silver upon signing the covenant, but that Ama-sukkal would continue to live with the household of her father until they consummated their marriage. The covenant also stipulated that either Enlil-issu or Ama-sukkal had the right to abrogate the covenant. After ten years their marriage had still not been ratified, so the couple appeared in court seeking a divorce. As the Code of Hammurabi (CH #130) indicates, lengthy delays between contracting a marriage and consummating a marriage were not unusual.

Enlil-issu accused Ama-sukkal of sexual promiscuity and misrepresenting her eligibility for marriage; Ama-sukkal accused Enlil-issu of slandering her. If Enlil-issu prevailed, he would not have to return the dowry to the household of Ama-sukkal, and he would not have to pay a cancellation penalty of eleven ounces of silver to divorce her. If he did not prevail, Enlil-issu would have to ratify his marriage to Ama-sukkal and pay a fine for the false accusation. A cuneiform tablet (UET 5) preserves the transcript of the trial (Hilprecht 1893–1914, 6/2:58; Gadd, Legrain et al. 1928, 5:256; Hallo and Younger 2003, 3:199). The trial is significant for the understanding of both ancient Near Eastern legal systems in general and legal systems in the Bible in particular (Hallo 1964, 95–105).

Village (Akkadian: *babtum*) assemblies in the world of the Bible were typically composed of fathers of households. Here, however, Enlil-issu and Ama-sukkal appear before an assembly composed of mothers of households (Akkadian: *sibatum*). The village assembly was the court of first resort. Here citizens were judged by their neighbors. So there must have been good grounds for them to argue their cases before an assembly of mothers rather than fathers. Since Enlil-issu is alleging that Ama-sukkal lied to him about her virginity, women, rather than men, were more appropriate jurors to determine physically whether his accusation was true or false.

To call the court to order, the bronze *Sharur* scepter of Ninurta—the divine patron who fed and protected Nippur—was placed in its stand; and the mothers of the households in the neighborhood took their places. The mothers did not find Ama-sukkal guilty of slander against Enlil-issu; they did, however, find Enlil-issu guilty of slander against Ama-sukkal. When he heard the verdict, Enlil-issu addressed the court. "You may convict me of slander, but I will not ratify my marriage covenant with her. I would rather go to jail and pay a fine."

There is also a teaching on a slandered bride in the book of Deuteronomy (Deut 22:13-21). In Babylon, the woman was physically examined by the mothers of households before the marriage was consummated. In the Bible, the fathers of households examined the blood-stained sheets after the marriage was consummated. According to biblical teaching, a husband convicted of falsely accusing his wife of adultery was flogged, paid a fine of thirty-six ounces of silver, and could not divorce his wife. In Babylon, a husband convicted of falsely accusing his wife of lying about her virginity was required to return his wife's dowry, pay a fine for false accusation, and consummate their marriage.

There is also a teaching concerning false witness in the book of Deuteronomy (Deut 19:16-21): "you shall punish the witness just as the witness intended to punish the defendant" (v. 19). If this teaching were applied in the case of the slandered bride, the husband bearing false witness against the wife for adultery would be sentenced to death.

Nonetheless, the trial of the slandered bride from Nippur demonstrates that men and women convicted of false witness were subject to a variety of sentences. For example, the village assembly sentenced Enlil-issu to ratify his marriage covenant with Ama-sukkal. They could also have sentenced him to pay a fine or to go to jail. Enlil-issu did not appeal his conviction, but he did appeal his sentence. He wanted to pay a fine or go to jail. He did not want to consummate his marriage with Ama-sukkal.

In the teachings on slander and premarital promiscuity in the book of Deuteronomy the sentence imposed on the husband may also demonstrate that death is the maximum sentence, not the only sentence. The husband is convicted of slander and sentenced to be shamed—to lose his social status—by flogging, by paying a fine, and by losing his right to divorce his wife (Wells 2005). He could have been sentenced to death but was not. If the wife had been guilty of adultery, she could have been sentenced to death, but, like her husband, could also receive a lesser sentence.

The ability of archaeologists to read cuneiform tablets from the world of the Bible enriches the understanding of the legal system in ancient Israel. There is now less evidence that the legal system lacked gender equality or that it required mandatory sentencing. Parallels such as the tablet from Nippur demonstrate that the intention of the legal teachings may not have been to instruct village assemblies to punish women more severely than men or always to impose the death penalty for capital offenses. The teachings may simply instruct village assemblies to punish men and women appropriately and to choose among sentences, not automatically impose a single sentence.

CONCLUSION

The archaeology of languages begun by European emperors and continued today by university museums is an important partner in any reliable interpretation of the Bible. Using archaeology and the Bible together, for example, makes it clear that legal systems in Judaism, Christianity, and Islam that impose cruel and unusual punishments on women for their sexual behavior cannot appeal to the Bible or to the world of the Bible to justify their legal practice. The archaeology of language is intensive; biblical exegesis is complex. The results, however, could ultimately separate religion from violence.

WHAT YOU HAVE LEARNED

- Unfortunately, emperors used archaeology to link the accomplishments of the empires of Mesopotamia and Egypt with their empires and to justify their desires to rule to world.
- Fortunately, emperors enriched the understanding and appreciation of the world of the Bible by creating collections of artifacts in their national museums and by making it possible for scholars to translate ancient languages.
- In 1822 French linguist Jean-François Champollion (France) used an inscription on the Rosetta Stone to decipher hieroglyphic Egyptian.
- Beginning in 1839 George F. Grotefend (Germany), Henry Rawlinson (Britain), Edward Hincks (Ireland), and Jules Oppert (German) used an inscription on Mt. Behustin (Iran) to decipher Mesopotamian cuneiform.
- Scholars working on the Chicago *Assyrian Dictionary* (University of Chicago) and the Pennsylvania *Sumerian Dictionary* (University of Pennsylvania) continue the work of these early archaeologists of language to better understand cuneiform cultures in the world of the Bible in both simple and profound ways.

STUDY QUESTIONS

1. Have you visited a museum with an Egyptian collection? What kinds of artifacts did you see?
2. How did Napoleon contribute to archaeological knowledge of the ancient Near East?
3. What is the significance of the Rosetta Stone?
4. What were the important languages in the world of the Bible? Give some examples of writings preserved in those languages.
5. Name two individuals who played a role in deciphering ancient languages and describe their contributions.
6. How do ancient Near Eastern writings contribute to the understanding of the Bible?

PREVIEW: ARCHAEOLOGY OF TRAVELERS

- Travelers and Orientalism
  - Edward W. Lane
  - David Roberts
- Archaeologists and Museum Curators
  - Gertrude Bell
  - Donny George Youkhanna
- Nineveh in the Bible
  - Nineveh in the Book of Jonah

Chapter 3 explains the difference between good orientalism and bad orientalism and what inspired travelers to visit the world of the Bible. It also explains the connection between Gertrude Bell the traveler and Gertrude Bell the archaeologist, discussing who continued to care for the artifacts of Babylon and Nineveh when foreign travelers and archaeologists were no longer welcome in Iraq. Finally, it shows why Westerners idealize archaeologists working in Iraq but demonize the people of the ancient cultures they are studying, and how archaeology contributes to the understanding of the role that Nineveh plays in the book of Jonah.

3

Archaeology of Travelers

Faith inspired pilgrims to leave their homes in Europe and Africa and go to the lands where the ancestors of their religious traditions had lived and taught. The quest for military and economic power inspired emperors to send their armies into the world of the Bible. Curiosity and adventure inspired travelers to leave their homes for the world of the Bible faraway.

TRAVELERS AND ORIENTALISM

Travelers often shared the view that the Orient that inspired them was a fragile world that was rapidly being destroyed. What they were traveling to see would soon be gone. To preserve their experience for those who would be unable to follow in their footsteps, pioneering travelers often committed themselves not only to visiting but also to immortalizing these wonderful worlds through writings and art. Edward W. Lane (1801–1876) recorded his travels in monumental cultural studies such as *Description of Egypt* (edited and published in 2000) and an *Arabic-English Lexicon* (1863). David Roberts (1796–1864) preserved his travels in paintings. Gertrude Bell (1868–1926) founded the Baghdad Archaeological Museum, known today as the Iraq Museum, Baghdad.

Regardless of how travelers preserved the material remains of the cultures they admired, their memorials reflect as much about their own attitudes as about the cultures themselves. The orientalism of David Roberts, for example,

> **Orientalism** *has two meanings (Said 1978–2003).*
>
> *First, orientalism or Assyriology refers to the academic discipline that studies the Near Eastern cultures of Mesopotamia and its neighbors. William Foxwell Albright, for example, considered himself to be an orientalist, a student of Near Eastern cultures. Second, "orientalism" refers to a racial prejudice that developed after 1900 against cultures in the Middle East. This orientalism considers western European cultures to be intellectual, dynamic, and inclusive. In contrast, it considers cultures of the Middle East to be impulsive, stagnant, and intolerant. As a prejudice, orientalism influences not only public opinion but also scholarship and art.*

portrayed the people and places of the world of the Bible as much less sophisticated and less corrupted than his European contemporaries. His paintings idealized an innocent world, and he depicted its passing with a mood of melancholy. Bell saw the cultures of Mesopotamia as prototypes of the British Empire, which was her home. She sponsored excavations to recover and restore the material remains of the grandeur of ancient times as an endorsement of her own era. She seemed to be more comfortable with the ancestors of Britain's greatness than with her contemporaries.

Edward W. Lane (1801–1876)

Edward W. Lane visited Egypt for the first time in 1825 about which he wrote

> I was not visiting Egypt merely as a traveler, to examine its pyramids and temples and grottoes, and, after satisfying my curiosity, to quit it for other scenes and pleasures; I was about to throw myself entirely among strangers; to adopt their language, their customs and their dress; and, in associating almost exclusively with the natives, to prosecute the study of their literature. (Jason Thompson 2008, x)

Lane became a renowned student of the culture of Egypt. His fascinating study of Egyptian society, *An Account of the Manners and Customs of the Modern Egyptians* (1836), is a classic that is still in print. His Arabic-English dictionary continues to be a basic reference work.

David Roberts (1796–1864)

Napoleon's highly publicized conquest of Egypt in 1798 greatly increased the interest of European artists in the world of the Bible. One was Scotland's David Roberts, who was a friend of Edward Lane and sought his advice to prepare for his own travels into the world of the Bible. When Roberts was forty-two years old, he traveled to Egypt and Syria-Palestine. He kept a journal of his travels in pictures of places mentioned in the Bible. In 1838 he exhibited *Departure of the Israelites from Egypt* and subsequently published his drawings as lithographs made with Louis Haghe (1829–1898). Eventually Roberts published six volumes of illustrations entitled *The Holy Land, Syria, Idumea, Arabia, Egypt, and Nubia.* His work not only reflected the romantic influence of orientalism but also offered a unique record of the condition of major archaeological sites before their restoration or disappearance.

Roberts's extensive work brought him great renown, and the popularity of his drawings inspired a group of academics and clerics to establish the British Palestine Exploration Fund (PEF) in 1865 (http://www.pef.org.uk; Chapman 1990, 8–36). The purpose of the PEF is to promote research into the archaeology, history, manners, customs, culture, topography, geology, and natural sciences of Syria-Palestine.

The PEF's most significant project was mapping the British Mandate of Palestine. The Survey of Western Palestine was conducted by H. H. Kitchener (1850–1916), among others. This survey became an invaluable resource for archaeologists, botanists, geologists, and geographers. General Edmund H. Allenby (1861–1936) used these maps when the British army occupied Jerusalem in 1917 (Isbouts 2007:344–51).

ARCHAEOLOGISTS AND MUSEUM CURATORS

Gertrude Bell (1868–1926)

In 1921 Winston Churchill assembled a commission of experts on the Middle East to determine

David Roberts. Remains of the great colossus of Thebes (Ramesseum). Location: Victoria and Albert Museum, London, Great Britain. Photo Credit: Erich Lessing / Art Resource, NY.

the future of Iraq. He invited ninety-nine men and one woman—Gertrude Bell. Bell almost single-handedly drew the borders of Iraq for Churchill's government. She also chose Faisal ibn Hussein (1883–1935) to be its first ruler. Bell remained in Iraq for years after Faisal's coronation in 1923 as his personal adviser.

Bell was born in England (Cohen and Joukowsky 2004). Her grandfather was Isaac Lowthian Bell, a wealthy manufacturer. When she was only sixteen, she enrolled in Oxford and graduated just two years later *summa cum laude* in history. Bell began her career as an intrepid world traveler. She spoke English, Arabic, French, German, Italian, Persian, and Turkish, and she became an accomplished mountaineer in Switzerland's Alps.

After Bell graduated from Oxford, she traveled to Tehran (Iraq) where her uncle, Frank Lascelles, worked for the British government. Bell kept a journal of her experiences which she later published as *Persian Pictures* (1894). In 1899 Bell traveled through Syria-Palestine. On one trip she disguised herself as a Bedouin male and went in search of the Druze Bedouin. She succeeded in reaching the sacred mountain of

Gertrude Bell

the Druze (Arabic: Jebel Druze), and became a close friend of Yahya Beg, the Druze ruler.

Bell made a second trip to the lands of both the Druze and Beni Sakhr Bedouin, who treated her as an honored guest. Bell's travel diaries such as *The Desert and the Sown* (1907) were filled with riveting images of daily life in the desert and captured the imaginations of Western travelers.

Bell evolved from being an observant traveler into an archaeologist of some accomplishment on her trip to Turkey with William M. Ramsey (1851–1939). Ramsey was a classical scholar and archaeologist who specialized in the geography, antiquities, and history of Asia Minor (Turkey). Bell co-authored their excavation report—*A Thousand and One Churches* (1909).

In 1909 Bell traveled to the Hittite city of Carchemish (Turkey) and located the ruins of Ukhaidir, a palace southwest of Baghdad built in 774–775 by Isa ibn Musa, a nephew of Caliph Al-Mansur (712–775) (Saoud 2002). At Carchemish, she worked closely with T. E. Lawrence (1888–1935). Bell was also only the second European woman after Anne Blunt (1837–1917) to visit Ha'il (Saudi Arabia). The Ha'il is a rest stop for Iraqi pilgrims en route to Mecca.

During World War I (1914–1918), Bell worked as a British intelligence officer and helped T. E. Lawrence, her former colleague from the excavation at Carchemish, to organize the Arab Revolt against the Turkish government. Britain awarded Bell the Order of the Empire for her service.

After the war Bell founded the Baghdad Archaeological Museum, today known as the Iraq Museum. The museum opened in June 1926. Bell was the first director of the museum. As director, she insisted that artifacts remain in Iraq and not be exported to collections in Europe.

In the 1920s George A. Barton (1859–1942) asked the Archaeology Institute of America (AIA) to found a school of archaeology in Baghdad. The AIA sent Albert T. Clay (1866–1925) to Baghdad to establish the school. He proposed that the school open with a director and an annual professor. Curiously, Clay decided to affiliate the school with the American Schools of Oriental Research (ASOR), rather than with AIA.

Bell, who was not only director of the Baghdad Museum but also Honorary Director of Antiquities in Iraq, was sympathetic to the need for a school of archaeology in Baghdad, and she provided ASOR with office, classroom, and library space at the museum. She was not, however, impressed with Clay.

DIARY OF GERTRUDE BELL

October 31, 1923 . . . Professor Clay is going to inaugurate an American school of archaeology. He has no money until several people die who have life interests in the sum that is ultimately to come to the school, and he's quite vague about everything, however that's his business not mine. He gave a lecture on Babylonian archaeology on Monday, under my auspices. We had an enormous audience including lots of Baghdadis. How much even the English people understood I don't know. He's the most muddly old thing and incidentally never finishes a sentence. I was of the opinion that you had to know a considerable amount yourself to be aware of what he was driving at. But there's a very genuine interest here in the ancient history of the country and people always flock to lectures.

In 1924–1925, Edward Chiera (1885–1933) was Annual Professor at ASOR. He had studied Semitic languages at the University of Pennsylvania and had worked on the University of Chicago Assyrian Dictionary project. Chiera planned to survey southern Iraq, but Bell asked him to direct a salvage excavation at Nuzi (Arabic: *Yorghan Tepe*). The site was being looted for Baghdad's antiquities markets. So he excavated at Nuzi (1927–1928) and then at Khorsabad (1928–1929).

DIARY OF GERTRUDE BELL

April 22, 1925 . . . I have just been up to Kirkuk. J. M. [Wilson] and I flew up there by air mail yesterday morning and came back today. We went up to inspect a little excavation which is being done under the auspices of the Museum by . . . Chiera, an Italian who is professor of Assyriology at some American university. It is the home of some rich private person who lived about 800 B.C., very comfortable, with a nice big bathroom lined with bitumen so that you could splash about . . . we discovered the drain the afternoon we were there. It has fine big rooms and an open courtyard but it all came to a bad end for in every room the floor is covered with a thick layer of ashes, the remains of the wooden roof which fell in when the house was burnt down. Dr. Chiera has found a great quantity of tablets and we hope when they are deciphered to get the history of the well-to-do family which built and lived in the house. There are other similar houses round, forming the suburbs of a town represented by a comparatively big mound a couple of hundred yards away or more. Nothing in this part of the world has been excavated ever; it is all full of unanswered questions and I hope this tiny trial dig may turn people's minds in this direction.

Chiera had an ardent desire to make research interesting to the general public, and he had the skills of a good teacher to make it happen. *They Wrote on Clay* (1938), his introduction to archaeology, is a fascinating combination of archeology and storytelling. He describes a find of clay tablets that had been recently discovered in Iraq as part of an absorbing excursion into the daily life of the ancient culture of Babylon. This remarkable little volume opens with a letter to his wife.

A LETTER OF EDWARD CHIERA TO HIS WIFE

This evening I made my usual pilgrimage to the mound covering the ancient temple tower. It is only a few hundred yards from our camp, and it is pleasant to ascend to the summit of that tower, which dominates the landscape. This I generally do in the evening, after supper, in the bright moonlight. Today I have come with the ambition of jotting down my impressions, for the spectacle moves me deeply.

Seen from below, it does not look so high as might be expected of a Babylonian temple tower. Did not that of Babylon pretend to reach to heaven? One gets the answer after ascending it. Though rather low (it can hardly be more than five hundred feet), still from the top the eye sweeps over an enormous distance on the boundless, flat plain. Nothing breaks the view, and the plain finally melts into the horizon. About twenty miles away rises the high mound of Cutha. This city was sacred to Nergal, the god of pestilence and of the underworld. The ruins of Babylon are nearer. All around the tower small heaps of dirt represent all that remains of Kish, one of the oldest cities of Mesopotamia.

On all sides is desert. The yellowish soil is arid and thirsty, and no plant can survive the parching heat of the summer; sheep and camels must feed on whatever remains of the grass that has managed to sprout in the few weeks after the rains. The large network of canals, which in ancient times distributed the waters of the Euphrates over all this land, is now represented by a series of small mounds of dirt, running in all directions. Even the Euphrates has abandoned this land by changing its course. In ancient times it came very near to the city, giving water in abundance and affording an easy way of communication.

. . . Not a column or an arch still stands to demonstrate the permanency of human work. Everything has crumbled into dust. The very temple tower, the most imposing of all these ancient constructions, has entirely lost its original shape. Where are now its seven stages? Where the large stairway that led to the top? Where the shrine that crowned it? We see nothing but a mound of earth—all that remains of the millions of its bricks. On the very top some traces of walls. But these are shapeless: time and neglect have completed their work.

. . . It is now quite dark. . . . But a certain fascination holds me here. I should like to find a reason for all this desolation. Why should a flourishing city, the seat of an empire, have completely disappeared? Is it the fulfillment of a prophetic curse that changed a superb temple into a den of jackals? Did the actions of the people who lived here have anything to do with this, or is it the fatal destiny of man-kind that all its civilizations must crumble when they reach their peak? And what are we doing here, trying to wrest from the past its secrets, when probably we ourselves and our own achievements may become an object of search for peoples to come? (Chiera 1938, xi–xv)

Chiera's pioneering work at Nuzi motivated ASOR to partner with various universities in a series of important excavations through-out Iraq. Harvard University joined ASOR to continue his excavations at Nuzi (1927–1931). The University of Pennsylvania joined with ASOR to excavate Tepe Gawra (1927–1938), Tell Billa (1930–1937), Khafajah (1937–1938), and Fara (1931).

ASOR's roster of directors and annual professors includes E. A. Speiser, Nelson Glueck, Samuel Noah Kramer, Albrecht Goetze, and Thorkild Jacobsen. Their work is still the foundation for Near East-ern studies today. The ASOR library, endowed by Morris Jastrow, Jr. (1866–1921), was one of the first research libraries in Iraq and the core of the library at the Iraq Museum today.

Bell committed suicide in Baghdad on July 12, 1926. She had never married, nor had any children. She was buried at the British cemetery in Baghdad's Bab al-Sharji district. Her funeral was a major event. The

Ivory plaque of a lioness devouring a boy. From Nimrud, Iraq, 800-750 B.C.E. The carving, Phoenician in style, shows an African boy with jewelled armlets and bracelets being attacked by a lioness. Inv. 127412. Location: British Museum, London, Great Britain. Photo Credit: © British Museum / Art Resource, NY.

museum which she founded is a legacy not only to this remarkable woman, but also to all the archaeologists whose artifacts fill its halls and vaults. For all the riches of the British Museum, the Louvre, the Metropolitan Museum and other Western collections, the Iraq Museum has primacy.

Among the unique antiquities in the Iraq Museum are artifacts from the throne room of Ashunasirpal II at Nimrud. The site was discovered by Austen H. Layard (1817–1894) in 1848, and then excavated by Max Mallowan (1904–1978) in 1950. Its collection also includes exquisite artifacts from the royal tombs of Nimrud, excavated by Muzahim Mahmu in 1989–1991.

The Iraq Museum is the best place in the world to understand and to appreciate the cultural grandeur of Mesopotamia. Unfortunately, since its foundation few westerners have had the chance to visit the museum. The last traveling exhibition from the Iraq Museum visited only Geneva (Switzerland) and Hildesheim (Germany) in 1977–1978. Most of the museum's most significant holdings—the Warka Mask and Warka Vase from Uruk, the pottery from Samarra, the gold from Nimrud, and the copper head of Naram-Sin from Nineveh—remained in Baghdad.

After 1968, the Baath government of Saddam Hussein (1937–2006) restricted the work of European and North American archaeologists and universities in Iraq. Consequently, ASOR redirected its funding and faculty from Iraq to Lebanon, Syria, Turkey, and Iran. The government eventually did allow ASOR to resume excavations at Tell Hamide, Tell Abu Duwari, Abu Salabikh, and Tell al-Deylam. Work continued at these sites intermittently until the war between Iraq and Iran (1980–1988) and the Gulf Wars (1990–1991, 2003–) when all foreign archaeologists left Iraq.

Donny George Youkhanna

After foreign archaeologists left, Iraqi archaeologists and curators at the Iraq Museum continued the work of recovering and preserving the country's cultural heritage. Donny George Youkhanna is perhaps the most well known and respected of these archaeologists. For more than thirty years George—as he is known outside Iraq—was a constant presence in the work of the museum.

As a respected member of the international community of museum curators, George succeeded in acquiring grants for the museum from

---

In 1991, during the first Gulf War, the Iraq Museum was closed, and it did not reopen until 2000. When the second Gulf War was imminent, Donny George Youkhanna unsuccessfully tried to convince the board of directors to protect its collection. Consequently, in April 2003 the museum was looted and some fifteen thousand artifacts were lost (http://oi.uchicago.edu/OI/IRAQ). Subsequently as Director General of Iraq's Museums and chair of the Iraqi State Board of Antiquities and Heritage, George worked with the American military and civil command in Iraq and played an important role in the recovery or location of almost half of the stolen artifacts. Some of the stolen objects turned up for sale on eBay. In addition, gold jewelry and other precious items from the royal tombs at Nimrud, and objects from the royal cemetery at Ur were found in a vault below the Central Bank in Baghdad, where they had been hidden before the onset of the first Gulf War in 1990. ∎

the U.S. State Department, the Packard Humanities Institute of Los Altos, California (http://www.packhum.org), and the Iraqi Culture Ministry. These funds were used to repair some of the damage done to the museum in the Iraq War. The roof has been repaired, the telephone system updated, the fences upgraded, guard houses built, the plumbing fixed, the windows washed, the locks coordinated, the air-conditioning repaired, surveillance cameras installed, an electronic security system activated, and date palms planted in the courtyards. With the help of Iraqi curators newly trained in Jordan and Italy, the Centro Ricerche Archeologiche e Scavi di Torino per il Medio Oriente e l'Asia (Italy) restored both the Assyrian and the Islamic galleries at the museum (http://www.centroscavitorino.it/en/progetti/iraq/baghdad_museo.html). These two galleries contain large and almost immovable objects. The Assyrian Hall has monumental sculptures, including stone panels from the royal palace at Nineveh and two winged bulls. The Islamic Hall contains an ancient *mithrab*—the niche in a mosque that indicates the direction of Mecca—from the Al-Mansur Mosque in Baghdad.

Despite George's personal desire to play a leading role at the Iraq Museum after Saddam Hussein, he made the decision on July 30, 2006, to retire from the Iraq Museum, to take his family out of Iraq, and to accept a teaching position at the State University of New York at Stony Brook.

After the museum was turned over to the party of Moqtada al-Sadr, policy and personality disputes began to develop between George and the Ministry of Tourism and Antiquities. Al-Sadr, a Shiite cleric from a poor neighborhood of Baghdad, opposed the U.S. occupation of Iraq. He drew much of his popularity from the reverence many Iraqi Shiites felt for his father, Grand Ayatollah Mohammed Sadiq Sadr, who was assassinated in 1999 by Saddam Hussein. George had been a member of the Baath Party of Sadam Hussein, so the ministry considered him politically suspect. He was also an Orthodox Christian, not a Muslim, so he was religiously suspect. He had extensive international contacts, so he was patriotically suspect. The ministry also failed to fully fund the salaries for the fourteen hundred antiquities police who guarded sites throughout the country; consequently, looting resumed. Moreover, George was under pressure to focus the resources of the museum on Islamic heritage and away from the Bronze Age cultures (3400–1200 B.C.E.) for which the museum is famous. As public safety in Baghdad became worse, George had his staff move the museum's collection into vaults, and then he had the doors welded shut. He turned the entire museum into a vault, just as the ministry wanted him to reopen it to the public.

NINEVEH IN THE BIBLE

The Iraq Museum preserves artifacts from cultures as diverse as Uruk, Elam, Akkad, Assur, Babylon, Urartia, Medea, and Persia. Assyria and the Assyrian city of Nineveh had a major impact on the world of the Bible. Assyria was a port of trade during the Middle Bronze period (2000–1500 B.C.E.), a warrior state in the Late Bronze period (1500–1200 B.C.E.), and an empire during the Iron Age (1000–600 B.C.E.). Politically, Assyria reinvented itself again and again, and its material culture is both impressive and aesthetic. Nonetheless, to achieve the beauty of its art and the sophistication of political administration Assyria was obsessed with unparalleled violence in deeds, words, and images. This was the side of Nineveh and Assyria that the Bible remembers.

Biblical traditions like the Trial of Nineveh in the book of Nahum not only indict states like Assyria for their political crimes but also have contributed to a barbaric legacy against women and women's bodies in Western cultures influenced by the Bible. The metaphors of Yahweh portrayed as male punishing Nineveh portrayed as female have created an unfortunate precedent in Western cultures for identifying all that is male as good and all that is female as bad. Because the Bible uses male metaphors for Yahweh, it is easy for males to feel empowered brutally to control women and their sexuality. Such misuse of the Bible against women is an important focus of feminist biblical scholarship today (Keefe 2001, 9–35). ■

A TRIAL OF NINEVEH
(Nah 3:1-7)

Indictment

Nineveh—City of Blood! City of Lies! City built on the plunder of others—endless plunder! The crack of whip, the rumble of wheel, the galloping horse and the bounding chariot! Cavalry charging, swords flashing, spears shining, the dead in piles, heaps of corpses, dead bodies without end—they stumble over the bodies! Your countless, gracefully alluring affairs have made you the Witch Queen. Therefore, Yahweh Sabaoth indicts you for seducing and enslaving nations and peoples.

Sentence

I will lift up your skirts over your head. I will let the nations see your breasts and all peoples see your reproductive organs. I will throw excrement at you to shame you, and make an example of you. Then all who see you will shrink from you and say, "Nineveh is dead. Who will mourn for her?" Where shall I seek mourners for you?

In this prophetic trial, Nineveh is to be shamed as a prisoner of war. Nineveh will be paraded naked before all the states in the Assyrian Empire so that they can publicly insult and torture the formerly powerful city (Sweeney 2000, 436–46; Abusch 2002).

Interpretations of Nineveh in particular and of Assyrian culture in general show a long history of contradictory opinions in both general and scholarly arenas in Europe and North America (Frahm 2006).

Until 1800 information about Near Eastern cultures like Assyria was derived solely from the Bible and Greek and Roman writings. Jerusalem, Athens, and Rome were considered to be noble cities. Nineveh was an outsider, a city of chaos. Jerusalem taught Europe its faith. Rome taught Europe how to think and how to govern. Nineveh, in contrast, demonstrated how power could be abused. Although Europeans were shocked by the brutality of Nineveh, they nonetheless admired its military, political, and architectural accomplishments. For prophets like Isaiah, Jeremiah, and Ezekiel, Nineveh was the worst of enemies; nonetheless these prophets announced that Yahweh had sent Assyria to punish the people of Judah for their breach of covenant.

In time archaeologists like Paul-Émile Botta and Austen H. Layard excavated the material remains of Assyrian cultures at Khorsabad (Arabic: *Dur Sharrukin*), Nimrud (Arabic: *Kalhu*), and Nineveh (Arabic: *Tell Kuynjik; Nebi Yunus*). Likewise, their languages were translated, and their works of art were restored. Yet even after these ancient peoples began to speak for themselves, the interpretation of Assyria's material remains was far from uniform. Pastors and biblical scholars argued that Assyria's material remains confirmed the historical reliability of the Bible. Art historians argued that the architecture and sculpture of Assyria were inferior and primitive compared with those of Greece and Rome. Nineveh was still a city both despised and admired.

Curiously, although popular orientalism romanticized archaeologists working at Khorsabad, Nimrud, and Nineveh, Assyrian culture as a whole was demonized. The greatest obstacles to romanticizing Assyrian culture were the annals of the great kings of Assyria, which glorified the horrors of war and the torture of prisoners. These annals were the earliest traditions recovered and translated, and they scandalized Westerners who viewed war as an honorable competition governed by humane rules of engagement. The reality of war, of course, was neither honorable nor humane. The great kings, in contrast, were brutally honest about the price of peace and the cost of power. They had paid a great price to feed their people and protect their land, and they recorded that price in gruesome detail.

When Ashurnasirpal II (883–859 B.C.E.) conquered Tela, his annals reported that he beheaded some of his prisoners of war and stacked their heads in piles or hung them from trees; that he maimed other prisoners by cutting off their noses, or their ears, or their thumbs, or gouging out their eyes; that he burned teenage boys and girls alive; and that he razed the city to the ground. When Sennacharib conquered Lachish in 701 B.C.E. during his campaign in Judah, he ordered reliefs of his victory recorded in his trophy room at Nineveh. The reliefs, showing starving women and children

Assyrian warriors impaling Jewish prisoners after conquering Jewish fortress of Lachish in 701 B.C.E. Part of a relief from the palace of Sennacherib, Nineveh, Mesopotamia (Iraq). Assyrian, 8th century B.C.E. Location: British Museum, London, Great Britain. Photo Credit: Erich Lessing / Art Resource, NY.

The Nimrud ivories, like much else in the Iraq Museum, suffered as a result of the Gulf Wars and the looting of the museum. Some ivories, such as the *Lion Attacking a Nubian*, were stolen and have not yet been returned. Others such as the *Mona Lisa of Nimrud*, which is now split vertically into three pieces, have been damaged from being packed, stored, and unpacked. Some of the finest ivories were stored in water-tight containers in the vaults of the Central Bank in Baghdad during the first Gulf War. Those vaults were flooded to protect their contents from looters during the second Gulf War. The water hid the containers, and created a barrier making it impossible for the antiquities to be easily recovered by looters. ■

Ivory head of a woman (the "Mona Lisa" of Nimrud). Assyrian, 720 B.C.E. Location: Iraq Museum, Baghdad, Iraq. Photo Credit: Scala / Art Resource, NY.

evacuating the city and prisoners being impaled and skinned alive, were carved into the walls on alabaster panels.

Archaeological finds, however, not only pointed to a glorification of violence but also reflected gentleness and civility. Some Assyrian artifacts called into question the caricature of Nineveh as an oriental power that existed only to conquer, enslave, and plunder its neighbors. Assyrian masters produced exquisite miniatures in ivory and elegant jewelry in gold. Assyrian ivory work is unsurpassed in the Near East. Layard recovered a small ivory inlay just over four inches high. The inlay was originally installed in a piece of wooden furniture. The inlay depicts a woman of the ruling household wearing an Egyptian wig looking over the banister of a second story window. She is a strong woman behind a strong man; one thinks of Bathsheba behind Solomon or Jezebel behind Ahab.

From the sludge at the bottom of a well at Nimrud, Max Mallowan recovered another ivory inlay that he called the *Mona Lisa of Nimrud* because of her subtle smile. The artist rendered the features of this royal woman in stunning detail. Her full wig is topped with a crown inlaid with jewels. Like the *Woman at the Window,* the *Mona Lisa of Nimrud* was originally set into a piece of wooden furniture.

Eventually archaeologists began to recover not only royal annals but also creation stories from Nineveh (G. Smith 1872). George E. Smith (1840–1876) translated some ten or twelve baked clay tablets about six inches high that were recovered by Layard during the 1848–1849 season at Nineveh. The creation stories on the tablets were written in Akkadian cuneiform and were about three hundred lines long. These *Stories of Gilgamesh*, the origins of which date to the Early Bronze period (3400–2000 B.C.E.), were popular during the reign of Ashurbanipal (668–627 B.C.E.).

In the stories, Gilgamesh rules Uruk (Iraq) with too firm a hand, so the divine assembly sends Enkidu to be his companion on a journey of self-discovery. Their heroic exploits teach Gilgamesh how to rule himself so that he will better rule his people. He experiences powerlessness, loneliness, friendship, love, loss, revenge, and finally, when Enkidu is killed, death (S. Mitchell 2004, 1–64; Abusch 2001). Portions are parallel to the flood story in the book of Genesis (Gen 6:1—11:26) and reveal a softer, gentler side of Assyrian culture than the annals of its great kings.

Nineveh in the Book of Jonah (Jonah 1:1—4:11)

The book of Jonah reflects the same painful contradictions about Nineveh in the world of the Bible that have appeared in popular and academic attitudes toward Assyria in the past two hundred years. The book is a theodicy that struggles to reconcile faith in the divine patron, who is good, with a world that is evil. Jonah wants Nineveh punished; Yahweh wants Nineveh forgiven. The book of Jonah leaves it to the audience to decide which is most fitting.

The book of Jonah begins, as all stories begin, when a crisis disturbs the peace. Again and again, the Hebrews have become strangers in strange lands: when the Assyrians destroyed Samaria in 721 B.C.E., when the Babylonians destroyed Jerusalem in 586 B.C.E., and when the Greeks conquered Syria-Palestine in 332 B.C.E. They were outraged that Yahweh had not protected them from their enemies. Jonah is their voice.

The life of the faithful prophet is turned upside down when the Creator of the heavens, the sea, and the land commissions him to preach against Nineveh. The Great City represents not only the city of Nineveh but also all the enemies from whom Yahweh did not protect Judah.

Jonah flees on board the ship *Sea Dragon* bound for Tarshish—the end of the earth. He will not give Nineveh the opportunity to repent. The Creator pursues Jonah with a storm, and Jonah offers himself as a human sacrifice to save the crew, who throw him overboard. Before Jonah drowns, the Creator sends a Great Fish—a Sea Dragon—to fetch Jonah. Once Jonah is safely on dry land, the Creator repeats the commission: "Go to the Great City. Cry out against Nineveh!"

Reluctantly, Jonah gets up and goes to Nineveh. For three days he preaches: "You have only forty days to turn around!" The people of Nineveh, whose reputation for arrogance was legendary, repent in sackcloth and ashes. Even the Great King of Nineveh takes off his robes, puts on burlap, and sits with the beggars in the city's garbage. He also issues a proclamation: "By order of the Great King and the city assembly no human or animal, large or small, will eat or drink anything. Every human and animal will wear nothing but burlap. They will cry out as loud as they can to the Creator of the Heavens, the Sea, and the Land. All the citizens of Nineveh will turn from evil and from violence. Who knows? Perhaps the Creator of the Heavens, the Sea, and the Land will turn around, will change heart, and will recall this burning anger so that we will not be annihilated?" (Jonah 3:7-9).

> A **theodicy** is an attempt to reconcile the idea of a good deity with the reality of evil in the world. Both the book of Job and the book of Jonah are theodicies (Benjamin 2004, 450–59). The book of Job asks, Why do good people suffer? The book of Jonah asks, Why do bad people go unpunished?

During only one brief period was Assyrian culture considered superior to the cultures of the Bible or those of Greece and Rome. From 1900 until the defeat of the Nazi Third Reich at the end of World War II (1939–1945), an approach called "pan-Babylonianism" influenced the study of the ancient Near East. Friedrich Delitzsch (1850–1922) especially is associated with this idea. He argued that since Assyria was an older culture than the worlds of ancient Israel, Greece, and Rome, it reflected a less contaminated, more pristine example of human life. In fact, his lecture entitled *Babel und Bibel* suggested that the only value in the Bible was what it had inherited from Assyria (Delitzsch 1902). Delitzsch's work was fundamentally anti-Semitic. He wanted to show that non-Semitic or Aryan cultures such as Sumer and Mitanni—and not Semitic cultures such as Assyria and ancient Israel—laid the foundation for human society. ■

Islam pays tribute to Jonah at the Mosque of Nabi Yunis—the Mosque of Prophet Jonah—where Nineveh once stood. For Muslims, Nineveh not only was the city where Jonah preached, but it is now the place where, according to Muslim tradition, he is buried. Like his Creator, the faithful prophet obviously forgave the great city. ■

The people of Nineveh turn away from the evil destroying their lives, and Yahweh turns away from the evil destroying their city. Jonah, ironically, turns against Yahweh in anger not back to Yahweh in repentance. Each figure in the story acts in exactly the opposite way that the audience expects.

In most stories, the denouement repairs the damage caused by the crisis and climax episodes. Parables, in contrast, are consciously thought provoking. They simply end with a question. The parable of Jonah asks: *Should the Creator, who forgives the faithful prophet, not forgive the city?*

CONCLUSION

People who burn books, loot museums, or steal artifacts destroy the collective memory of humanity's past. They seal the door to the past, condemning the present to begin again the slow and painful evolution from chaos to civility. Destroying the memory of a culture strips the present of its identity as mercilessly as Alzheimer's disease. The archaeology of travelers is the priceless record of what it was like to go where they went and to see what they saw. That memory offers people today the opportunity to see more clearly just how important it is for humans to know who they were, so that they can better identify who they should be in order to survive.

The archaeology of travelers such as Lane, Roberts, and Bell not only preserved records of how the world of the Bible appeared in their time but also made an ongoing contribution to how cultures and faith traditions think about themselves today. The archaeology of travelers opens a door in the wall separating the past from the present. The access of the present to the opening of the past and the past to the present provide one of the most important guarantees that what people have learned in the past will continue to enrich the present. The journals, photographs, paintings, and creations of travelers allow the past to endure in the present, and the present to look back into the past for guidance. The relationship between the present and the past is not static. What Lane, Roberts, and Bell saw when they looked at the past is not what travelers and archaeologists today see when they look at that same past. Each generation sees its past with different eyes. By handing on their experience, travelers in the past allow those in the present to sharpen their vision about what it means to be human.

WHAT YOU HAVE LEARNED

- Good orientalism is an academic discipline that studies the cultures of Mesopotamia; bad orientalism is a racial prejudice that depicts Near Eastern culture as primitive and barbaric in contrast to Western cultures.
- Curiosity and adventure inspired travelers to leave their homes for the world of the Bible.
- Gertrude Bell began her career as an intrepid world traveler. She spoke English, Arabic, French, German, Italian, Persian, and Turkish. She became an accomplished mountaineer in Switzerland's Alps. She developed into an archaeologist of some accomplishment and specialized in Roman and early Islamic architecture in Anatolia, Syria, Jordan, and Iraq. Bell founded the Baghdad Archaeological Museum.
- Westerners demonized Assyrian culture because the earliest artifacts recovered were the annals of the great kings of Assyria, which glorified the horrors of war and the torture of prisoners. Westerners viewed war as an honorable competition governed by humane rules of engagement.
- The book of Jonah reflects the same painful contradictions about Nineveh that have appeared in popular and academic attitudes toward Assyria in the past two hundred years. Jonah wants Nineveh punished; Yahweh wants Nineveh forgiven. The book of Jonah leaves it to the audience to decide which is most fitting.

STUDY QUESTIONS

1. What was David Roberts's contribution to the archaeology of travelers?
2. Describe three important accomplishments of Gertrude Bell.
3. Who is Donny George Youkhanna?
4. How is Nineveh portrayed in the Bible? Is this an accurate depiction?
5. What are the *Stories of Gilgamesh*?

PREVIEW: ARCHAEOLOGY OF ANTIQUITIES DEALERS

- Giovanni Battista Belzoni
  - Valley of the Pharaohs
  - Tomb of Seti I
  - Egyptian *Book of the Dead*
- Moshe Dayan
  - Collecting Antiquities
  - Dayan and the World of the Bible
  - Contribution to Archaeology
- Roderick J. McIntosh and Susan Keech McIntosh
  - Jenne-jeno
  - Ethical Collecting of Antiquities

Chapter 4 explains what collectors and antiquities dealers have done for and against the understanding of the world of the Bible, and how eighteenth-century antiquities dealers like Giovanni B. Belzoni inspired Europeans with a desire for things Egyptian. It also describes how the twentieth-century war hero and politician Moshe Dayan became a notorious antiquities dealer, and what archaeologists like Roderick McIntosh and Susan McIntosh mean by good antiquities dealers.

4

Archaeology of Antiquities Dealers

GIOVANNI BATTISTA BELZONI (1778–1823)

Giovanni B. Belzoni was born in Padua (Italy). He left there to seek his fortune in Rome, where he studied at a Franciscan monastery to learn how to maintain and repair Rome's fountains. When Napoleon invaded Italy, Belzoni fled to England, where he made his living as a circus strongman. Belzoni was six feet, seven inches tall. He was billed as *The Great Belzoni* or *The Patagonian Samson*. As a finale to his strongman act, Belzoni would lift a dozen people sitting on platform, including his wife, into the air and then walk around the stage.

Belzoni left the circus in 1815 and went to Cairo to market an ox-driven water pump he had invented to Muhammad Ali (1769–1849), the pasha of Egypt. Ali governed Egypt for the Ottoman emperor in Constantinople. (The Ottoman Empire was founded in the fifteenth century and lasted until 1922 when it was replaced by the Republic of Turkey.) Muhammad Ali had unified Egypt under a strong central government. He was committed to developing Egypt into a state as technologically advanced as any in Europe. In 1835, William Brown Hodgson, an attorney from Savannah (Georgia) wrote: "He desires to raise Egypt to the level of European civilization. . . . The patronage which he gives to the arts and sciences; his encouragement of Europeans of talent; his printing presses; polytechnic, elementary, and medical schools; his factories and internal improvements, are evidence of enlightened views in civil administration" (http://www.sunnah.org/history/mhdalip.htm).

Although Ali was not interested in Belzoni's pump, Belzoni stayed in Egypt. Here he met Johann Ludwig Burckhardt (1784–1817), a daring Swiss traveler who had taught himself Arabic, the Qur'an, and Islamic law. Burckhardt disguised himself during his journeys; sometimes he was an Arab sheikh; sometimes a merchant; sometimes a teacher. He was the

Giovanni Battista Belzoni

Patagonia is a remote area of Argentina. Ferdinand Magellan (1480–1521) named the region (Portuguese: *Patagao*). Antonio Pigafetta (1491–1534), one of only eighteen sailors who survived Magellan's voyage, describes in his journal an indigenous Tehuelche male as "so tall that we reached only to his waist."

JOURNAL OF ANTONIO PIGAFETTA

One day we suddenly saw a naked man of giant stature on the shore of the port, dancing, singing, and throwing dust on his head. The captain general sent one of our men to the giant so that he might perform the same actions as a sign of peace. Having done that, the man led the giant . . . into the presence of the captain-general. When the giant was in the captain-general's and our presence, he marveled greatly, and made signs with one finger raised upward, believing that we had come from the sky. He was so tall that we reached only to his waist, and he was well proportioned. His face was large and painted red all over, while about his eyes he was painted yellow; and he had two hearts painted on the middle of his cheeks. His scanty hair was painted white. He was dressed in the skins of animals skillfully sewn together. (Pigafetta 1969, 51–52)

"Patagonian" became a synonym in Europe for "giant." European maps of Patagonia labeled it the "Land of Giants" (Latin: *regio gigantum*). By Shakespeare's day (1564–1616) Patagonia was familiar enough for him to include Setebos, the divine patron of the Tehuelche people, in his play *The Tempest* (1611).

The Tehuelche people were tall by European standards, but they were not giants. They were about five feet, nine inches tall; Europeans of the period were five feet, five inches tall. ∎

first Westerner to visit Petra (Jordan) and the temple built by Ramesses II at Abu Simbul (Egypt).

Burckhardt fascinated Belzoni with stories of his travels and his description of a colossal bust of Ramesses II in the Valley of the Pharaohs. Belzoni asked Henry Salt (1780–1827), then British consul in Egypt, to hire him to move the statue to the British Museum. Salt was not only a diplomat but also a portrait painter and, like Belzoni, a collector of Egypt's antiquities. Salt amassed three significant collections of Egyptian antiquities. He sold one to the British Museum; another to the Louvre Museum; and the third was auctioned to the public.

Salt authorized Belzoni to move the statue of Ramesses to the British Museum. Belzoni was a maverick; he could think outside the box. His skills were suited to the challenges posed by Egypt's antiquities. He knew how to use his physical strength and his knowledge of engineering to move massive pieces. In just three weeks, with only four poles and some rope, Belzoni lifted several columns out of the way and loaded the statue safely on a boat bound for England. Burckhardt wrote, "He handles masses of this kind with as much facility as others handle pebbles, and the Egyptians who see him a giant in figure, for he is over six feet and a half tall, believe him to be a sorcerer." Salt subsequently hired Belzoni to collect and ship artifacts from the temples at Edfu, Philae, and Elephantine for the British Museum. Belzoni was also the first European to visit the oasis of Siwah and to identify the city of Berenice on the Red Sea.

Belzoni also worked in the Valley of the Pharaohs (Hobson 1987, 94–95). He located the forty-seven tombs counted in antiquity by Strabo (64 B.C.E.–24 C.E.) and Diodorus Siculus (90–30 B.C.E.). Belzoni also identified eight more tombs. In 1816, Belzoni discovered the tomb of Aya (ruled 1323–1319 B.C.E.), designated WV 23, and carved his name and the date of his discovery on a rock near the entrance to claim his prize. Aya and his wife, Tiya, were the parents of Nefertiti, the wife of Akhenaton (ruled 1353–1335 B.C.E.). Aya's tomb has a simple, straight axis with an offset burial chamber. There are no great halls with pillars and no ritual shafts, which were common in royal tombs of the period.

Another remarkable monument identified by Belzoni in the Valley of the Pharaohs was the tomb of Seti I (KV 17). Seti I (ruled 1306–1290 B.C.E.) was the predecessor of Ramesses II, who was most likely the pharaoh in the biblical book of Exodus. Ramesses I inaugurated the Nineteenth Dynasty (1307–1196 B.C.E.) and was its first pharaoh. Seti, however, was the actual political, military, and cultural genius of the New Kingdom (Stierlin 1995, 142). He led a successful campaign into Syria-Palestine (1312 B.C.E.), conquering Kadesh (Syria) and reestablishing Egypt's dominance in the region. He cut a covenant with Mursilis, Great King of the Hittites (Turkey), establishing a peace in Syria-Palestine that allowed trade to flourish (Collins 2007). He revived the arts by launching building projects throughout Egypt. Seti's tomb was his finest work.

Few of the tombs in the Valley of the Pharaohs were finished at the time of the decedent's burial. This may have been because the pharaoh building the tomb died before the work was completed and once the funeral took place the tomb was sealed. It is also possible, however, that the tombs were deliberately left unfinished because of a tradition that the work would be completed in the afterlife. This idea reflects the Egyptian belief in the continuity between the human plane and the divine plane.

The tomb of Seti I is one of the few tombs in the Valley of the Pharaohs that was actually completed before it was sealed. It is also the longest tomb—more than 130 yards—and goes deeper into the ground than any other tomb.

In the tomb Belzoni found an elegant empty alabaster sarcophagus—a translucent stone coffin. The alabaster in Seti's coffin allowed the light to shine through it illuminating the passages advising him on how to move safely from the human plane into the afterlife carved into the coffin.

JOURNAL OF GIOVANNI BATTISTA BELZONI (1778–1823)

... what we found ... merits the most particular attention, not having its equal in the world, and being such as we had no idea could exist. It is a sarcophagus of the finest oriental alabaster, nine feet five inches long, and three feet seven inches wide. Its thickness is only two inches; and it is transparent when a light is placed in the inside of it. It is minutely sculptured within and without with several hundred figures, which do not exceed two inches in height, and represent as I suppose, the whole of the funeral procession and ceremonies relating to the deceased. I cannot give an adequate idea of this beautiful and invaluable piece of antiquity, and can only say that nothing has been brought into Europe from Egypt that can be compared with it. (Belzoni 1820)

The Egyptians developed a number of handbooks describing the journey from death to life. The best known is the *Book of Coming Forth by Day*, or the *Book of the Dead*. Other traditions are preserved in the *Pyramid Texts*, the *Coffin Texts*, and, here on the sarcophagus of Seti, the *Book of the*

John Gardner Wilkinson (1797–1875) developed the system of identifying the royal tombs in the Valley of the Pharaohs with the labels KV for King's Valley or WV for West Valley (Arabic: *Wadi el-Gurud*). The tombs are numbered in the order of discovery beginning with Ramesses VII (KV 1). As many as sixty-four possible tombs have been identified by archaeologists. Wilkinson was English, and his travels in Egypt for more than a decade earned him the title *Father of British Egyptology*, to distinguish him from Jean-François Champollion, the French scholar honored as the *Father of Egyptology*. Wilkinson's notes and paintings of Egypt's antiquities are still a valuable archive of the condition of these monuments in his day. His *Manners and Customs of the Ancient Egyptians* (1837) was the standard introduction to ancient Egypt until the beginning of the twentieth century (Jason Thompson 1992). ∎

Alabaster is a form of gypsum—a smooth, white stone. The Egyptians used it for lamps because light shined through the stone highlighting its grain. ∎

View of the ceiling of the sarcophagus hall in the tomb of Seti I, with the list of the Northern Constellations and stars. Egypt, Pharonic. 19th Dynasty, 1305–1290 B.C.E. Location: Tomb of Seti I, Valley of the Kings, Thebes, Egypt. Photo Credit: Werner Forman / Art Resource, NY.

Gates. Egyptians patterned their descriptions of the journey from death to the afterlife on the journey of the sun from dusk to dawn. It took twelve hours; each hour was a gate, and each hour had its divine guardians. The guidebooks would tell the dead which members of Egypt's divine assembly guarded each gate. The handbooks would also tell the dead what questions these members of the divine assembly would ask, and how one should answer their questions correctly. These directions were written on the inside of the coffin lid, where the decedent could easily refer to them during the journey.

If the dead person followed the directions in the *Book of the Gates*, greeted the members of the divine assembly respectfully, and answered their questions correctly, the deceased could proceed into the next hour of the journey. The decedent who cleared all twelve gates would arrive successfully in the afterlife. A decedent who did not would be condemned to a life of exile from both the human plane and the divine plane.

The sarcophagus of Seti I is preserved today in Sir John Soane's Museum in London. Soane was a famous British architect and antiquities collector whose own house is an architectural masterpiece. Soane himself designed the house and lived there among his art and antiquities. When he died in 1815, the house and his collections became a public museum (http://www.soane.org/).

When Belzoni returned to England in 1821 he built full-scale replicas of the royal tombs he had uncovered in the Valley of the Pharaohs. Thousands of people paid to visit these exhibits, which he constructed in Piccadilly Circus. He also published his *Narrative of the Operations and Recent Discoveries Within the Pyramids, Temples, Tombs and Excavations in Egypt and Nubia* (1820).

MOSHE DAYAN (1915–1981)

Flamboyant collectors like Belzoni continue to punctuate the history of archaeology in the world of the Bible. Perhaps the most controversial collector of the twentieth century was Moshe Dayan.

Dayan was born in Kibbutz Degania Alef (Israel). Before World War II he fought for Jewish independence against the British in Palestine. He was captured and spent three years in prison (1939–1941). The British released him to fight for them against the French forces fighting the Germans in Syria and Lebanon (1941–1945). He lost an eye during this campaign and subsequently wore a signature black eyepatch.

During Israel's War of Independence (1948), the Sinai Campaign (1956), and the Six Days' War (1967), Dayan distinguished himself as a commander. During the Yom Kippur War (1973), however, he was minister of defense, and many Israelis held him responsible for Israel's lack of preparedness and poor performance. His reputation never recovered. Nonetheless, Dayan returned to politics as foreign minister (1977–1980) with Prime Minister Menachem Begin (1913–1992). As foreign minister, he was instrumental in drawing up the Camp David Accords (1978), a peace agreement with Egypt. Begin, however, did not entrust Dayan with the responsibility of implementing the historic agreement, so he resigned.

Moshe Dayan

In addition to his military and political activities, Dayan collected antiquities and also bought, exchanged, sold, and was given antiquities in Israel and abroad (Kletter 2002). Dayan's thirty-year collecting career (1951–1981) began at Tell el-Hesi, the same site where W. M. Flinders Petrie directed the first archaeological excavation in Israel in 1890. A chance find of an Iron Age jar ignited Dayan's lifelong passion for collecting. In the beginning he collected from sites in the Negev and the Sinai that were under his military command. Later he collected from sites throughout Israel, the West Bank, and Gaza. As a general, Dayan had access to sites that were off-limits to civilian archaeologists. He also commanded resources—soldiers, trucks, helicopters, warehouses—that civilian archaeologists could not afford. Moreover, he enjoyed private resources—his family helped him as did antiquities dealers.

The public loved Dayan, and no one in the government, in the legal system, or in the professional community of archaeologists could successfully challenge his antiquities collecting. Even archaeologists of the stature of Yigael Yadin (1917–1984) and Avraham Biran (1909–2008), were powerless to control his collecting and dealing in antiquities (Slater 1992, 326–27). A conspiracy of silence allowed him to remove antiquities from more than thirty-five sites over a period of some thirty years.

Dayan often competed with archaeologists excavating at the same sites where he was collecting. He had a passion for the hunt and for possessing ancient material remains. He had no interest in understanding either the ways in which the artifacts he collected were manufactured, or how they reflected the worldviews of the cultures that produced them. Unlike Belzoni, who recorded when and where he collected his artifacts, Dayan collected, but he did not locate, date, or interpret the artifacts in his collection. There was no official inventory of his personal collection,

Jar with traces of paint, composed of three segments. Egyptian find at Deir el-Balah, Gaza Strip, Israel. Alabaster, New Kingdom. The Dayan Collection. Location: Israel Museum (IDAM), Jerusalem, Israel. Photo Credit: Erich Lessing / Art Resource, NY.

65

Three coffins with anthropoid lids, grotesque style, from Deir el-Balah, Gaza Strip, Israel. Clay. 1550–1200 B.C.E. Late Bronze Age. The Dayan Collection. Philistine. Location: Israel Museum (IDAM), Jerusalem, Israel. Photo Credit: Erich Lessing / Art Resource, NY.

and there is no official record of where the pieces in his collection were found. He enjoyed the antiquities that he stored and restored in warehouses and on display in his house in the Zahala neighborhood of Tel Aviv (Israel), but he did not share them with the public.

Like many collectors, Dayan had an uncanny ability to know where to dig for antiquities. He also had a very accurate ability to recognize forgeries. He knew the market value of the antiquities he collected, and where to find the buyers who would pay the most.

Dayan demonstrated a fierce identification with the world of the Bible. He understood himself as the heir of the past that he collected. Nonetheless, he was not a person of faith. Devout Jews, Christians, and Muslims also identify with the world of the Bible. Their identification defines both what they teach and how they act. His identification was historical. His knowledge of the world of the Bible was mostly a projection of his own experience. What he did, he assumed that the great figures in the world of the Bible had done. Few other cultures have such a magnetic hold on their students as the world of the Bible. The way of life of the Maya in the Americas does not become a way of life for those who study them. Nor does the world of the pharaohs of Egypt create faith traditions in the world today, nor historical admirers like Dayan. The material remains from the world of the Bible have a remarkable power to inspire even outside Judaism, Christianity, and Islam.

Dayan considered his collecting to be humanitarian. He told both his friends and his accusers in the Israeli Knesset that he was rescuing antiquities that would otherwise be ignored or destroyed, and that he intended to donate his collection to the Israel Museum.

Except for a few gifts that Dayan gave to private individuals, his collection remained intact until his death. His wife then negotiated with the Israel Museum for the collection (Silberman 1989, 127–28). She appraised the artifacts to be worth two million dollars. (Two million dollars in 1981 was the equivalent of 4.5 million in 2006.) Eventually she accepted a million dollars for the collection and donated the rest. The purchase was privately funded. Nonetheless, public and private pressure from both archaeologists and ordinary Israelis influenced the Israel Museum's decision neither to display Dayan's collection as a whole, nor even to identify pieces from the collection in its catalogues. The Internet archive Art Resource, however, still labels some thirty images as *The Dayan Collection* (http://www.artres.com).

Although antiquities collectors like Dayan made few direct contributions to the interpretation of the Bible, they did contribute to the development of the discipline of archaeology, sometimes indirectly. Dayan's collecting, for example, contributed a great deal to the development of public policies concerning the collecting, buying, and selling of antiquities. Israel finally passed a comprehensive antiquities law in 1978, but even that law does not prohibit dealing or selling antiquities. The collecting begun by antiquities dealers like Belzoni was either ignored altogether or tolerated. The trafficking in antiquities by dealers like Dayan outraged both professionals and the general public. The free market for antiquities needed regulation, and perhaps no one more than Dayan demonstrated that need for antiquities from the world of the Bible.

By today's standards what antiquities dealers did—and what some continue to do—is a scandal. Nonetheless, scandal often sheds light on what needs to be done. Condemning the past or the people of the past distracts from the commitment of creating more effective policies for the preservation and distribution of cultural heritage. What was learned from what Dayan did, or what his contemporaries failed to do to stop him, is infinitely more important than condemning him or them.

RODERICK J. MCINTOSH AND SUSAN KEECH MCINTOSH AND THE ETHICS OF COLLECTING ANTIQUITIES

The American Schools of Oriental Research, a professional organization of archaeologists and biblical scholars working in the world of the Bible, have a zero-tolerance approach to collecting antiquities. As an organization, ASOR does not accept advertising or endorsements of any kind from collectors of antiquities, and there are no advertisements from collectors in ASOR's journal for the general public—*Near Eastern Archaeology* (1998–present), formerly *Biblical Archaeology* (1938–1997).

Hershel Shanks, the editor of the popular *Biblical Archaeology Review*, continues to do investigative reporting on unethical collectors of antiquities from the world of the Bible. The *Biblical Archaeology Review* and its parent corporation, the Biblical Archaeology Society, however, accept endorsements and advertising from reputable collectors (http://www.bib-arch.org).

In 1977, 1981, and 1994 Roderick J. McIntosh and Susan Keech McIntosh excavated Jenne-jeno and neighboring sites (http://www.ruf.rice.edu/~anth/arch/brochure) in Mali (Africa). The city of Jenne on the Niger Delta of the Middle Niger River between Mopti and Segou was a major trade depot for five hundred years. Today, the stunning mud architecture of Jenne is a legacy of its early trade ties with North Africa. Less than two miles southeast of Jenne is the tell of Jenne-jeno—*Old Jenne*. The site was settled in 200 B.C.E. and was occupied for some sixteen hundred years. The archaeology of Jenne-jeno clearly shows that a city with extensive trade routes developed there long before the arrival of Arab peoples from North Africa in 700. Terra-cotta statues from Jenne-jeno are quite detailed. They have jewelry, clothing, and body art created by scarring. The statues may represent human ancestors or divine patrons.

Illegal trade in antiquities from Jenne-jeno and other sites in Mali is rampant. Consequently, the McIntoshes have been consistently proactive with the government of Mali and the United Nations Educational, Scientific and Cultural Organization (http://whc.unesco.org/) to help safeguard Mali's rich heritage. The endeavor has led to the development of a policy for identifying and working with *good collectors* of antiquities to eliminate illegal collecting and trafficking in antiquities (McIntosh, McIntosh and Togola 1995). Alpha Oumar Konare, president of Mali (1992–2002), said that Mali regards good collectors and public trust museums as natural partners in its goal of sharing Mali's antiquities with the world.

The policy of identifying good, or ethical, collectors is not widely embraced by archaeologists (McIntosh 2000). Many consider all collectors to be relics of an era when empires exploited the resources of their colonies. For archaeologists, however, the value of any artifact is defined by its place in the cultural heritage in its country of origin, not by the aesthetic value assigned to it by art collectors.

For the McIntoshes, good collectors must begin collecting because of their admiration for the maker culture and because they want to use their collection to help others better understand and appreciate the worldview of that culture.

Consequently, good collectors allow both scholars and the public access to their collections. They do not hide their collections just for their own personal enjoyment or for fear of public criticism.

In addition, good collectors buy only artifacts that have been both legally and professionally excavated. They do not collect beautiful artifacts that have been looted. The reputation of a seller is never a substitute for the documentation of the origin of any artifact or for appropriate export permits. Moreover, good collectors do not destroy duplicate artifacts to increase the value of the artifacts in their collections.

Good collectors are committed to policing the collecting community in order to prevent the development of syndicates that traffic in illegally obtained antiquities that are procured by the wanton destruction of ancient sites. Consequently, they support enforcement of policies such as the 1970 UNESCO Convention on Cultural Property, the 1970 University of Pennsylvania Museum's "Philadelphia Declaration," and the 1989–1994 International Council of Museums Code of Professional Ethics. Good collectors are also proactive in opposing any policy or practice in their own countries that allows for one government to remove the cultural property of others. Cultural property is neither plunder nor the spoils of war.

Good collectors actively encourage departments of antiquities to station representatives in communities near ancient sites to develop education and outreach programs with local leaders, schools, and citizens' groups to raise the awareness of the public and to preserve the sites. Departments of antiquities need to demonstrate to local communities that they are committed to the preservation of cultural property and to the prosecution of those who plunder and destroy the cultural heritage of their country. Good collectors help these departments educate the public to realize that their cultural heritage defines their culture today, and that preserving and studying their cultural property also contributes to their local economy through tourism.

CONCLUSION

The evolution of the archaeology of collectors is a work in progress. The legacies of Belzoni, of Dayan, and of the good and bad collectors today have contributed significantly to our understanding of the world of the Bible. The question today for museum curators, professors, publishers, and the museum-going public, however, is *At what cost?* The ongoing challenge for both collectors and archaeologists is still to find effective and responsible ways to recover the past, to interpret the past, and to publicize the past. Otherwise the material remains of past cultures will continue to be destroyed either through ignorance or through greed.

WHAT YOU HAVE LEARNED

- Giovanni Battista Belzoni created markets of fascination for the antiquities he collected and brought to Europe. In response, patrons of the arts sponsored exhibits at museums and in departments of Near Eastern studies at universities. Even the general public began to travel to the world of the Bible.
- Trafficking in antiquities by high-profile antiquities dealers like Moshe Dayan outraged both professionals and the general public. The free market for antiquities needed regulation, and perhaps no one more than Dayan demonstrated that need for antiquities from the world of the Bible.
- Roderick McIntosh and Susan Keech McIntosh developed a code of ethics for good collectors. They must, among other things, begin collecting because of their admiration for the maker culture and because they want to use their collection to help others better understand and appreciate the worldview of that culture.

STUDY QUESTIONS

1. Do you think that Giovanni Belzoni had any second thoughts about removing antiquities from Egypt?
2. How are royal tombs identified in Egypt?
3. How do the burial practices of the ancient Egyptians reflect their beliefs about the afterlife?
4. What was the negative contribution to archaeology made by Moshe Dayan's collecting of antiquities?
5. What are the characteristics of a good, or ethical, collector of antiquities?

PREVIEW: ARCHAEOLOGY OF MISSIONARIES

- Missionaries as Ethnoarchaeologists
- Annals of Mesha
  - F. A. Klein
  - Charles Clermont-Ganneau
  - Charles Warren
  - Hearth Sanctuaries
  - Altars of Sacrifice
  - Massebah Standing Stones
- Annals of Jehoram of Israel
  - River of Blood
  - Human Sacrifice
- Stories of Atrahasis

Chapter 5 explains why Christian missionaries made the same journey as pilgrims who walked the lands of the Bible to understand better their Jewish, Christian, and Muslim faith. It also describes how an inscription recovered by a missionary in Jordan in 1868 continues to influence the study of the culture, languages, politics, and worship of ancient Israel and its neighboring states. The chapter also shows how fire pits, altars, and pedestals represent the presence of a divine patron in the world of the Bible, and how the erosion of red clay by sudden and unexpected floods during an invasion of Moab convinced the ruler of Israel that he was a new Moses. Finally, it describes what modern missionaries have contributed to successful archaeological excavations.

5

Archaeology of Missionaries

In the nineteenth century, missionaries from Europe, the United States, and Canada set out for the world of the Bible inspired by their Christian faith. Included among these intrepid Christians were women who traveled to Egypt, Sinai, and Syria-Palestine to minister to women and their children (Warzeski 2005).

Although missionaries set out to convert peoples of Muslim faith to Christianity, even the most zealous often found themselves influenced by the people they set out to convert. They did not abandon their faith, but they did abandon their colonial attitudes that the peoples of the world of the Bible in their day were primitive and pagan. They learned the languages of the places where they went on their missions and developed a profound respect for the peoples among whom they worked.

In many ways Western missionaries were ethnoarchaeologists. They recognized a cultural link between the nineteenth-century peasants in the world of the Bible and the way of life in Israel, Judah, Moab, and Edom during the Iron Age. Consequently, they developed a spirituality of respect for the people whom they considered to be living descendants of the biblical households of Abraham and Sarah and of Jacob, Leah, and Rachel. These people offered their Western visitors a living connection with the Bible and brought the world of the Bible to life.

Stela of Mesha, King of Moab. It relates to the defeat inflicted on to the Kingdom of Israel shortly before 842 b.c.e., and the pillaging of the town of Nebe and the temple of Yahweh. Constructed c. 830 b.c.e. Basalt. Dhiban, Jordan. Location: Louvre, Paris, France. Photo Credit: Réunion des Musées Nationaux / Art Resource, NY.

THE ANNALS OF MESHA

One missionary who made a significant archaeological contribution to the understanding of the world of the Bible was F. A. Klein. His respect not only for the Bedouin with whom he lived but also for their past was obvious to his hosts. Therefore,

Bedouin or *Bedu* in Arabic means "people of the desert." Today most of Jordan's Bedouin live east of the Desert Highway that runs north and south along the ridge above the Dead Sea. The clan is the base community in Bedouin culture. Bedouin who belong to the same clan consider themselves to be one large family. Each clan has a sheikh responsible for making decisions and resolving conflicts. A tribe (Arabic: *qabilah*) is an alliance of clans committed to protecting one another from their enemies. ∎

Four hundred U.S. dollars in 1868 would be the equivalent of $5,600 in 2006; $480 would be $6,700; and $4,000 would be the equivalent of $56,000 (http://oregonstate .edu/cla/polisci/faculty-research/ sahr/sahr.htm). ∎

in 1868 they took him to see writing on a stone, and he became the first European to see the Annals of Mesha, the so-called Moabite Stone, the longest inscription recovered thus far in Syria-Palestine.

F. A. Klein was an Anglican missionary born in Alsace-Lorraine (now in France). He went to Syria-Palestine as a medical missionary with the Church Missionary Society (Horn 1986). He lived in Jerusalem, but traveled on both sides of the Jordan River. He spoke Arabic and was one of the few Westerners who could travel safely east of the Jordan River. Not even the Turkish government could guarantee the safety of visitors traveling among the Bedouin peoples there. In August 1868, Klein rode on horseback to treat sick Bedouin around Dhiban (Hebrew: *Dibon*) in the biblical land of Moab (Morton 1985, 239–46; Routledge 2004).

Klein reached the camp of the Beni Hamidan Bedouin just north of the Arnon River. He was escorted by the son of the sheikh of the Beni Sakhr, the most powerful Bedouin tribe east of the Jordan River. The Beni Hamidam told Klein that there was a stone with writing on it in the ruins of Dhiban, and they took him to see the stone. He could not read the writing, but he drew a sketch of the inscription and offered to buy the stone from the Beni Hamidam for four hundred dollars. They agreed.

Klein returned to Jerusalem and asked J. Heinrich Petermann, the consul of Prussia (Germany), to ask the Berlin Museum if it wanted to purchase the stela. The museum agreed, Klein and his friend the sheik of the Beni Sakhr failed to finalize the sale with the Beni Hamidan. Subsequently, the Bedouin raised their asking price from four hundred to four thousand dollars. The consul hired Saba Qa'war, who was teaching in Jerusalem, to meet with the Beni Hamidan. Although it took months, the Beni Hamidan eventually agreed to sell the stela for $480. Arrangements were made to ship the stela from the land of the Beni Hamidan through the land of the Beni Attiyah to Jerusalem. When the time came, however, the Beni Attiyah refused to permit the caravan to cross their land, so the deal collapsed for a second time and the Prussian government dropped the project.

Subsequently, Charles Clermont-Ganneau (1846–1923), a scholar from France who was working in Jerusalem as a translator, took an interest in the stela. In 1869 he arranged for Salim el-Qarigo to travel to Dhiban and copy seven lines of the inscription. When he saw the copy, Clermont-Ganneau knew the artifact was authentic. So he hired Ya'qub Karavaca to go to Dhiban and make a paper squeeze of the inscription. Although the Beni Hamidan agreed to let Karavaca make the squeeze, a fight broke out while he was working and Karavaca was wounded. Before escaping, he tore the paper off the stela while it was still wet.

The attention that the Europeans were giving the stela convinced the Beni Hamidan that the stone had life-giving power. They decided to heat the stela in a fire and then smash it into pieces with cold water. Each clan took fragments of the stela and buried them in their grain siloes to transfer the living-giving power of the stone into the seed they would plant (Horn 1986, 52–53).

Clermont-Ganneau and Charles Warren, a British officer who was conducting an excavation in Jerusalem, tried to recover as many fragments of the stela as possible. Clermont-Ganneau bought thirty-eight fragments of the stela containing 613 letters out of a total of about one thousand letters. Warren bought eighteen fragments containing fifty-nine letters. Konstantin Schlottmann (1819–1897), a professor from Germany, bought one additional fragment.

A third of the stela had been permanently destroyed. Nonetheless, by 1870 Clermont-Ganneau had reassembled the fragments. Using the damaged squeeze, he reconstructed the stela and most of the inscription for the Louvre Museum. In subsequent years, archaeologists who are cultural historians have studied the Annals of Mesha to understand the events they describe and to reconstruct the thinking of the great men who caused these events (Miller 1989).

A squeeze is created by pressing a sheet of soft, wet paper into the engraved writing on a stone with a brush. When the paper has dried, it can be peeled away from the stone producing a reverse image of the inscription. ∎

Charles Warren (1840–1927) was an officer in the British Royal Engineers. In 1867 the Palestine Exploration Fund sent Warren to Jerusalem where he met Clermont-Ganneau. Warren conducted the first major excavations of Jerusalem. His most significant discovery was a tunnel leading under the ancient city wall to the Gihon Spring, now known as *Warren's Shaft*. Later in life Warren was chief of the London Metropolitan Police when the Jack the Ripper murders were committed (1886–1888). ∎

About 835 B.C.E. Mesha, the ruler of Moab, inscribed his annals on a curved topped, rectangular block of basalt stone (Smelik 1992, 82). The stela is three feet high and two feet wide (Smelik 2003, 137–38). The thirty-four lines are written in the Moabite language which used an early alphabet also used for Hebrew. The grammar, syntax, and vocabulary of Moabite and Hebrew are also very similar (Jackson 1989, 96–130; Garr 1985). Today the stela is known as the *Moabite Stone* or the *Mesha Stela*. ∎

ANNALS OF MESHA

(Matthews and Benjamin 2006, 167–69, revised)

I am Mesha, ruler of Moab and conqueror of Dibon. My father, Chemoshyat, ruled Moab for thirty years, and then I became ruler. . . . Omri, ruler of Israel, invaded Moab year after year because Chemosh, the divine patron of Moab, was angry with the people. When the son of Omri succeeded him during my reign, he bragged: *I too will invade Moab.* However, I defeated the son of Omri and drove Israel out of our land forever. Omri and his son ruled the Madaba plains for forty years, but Chemosh dwells there in my time. I built the city of Baal-Ma'on with its reservoir and the city of Qiryaten. Long ago the tribe of Gad conquered Ataroth, but I defeated the tribe and captured the city of Ataroth which the ruler of Israel had fortified. I sacrificed all of the people of Ataroth to Chemosh. I brought the altar of Israel (Moabite: *ʿarʿal dwdh*) from the sanctuary of Ataroth and installed it before Chemosh in the sanctuary of Qiryat. Finally, I settled the tribes of Sharon and Maharith in the land which I had taken from Israel to claim it for Moab. At that time, Chemosh said to me, *Go and take Nebo from Israel.* So I deployed my soldiers at night and attacked Nebo from dawn until

> noon. I won a great victory and I sacrificed seven thousand men, women, and children from Nebo to Chemosh. I brought sacred vessels from the sanctuary of Yahweh at Nebo and laid them before Chemosh. The ruler of Israel was invading Moab from Jahaz, which he had fortified. Chemosh, my divine patron, drove him out before me. I settled the households of two-hundred of my best soldiers in Jahaz to claim it for Dibon.
>
> I built Qarhoh with gates and towers, a palace and reservoirs. I also decreed: *Every household in Qarhoh is to have its own cistern.* I had my prisoners of war from Israel dig the cisterns of Qarhoh. I built Aroer and a highway through the Arnon valley. I also rebuilt the cities of Beth-bamoth and Bezer for fifty households from Dibon. I reigned in peace over hundreds of villages which I had conquered. . . . Chemosh was lord in Moab during my time. . . .

F. A. Klein's relationship with the Bedouin peoples of Jordan set in motion a dynamic and ongoing current of study in a wide variety of fields. Recovering, restoring, and translating the Annals of Mesha allowed archaeologists of language and historians of ancient Israel to understand better its relationship to surrounding states. Moab and Israel, for example, use almost the same language, have remarkably similar understandings of their divine patrons, and wage war using almost identical strategies. Comparing and contrasting the Annals of Mesha, ruler of Moab, with the Annals of Jehoram, his counterpart in Israel, continues to provide insights into the ways in which ancient rulers told the stories of their reigns. For example, Jehoram wanted not only to be remembered for protecting the land and people of Israel from Moab but also to be remembered as a new Moses leading the Hebrews out of Egypt and into the promised land. Finally, Klein's own faith-based ministry almost 150 years ago continues to contribute to the study of how the Hebrews worshiped Yahweh. The Moabite Stone, revealed by the Bedouin people to their Western physician and friend, continues to be a rich source of understanding and appreciation of the world of the Bible.

Hearths

One of the most fascinating phrases in the Annals of Mesha is the two-word description of a piece of liturgical furniture (Moabite: ʿarʿal dwdh) that Mesha confiscated from the sanctuary of Yahweh in Ataroth (Arabic: *Khirbat ʿAtaruz*) and transported to the sanctuary of Kemosh in Qiryat. The first word, ʿarʿal, identifies the piece of furniture; the second word, dwdh, identifies either the household that donated it to the sanctuary or the member of the divine assembly to whom it is dedicated. There are varying translations of the passage from the Moabite inscription:

Klass A. D. Smelic translates, "I brought back the fire-hearth of his Uncle from there, and I hauled it before the face of Kemosh in Kerioth" (2003, 137–38), thus identifying the furniture as a hearth dedicated to Yahweh, the Uncle or divine patron of Israel. Anson F. Rainey and R. Steven Notley identify the furniture as a hearth donated to the sanctuary of Yahweh by the household of David or in honor of the household of David: "I confiscated from there its Davidic altar hearth and I dragged it before Chemos in Kerioth" (Rainey and Notley 2006, 211–12). The translation offered here, "I brought the altar of Israel from the sanctuary of Ataroth and installed it before Chemosh in the sanctuary of Qiryat," simply identifies it as treasure taken from Israel, Moab's enemy, leaving open the question of whether it was donated by the household of David or dedicated to Yahweh, Israel's divine patron or uncle. This translation is a dynamic equivalent. It focuses on the audience and uses language that will help them better understand the connotations of the inscription. What was important to Mesha was that the trophy belonged to Israel, not who donated it or to whom it was dedicated.

Archaeologists uncovered a hearth at the north end of the main hall of Building 350 at Tel Miqne (Dothan 1990). The hearth sanctuary first installed about 1125 B.C.E. and was reinstalled at least three times. The floor of each hearth was paved with river rock. The thick layer of ashes and charcoal covering the floor of the hearth contained animal bones, including the only chicken bones recovered in Syria-Palestine. By 1000 B.C.E. it had been decommissioned.

The only known parallel in Syria-Palestine to this sanctuary hearth at Tel Miqne is a sanctuary hearth at Tel Qasile. Like Ekron, Tel Qasile was a Philistine city. Since Ataroth was not a Philistine city, it is unlikely that there was a hearth sanctuary at Ataroth that Mesha dismantled and then reassembled at Qiryat. Nonetheless, he may have confiscated an altar of sacrifice or a pedestal like the ark of the covenant.

Hearth sanctuaries were common in western Mediterranean cultures. At Pylos (Greece), for example, a hearth sanctuary was part of a megaron—a building with a large central hall, side rooms, and an open porch. ■

Altar of Sacrifice

The altar of sacrifice at Ataroth may have looked like the altars at Beersheba and Arad that were excavated by Yohanan Aharoni (1913–1976). Beersheba and Arad were fortresses guarding the southern border of Judah.

Those entering Judah were, no doubt, required to pay their respects to Yahweh at these altars to guarantee their good conduct during their stay. These sanctuaries are an institution similar to passport control stations at national borders today. By removing the altar at Ataroth, Mesha was removing the border station and reincorporating the city into Moab.

The Beersheba altar is a cube a little more than five feet square (Aharoni 1974). The corners on the top course of sandstones are raised to form horns (Exod 27:1; 2 Chr 6:13). There is a snake engraved on one of the stones at the base of the altar (Num 21:8-9; Kgs 18:4). The altar had been taken apart and recycled to repair a warehouse wall. The warehouse was subsequently destroyed during the invasion of Judah by Sennacherib, Great King of Assyria, in 701 B.C.E. (2 Kgs 18:22). The Arad altar stood in the courtyard (Hebrew: ʾûlām) of a sanctuary to Yahweh (Aharoni 1968, 18–31). The base of the altar was almost nine feet square. It was some five feet high.

Scenes from Synagogue at Dura Europos, c. 239 C.E. The Ark versus paganism. Location: Dura Europos, Syria. Photo Credit: Princeton University Press / Art Resource, NY.

Pedestal for Yahweh

If the furniture that Mesha confiscated at Ataroth was not an altar of sacrifice, it may have been a pedestal for Yahweh. The ark of the covenant was a portable pedestal on which Yahweh was believed to stand (Benjamin 2004, 181–83). Cultures in the world of the Bible carried their divine patrons on pedestals in processions to visit the land and their people. These pedestals were not images but vehicles. In Egypt the pedestals were shaped like boats; in Syria-Palestine they were great lions or bulls.

Yahweh rode on two different pedestals. One was the ark of the covenant, a gold-plated dais or platform on which Yahweh stood, invisible, between two cherubim having the faces of humans, the bodies of lions, the feet of oxen, and the wings of eagles. Yahweh's other pedestal was a great bull. In the story of the incident of the golden calf in Exod 32:1–35, Aaron uses the jewelry of the Hebrews to plate in gold a wooden statue of a great bull, on whose back Yahweh would ride into battle. Jeroboam of Israel commissioned two bull pedestals for Yahweh; he erected one in the sanctuary at Dan and the other in the sanctuary at Bethel.

In the account of the commissioning of Isaiah at Jerusalem (Isa 6:1-13), seraphim snakes, rather than cherubim, guard Yahweh (Benjamin 2004, 342–46). The seraphim are comparable to the *uraeus* snakes that guard pharaoh. Like a hearth, the seraphim are associated with fire. They have the body of a snake with the flames of a fire and the wings of an eagle. When Yahweh calls Isaiah, the prophet is outfitted by the seraphim with lips of iron, manufactured using the charcoal burner in the

The storm-god Adad standing on a bull, brandishing a flash of lightning. Basalt bas-relief on a stela from Arslan-Tash, North Syria. 8th century B.C.E. (138 x 56 cm). Location: Louvre, Paris, France. Photo Credit: Erich Lessing / Art Resource, NY.

Gold-plated bronze young bull representing the animal form of the warrior god Reshef, or Baal. The prophets of Israel condemned the idolization of the "golden calf" and the Baal-cult. From Byblos, Lebanon. Bronze and gold. Bronze Age. Location: Louvre, Paris, France. Photo Credit: Erich Lessing / Art Resource, NY.

Horned altar, from Megiddo. Limestone (around 900 B.C.E.). Location: Israel Museum (IDAM), Jerusalem, Israel. Photo Credit: Erich Lessing / Art Resource, NY.

Statues of the deities were dedicated by placing a weapon in their upraised hand or inlaying their eyes with semiprecious stones. When warriors overran a city, they executed the statue of its divine patron by cutting off its hands, its nose, its eyes, or its head. Archaeologists have recovered a decapitated basalt statue of the divine patron of Hazor, a city overlooking the Huleh plain north of the Sea of Galilee. ■

sanctuary as a forge. Ironworking played a significant role in the development of cultures in Syria-Palestine. Iron became a metaphor for states that were economically sound. These new iron lips prepared Isaiah to help the rulers of Judah make economically sound decisions in their struggle with Assyria.

In the stories of the ark of the covenant (1 Sam 4:1—7:1), the Philistines defeat the Hebrews on the first day of battle. The next day Hophni and Phinehas carry the ark of the covenant into battle to force Yahweh to defend them. Their plan fails. Yahweh will lead the Hebrews, but will not be led by them. Hophni and Phinehas are killed, and the Hebrews retreat. Just as Mesha captures his trophy and places it like a prisoner of war before Chemosh in Qiryat, the Philistines capture the ark of the covenant and place it like a prisoner of war at the feet of Dagon. During the night, however, the statue of Dagon falls prostrate before the ark of the covenant. The people of Ashdod put the statue back on its pedestal. The next night the statue of Dagon again prostrates before the ark, breaking off its hands and head in the process.

Chang-Ho Ji is currently directing excavations at *Khirbat ʿAtaruz* (Jordan). The site may well prove to be the location of Israel's sanctuary at Ataroth, mentioned in the Annals of Mesha.

The identity of Mesha's war prize may be easier to establish once the excavations there are complete. Among the liturgical furniture recovered at the sanctuary to date are a hearth and two large inscribed pots used to burn incense before a set of *maṣṣebôt*, standing stones, that is, stones set up for worship or as memorials. One *maṣṣēbâ* is still on the site; the other is missing. The missing stone may have been the trophy claimed by Mesha.

THE ANNALS OF JEHORAM OF ISRAEL

There are parallels between the Annals of Mesha and the Annals of Jehoram of Israel, who ruled from 849 to 842 B.C.E. (2 Kgs 3:1-27). Both traditions describe Mesha as a covenant partner of Omri of Israel (ruled 886–875 B.C.E.). Both explain military defeat as a divine punishment (Judg 3:12); both describe sacrificing prisoners of war; and both describe using prisoners of war to rebuild captured cities.

The Annals of Mesha, however, describe events not mentioned in the Bible and the Bible describes events not mentioned in the Annals of Mesha. The Annals of Jehoram of Israel describe a campaign against

Mesha by Israel, Judah, and Edom to punish Mesha for abrogating his covenant with them (2 Kgs 3:4). Israel and Judah were covenant partners during the reigns of Ahab, Ahaziah, and Jehoram. The covenant between Israel and Judah was ratified by the marriage of Ataliah, a daughter of Ahab and Jezebel,

Assyrian soldiers of Tiglath-Pileser III carrying away the statues of the gods from a captured city; from Nimrud.

and Jehoram, heir to the throne of Judah (2 Kgs 3:16-26). The Annals of Mesha say nothing about a military campaign by Israel, Judah, and Edom against Moab. Instead, they describe Mesha's invasion of Israel and occupation of the province of Gad (Jordan). In the Annals of Mesha, Israel invades Moab from the north; in the Annals of Jehoram, Israel, Judah, and Edom invade Moab from the south.

ANNALS OF JEHORAM OF ISRAEL
(2 Kgs 3:1-27)

¹In the eighteenth year of Jehoshaphat of Judah [874–850 B.C.E.], Jehoram, heir of Ahab [873–851 B.C.E.], became ruler of Israel in Samaria [849–842 B.C.E.]. . . . ⁴Now Mesha of Moab was a great herder, who paid the ruler of Israel the lambs' and rams' wool of one hundred herds every year. ⁵But when Ahab died, the ruler of Moab rebelled against the ruler of Israel. ⁶So Jehoram marched out of Samaria and mustered all Israel. ⁷He sent a message to Jehoshaphat, the ruler of Judah, "The ruler of Moab has rebelled. Will you go with me into battle against Moab?" Jehoshaphat answered, "I will. I am with you. My army is your army. My horses are your horses." ⁸Then he asked, "By which way shall we march?" Jehoram answered, "Along the Edom Highway."

⁹So the rulers of Israel, Judah, and Edom set out to war. When they had force marched for seven days, there was no water left for their soldiers or for their animals. ¹⁰Then the ruler of Israel said: "Yahweh intends to hand the three of us over to Moab." ¹¹But Jehoshaphat said, "Is there no prophet of Yahweh here, through whom

---

we determine what Yahweh wills?" Then a slave of the ruler of Israel answered, "Elisha son of Shaphat, who is a follower of Elijah, is here." ¹²Jehoshaphat said, "The word of Yahweh is with him." So the rulers of Israel, Judah, and Edom went to meet with him.

¹³Elisha said to the ruler of Israel, "I do not want anything to do with you. Go to your father's prophets or to your mother's prophets." But the ruler of Israel asked him, "Does Yahweh intend to hand the three of us over to Moab?" ¹⁴Elisha said, "I swear on the life of Yahweh Sabaoth, my divine patron, if it were not because of my respect for Jehoshaphat of Judah, I would not even look at you. Nonetheless, ¹⁵get me a musician." While the musician played, the spirit of Yahweh came on the prophet, ¹⁶who said: "Thus says Yahweh: 'I will fill this dry river bed with pools of water. ¹⁷You shall see neither wind nor rain, but the river bed shall be full of water, so that you and your animals can drink.' ¹⁸This is nothing for Yahweh, who will also hand Moab over to you. ¹⁹You shall conquer every fortified royal city. You shall cut down every good tree. You shall damn up every spring of water. You shall dump rocks on every farm's land." ²⁰The next day, about the time of the morning offering, water suddenly began to flow from the direction of Edom, until the river bed was filled with water.

²¹When the people of Moab heard that three armies had come up to attack them, they called up every able-bodied man. They sent these soldiers, from the youngest to the oldest, to the border. ²²When the soldiers of Moab rose early in the morning, and the sun shone upon the water, they saw it was as red as blood. ²³They said, "This is blood. The three rulers must have fought and killed one another.

So we can plunder their camps." ²⁴When the soldiers of Moab entered the camp of Israel, the Israelites ambushed and routed them. The Israelites continued the attack by invading Moab. They conquered every fortified royal city. ²⁵They dumped rocks on every farm's land. They damned up every spring of water. They cut down every good tree. Only the walled city of Kir-hareseth remained under the control of the ruler of Moab, and even it was surrounded and under attack by slingers. ²⁶When the ruler of Moab saw that the battle was going against him, he ordered seven hundred soldiers to break through Edom's line, but they could not. ²⁷Then the ruler of Moab took his firstborn son and sacrificed him on the wall of Kirhareseth. Divine wrath came upon the soldiers of Israel, so they withdrew from Moab and returned to their own land.

The Annals of Mesha and the Annals of Jehoram are describing the same military campaign, but from different perspectives (Smelik 1992, 73–74). The Annals of Jehoram describe the campaign as the exodus revisited (Smelik 1992, 89–90). Since Moses marched the Hebrews from south to north, Jehoram marches his armies from south to north. Just as Yahweh miraculously delivered the Hebrews from dying of thirst in the desert, Yahweh saves the armies of Jehoram from dying of thirst. Just as Yahweh turned the Nile River blood red, Yahweh also turns the water in Moab blood red. Just as Moses and the Hebrews routed their enemies east of the Jordan River, Jehoram and his armies rout the army of Mesha. And just as it was only after Pharaoh sacrificed the firstborn of Egypt, including the heir to his own household, that the Hebrews withdrew, so only after Mesha sacrifices his firstborn do the soldiers of Israel withdraw. The description of the war in the Annals of Jehoram is symbolic, not strategic, but the events such as the unexpected appearance of a river of blood and the offering of a human sacrifice are credible in the world of the Bible.

A River of Blood

Landscape archaeologists studying the climate and land east of the Jordan River have reconstructed how a river of blood could suddenly fill a dry riverbed. During the wet season (Hebrew: *hōrēp*), from October to March, winds moving from west to east across the Dead Sea create microburst storms that dump inches of water on the high, treeless plateaus in such a short period of time that most runs off into the valleys below (Frick 1992). With little vegetation to slow the water long enough for it to soak into the shallow highland soil, the normally dry riverbeds are quickly and unexpectedly flooded. In the Annals of Jehoram the event miraculously provides the armies of Israel, Judah, and Edom with badly needed water, and temporarily cuts the army of Moab off from their camps.

The heavy rains also cut into the red soil (Hebrew: *ădāmâ*) for which Edom is named. As in the story of the exodus (Exod 7:14-24), when the Nile River and its canals were "turned to blood," the suspended soil here turns the water red. The soldiers of Moab assumed that a civil war had broken out in the armies of Israel, Judah, and Edom and that the dead had stained the water with their blood.

Assuming that the camp of Israel has been abandoned, the soldiers of Moab are easily ambushed as they rush in to plunder it. The counterattack continues until the army of Moab is surrounded behind the walls of Kir-hareseth.

Human Sacrifice

Mesha orders his soldiers to break through the siege line, but the attempt fails. Having exhausted all human alternatives, Mesha throws the people of Moab on the mercy of Chemosh, their divine patron. He sacrifices his heir on the city wall in full view of Israel, Judah, and Edom. Chemosh intervenes, and the armies of Israel, Judah, and Edom withdraw.

Archaeologists working in Mediterranean and Mesoamerican cultures, as well as a variety of other cultures, have studied the significance of human sacrifice (Bremmer 2007). Some studies of human sacrifice in western Mediterranean cultures connect the ritual with the evolution of humans as hunters (Burkert 1972). Sacrifice processed the guilt that humans incurred by killing fellow animals. It allowed humans to deify their victims as an act of reconciliation and to reaffirm their common bond as fellow animals. Other studies of human sacrifice in western Mediterranean cultures argue that sacrifice was a strategy for controlling aggression or competition, which consistently threatens to destroy human communities (Girard 1972). Human sacrifice focused this aggression on a single member of the community. By sacrificing one human being the community vented its hostility, thereby protecting other members. Once the victims were dead, they were often deified as an act of restitution. The portion served to each household during the meal following the sacrifice reestablished the social structure that was threatened by the violence neutralized by the sacrifice.

Studies of human sacrifice in Mesoamerican cultures focus on the ritual of Atl Caualo for Tlaloc, the divine patron of nature in Aztec culture. The Aztecs ate the produce of Tlaloc, and then Tlaloc ate the children of the Aztecs. The ritual was performed at the end of the dry season to pray for enough rain to ensure successful harvests and to remind the people that only life creates life (Arnold 1991, 226). The creation stories for Atl Caualo taught that for Tlaloc to be able to release life-giving power, she had to be dismembered. In order to give birth, she had to be split in two (Sullivan 1972). In these stories the creators, Quetzalcoatl and Tezcatlipoca, change into great snakes. Like midwives they take Tlaloc's arms as her legs split and she gives birth. The violence here is not only murder but labor.

Human sacrifice was a reenactment of the labor that gave birth to the earth. Mother Earth labors to bring forth her children. Evidence of the violence or labor of creation is reflected in the landscape. When Tlaloc writhed in labor, the earth quaked and volcanoes erupted. Therefore, at these points of pain the Aztecs offered human sacrifice to reenact the labor of their birth (Arnold 1991, 225).

Everything the Aztecs needed grew from the body of Tlaloc. Trees, flowers, and plants were the hair on her head and skin. Springs and waterfalls flowed from her eyes. Rivers flowed from caves that were her mouth. The mountains and the valleys were her nose. Aztec culture transformed these natural features into sacred space (Carrasco 1991, 33). They changed these natural places into sacred places—places where they as humans assumed divine roles by reenacting the creation of the land and their own human creation.

Human sacrifice in Aztec culture also created parallels between rain and blood. Blood was the water that supported human life. Rain was the blood that supported the land's life. To obtain the rain needed to water the land required watering the land with their children's blood (Arnold 1991, 227). The weeping that accompanied human sacrifice was another sympathetic ritual that brought the land back to life. Shedding human blood and crying human tears brought the rain that brought the land back to life (Arnold 1991, 228).

Perhaps the most helpful parallels for understanding human sacrifice come from Near Eastern

---

STORIES OF ATRAHASIS
(Matthews and Benjamin 2006:33–42)

Nintu said to the divine assembly: *I cannot do Ea-Enki's work.*
　　Only Ea-Enki has the clay to create.
　　Let him give me clay to create.
Ea-Enki spoke: *I will bathe to mark my time. . . .*
　　At the new moon, the seventh day, and the full moon, I will wash.
Let the divine assembly sacrifice We-ila.
　　Let them bathe in his blood.
Let Nintu thin my clay with his blood.
　　Let Nintu mix clay with blood, the human with the divine.
Let the drum mark off the days,
　　Count down the time.
Let We-ila's blood give these workers life,
　　Let the spirit within allow them to live.
The divine assembly agreed,
　　The anunnaki elders consented.

creation stories recovered by archaeologists working in Mesopotamia. In the Annals of Jehoram and the hero story of Jephthah delivering Israel from Ammon (Judg 11:1-40) a human sacrifice is offered during a war. In creation tales such as the Stories of Atrahasis, human sacrifice is offered during creation. These parallels suggest that human sacrifice is a ritual of new beginnings. The chaos of the old world—war—is ending; the cosmos of the new world—creation—is beginning.

The Stories of Atrahasis begin in a world populated only by divine warriors (Akkadian: *iggigi*) and elders (Akkadian: *anunnaki*). Eventually the divine warriors revolt, refusing to do all the work necessary to keep their world running properly. Ea-Enki negotiates a settlement with them, in which workers (Akkadian: *lullu*) will be created to take care of the world, especially by dredging its canals. The elders ratify Ea-Enki's proposal but assign Nintu-Mami the actual task of carrying out the project.

The stories describe the labor of Nintu-Mami with different accounts of how she carried out the task. One account compares Ea-Enki with a menstruating woman, who bathes three times during the menstrual cycle: first when the new moon appears, then seven days later, and finally fourteen days later when the full moon appears. Then the divine assembly sacrifices Wei-la, one of its own, to create the *lullu*, the people primeval. Life comes from life. The life of We-ila becomes the life of the *lullu*. Human sacrifice is the intercourse that mixes the body of Ea-Enki with the blood of We-ila.

Generally, fathers of households in the world of the Bible did not sacrifice their firstborn. They sacrificed animals or took vows instead. But some, like Jephthah and Mesha, did (Levenson 1993, 17). Even in ancient Israel the firstborn belonged to Yahweh (Exod 22:28). Repeated denials in the Bible that only strangers and heretics offered human sacrifice make it more likely that the Hebrews themselves offered human sacrifices to Yahweh (Noort 2007; Sales 1957; Mosca 1975; Heider 1985).

The careful work of archaeologists in the Mediterranean and Mesoamerica has made it clear that Mesha's human sacrifice was regarded in his world as something extreme or barbaric; it was an act of faith that demonstrated the complete dependence of his household upon Chemosh, its divine patron. Human sacrifice in the world of the Bible was a profession of faith that the life of the household was a divine gift, not a human accomplishment. Although human sacrifice itself is no longer an acceptable ritual today, ongoing research, inspired in part by the Annals of Mesha, results in a better understanding and appreciation of the sentiments that inspired human sacrifice in past cultures.

CONCLUSION

F. A. Klein was a missionary, not an archaeologist. Nonetheless, his patient commitment to understanding the Bedouin people who showed him the Annals of Mesha led to one of the most significant archaeological discoveries in the last 150 years. The Bedu people who helped the archaeologists of Klein's day continue to help today's archaeologists to better understand the world of the Bible. In the present time, archaeologists do not go into the field to convert the people who live around ancient sites, but because of the influence of missionaries like Klein most archaeologists allow local people to collaborate in various ways in their excavations. A patient commitment to understanding and learning from the local people around a site is essential to the success of any excavation.

WHAT YOU HAVE LEARNED

- Christian missionaries from Europe and the Americas came to the world of the Bible to convert Muslims to the Christian faith.
- F. A. Klein was a missionary to the Bedouin in Jordan, and in 1868 he was the first Westerner to see the Annals of Mesha carved on a black basalt stela. It is the longest inscription recovered from Syria-Palestine to date.
- Archaeologists continue to study the language and contents of the Annals of Mesha to better understand the cultures that the inscription reflects.
- Cultures that, like ancient Israel, prohibit making images of their divine patrons often kindle fires, build altars, or construct pedestals to indicate that their divine patron is present.
- The stories of the plagues in the book of Exodus (7:14—13:10) describe Moses turning the Nile River blood red. When red clay suspended in floodwater surrounded the army of Israel protecting it from the army of Moab, Jehoram, the ruler of Israel, considered it a repetition of the plague on Egypt and considered himself to be the new Moses.
- Missionaries demonstrated that a patient commitment to understanding and learning from the local people around a site is essential to the success of any excavation.

STUDY QUESTIONS

1. What is the significance of the Annals of Mesha?
2. What was the function of altars in ancient Israelite cities?
3. Why did the Israelites make pedestals for Yahweh?
4. How does the description of the military campaign in the Annals of Jehoram differ from that in the Annals of Mesha?
5. What do we know about human sacrifice in ancient cultures?

Part 2

Cultural History

- Part 2 is an introduction to the School of Cultural History.
- Chapter 6 describes how cultural historians reconstruct the important political and military events at a site using written artifacts to interpret the material artifacts they recover.
- Chapter 7 describes a specific kind of cultural history called *biblical archaeology*. Biblical archaeologists use the Bible to interpret material artifacts.
- Chapter 8 describes the Wheeler-Kenyon method, which every school of archaeology today uses to recover and record artifacts.
- Chapters 9–10 look at Arad and Qumran, two important sites excavated by biblical archaeologists and what these sites contribute to the understanding of the Bible.

PREVIEW: CULTURAL HISTORY

- Stories Interpret Stones
  - Taylor Prism
  - Lachish
- Story Calendars and Stone Calendars
  - William Matthew Flinders Petrie
  - Pottery
- Stones versus Stories; Stories versus Stones
  - Tutankhamen

Chapter 6 describes how cultural historians and biblical archaeologists use written artifacts to interpret the material remains they recover and how this contributes to the interpretation of the Bible. It explains what cultural historians do when written artifacts and material artifacts tell different stories and how cultural historians use written artifacts to interpret material artifacts. Finally, the chapter shows how cultural historians used written artifacts to interpret the material artifacts recovered at Lachish (Israel) from the layers of destruction from 701 B.C.E. and 586 B.C.E.

6

Cultural History

Archaeology has partnered both with history and with anthropology. In North America, with the notable exception of Boston University, archaeology is taught in anthropology departments. At Boston University and at universities in Europe archaeology is taught in history departments. Cultural History (German: *Kulturgeschichte*) is a school of archaeology that partners with history or political science (Webster 2008; Rouse 1953). History is the study of the human past using written records (J. Maxwell Miller 1988, 3). Cultural historians considered writings to be their primary tool for understanding material remains (Jamieson-Drake 1997, 3:28–30).

Biblical archaeologists are cultural historians who use the Bible to interpret the material remains from ancient Israel and surrounding cultures. After 1918, most archaeologists working in the world of the Bible were cultural historians or biblical archaeologists. The Bible took priority in the research agendas and the paradigms they created to interpret the artifacts they recovered.

STORIES INTERPRET STONES

For biblical archaeologists, the Bible and other ancient Near Eastern writings were the primary interpretive tools in their analysis of material remains. The invention of writing in Mesopotamia, Egypt, and Syria-Palestine; the development of the Bible; and the remarkable archive of Near Eastern traditions recovered by archaeologists between 1800 and the present are among the most important reasons for giving these writings pride of place in interpreting material remains in the world of the Bible. This cross-fertilization has dramatically increased the understanding of both the world of the Bible and the Bible itself for cultural historians and for the general public.

For example, Sennacherib, the Great King of Assyria, inscribed annals for eight military campaigns on a six-sided clay prism about fifteen inches high. The record is written in the Assyrian dialect of the

The Taylor Prism, Neo-Assyrian, from Nineveh, northern Iraq, 691 B.C.E. This six-sided baked clay document is a foundation record, intended to preserve Sennacherib's achievements for posterity and the gods. The prism records Sennacherib's third campaign, the destruction of forty-six cities in Judah and the deportation of 200,150 people. Hezekiah, king of Judah, is said to have sent tribute to Sennacherib. ANE 91032. Location: British Museum, London. Photo Credit: Erich Lessing / Art Resource, NY.

Akkadian language using the cuneiform script. Colonel R. Taylor, British consul general in Baghdad, acquired the prism in 1830, and the British Museum bought it from his widow in 1855.

According to the prism, Hezekiah declared Judah's independence from Assyria after 715 B.C.E. Consequently, Sennacherib sent an army into Judah in 701 B.C.E. to put down the revolt. He laid siege to Jerusalem and devastated the surrounding countryside. Biblical archaeologists used the Taylor Prism and the Bible to interpret the material remains recovered from destruction layers at sites like Lachish.

THIRD YEAR OF THE REIGN OF SENNACHERIB
(Matthews and Benjamin 2006, 190–92)

Because Hezekiah of Judah did not submit to my yoke, I laid siege to forty-six of his fortified cities, walled forts, and to the countless villages in their vicinity. I conquered them using earthen ramps and battering rams. These siege engines were supported by infantry who tunneled under the walls. I took 200,150 prisoners of war, young and old, male and female, from these places. I also plundered more horses, mules, donkeys, camels, large and small cattle than we could count. I imprisoned Hezekiah in Jerusalem like a bird in a cage. I erected siege works to prevent anyone escaping through the city gates. The cities in Judah which I captured I gave to Mitinti, king of Ashdod, and to Padi, king of Ekron, and to Sillibel, king of Gaza. Thus I reduced the land of Hezekiah in this campaign, and I also increased Hezekiah's annual tribute payments.

Hezekiah, who was overwhelmed by my terror-inspiring splendor, was deserted by his elite troops, which he had brought into Jerusalem. He was forced to send me four-hundred twenty pounds of gold, eleven-thousand two-hundred pounds of silver, precious stones, couches and chairs inlaid with ivory, elephant hides, ebony wood, box wood, and all kinds of valuable treasures, his daughters, wives, and male and female musicians. He sent his personal messenger to deliver this tribute and bow down to me.

The annals report that, because Hezekiah had not submitted to Assyria, Sennacherib laid siege to forty-six fortified cities in Judah, deported 200,150 people and laid siege to Jerusalem (T. C. Mitchell 1988, 59). The annals of Hezekiah for this war of independence are reported in the books of Samuel–Kings (2 Kgs 18:17—19:36) and the book of Isaiah (Isa 36:1—37:37). The Bible reports that the Assyrians suffered staggering casualties during a mysterious night event, and then lifted the siege of Jerusalem. Sennacherib does not report that he took Jerusalem, but makes an inventory of the ransom in gold, silver, iron, precious stones, woods, ivory inlaid furniture, weapons, and musicians that Hezekiah paid for the city. Curiously, the annals on the prism do not mention the siege and capture of Lachish by Sennacherib, which are described in vivid detail on reliefs in the trophy room at Nineveh.

Cultural historians like James L. Starkey (1895–1938), G. Lankester Harding, and Olga Tufnell (1905–1985) excavated at Lachish from 1932 to 1938. David Ussishkin, Gabriel Barkay, Christa Clamer, Yehudah Dagan, John Woodhead, and Orna Zimhoni excavated there from 1973 to 1983. Both teams relied closely on the time line and description of events in the written artifacts for their interpretation of the material remains from Lachish.

According to the reconstruction of events using both material remains and biblical tradition, Nebuchanezer laid siege to Jerusalem, Lachish, and Azekah. Azekah is eighteen miles southwest of Jerusalem, and Lachish is thirty miles away. At some point during the siege, the citizens of Jerusalem released their slaves in hope of deliverance, and, in fact, the Babylonians withdrew. But the citizens of Jerusalem broke their oath and retook their slaves. The Babylonian withdrawal, however, was not an answer to their prayer but Nebuchadnezzar's decision to use the soldiers surrounding Jerusalem in the final assault on Lachish. The Babylonians returned after the fall of Lachish to resume their assault on Jerusalem.

In one of the Lachish Letters recovered by Starkey (see sidebar), the commander of Lachish writes, "this letter certifies to the commanding officer in Jerusalem that I remain on duty to carry out your orders. Judah's signal fire at Lachish still burns, even after the only other remaining signal fire at Azekah has gone out." This written artifact is used to argue that Azekah fell before Lachish. Therefore, the sequence can be reconstructed as first Azekah, then Lachish, then Jerusalem.

STORY CALENDARS AND STONE CALENDARS

A significant contribution of cultural historians to the study of the world of the Bible is the calendar that they have reconstructed. Calendars are an important tool for sorting material remains and for focusing the interpretation of a site. Gradually, the calendars built around

LACHISH

The biblical site of Lachish has been identified with Tell ed-Duweir, located about thirty miles southwest of Jerusalem. The site was occupied from as early as the fourth millennium B.C.E. One of the most important discoveries of the excavations at Lachish was twenty-one ostraca (pottery fragments) inscribed in classical Hebrew. These inscribed fragments are known as the Lachish Letters. Dating to around 590 B.C.E., these letters offer insights into the reign of King Zedekiah and the activities of the prophet Jeremiah. For example there is a brief mention of the siege in a trial of Jerusalem in the book of Jeremiah (Jer 34:1—35:19). Jeremiah promulgates the verdict when "the Great King of Babylon had laid siege to Jerusalem, Lachish, and Azekah—the only walled cities left in Judah" (Jer 34:7). In the indictment Jeremiah charges that the citizens of Jerusalem freed their slaves as a ritual of repentance asking Yahweh to deliver the city. Then, once the siege was lifted, they enslaved them again. ■

Letter from the commander of the fortress of Lachish to his commander in Jerusalem, reporting that he can no longer see the signal fire at Azekah, another outpost on the road to Jerusalem, because the Babylonians have overrun the city. Clay sherd covered with reed-pen and carbon ink writing. 6th century B.C.E. Location: Israel Museum (IDAM), Jerusalem, Israel. Photo Credit: Erich Lessing / Art Resource, NY.

political and economic events in written artifacts have been replaced by calendars based on ceramics, the shape and decoration used in pottery. Repeated, careful excavations have developed sequences for the evolution of pottery types from the first appearance of pottery in the Neolithic period (6000–3800 B.C.E.) to the ceramics used in Syria-Palestine during the Crusades (1096–1291). Pottery not only provides a chronology for a particular site, but the chronologies from other sites can be used to recreate the time line of an entire region (Wright 1962, 24).

William Matthew Flinders Petrie (1853–1942)

William Matthew Flinders Petrie

Flinders Petrie began his career in archaeology as a surveyor. Petrie's father, too, was a surveyor, and he taught his son how to use the most advanced equipment of the time. This early training instilled in Petrie a respect for measurement and accuracy that would influence his work in archaeology.

Petrie pioneered archaeology as a science by carefully identifying settlement layers. He was among the first to map the exact location of the material remains that he excavated. He also recognized that pottery could be used to create a calendar for dating remains. Finally, Petrie discovered the earliest form of the Proto-Sinaitic alphabet, which was a major contribution to the study of the origins of writing in the ancient Near East. He is honored today as the *Father of Modern Egyptology*—to distinguish him from Jean-François Champollion, who is honored as the *Father of Egyptology* and John Gardner Wilkinson who is honored as the *Father of British Egyptology*. The measurement of ancient monuments always fascinated Petrie, and from 1880 to 1883 he surveyed the pyramid of Khufu (2551–2528 B.C.E.) on the Giza Plain. Petrie became Edwards Professor of Egyptian Archaeology and Philology at University College (London). His collection of Egyptian artifacts is preserved today in the Petrie Museum at University College.

Pottery

Petrie excavated many important sites in Egypt: Hawara, Meydum, Abydos, Amarna, Ballas, Naqada, Gerza, and Tarkhan. There were over two thousand undated graves at Naqada. While excavating these graves Petrie began to classify them by the different styles of pottery placed with the bodies as grave goods. The first benchmark he established was the difference in style between pre-dynastic pottery (4500–3000 B.C.E.), from before Pharaoh Narmer (3000 B.C.E.) united southern and northern Egypt into a state, and dynastic pottery (2920 B.C.E.–311). The signature of pre-dynastic pottery is a ledge-shaped wavy handle on either side of the upper body of a pot. These handles were finger grips. Over time, the wavy handles became narrower. The body of the pre-dynastic pots also evolved. In the beginning, the body of these pots was round. By the end of the period, the body was cylinder shaped. Petrie dated the round-shaped pottery with large wavy handles earlier than the cylinder shaped pottery with narrow handles. He also noted that the crossed-line decoration on the cylinder-shaped jars was a later addition. This design imitated the knotted cord slings that formed a net to

Replica of a household cave tomb with grave goods. Royal Ontario Museum. Photo by the author.

hold vessels for carrying or for hanging. Petrie designed a pottery sequence labeling the oldest pottery 80 and the latest pottery 30.

Pre-dynastic pottery was manufactured by kneading clay tempered or strengthened with sand. Potters rolled the clay into a rope and then coiled it on a flat stone to shape the pot. The surface of the jar was polished to seal it, and then air-dried to a leathery consistency, decorated with paint, and fired. The wavy-handle design on the upper body was produced by pinching the wet clay.

Petrie left Egypt and directed the first American excavation in Syria-Palestine at Tel el-Hesi (Israel) in 1890. There he found many of the same types of pottery that he had dated in Egypt. Petrie continued to develop his pottery chronology, which soon replaced written artifacts as the most reliable tool for dating material artifacts (Currid 1999, 79–88).

During four seasons (1926, 1928, 1930, 1932) of excavating Tell Beit Mirsim, William Foxwell Albright completed the Petrie pottery calendar for the Bronze Age and the Iron Age in Syria-Palestine (Running and Freedman 1975, 143–63). Albright's student G. Ernest Wright (1909–1974), continued to refine the calendar. The pioneering work of Petrie, Albright, and Wright was eventually synthesized in *Ancient Pottery of the Holy Land from Its Beginnings in the Neolithic Period to the End of the Iron Age* (1970) by Ruth Amiran. Amiran's work is still a basic handbook for dating pottery in Syria-Palestine.

Pottery in the world of the Bible was functional. Clay vessels were produced to be useful rather than decorative. There were pots for storing grain and liquids; pots for cooking, eating, or mixing; and small pots for storing cosmetics and perfumes (Borowski 1982). Pottery can break, but it is seldom destroyed. Pieces of broken pottery, or sherds, reveal something about the composition, shape, decoration, and purpose of the original pot. Diagnostic sherds—rims, handle, and bases—allow archaeologists to reconstruct the original pot. Body sherds—from any other part of the pot except its rim, handle, or base—are less informative about the original.

Pottery making was a trade that passed from one generation to the next, perpetuating the shapes of pots and the methods of production. The evolution of pottery, however, was slow. Archaeologists can date pots by their shape and manufacturing characteristics. A pot is unique to the culture that makes it or to the time period in which it is made. The kind of clay, the additives that harden the clay and keep it from shrinking and cracking, the shape of pots, and the decoration all are culture specific or time specific. Therefore, once these indicators are linked to a particular culture or a particular period of time, they create a reliable calendar for dating other artifacts that are found at the same level, or stratum, of an excavation. The date of a stratum corresponds to the latest piece of pottery found there. The most recent pottery found on a floor indicates the most recent date when the building was occupied.

During excavation, sherds are collected into buckets. Each bucket has a number identifying the place or locus where the pottery was collected. Each piece of pottery is dipped in water to see if the water highlights any writing. If the sherd is blank, then it is brushed clean and laid out in a tray with the other pieces of pottery from the same bucket. When the pieces are dry, pottery experts on the excavation team date or read the pieces in the tray. Generally all the pieces are similar in construction and decoration, but occasionally there will be pieces from another culture or time period. These pieces are noted, and a reason for their presence in the tray is suggested. For example, they may have been heirloom or keepsake pieces; they may have been imported pieces; or the stratum to which they originally belonged may have been disturbed by digging.

STONES VERSUS STORIES; STORIES VERSUS STONES

An ongoing challenge for cultural historians working in the world of the Bible is how to resolve contradictions between material remains and written remains. For example, the preached tradition understands the books of Joshua and Judges to be a description of how miraculous military victories confirmed the Hebrews' faith in Yahweh. Nonetheless, Kathleen Kenyon (1906–1978), who excavated Jericho from 1952 to 1959, could not confirm that there was a city at the site when the Hebrews were in Syria-Palestine. Instead, the material remains indicate that the Hyksos' city of Jericho was destroyed in 1350 B.C.E.—more than 250 years before Joshua (1200–1000 B.C.E.)—and that the site remained abandoned until 716 B.C.E., when Hezekiah of Judah rebuilt it. Some archaeologists working in the Near East resolve the conflict by separating the study of written artifacts from the study of material artifacts altogether. They emphasize that written artifacts and material artifacts have too little in common to accurately interpret one another.

Among the striking differences between written and material remains is the fact that written artifacts reflect the worldview of the elite but not the worldview of the culture as a whole. Material remains reflect a more populist worldview. The book of Deuteronomy, for example, holds the elite view that the Hebrews should worship Yahweh and celebrate Passover only in Jerusalem. Material remains from Arad (Israel) and Elephantine (Egypt), however, show that Hebrews worshiped Yahweh and celebrated Passover not only in Jerusalem but also in Arad and Elephantine. Likewise, according to the Bible, Yahweh, the divine patron of ancient Israel, is unmarried and male. Nonetheless pilgrims who visited the sanctuaries at Kuntillet ʿAjrud and

Khirbet el-Qom addressed Yahweh as part of a divine couple. They wrote their prayers on broken pieces of pottery to both Yahweh—their Godfather—and Asherah—their Godmother (Zevit 2001, 350–438). (See p. 219 below.)

Similarly, material remains are artifacts of a single time and place. Written remains, however, reflect multiple times and multiple places: the time and place when and where written remains developed; the times and places that appear in the written remains themselves; and the times and places where the written remains, as they appear in the Bible today, were told. Each of these calendars and geographies must be taken into account when interpreting written remains. Establishing a reliable interface between the complex calendars and geographies of written artifacts and the contrastingly simply calendar and geography of material artifacts is a complicated project.

Another significant difference between written and material remains is that chance determines what material remains are preserved. Settlement layers at a site are haphazard, not choreographed. The artifacts of ordinary people may be preserved while those of the elite may perish, or the elite may survive and the ordinary perish. What is recovered from an excavation is also, regardless of the expertise of the excavation team, haphazard. The Dead Sea Scrolls were discovered by herders looking for lost sheep. Howard Carter (1874–1939) was looking for the tomb of Tutankhamen, had given up hope of finding it, but then unexpectedly, he found it.

During the Middle Bronze period, colonists and warriors from Syria-Palestine, whom native Egyptians despised as Hyksos or northerners, occupied the delta where the Nile River flows into the Mediterranean Sea. From there the Hyksos ruled Egypt as far as Thebes, three hundred miles to the south, from 1630 to 1539 B.C.E. ■

THE TOMB OF TUTANKHAMEN
Howard Carter (1954:31)

The history of the Valley, as I have endeavoured to show . . . has never lacked the dramatic element, and in this, the latest episode, it has held to its traditions. For consider the circumstances. This was to be our final season in the Valley. Six full seasons we had excavated there, and season after season had drawn a blank; we had worked for months at a stretch and found nothing, and only an excavator knows how desperately depressing that can be; we had almost made up our minds that we were beaten, and were preparing to leave the Valley and try our luck elsewhere; and then—hardly had we set hoe to ground in our last despairing effort than we made a discovery that far exceeded our wildest dreams. Surely, never before in the whole history of excavation has a full digging season been compressed within the space of five days.

In contrast, conscious editorial choice determines what written artifacts are preserved. The Bible is the work of decision making. What was chosen and what was left created the canon of the Bible. The traditions that were chosen were not necessarily the best traditions. How the traditions are used in the Bible does not necessarily reflect the intentions of those who developed the traditions. Again, trying to establish a productive relationship between artifacts of chance and artifacts of purpose is a challenging project.

Historical models of ancient cultures in written remains are different from archaeological models in material remains. Historical models are designed around the lives of great men and the events to which they contribute. Archaeological models are designed around the artistic development of styles of architecture, pottery, or metalwork that define a particular stratum or settlement layer. Most material artifacts are records of daily life, not spectacular events such as are preserved in the written accounts. Focusing only on the material remains that illumine the lives of the rich and famous ignores most of what archaeologists recover in the field. The Bible, for example, narrates not only Solomon's rise to power as the successor of David, but also attributes to him teaching traditions such as the book of Proverbs, Ecclesiastes, and the Song of Solomon. The material remains from the city of Gezer, described by the Bible as the dowry of a pharaoh's daughter to Solomon, clarifies little and confirms little about this biblical Solomon.

Finally, written artifacts are permanent. They can be studied and restudied by scholars with different abilities and different methods. Feminist scholars reconstruct the character of Bathsheba in a Trial of David (2 Sam 10:1—12:31) much differently from their patriarchal colleagues. Nonetheless, interpretations of written artifacts do not destroy the artifacts. Feminist scholars do not have to wonder what text was previously read and interpreted by their patriarchal colleagues. The artifact remains constant.

The context of material artifacts (Latin: *in situ*) is destroyed by the archaeologists who excavate the site. Even the records of archaeologists, no matter how carefully kept, preserve only what *they* did, what questions *they* asked, what artifacts *they* studied. The rest is lost. Archaeologists with better tools, better skills, and different questions cannot ever see what their predecessors saw or dig where their predecessors dug.

CONCLUSION

Today cultural historians still consider the relationship between written artifacts and material artifacts to be important for accurately understanding maker cultures. They do not ignore the Bible in interpreting material remains, but they no longer use the Bible as their primary tool for interpreting material remains—and they no longer use material remains only to prove the historicity of the Bible. The Bible is a cultural artifact of an Iron Age culture, just like other material remains recovered by archaeologists. Cultural historians construct their models from the ground up, initially using only material remains. Once that artifact model is in place, they can evaluate it both for its historical significance and for its relationship to the Bible

Likewise, cultural historians today place less emphasis on events and more emphasis on social systems. Cultures develop not so much in response to what strong men do, as in response to how environments change. An earthquake had a greater impact on life in Judah from 740 to 700 B.C.E. than did the prophet Isaiah.

Social institutions and behavioral patterns adapt in response to ecological changes such as drought or social developments such as ironworking technology. Environmental change is seldom simple. More often environmental changes interact with one another producing compound change agents to which cultures must respond in order to survive. To understand a culture it is less important to understand its great men than to understand the systems it developed to survive and flourish as its environment changed. Therefore, cultural historians are equally sensitive to how cultures responded to changes in their environments and to how they responded to political or economic changes.

Originally, cultural historians immediately brought written and material artifacts into conversation with one another to establish an interpretation of a site. Cultural historians today develop two separate models for interpreting a site—a model based on written artifacts, and a model based on material artifacts. Once these two models have been developed and tested, cultural historians begin to draw them into conversation with one another. The result is the creation of various paradigms for understanding a single site, rather than the creation of a single definitive interpretation.

WHAT YOU HAVE LEARNED

- For cultural historians, written artifacts are the most important resource for interpreting material artifacts.
- For biblical archaeologists, biblical traditions are the most important resource for interpreting material artifacts.
- Cultural historians used the Bible, the Annals of Sennacharib, and the Lachish Letters to interpret the two destruction layers at the site of Iron Age Lachish.
- Today cultural historians first reconstruct the story in the material artifacts, and only then use written artifacts to evaluate it.

STUDY QUESTIONS

1. Describe the approach to archaeology of the School of Cultural History.
2. What is the importance of the Taylor Prism?
3. How is pottery used to establish chronologies?
4. What are some of the differences between material remains and written remains?

PREVIEW: BIBLICAL ARCHAEOLOGY

- The Biblical Archaeology Movement
  - William Foxwell Albright
  - George Ernest Wright
  - John Bright
  - Kenneth A. Kitchen
- The Origins of Early Israel
  - ʿApiru
  - Sethos I
  - Israel and Neighboring States
- The Settlement of Syria-Palestine
  - The Conquest Theory
  - The Settlement Theory
  - The Social Revolution Theory
  - The Evidence of Archaeology

Chapter 7 describes how William Foxwell Albright defined the goal of biblical archaeology, and how biblical archaeology related to biblical theology. It also explains how biblical archaeologists reconstruct the origins of ancient Israel, and how the ʿapiru were related to the Hebrews. Finally, the chapter shows how the Annals of Merneptah contribute to the understanding of the origins of Israel and why biblical archaeologists now describe the Hebrews as farmers and herders rather than as warriors.

7

Biblical Archaeology

THE BIBLICAL ARCHAEOLOGY MOVEMENT

William Foxwell Albright

As the director of the American School of Oriental Research at The Johns Hopkins University (1929–1959), **William Foxwell Albright** pioneered the biblical archaeology movement. The first American to excavate in Syria-Palestine was William Matthew Flinders Petrie. He began his work at Tell el-Hesi in 1890. Before Albright, however, few biblical scholars were archaeologists. They let others dig, and then applied the findings to the world of the Bible. Albright inspired biblical scholars to direct their own excavations. He convinced them that archaeology was crucial to an accurate understanding of the world of the Bible.

William Foxwell Albright

Albright was born in Chile to Methodist missionary parents: Wilbur Finley and Zephine Viola Foxwell Albright. In 1913 Albright earned his Ph.D. from Johns Hopkins University under the direction of Paul Haupt (1858–1926) and became an expert in Semitic languages and pottery analysis. In 1921 he married Ruth Norton, who also had earned her Ph.D. from Johns Hopkins. She was a specialist in Sanskrit linguistics and folklore.

Books by Albright such as *The Archaeology of Palestine* (1949), *From the Stone Age to Christianity* (1940), *The Biblical Period from Abraham to Ezra* (1963), and *Yahweh and the Gods of Canaan* (1968) dominated biblical scholarship in the United States during much of the twentieth century. Albright's students like G. Ernest Wright, Frank M. Cross, David N. Freedman, and Cyrus Gordon (1908–2001) became internationally respected scholars of the world of the Bible.

Albright launched the biblical archaeology movement to demonstrate that the Bible was historically reliable. This was the defining characteristic of biblical archaeology. For example, he used archaeology to argue that Abraham and Sarah, Isaac and Rebekah, and Jacob, Leah, and Rachel were real people who lived during the Middle Bronze period (2000–1550 B.C.E.). For him, archaeology demonstrated that the ancestor stories in the book of Genesis

(Gen 11:27—37:2) were historically reliable biographies. Similarly, Albright identified the destruction layers in Syria-Palestine during the Iron IA period (1200–1100 B.C.E.)—such as those at Tell Beit Mirsim near Hebron where he excavated from 1926 to 1932—as evidence that the hero stories in the books of Joshua–Judges are historically accurate reports of the invasion of Syria-Palestine by the Hebrews.

The inspiration for biblical archaeology came from the biblical theology movement. For biblical theologians, a foundational teaching of both Judaism and Christianity is that God intervenes in human history (Davis 2004, viii). They consider Judaism and Christianity to be historical or linear religions, in contrast to faith traditions that are mythical or cyclical (Eliade 1959, 67–113). According to biblical theology, the record of God's intervention is the Bible, and biblical archaeology is used to support this preached interpretation. The Bible sets the agenda for biblical archaeology, and the goal is to demonstrate that the Bible is a historically reliable witness to the events it describes. This is a basic teaching of churches in the tradition of Reformation Christianity in the United States, for which biblical archaeologists sought to provide evidence. For example, in 1922 Leonard Woolley was directing an excavation of the royal tombs at Ur (Arabic: *Tell al Muqayyar*) north of Basra (Iraq), when he uncovered an eight-foot-thick layer of clean clay. He considered this layer unmistakable evidence that the flood stories in the book of Genesis (Gen 6:1—11:26) were historically accurate. For a time biblical archaeologists and the general public almost universally agreed with him.

Archaeology, for Albright, could not prove Israel's faith, but it could demonstrate that Israel's faith was not mindless superstition. Books on archaeology and the Bible published from 1950 to 1970, such as *The Archaeology of Palestine* (1949) by Albright, *Archaeology in the Holy Land* (1960) by Kathleen Kenyon, and *The Archaeology of the Land of Israel* (1982) by Yohanan Aharoni, use archaeology to demonstrate the historical accuracy of the Bible. These works are political histories of Syria-Palestine that highlight ancient Israel, refining the time lines and significant events identified in the Bible with archaeology. These archaeologists accepted the biblical traditions as reliable reflections of past events and their relationships with one another (Alhstrom 1993, 10).

Until 1970, biblical archaeology was the unchallenged paradigm for excavations in Syria-Palestine. Since then the paradigm has been continually revised by archaeologists, anthropologists, historians, and biblical scholars. Signs of significant change are reflected in name changes for the discipline. The *biblical archaeology* of yesterday is the *archaeology of Syria-Palestine* today. Yesterdays courses in *biblical archaeology* are today's courses in *archaeology and the Bible*.

Nonetheless, the general public, and not a few archaeologists, remain as unwaveringly enthusiastic about Albright's biblical archaeology as it has ever been (Henry O. Thompson 1987, 281–418). Publications such as the *Biblical Archaeology Review*—founded by Hershel Shanks in 1976—are widely read. Popular presentations by archaeologists working in Syria-Palestine are well attended. Travel study programs to the world of the Bible are well enrolled. Likewise, in North America financial support for excavations in the world of the Bible continues to be strong from religiously affiliated institutions and individuals. These generous sponsors expect their protégés to focus their fieldwork on improving the understanding of the Bible.

George Ernest Wright

George Ernest Wright (1909–1974) was one of Albright's early students and became a leading biblical archaeologist, especially skilled in the study and dating of pottery. For Wright the historical reliability of the Bible was a pillar of the Christian faith. Wright graduated from the College of Wooster (Ohio) and from McCormick Theological Seminary (1934) and was ordained in the Presbyterian Church. He studied with Albright at Johns Hopkins University, where he received his master's degree in 1936 and his doctorate in 1937. He taught Old Testament history and theology at McCormick Seminary (1939–1958) and then became Parkman Professor (1958–1974) and Curator of the Semitic Museum (1961–1974) at the Harvard Divinity School. Like Albright, his mentor, Wright published to prove the historical reliability of the Bible: *God Who Acts: Biblical Theology as Recital* (1952); *Biblical Archaeology* (1957); *Shechem, the Biography of a Biblical City* (1965); and *The Old Testament and Theology* (1969). He directed the Drew-McCormick Archaeological Expedition to Shechem in Israel (1956–1974); the Hebrew Union College Biblical and Archaeological School Expedition at Tel Gezer in Israel (1964–1965); and the Joint American Expedition to Idalion in Cyprus (1971–1974).

John Bright

Another influential Albright student was **John Bright** (1908–1995), who earned his bachelor of divinity at the Union Theological Seminary, Virginia (1931). Bright was the Cyrus H. McCormick Professor of Hebrew and the Interpretation of the Old Testament at Union Theological Seminary in Virginia (1940–1975). His books include *The Kingdom of God: The Biblical Concept and Its Meaning for the Church* (1953) and *Covenant and Promise: The Prophetic Understanding of the Future in Preexilic Israel* (1976). But the work for which Bright is most well known is *A History of Israel* (1959 and many subsequent editions). It is a consistent application of Albright's assumption that what the Bible describes is historically reliable.

Kenneth A. Kitchen

Kenneth A. Kitchen is a scholar of ancient Egypt. His work focuses on the reign of Ramesses II (1290–1224 B.C.E.) and the Third Intermediate Period in Egypt (1100–650 B.C.E.). His publications include *Ramesside Inscriptions* (2000), *The Third Intermediate Period in Egypt 1100–650 BC*

EGYPTIAN CHRONOLOGY

Between 384 and 343 B.C.E., Manetho, an Egyptian priest, compiled a history of Egypt. His work has not survived, but it is widely quoted in ancient sources. Scholars today follow Manetho's outline in dividing ancient Egyptian history into a series of thirty-one dynasties, beginning with Menes, who united southern and northern Egypt in 2920 B.C.E., and ending with Alexander's conquest of Egypt in 332 B.C.E. The following dates are B.C.E. (Brewer and Teeter 2007: 30-59)

Pre-Dynastic Period	3400–*ca.* 3100
Early Dynastic Period	2920–2650
1st and 2nd Dynasties	
Old Kingdom	2649–2134
3rd through 8th Dynasties	
First Intermediate Period	2134–2040
9th through 11th Dynasties	
Middle Kingdom	2040–1640
11th and 12th Dynasties	
Second Intermediate Period	1783–1539
13th through 17th Dynasties	
New Kingdom	1550–1069
18th through 20th Dynasties	
Third Intermediate Period	1069–664
21st through 25th Dynasties; Kings of Sais	
Late Period	664-525

(1996), and *Poetry of Ancient Egypt* (1999). In 2003, however, he published *On the Reliability of the Old Testament*, a defense of the historical and chronological reliability of the Bible in a style reminiscent of the biblical archaeology of Albright and Wright.

In *On the Reliability of the Old Testament* Kitchen targets the positions of Niels Peter Lemche, Thomas Thompson, Philip Davies, Keith Whitelam, and Israel Finkelstein, who argue that the Bible was developed by Jews attempting to avoid assimilation into the Hellenistic culture that Alexander of Macedonia (ruled 356–323 B.C.E.) brought to the ancient Near East (on Lemche, see http://www.bibleinterp.com/articles/Long_Conservative_Critical_Scholarship.shtml). For them the traditions in the Bible created an identity for Hellenized Jews but had little or no historical content. This school of biblical interpretation is called *biblical minimalism* (see Davies, http://www.bibleinterp.com/articles/Minimalism.htm).

THE ORIGINS OF EARLY ISRAEL

An early and ongoing focus for biblical archaeologists has been the search for evidence that there were Hebrew slaves in Egypt who at some point fled into Syria-Palestine. Their research has greatly enriched the understanding of the Iron I period (Iron IA: 1200–1100 B.C.E.), which represented a recovery in Syria-Palestine from the chaos of the Late Bronze period (1500–1200 B.C.E.).

At the beginning of the Late Bronze period, Syria-Palestine belonged to Egypt's sphere of influence. Egyptian troops stationed throughout the region maintained an order that allowed farmers and herders to tend their fields and flocks; allowed merchants to move their goods safely along caravan routes; and, most important, allowed Egypt to tax the produce of Syria-Palestine. As political

and social conditions in Egypt itself deteriorated, however, law and order in Syria-Palestine vanished. Egyptian troops were recalled, and rogue bands of warriors raided and pillaged the land, making it almost impossible for farmers, herders, and tax collectors to carry on.

ʿApiru

Late Bronze period pharaohs like Amenophis II (1427–1401 B.C.E.) conducted military campaigns in Syria-Palestine. Amenophis waged his first campaign in 1420 B.C.E. and the second in 1418 B.C.E. His annals list 3,600 *ʿapiru* and 15,200 *shasu* among his prisoners of war. Amenophis II reenacted his battles with his *ʿapiru* and *shashu* prisoners. Some were publicly hung on the bow of his barge or the walls of temples; others were beheaded.

THE ANNALS OF AMENOPHIS II
(Memphis Stela: 2933)

Amenophis II returned to the city of Memphis, after he had conquered every foreign state and land.

Through the power of AmunRe, our Godfather, who loves him and who delivers him from his enemies, and who gave him victory, His Majesty brought with him:

127 *Retunu* prisoners from Syria-Palestine
179 covenant partners of the *Retunu*
3,600 *ʿapiru* prisoners
15,200 *shasu* prisoners
36,000 prisoners from Damascus
15,070 prisoners from Nagasu . . . .
household belongings too numerous to count
goats, sheep, and cattle too numerous to count
60 gold and silver chariots
1,032 painted chariots
13,500 weapons

Relief showing the military campaigns of Seti I into Syria and Palestine (1304-1290 B.C.E.),
detail. Great Hypostyle Hall, Outer wall north. Location: Temple of Amun, Karnak, Thebes,
Egypt. Photo Credit: © DeA Picture Library / Art Resource, NY.

The Akkadian words *ʿapiru* or *habiru* (or *hapiru*) do not refer to a
particular people, but they are derogatory terms applied to a particular
social class. The common bond between the *ʿapiru* was social, not ethnic. They were herders and farmers who had abandoned their pastures
and farms and fled the settled areas of Syria-Palestine for remote locations. They were a people out-of-place, who supported their households
by raiding herds, harvests, and caravans. The Egyptians also used the
word to identify any peoples who lived in the deserts or wilderness areas.
Etymologically there is no connection between the words *ʿapiru* and
"Hebrew." The words sound alike, but they are not related in their original languages. Sociologically speaking, the Hebrews in the villages that
appeared during the Iron I period in the hills north of Jerusalem were
ʿapiru. The *ʿapiru*, however, appear in too many different regions of Syria-
Palestine and during too many different time periods for this one word
to have referred only to the Hebrews in the Bible.

Great columns of the Hypostyle Hall in the Temple of Amun at Karnak, built and enlarged by Ramesses I, Sethos I, and Ramesses II. Photo Credit: Erich Lessing / Art Resource, NY.

The word *shasu* is not Semitic; it is an Egyptian word meaning "landless." Egyptians used it to refer to a variety of nomadic or seminomadic people. There is no evidence, however, that the Egyptians referred to the Hebrews as *shasu*. The word also appears in the Annals of Sethos I (1294–1285 B.C.E.), which were inscribed on either side of the north doorway into the Great Hypostyle Hall of the temple at Karnak in Thebes (Egypt). The first three scenes describe Sethos's march across the Sinai north along the coastal highway. His army clears the area of *shasu*, who were raiding caravans from the Delta into the Philistine plain (Hallo and Younger 2003, 2:23).

As the situation worsened, Egyptian governors in Syria-Palestine like Biridiya, the governor of Megiddo, and Labayu, the governor of Shechem, wrote urgent letters to Pharaohs Amenophis III and Akhenaten (1353–1335 B.C.E.) accusing them of treason and pleading with the pharaohs to send troops (Matthews and Benjamin 2006, 146–50).

Sethos I

The material remains recovered by archaeologists from Late Bronze period sites create an epitaph for the once-great

---

ANNALS OF SETHOS I, YEAR ONE
(1306 B.C.E.)
(Karnak Temple, KRI I 6.157.9)

With the help of Re, our Godfather who is the Sun of Egypt and the Moon of All Lands,
    And Montu who cannot be defeated by any enemy,
And Baal the Brave, who does not leave a single survivor on the battlefield,
    Sethos I extended the boundaries of Egypt to every horizon.

Not a single caravan could get past the bandits along the Coast Highway
    Without being attacked from the hills by *shasu* outlaws,
Until His Majesty captured every last one of them,
    Not a single *shasu* escaped.

Bronze Age culture. The trade empires of Mycenae, Hatti, and Egypt collapsed, setting in motion massive migrations of populations, military disasters, and the destabilization of Egypt's empire in Syria-Palestine. Cities were destroyed and not rebuilt. Potters returned to hand-shaping thick-walled pots from clays that were full of impurities, that cracked when fired, and that were poorly mended. As the empires died, the people over whom the empires had ruled for so long were plunged into a life-or-death struggle with an unkind land in a dangerous world.

During the Iron I period longtime peoples of Syria-Palestine tried new ways of living to renew the vitality of this dying land. A major element in this transition to the Iron I period cultures from Bronze Age cultures was the establishment of hundreds of small villages, renewing a landscape that had been sparsely inhabited in the Late Bronze period.

Adaptation was the signature of the cultures of the Iron I period. Cultures with distinct social, economic, and political institutions appeared. Bronze Age culture in Syria-Palestine was homogenous. Iron I cultures, in contrast, were diverse. The peoples of each region of Syria-Palestine developed unique ways to adapt to their life in different lands. There was no dominant political or economic system. The business of feeding and protecting the people and of caring for the land and its people was local.

During the Iron II period (900–586 B.C.E.), the diverse cultures of the Iron I period would become the states of Ammon, Moab, and Edom east of the Jordan River; Israel and Judah west of the Jordan River; and Philistia, Tyre, and Sidon along the coast of the Mediterranean Sea. The social world of each was customized to fit its unique geography and population (Bloch-Smith and Nakhai 1999).

Israel and Neighboring States

The states that were developing in Ammon, Moab, Edom, Israel, and Judah were innovative. Their institutions had not previously appeared in Syria-Palestine. The states that were developing in Philistia, Tyre, and Sidon, however, were conservative, following models developed during the Bronze Age. Although life shifted from the macroeconomics of the Egyptian empire to the microeconomics of Gilead, the Jezreel Valley, or the Shephelah foothills, there is a clear continuity between the culture of the Late Bronze period and the Iron I period. The only clearly identified outsiders were the Sea Peoples who settled the plain along the coast of the Mediterranean Sea.

SEA PEOPLES

The term *Sea Peoples* first appears in the Annals of Merneptah (1224–1214 B.C.E.). The Egyptians and the Hittites identified at least nine groups of Sea Peoples: the Karkisa, Labu, Lukka, Meshwesh, Shardana, Shekelesh, Tjakkar, and Philistines. The Sea Peoples had been uprooted from their homelands by the collapse of the great empires of Egypt, Hatti (Turkey), and Mycenae (Greece). They migrated from Mycenae, Troy (in Turkey), and Crete through Cyprus and then on to Syria-Palestine and Egypt. After a fierce battle on Egypt's Mediterranean coast, Ramesses III (1194–1163 B.C.E.) ceded control of much of the southern coast of Syria-Palestine, including Tel Miqne, to the Sea Peoples. ∎

Two common social institutions shared by all microcultures in Syria-Palestine were villages and states. Villages are a social institution in a decentralized and subsistence culture. States are a social institution in a centralized and surplus culture. Both appear in the Bible (Matthews and Benjamin 1993). The social world of early Israel was a village culture that developed during the Iron I period (1200–1000 B.C.E.). The monarchy was a city culture or state that developed during the Iron II period (900–586 B.C.E.).

The first Hebrew villages appeared in the hills of Judah, west of the Jordan River and north of Jerusalem. Their initial growth took place around 1200 B.C.E. Dates for trends or events in the ancient world are not absolutely accurate, but three prominent wars help calendar the appearance of these Hebrew villages: the Battle of Kadesh (1286 B.C.E.), the wars of Merneptah (1224–1214 B.C.E.), and the battle between Ramesses and the Sea Peoples (1190 B.C.E.).

The Battle of Kadesh took place around 1286 B.C.E. Pharaoh Ramesses II of Egypt and Hattusilis III, the Great King of the Hittites, battled on the Orontes River in Syria. For more than one hundred years, Egypt and Hatti had wrestled for political and economic control of Syria-Palestine. The conflict drained the resources of both states. Following this famous, but inconclusive, battle at Kadesh a treaty was negotiated.

Battle of Kadesh against the Hittites: Chariots, horses, dead and dying on the battlefield. Relief from the Ramesseum. Ramesses II claimed a decisive victory, as did the Hittites. Egyptian, 1290–1224 B.C.E. Location: Ramesseum (Mortuary Temple of Ramesses II), Thebes, Egypt. Photo Credit: Erich Lessing / Art Resource, NY.

Both Egyptian and Hittite versions of the treaty have been recovered. Ramesses II had the treaty carved in hieroglyphics on the walls of no fewer than five temples (Hornung and Bryan 2002, 20). One was on the walls of the Temple of Amon in Karnak and another on the walls of the Ramesseum, his funeral chapel in the Valley of the Pharaohs. The Hittite version is written on clay tablets in Akkadian cuneiform, which was the diplomatic language of the ancient Near East. Archaeologists recovered these tablets from the archives of Hattusas, the Hittite capital.

The Treaty of Ramesses II and Hattusilis III was a remarkable political and military accomplishment (Matthews and Benjamin 2006, 91–96). It was motivated both by the need of Egypt and Hatti for economic recovery and by the increasing military threat of the Sea Peoples migrating into the eastern Mediterranean. The treaty ended the war and liberated the people of Syria-Palestine from both Egyptian and Hittite domination. Peace ensued for virtually the next fifty years.

The withdrawal of the Egyptians and the Hittites from Syria-Palestine was not an unqualified blessing for its indigenous peoples. Populations dropped dramatically. Cities and villages were destroyed, trade caravans vanished, and 60 percent of the people of Syria-Palestine died from starvation as a result of crop failures. Famine led inevitably to the outbreak of wars and endemic diseases aggravated by shifting populations. These disasters were not isolated and sporadic but ongoing. Some villagers in Syria-Palestine took advantage of their freedom and tried to protect their households against an uncertain future by migrating into the hills, where they reestablished abandoned villages or founded new ones of their own. Among these refugees were the Hebrews, the ancestors of biblical Israel.

Merneptah (1224–1214 B.C.E.) celebrated his wars on a stela originally inscribed by Amenhotep III (1398–1361 B.C.E.). In 1896, excavators recovered this granite column, which is more than seven feet high and three feet wide, from Merneptah's funeral chapel in the Valley of the Pharaohs. It is now in the Egyptian Museum in Cairo. The stela contains the only mention of Israel yet discovered from the Egypt of this period. As a result, it has been used to argue that the Israel which Merneptah encounters in Syria-Palestine before 1200 B.C.E. was founded by the Hebrews who must have fled Egypt.

The battle with the Sea Peoples (1190 B.C.E.) is celebrated on the outside walls of Medinet Habu, the funeral chapel of Ramesses III (1194–1163 B.C.E.) in the Valley of the Pharaohs. Following their invasion of Egypt, some of the Sea Peoples settled along the coast of Syria-Palestine to become the Philistines of the Bible.

THE SETTLEMENT OF SYRIA-PALESTINE

Based on archaeological dates for the Battle of Kadesh (1286 B.C.E.), the wars of Merneptah (1224–1214 B.C.E.), and the battle with the Sea Peoples (1190 B.C.E.), the appearance of the Hebrews in Syria-Palestine is now dated to 1200 B.C.E. after the end of the Late Bronze period and before peoples such as

William Flinders Petrie excavated this stela of Pharaoh Merneptah in 1896. Merneptah's claim to have defeated Israel in the fifth year of his reign (1207 B.C.E.) is the earliest mention of Israel outside the Bible: "I slaughtered the people of Israel and burned their grain." Photo © The Art Archive/Egyptian Museum, Cairo/Dagli Orti.

the Philistines and the Hebrews began to affect seriously the foreign policies of Egypt in Syria-Palestine.

INAUGURATION OF JOSHUA
(Josh 1:1-9)

[1]After the death of Moses, the servant of Yahweh, Yahweh spoke to Joshua son of Nun, who had helped Moses. [2]"My servant Moses is dead. Now cross the Jordan River with the people into the land. . . . [3]You will walk the land I promised to Moses. [4]The land of the Hittites will be your land—east to the Mediterranean Sea, south to the Sinai Desert, north to the Lebanon Mountains and the Euphrates River. [5]No one shall be able to stand against you all the days of your life. I was with Moses. I will be with you. I will not fail you or forsake you. [6]Be strong and courageous; for you shall put this people in possession of the land that I swore to their ancestors to give them. . . ."

The Conquest Theory

The biblical Hebrews were a microculture that settled hundreds of new villages in the hills along the west side of the Jordan River north of Jerusalem. A long-standing tradition of interpreting the books of Joshua–Judges describes the Hebrews as foreign warriors who invaded Syria-Palestine from the west, the so-called conquest. Some archaeologists and historians such as Albright, Wright, and Bright believed that the archaeology of Syria-Palestine supported the understanding of the appearance of the Hebrews in Syria-Palestine as a conquest.

The Settlement Theory

In contrast to the theory of Albright, Albrecht Alt (1883–1956) and Martin Noth (1902–1960) proposed that the Hebrews peacefully emigrated west from the Jordan River into unsettled areas of Syria-Palestine. There were few battles. Violence between these Hebrews and other peoples occurred only when the original Hebrew villages begin to expand.

Martin Noth was born in Germany; he considered himself to be a historian of ancient Israel. He argued that early Israel was an amphictyony—a league of twelve tribes whose lands surrounded a central sanctuary such as Shechem or Hebron. One tribe protected and provided

Albrecht Alt

for the sanctuary for one month each year. In *A History of Pentateuchal Traditions* (1948), Noth argued that the traditions of ancient Israel preserved in the first six books of the Bible—a hexateuch—were organized around five basic themes: *Guidance out of Egypt, Guidance into the Arable Land, Promise to the Patriarchs, Guidance in the Wilderness*, and *Revelation at Sinai*.

Martin Noth

The Social Revolution Theory

A third explanation of the appearance of the Hebrews in Syria-Palestine was presented by George Mendenhall and Norman K. Gottwald. Both described the appearance of the Hebrews in Syria-Palestine as a social revolution. Once Egypt's military support for the rulers of the states in Syria-Palestine was withdrawn, villagers stopped farming and herding for them. They revolted against the surplus state culture that had enslaved them during the Bronze Age. After the cities along the coast that governed their villages were destroyed, they moved east toward the Jordan River and established a decentralized or *retribalized* subsistence culture (Gottwald 1979).

The Evidence of Archaeology

The theories about the appearance of Israel in Syria-Palestine as a conquest, immigration, or revolt do not ignore archaeology, but none of these explanations uses archaeology as a central argument. These were theories drawn from biblical studies, not from archaeological fieldwork. As the material remains from excavations in Syria-Palestine were more closely studied during the last half of the twentieth century, however, it became more and more clear that the Bible is the only evidence for an invasion or conquest of Syria-Palestine by the Hebrews from the east during the Iron I period. Archaeology shows that herders migrated into Syria-Palestine from the Sinai Desert and elsewhere during both the Bronze Age and the Iron Age. Archaeology does not show that the villages in the hills of Judah were founded by foreigners or warriors. No material remains identify the Hebrews as warriors who invaded Syria-Palestine or as revolutionaries who overthrew its great cities. At least twice during the Iron I period, wars destroyed many cities and villages in Syria-Palestine, yet there is nothing in the archaeological record linking the Hebrews to these destructions. These native villagers in Syria-Palestine were farmers and herders; their economy was agricultural, not military. They left

Archaeologists have identified in the hills more than three hundred village sites that date from the Iron I period. Ninety percent were new foundations. For example, in one sample of 136 villages, 97 did not exist before 1200 B.C.E. Similar villages appear east of the Jordan, which the Bible calls the *Gilead*. The villages were small and scattered. Most were only one-acre parcels of land. There were some fifty to three hundred inhabitants per village. For example, Ai was a modest, two-and-three-quarter-acre village founded about 1220 B.C.E. on the site of a twenty-seven-and-a-half-acre city destroyed at the end of the Early Bronze period (3400-2000 B.C.E.). The nearest village was Khirbet Raddana, four miles west. ■

almost no weapons and built few fortifications or monumental buildings. Giloh, south of Jerusalem, is a major exception. The writing, language, and material culture of these villagers link them to cultures found throughout Syria-Palestine (Faust 2006).

Further, archaeology suggests that the Hebrews who founded the villages in the hills west of the Jordan River Valley were from cities along the coast, not nomads from the desert. The villages, however, were not founded by inhabitants of the cities of the plains along the coast of the Mediterranean Sea and in the foothills inland. These settlements had been destroyed before the villages began to appear. Consequently, these villagers did not wage war in the hills to the east; they survived the wars on the plains and foothills to the west. What these villagers had in common was that they were social survivors who fled the famine, plague, and war that brought the Bronze Age to an end. They were peoples who for environmental or economic reasons emigrated from the cities of Syria-Palestine and settled into a politically less complex culture in the hills. They left a centralized, surplus state culture and created a decentralized, subsistence village culture called *Israel* (Chaney 1983, 39–94). Politically they were *Israelites;* culturally they were *Hebrews*. They were adaptable; they were survivors; and they were masters at crafting the words that preserve their amazing worldview.

Archaeology shows that the Hebrews were remarkably successful at maximizing their labor and spreading their risks. Between 1000 and 800 B.C.E., their population expanded to eighty thousand, and more than one hundred new villages were founded in the hills of Samaria, Galilee to the north, and the Beersheba basin to the south. Every household shared in the labor-intensive work of terracing, planting, and processing grain and fruit. More and more agriculturally marginal land was turned into productive farms and vineyards. What was not consumed was stored in huge buildings like those at Raddana, Shiloh, and Tel Masos as a check against famine.

AMARNA LETTER 244:1–30
(Matthews and Benjamin 2006, 147–48)

To: Pharaoh, ruler of the heavens and earth
From: Biridiya, governor of Megiddo

I am your slave, and I renew my covenant with you as my pharaoh by bowing before you seven times seven times.

> Pharaoh should know that, since he recalled his archers to Egypt, Labayu, the governor of Shechem, has not stopped raiding the land of Megiddo. The people of Megiddo cannot leave the city to shear your sheep for fear of Labayu's soldiers.
>
> Because you have not replaced the archers, Labayu is now strong enough to attack the city of Megiddo itself. If Pharaoh does not reinforce the city, Labayu will capture it.
>
> The people of Megiddo are already suffering from hunger and disease. I beg Pharaoh to send 150 soldiers to protect Megiddo from Labayu or he will certainly capture the city.

The Hebrews cleared new areas of *maquis* brush and cultivated the land, using wooden or iron blades. They farmed a combination of wheat and barley, depending on the quality of the soil, temperature, and rainfall. They tended fig and olive trees and skillfully managed grapevines on terraced hillside plots.

The place where the early Israelites chose to live had a significant influence on the structure of their society. They fled from the coast with its trade routes, commercial centers, and farms, where no one was safe, and they founded new villages in the hills just north of Jerusalem. Here the land was safe, but it was barren and rugged and demanding, all of which would affect the society that developed and the roles that men and women would play in it. In the hills there would be no surplus to fuel the economy.

Maquis brush is a stand of various evergreen shrubs and trees from three to nine feet tall. These stands include carob (*Ceratonia siliqua*), pistachio (*Pistacia lentiscus*), buckthorn (*Rhamnus alaternus*), hawthorn (*Crataegus*), bay laurel (*Laurus nobilis*), myrtle (*Myrtus communis*), broom (*Spartium junceum*), and Sandarac (*Teraclinis articulata*). ■

CONCLUSION

During the Late Bronze period (1500–1200 B.C.E.) people in the panhandle of Syria-Palestine abandoned large cities (more than fifty acres) inland in the hills and migrated to unfortified smaller cities (less than twelve acres) dominated by Egypt along the coast. Population declined. The rich were very rich, and the poor were very poor. Sanctuary architecture was diverse. International trade increased. An alphabet replaced picture-writing. *Apiru* mercenaries terrorized governors loyal to Pharaoh Akhenaten (1353–1335 B.C.E.), and Pharaoh Merneptah conquered Ashkelon, Gezer, Yanoam, and Israel.

The stories of the death of the firstborn of Egypt (Exod 1:7—13:16) and the creation of the firstborn of Israel (Exod 13:17—Num 27:11) are

109

set in the Late Bronze period, although they appear in the Bible as they were told in the Iron II period (900–586 B.C.E.), when Israel built a fort near the largest and most plentiful spring in the Sinai at Kadesh Barnea, which is prominent in the stories.

The surplus economies of the Bronze Age were built by monarchs, taxes, soldiers, cities, and slaves. Monarchs provided a centralized government for the great cities. Soldiers controlled its population and expanded its borders. Slaves produced goods for trade. It was an efficient but brutal system. Taxation, slavery, and war painfully affected the lives of all but a minority of the people who lived in these states. When great wars of commerce and conquest brought down the international trade empires of Mycenae, Hatti, and Egypt about 1200 B.C.E., survivors in Syria-Palestine had neither the resources nor the desire to rebuild the social system that had enslaved them. Therefore, the economy of early Israel was not a surplus or slave economy but a subsistence economy. There would be no monarchs, no soldiers, no slaves, no taxes, no cities, and no standing army. It was a demanding and idealistic society. Nonetheless, it lasted almost two hundred years.

WHAT YOU HAVE LEARNED

- For William Foxwell Albright, the goal of biblical archaeology was to demonstrate that the traditions in the Bible were historically reliable.
- The biblical archaeology movement sought to provide concrete evidence for the idea of the biblical theology movement that Christianity was rooted in unique historical events, not in the recurring cycles of nature.
- Many biblical archaeologists today find the origins of the people of Israel in refugees who tried to protect their households against an uncertain future in the cities along the coastal highway in Syria-Palestine by migrating into the hills, where they reestablished abandoned villages or founded new ones of their own.
- The early Hebrews were displaced households whose common bond was not ethnic but social.
- The Annals of Merneptah describe this pharoah's conquest of the people of Israel, which helps archaeologists date and locate the first Hebrew villages in Syria-Palestine.
- The economy of the early Hebrew villages was agricultural, not military. The Hebrews left almost no weapons, and they built few fortifications or monumental buildings.

STUDY QUESTIONS

1. How does the biblical archaeology movement differ from the present approach of archaeologists to Syria-Palestine?
2. What are the three principal theories about how the Hebrews came to settle in Syria-Palestine?
3. What is the importance of the Battle of Kadesh for dating the early history of Israel?
4. What is the Merneptah Stela?
5. Does archaeology prove any of the three theories about the settlement of Syria-Palestine?

PREVIEW: THE WHEELER-KENYON METHOD

- The Development of Archaeological Method
  - William Matthew Flinders Petrie
  - George A. Reisner
  - William F. Badè
  - Mortimer Wheeler
  - Kathleen M. Kenyon
- Excavating a Site
  - The Proposal
  - The Staff
  - Preparing the Site
  - Surveying the Site
  - Beginning to Excavate
  - Record Keeping
  - Pottery Washing and Reading
  - Restoration and Preservation

Chapter 8 describes the goal of the Wheeler-Kenyon method, and the differences between the sondage, horizontal, and Wheeler-Kenyon methods of excavating a site, and why accurate record keeping is such an essential part of the Wheeler-Kenyon method. It also explains the important elements contained in an excavation proposal, how pottery is collected and analyzed during the excavation, and defines terms such as theodolite, probe trench, square, locus, balk, guffa, sifter, and dump.

8

The Wheeler-Kenyon Method

Regardless of what school of archaeology is used to interpret artifacts, all archaeologists follow some variation of the Wheeler-Kenyon method to excavate a site. The method is named for British archaeologists Mortimer Wheeler (1890–1976) and Kathleen Kenyon. Wheeler developed the method during 1930–1935 while excavating the Roman village of Verulamium (England). Kenyon was a member of Wheeler's team at Verulamium. She later refined his method and used it during her excavations at Jericho (1952–1958). Although Wheeler and Kenyon codified the various parts of the system into a coherent process, the method was the end result of the work of a number of archaeologists, including William Matthew Flinders Petrie, Augustus H. Pitt Rivers, William F. Badè, and George A. Reisner.

Portrait of Amenhotep III, from Amarna. http:// upload.wikimedia.org/ wikipedia/commons/2/2b/ PortraitStudyOf AmenhotepIII-Thutmose Workshop_Egyptian MuseumBerlin.png

THE DEVELOPMENT OF THE WHEELER-KENYON METHOD

William Matthew Flinders Petrie (1853–1942)

Petrie made several important contributions to the Wheeler-Kenyon method. Most of Petrie's predecessors were simply interested in salvaging museum-quality antiquities. He was much more interested in ordinary objects that helped reconstruct the history of a site. He considered small objects, like pottery, to be more useful than museum objects in interpreting a site. Excavations take artifacts out of context. Petrie realized that without a context artifacts are meaningless. Therefore, he stressed the importance of carefully recording the context from which artifacts were removed. Curiously, however, he was unfortunately selective in his own excavations. He did not record all the artifacts, but only those he identified as important to his pottery chronology (Davis 2004, 29). The first archaeologist to meticulously record his excavations was Augustus H. Pitt Rivers (1827–1900) (Wheeler 1954, 15–28).

> *Calendars based on political and economic events in written artifacts were replaced by* **ceramic calendars** *built around the raw material, the shape and the decoration used in pottery. Repeated careful excavations developed sequences for the evolution of pottery types from its first appearance in the Neolithic period (6000–3800 B.C.E.) to the pottery used in Syria-Palestine during the Crusades (1096–1291). Not only does pottery provide a chronology for a particular site, but the chronologies from more than one site can be used to recreate the chronology of an entire region.*

Using different styles of pottery, Petrie developed a ceramic calendar that allowed him to date the various levels of occupation at a site using differences in the clay used for pottery and in the shapes, the decoration, and the firing of the pieces. This pioneering work of Flinders Petrie in understanding the ceramic typology was perfected and put by use throughout Syria-Palestine by Louis-Hugues Vincent, William F. Albright, and Nelson Glueck.

As a surveyor, Petrie also began drawing top plans and taking topographical information to include in his excavation reports. He was also one of the first archaeologists to make extensive use of photography to preserve the context of the artifacts from a site. Petrie was also aware that tells were architectural, not geological features. They were created by successive eroded layers, or strata, of settlement.

Stratigraphy is one of the major interpretive principles of field archaeology, borrowed from geology. It is assumed that material remains left by human beings create levels like the sediment left in the geological record—one on top of the other. Each layer of material remains is called a "level" (Latin: *stratum* [singular] or *strata* [plural]) and is identified by a Roman numeral. Ground level, for example, is "Stratum I." Upper levels must have accumulated later than lower levels. The material from one level, however, can be mixed with another by earthquakes, burrowing animals, or humans burying garbage or recycling stones. (Kenyon and Moorey 1987, 185). ■

> *A* **tell** *(Hebrew: tel; Arabic: tell, tall) is an artificial hill or mound formed by the eroded debris from an ancient settlement.*

George A. Reisner (1867–1942)

George A. Reisner was the first to study a tell as a record of human occupation (Davis 2004, 42–44) when he excavated at Sebaste (1908–1910). The tell, for Reisner, was not just a series of artifacts; it was a record of human settlement. Only about 10 percent of a site is architecture; 90 percent is debris. By analyzing not only the architecture on the site but also the debris, Reisner reconstructed the process that formed the tell.

Reisner identified different types of debris. Geological debris is deposited by natural events such as wind and water. Building debris is left by workers, like the chips of stone masons. Garbage debris is the remains of livestock or meals. Unfortunately, Reisner's insights were overlooked and had to be rediscovered by Wheeler (Davis 2004, 44).

William F. Badè (1871–1936)

William F. Badè directed excavations at Mizpah of Benjamin (Hebrew: *Tell en-Nasbeh*) using what was then called the Reisner-Fisher method.

(Clarence H. Fisher was an accomplished archaeologist who focused on the architecture of a site. Albright studied with him in Jerusalem.) Badè cleared about two-thirds of a site and then divided a tell into squares thirty feet on a side. He excavated the squares in strips, which were then back-filled. Badè kept meticulous records, including plans, photographs, and descriptions of about twenty-three thousand artifacts. All of his drawings were to scale. Badè's fieldwork ranks above the fieldwork of Elihu Grant during the same period at Beth-Shemesh and that of Gerald M. FitzGerald at Beth-Shean.

Aaron Brody is now the director of the the Badè Project, a collaborative effort of students and faculty at the Graduate Theological Union and University of California at Berkeley to make available in digital format the holdings of the Badè Museum for study and teaching (http://bade.psr.edu). ■

Mortimer Wheeler (1890–1976)

Wheeler was born in Glasgow (Scotland) and became lecturer in archaeology at the University College of Cardiff (Wales) and then professor of Roman Archeology at the University of London (1948–1955), where he had studied. His fieldwork focused on both South Asia (India, Pakistan) and Great Britain at Verulamium, a city built by the Romans, and Maiden Castle (UK), the largest Iron Age hilltop fortress in Europe.

Wheeler's books—*Archaeology from the Earth* (1954), *Early India and Pakistan* (1959), *Civilizations of the Indus Valley and Beyond* (1966), *Still Digging* (1955), and *Alms for Oblivion: An Antiquarian's Scrapbook* (1966)—had a wide public audience. He was also a charismatic television personality who raised public awareness about all that can be learned about human development from archaeology and anthropology.

Mortimer Wheeler

Kathleen M. Kenyon (1906–1978)

Kenyon was the daughter of Frederick Kenyon, a distinguished biblical scholar and later director of the British Museum (Cohen and Joukowsky 2004). She did her undergraduate degree in history at Oxford.

Kenyon's first experience in the field was as photographer on the excavation of Gertrude Caton-Thompson at the Great Zimbabwe (1929). On her return to England, she joined Mortimer and Tessa Wheeler on their excavation at Verulamium in the summers from 1930 to 1935. In the same period, Kenyon worked with John and Grace Crowfoot at Samaria (1931–1934). There she cut a trench across the summit of the tell and down the northern and southern slopes using the techniques of the day. She exposed settlement layers in a sequence from Iron II to the Roman period. In addition to providing crucial dating material for the Iron Age in Syria-Palestine, she obtained key stratified data for the study of Roman terra sigillata pottery (Kenyon 1957).

Kathleen M. Kenyon

Kenyon was a member of the Council of the British School of Archaeology in Jerusalem, where she taught from 1948 to 1962. In 1962 she became president of St. Hugh's College, Oxford. She was also the first woman to become president of the Oxford University Archaeological Society. In January 1951, she traveled to Jordan and undertook excavations at Jericho (1952–1958) on behalf of the school. Her groundbreaking discoveries there revolutionized our understanding of Neolithic cultures in Syria-Palestine.

From 1961 to 1967 Kenyon excavated in Jerusalem. Her field school helped to train a generation of archaeologists, who went on to teach in Britain, Australia, Canada, the United States, Denmark, and elsewhere. Among those whom Kenyon mentored was Peter Roger Stuart Moorey. He was director of the Ashmolean Museum of Art and Archaeology at Oxford University for nineteen years (http://www.ashmolean.org). The Ashmolean Musem preserves an outstanding research collection of Near Eastern artifacts. Moorey wrote extensively on the archaeology of Iran, Iraq, Syria-Palestine, Egypt, and Turkey. *Ancient Mesopotamian Materials and Industries: The Archaeological Evidence* (1994) was among his significant publications.

Moorey collaborated with Kenyon on the excavations of the British School of Archaeology in Jerusalem—now the Kenyon Institute in the Council for British Research in the Levant (http://www.cbrl.org .uk/). She influenced his interest in archaeology and the Bible. The results of their collaboration enriched Moorey's publications for the general public: *Archaeology, Artefacts and the Bible* (1969) and his *Century of Biblical Archaeology* (1991). He edited a commemorative volume with Peter Parr for her: *Archaeology in the Levant: Essays for Kathleeen Kenyon* (1978), and published a revised edition of her book: *The Bible and Recent Archaeology* (1987). Kenyon encouraged Moorey to found the journal *Levant*, which he edited for eighteen years.

Terra sigillata *is bright red, polished pottery impressed with designs (Latin:* sigillata*) used throughout the Roman Empire from 100 B.C.E. until 300 C.E. The body of the ware was cast in a mold. Relief designs taken from a wide repertory of patterns were then applied to the ware. The style changes in these patterns and the potters' marks stamped on the vessels make terra sigillata pieces an important tool for dating other artifacts found with them. The quality of the pottery was high, considering that it was mass-produced.*

EXCAVATING A SITE

Archaeologists destroy the sites they excavate; they cannot go back to a previously excavated site and see exactly what the original excavators saw. Record keeping should provide all the information researchers who were not present at the original excavations would need to reconstruct the site in three dimensions. Therefore, the Wheeler-Kenyon method establishes guidelines for both digging and recording. Procedures for digging include identifying the site, choosing squares to excavate, and probing those squares. Records of an excavation include a survey of the site, square supervisors' journals, locus sheets, balk drawings, and photographs.

The Proposal

To begin the process of excavating, dig directors must select a site and submit a proposal to the authority responsible for the site. Requirements for proposals vary, but all require a clear statement of purpose. For example, a consortium of institutions under the direction of Steven M. Ortiz and Sam Wolff resumed work at Tel Gezer in 2006 (http://www.gezerproject.org/). The project is reinvestigating the Iron Age levels of occupation (strata V–XIII). Most departments of antiquities also require archaeologists to outline not only the schedule for their excavations but also the schedule for their publications. When archaeologists fail to publish their annual and final reports on a site, scholarly assessment of the work is crippled and popular appreciation of the site is manipulated by amateur enthusiasts (Cline 2007, ix–xv). The first excavations at Qumran (1951–1958), for example, were directed by Roland de Vaux. Unfortunately, the final report of de Vaux's excavations has yet to be published, and many artifacts and records from Qumran now at the Ecole Biblique in Jerusalem are still unavailable to scholars (Atkinson 2008). The painstaking work of completing the final report on de Vaux's excavations undertaken by Robert Donceel and Pauline Donceel-Voute may be more labor intensive than the original

excavations themselves (Donceel and Donceel-Voute 1994).

Proposals also must establish a formula for the preservation and display of both the artifacts and the site. International antiquities law reflected in the UNESCO Convention on Cultural Property (1970), the University of Pennsylvania Museum *Philadelphia Declaration* (1970), and the International Council of Museums Code of Professional Ethics (1989) clearly assign ownership of all artifacts to the government of the country where they are recovered. Nonetheless, proposals can negotiate long-term loans or traveling exhibitions of artifacts to museums and universities sponsoring the excavations.

The Staff

Some, but not all, departments of antiquities require that excavations proposed by foreign archaeologists and institutions include an archaeologist from their own country on staff in a senior position. In Israel this requirement is mandatory if the sponsoring institution does not have adequate laboratory and museum facilities on its campus to properly evaluate and preserve artifacts. Authorities also want to guarantee that the terms of the proposal or license will be fulfilled and that the cultural heritage of their country will be professionally preserved.

Dig directors are responsible for assembling a team for the excavation. Some team members are professional; some are not. Amateur team members include volunteers and hired workers. Historically, workers have been hired from communities near the excavation site. Today most excavations depend on student volunteers from the sponsoring universities, and volunteers from the general public for whom archaeology is a personal passion. Even excavations with volunteers from abroad, however, try to hire local workers in order to educate communities around the site on the importance of their cultural heritage. Students pay for their own transportation to the site. They also pay tuition to their universities in order to receive academic credit for their work. The work day for students is divided between classroom or travel study and the excavation.

The makeup of the professional staff for an excavation depends on the goals stated in the proposal. All teams will have professionals such as a ceramicist, a specialist in reading pottery recovered from the site. Some excavations, for example, like sites settled after the Persian period (539–323 B.C.E.) when coins came into use, will have a numismatist, a specialist in reading coins. The professional team excavating the bakeries in the workers' village on the Giza plain beside the pyramids included an archaeobotanist to study seeds found at the site.

Preparing the Site

The first step at the site itself is to clear off the overgrowth. The initial overgrowth at a site, when the excavation begins, and the seasonal overgrowth, when an excavation resumes, can prevent archaeologists from getting a clear picture of the site as a whole. Workers generally use only hand tools for the project. Power tools and tractors can inadvertently damage the surface of the tell or the artifacts themselves.

Once the site is cleared, the dig director needs to select a place to dump the soil removed from the squares. The dump should be easily accessible from the squares, and it should be at a location that will not itself need to be excavated at some later time. At some sites workers install a narrow gauge railroad and use mine carts to move the soil from the squares to the dump. Workers at most sites use wheelbarrows to move the soil.

Small finds such as seals, beads, pins, and whorls can often be overlooked during normal digging. Even though they are small, however, they still contribute to the overall understanding of a site. Therefore, the dig director also needs to find a site for sifting. The dig director establishes a formula for how many buckets of soil from each square will be sifted for small artifacts. The bucket of soil is dumped into a frame with a fine mesh screen bottom, and workers shake the frame back and forth. The soil drops through the screen as dust, leaving the small finds behind. As with the dump site, it is important to locate the sift site someplace that will not need to be excavated later.

THE SONDAGE METHOD

Prior to the work of Petrie, Wheeler, and Kenyon some archaeologists used the sondage method. They dug long, deep trenches through their tells. Petrie realized that these vertical trenches prevented archaeologists from accurately drawing top plans of the strata cut by the trenches. Other archaeologists excavated horizontally across the entire surface of a site. Layers of occupation were simply peeled off an excavation site. While horizontal excavations gave maximum exposure to a site, they destroyed the chronology of the site's development. The Wheeler-Kenyon method vertically excavates squares—most only fifteen feet on a side (Mazar 1990, 1–34; Laughlin 2000, 17–32). ■

Surveying the Site

After the site is clear, a surveyor lays a grid over the site using a theodolite. The theodolite is a small mounted telescope that rotates both horizontally and vertically. It is used to measure angles in surveying, meteorology, and navigation. Site surveyors create a geological top plan of the entire site, which will serve as a tool to identify the squares to be opened and to label the artifacts removed from each square. The grid also serves to locate the site within larger geological maps of the region and to position it correctly on Global Positioning Systems (GPS).

Significant artifacts and natural features of the tell can be accurately positioned also by using an infrared beam. The beam is focused on the artifact, and then its coordinates are read into the GPS, fixing its location. This database can subsequently be used to reconstruct accurate virtual models of the site and of artifacts once they have been removed.

Dig directors use the surveyor's grid to assign supervisors and their teams to excavate certain squares. The choices are determined by the goals of the excavation set down in the proposal. Usually the choices are a mix of squares from different areas of the site, which would be connected with different aspects of daily life. Historically archaeologists were interested primarily in large, public monumental architecture—the gates, the walls, the palaces, and the sanctuaries at a site. Today most directors include squares that will represent the lives of ordinary people as well.

Beginning to Excavate

Workers then open a probe trench to test if, in fact, there are remains in the square relevant to the goals of the excavation. A probe trench is typically three feet wide and fifteen feet long. For example, large public buildings are often found on the acropolis—the highest elevation on a site. Gates reflect not only the defensive capabilities of a city but generally also its judicial institutions. Sanctuaries are connected with the economic system. Once a square has been probed the square supervisor directs workers to carefully remove the top layer of soil from stratum I.

Workers use only simple hand tools to dig out a square. They use a traditional bucket made from an automobile tire (Arabic: *guffa*) or a contemporary plastic bucket to lift the soil out of the square and measure it. The dig director will stipulate that every fifth or eighth bucket of soil will be sifted or washed in a flotation tank.

Flotation is a method of separating carbonized plant remains, shells, small bones, and insect remains from soil. A bucket of excavated soil is dumped into a tank of water and stirred. The lighter seeds, shells, and bones float to the surface of the water and are collected with a sieve. The heavier soil sinks to the bottom of the tank (Darvill 2002, 148).

Each side of a square is five meters or some fifteen feet long. Each square is separated from the other by a balk of unexcavated soil that is one meter or some three feet wide. These balks preserve the chronology of a site. Archaeologists use balks to record the vertical relationship of one stratum or time period to another and the relationship of any buildings or architecture to each time period. This significantly improves the ability of the excavators to date artifacts (Callaway 1979). Balks also allow archaeologists to compare the location of artifacts in one square to the location of artifacts in another.

Record Keeping

Record keeping begins with the journal kept by the square supervisor. As workers dig, bucket, and brush their way through a settlement layer, the supervisor records not only the findings but also the first impressions of the team about what the findings reveal about life at the site. Another responsibility of the square supervisor is completing locus sheets. As each artifact is uncovered, the supervisor assigns it a number and then completes a detailed questionnaire about it. At some excavations these sheets are filled in by hand, other sites use computers.

THE LAHAV RESEARCH PROJECT

Since 1983 the Cobb Institute at Mississippi State University has been the major sponsor of the Lahav Research Project and its ongoing program of archaeological investigations at Tell Halif (Israel). The Lahav Project was organized in 1975, and by 1989 it had completed two major phases of excavation involving eight seasons of field research. Fifteen strata of occupation have been identified at the site of the tell, including major settlements from the Early Bronze period (3400–2000 B.C.E.) and from the Israelite Iron II period (900–586 B.C.E.). Significant finds also have been recovered from the Late Bronze period (1500–1200 B.C.E.), when the site was largely under Egyptian influence, and from the Late Roman/Byzantine periods (100 to 600) when the region was the scene of Jewish and Christian resettlement after the Roman destruction of Jerusalem. During the 1999 season of the Lahav Research Project at Tell Halif, Joe D. Seger, the dig director, tested newly applied digital methods of field recording and reporting, with the intention of better meeting the needs of archaeologists working in the world of the Bible.

When workers reach bedrock, square supervisors also draw the three-foot-wide balks framing the square. These balk drawings are like a slice of cake. Each layer of settlement is clearly indicated as are the artifacts connected with the stratum. In addition to artifacts that are still intact such as walls, wells, floors, pits, and silos, there are also destruction layers of ash or mud, and backfill used to level previous destruction before rebuilding. Robber trenches also appear in balk drawings. These silhouettes of stones in the soil were created when villagers recycled stones from old buildings or walls to construct new buildings or walls.

JOE D. SEGER, MISSISSIPPI STATE UNIVERSITY
Lahav Research Project

The 1999 field season of the Lahav Research Project at Tell Halif [LRP] was designed to test newly applied digital methods of field recording and reporting, with the intention of better meeting the needs of Middle Eastern archaeology at the end of the 1990s.

The quantity of artifacts recovered even by a small team often overwhelms traditional means of dissemination and sets a demand for new, efficient ways of reporting in visual, graphic form.

These were the questions which faced the LRP at the end of the 1993 season: how can we manage the data more efficiently while in the field, and how can we disseminate that data quickly and efficiently to others in the discipline?

We began the season, accordingly, with several notebook computers in the field, each linked to a server (also a notebook), a fact which permits both the control of the input of data and allows any member of the staff to track progress in laboratory treatment, photography, disposition, etc. Because the server assigns sequential numbers as requests from the field are made to register an object find, a material culture sample, or a new locus, the field and laboratory staff are guaranteed that accidents of duplicate numberings will not occur. Simultaneously, progress in the field and in the lab can be tracked from any of the several laptops on such matters as the drawing or photography of an object, as well as the formal description assigned by specialists. Every entry becomes part of the common database immediately and is available by search for a specific item or by browsing

the database entries. Significantly, reports on aspects of the excavation, recording, or reporting can, therefore, be generated quickly. And, we believe, the fact that a supervisor in the field—or an artist in the lab—can simply select descriptive terms from drop-down windows saves time and brings greater accuracy to the recording procedures.

Another important feature of the computerized database is that it allows the introduction of 3D analysis and simulation into a dig while it is still in progress. By using the data entered into the database by field personnel, we are able to construct a computerized view of the progress and finds in the field. Each area, locus, and basket is represented as a volumetric area. Each object, when found in-situ, is also recorded in three-dimensional coordinates and shown in the 3D browser window. The significant insights rewarded through use of the 3D display are magnified as the dig season progresses. Early, there is not enough data to create any kind of visual anomalies, but we have been using it as a visual error checking device for data entry and recording errors. Later, as more data are introduced to the system, visual clues are created by the grouping of objects and architecture. The 3D browser is still in its infancy and we are currently only tracking object finds found in-situ although we are planning to add architectural analysis and reconstruction to the program very soon. We will offer a complete description of our processes and methods as soon as possible.

Reporting responsibilities mark the other main problem this 1999 experimental season addresses. We have shown in previous work that modern digital communication devices permit archaeologists to report findings far more completely than ever before; in fact, in displaying the

Stone pillars from a storehouse at Hazor, Israel. Location: Hazor, Israel. Photo Credit: Erich Lessing / Art Resource, NY.

Persian and Iron Age figurines discovered in the 1992 and 1993 seasons on the DigMaster website, we made available to web browsers more than 5,000 color photographs and drawings and 84 QuicktimeVR object movies of the ceramic and stone figurines, something impossible except through digital and electronic media. This DigMaster web publication project, however, occurred well after the seasons had ended. In the 1999 LRP field season, the attempt is to prepare basic excavation data and graphic representations of all artifacts, architecture, and field photographs while yet in the field, all of which will be made available, as far as possible, on a daily basis on this web page.

The benefits of this experiment in dissemination of LRP excavation data are several. First, if successful, we will have demonstrated the viability of rapid (nearly immediate) reporting. Colleagues and staff members not on location will see high resolution images of the excavation as it progresses and of the artifacts recovered in the excavation; we believe that the images will be sufficiently detailed to permit close study on monitor. Second, the numbers of photographs that can be contained and disseminated in digital format will have demonstrated the viability of *total publication*, something not economically permitted in traditional publication (source: http://www.cobb.msstate.edu/dig/LRP-1999-01/overview.html).

After each stratum has been cleared, and the journal entries and locus sheets completed, then the site is carefully brushed and photographed. To get a good top plan photograph of a square, photographers have to be creative. Sometime they use scaffolding to construct towers. Sometimes they float their cameras above the square using a balloon. Special fish-eye lenses also allow photographers to capture the entire scope of the square and its surroundings.

Pottery Washing and Reading

At the end of each day in the field, workers wash and dry pottery, which the ceramicist will read. Pottery from each locus is carefully collected in buckets and taken back to camp. Each piece of pottery is dipped in water, which will highlight any writing if it was used as an ostracon. Blank sherds are then laid in trays along with their bucket tags to dry. Each tray is read by the ceramicist. Significant diagnostic sherds are drawn and photographed. The rest of the sherds are then bagged and labeled and stored for future reference.

> *A **potsherd** or **sherd** is a broken piece of pottery. An **ostracon** (plural **ostraca**) is a broken piece of pottery used as a writing surface.*

Restoration and Preservation

As the excavation proceeds sections of the site are designated for restoration and preservation. The artifacts are cleaned and repaired, and then either reinstalled on the site as part of an archaeological park, or moved to museums for display. At Hazor a particularly well preserved pillared warehouse or stable was moved off its original site and reconstructed elsewhere on the site. This allowed visitors to see a good example of this architecture, while archaeologists continued excavating the original site.

CONCLUSION

The Wheeler-Kenyon method stabilized the recovery of artifacts from ancient sites. It was a reliable scientific process for handling the cultural heritage of the past and preserving it responsibly for future study and enjoyment. Sadly, it did not put an end to the piracy and treasure hunting of antiquities by private collectors, but it did begin an entirely new era in Near Eastern studies. The development of the Wheeler-Kenyon method

Basalt sanctuary furniture from Hazor (Israel): flat incense altar (front), stelae (back), seated priest (left), lion guardian (right). Location: Israel Museum (IDAM), Jerusalem, Israel. Photo Credit: Erich Lessing / Art Resource, NY.

was an outstanding accomplishment of biblical archaeologists working in the world of the Bible during the twentieth century.

WHAT YOU HAVE LEARNED

- Sondage excavations cut a single trench across the entire site from the surface down to bedrock. Horizontal excavations remove one layer at a time across the entire surface of the site. Wheeler-Kenyon excavations open a series of squares fifteen feet on a side and separated from one another by a three-foot-wide balk.
- Excavations destroy the context essential for interpreting artifacts. The site survey, square supervisor's journal, locus sheets, balk drawings, and photographs required by the Wheeler-Kenyon method allow later scholars to reconstruct that context.
- Excavation proposals should identify a site, state a clear goal for the dig, list the names of the team, calendar the dig schedule and the publication schedule, and describe how the artifacts and the site will be preserved and publicized.
- Pottery from each statum in a square is collected in buckets and identified by a locus tag. At the pottery center, broken pieces are dipped in water to see if there is writing on them. The contents of each bucket are transferred to a tray and read by a ceramicist,

who dates the pottery, notes any unusual pieces, and identifies pieces that will be drawn. The contents of the tray are then bagged, tagged, and stored.

- A **theodolite** is a telescope used by surveyors. A **probe trench** is generally three feet wide and opened to test a site for a full square. A **square** is fifteen feet on each side and dug from the surface to bedrock. A **balk** is a three-foot-wide wall left between balks to provide a record of the strata excavated. A **locus** is the context where an artifact is found. A *guffa* is a bucket made from an automobile tire and used to remove dirt and pottery from a square. A **sifter** is a framed piece of narrow mesh screen that archaeologists use to recover small finds from a square. A **dump** is where dirt removed from squares is collected.
- The goal of the Wheeler-Kenyon method is to allow scholars to recreate a three-dimensional model of the site after the excavation is complete.

STUDY QUESTIONS

1. Why is record keeping important for an excavation?
2. What is the procedure for beginning an excavation?
3. What can be learned about chronology from pottery?
4. What sorts of specialists may be required on an excavation?
5. What is stratigraphy?

PREVIEW: ARAD

- Arad from 3100 to 2650 B.C.E.
  - Narmer Cartouche
  - Icons of Tammuz and Ishtar
  - Arad Seals
- Arad from 900 to 586 B.C.E.
  - Arad Sanctuary
  - Ostraca

Chapter 9 explains why the School of Annales Archaeology is the preferred method for interpreting the Chalcolithic and Early Bronze Age artifacts from Arad, and how the villagers who founded Arad exploited the natural geography. It also describes why the state of Judah wanted a military presence at Arad during the Iron II period and where to find the "House of Yahweh" referred to on one of the Arad ostraca. Finally, the chapter shows what was unusual about the sanctuary of Yahweh at Arad and when and by whom Arad was destroyed.

9

Arad

Arad, Lachish, Dan, and Qumran are among the most significant excavations conducted by biblical archaeologists during the twentieth century. The goal of the excavators was to reconstruct the history of human settlement at the particular site, and to use the Bible and other Near Eastern written artifacts to interpret the material remains they recovered.

ARAD FROM 3100 TO 2650 B.C.E.

From 1962 to 1967, Yohanan Aharoni and Ruth Amiran directed large, general excavations at Tel Arad. In 1977, Ze'ev Herzog directed a smaller, more focused excavation. Aharoni and Amiran excavated the five Chalcolithic and Bronze Age villages and cities at Tel Arad in the Negev desert using the methods of the schools of cultural history, biblical archaeology, and Annales archaeology (see part 3 below). Each school expects archaeologists to carefully remove and record each settlement stratum. The goal for cultural historians is to link the material remains with written artifacts. The goal for biblical archaeologists is to link the material remains with the Bible. The goal for Annales archaeologists is to understand the long-term development of social institutions such as trade, architecture, village and city development, water management, military science, and daily life.

The large fortified city of Iron II Arad, Israel, as seen from the ruins of the Early Bronze period settlement. Photo: Erich Lessing / Art Resource, NY.

The Narmer Palette honors Pharaoh Narmer, who united southern and northern Egypt in 2920 B.C.E. In the top register he is flanked by two great bulls; in the second register he looks on the bodies of Egypt's enemies; in the third, gamekeepers tame creatures representing northern and southern Egypt; in the bottom register, Narmer, represented as a great bull, attacks an enemy city. h=63, w=42cms. Location: Egyptian Museum, Cairo, Egypt. Photo Credit: Werner Forman / Art Resource, NY.

Tel Arad is a unique, twenty-five-acre geological site in the Negev desert. The landscape is a natural fan-shaped amphitheater. The soil just below the surface hardens when wet allowing rainwater to sheet off the slopes and into a large circular cistern constructed between 3100 and 2650 B.C.E. (EBII) at the base of the amphitheater. The cistern held sixty-six thousand gallons of water (King and Stager 2001, 127–29). The quality of this soil and the sophistication of the water management system developed at Arad during the Bronze Age took the best possible advantage of the seven inches of rainfall at the site each year (Ornit and Amiran 2006, 1:169–74).

Like the villages in the Beersheba Valley less than twenty miles away, the earliest villages at Tel Arad (Stratum V) were built in clusters between 4000 and 3400 B.C.E. during the Chalcolithic Age. There were no large public buildings; there was no wall; and there was no overall plan orienting one village with the other.

The first written artifact was recovered from the second settlement at Tel Arad (Stratum IV). The artifact was a broken piece of Egyptian pottery with an oval cartouche containing the name of Pharaoh Narmer drawn on it. Aharoni and Amiran used written artifacts like the Narmer cartouche to reconstruct the significant events in the development of a site. This written artifact told them two things about the village that would play a critical role in the interpretation of the material remains at the site. First, the second human settlement at Arad was built during the Early Bronze Age (3200–3000 B.C.E.) when Narmer was pharaoh of Egypt. Arad was in existence at that point, when the villages along the Nile were being united into a state that would last three thousand years. Second, the village traded with Egypt's copper mining communities, which were more than 180 miles away in the Sinai. The jar with Pharaoh Narmer's name on it was manufactured by Egyptians from Sinai clay and contained Egyptian goods sent to the village to trade for wine and olive oil. Although the people at Arad lived in the desert, they were not isolated. The village was an integral part of an important political and economic network.

The third and fourth settlements (Strata III-IV) were cities. There were public buildings—a palace and a sanctuary—there was a wall, and there was a sophisticated water system.

The sanctuary provided a second written artifact from Arad—a shaped stone that had been erected in the ground of the great room in the sanctuary. Artists had carved on the stela two stick figures with human bodies and ears of grain for heads. One figure was lying down; the other was standing up. These drawings on the Bronze Age stela at Arad may be icons for the stories of Tammuz and Ishtar known from written artifacts from Mesopotamia (Matthews and Benjamin 2006, 329–34). Tammuz, or Dumuzi, is the divine gardener who, at the end of the dry season in the world of the Bible, waters the parched soil of Ishtar, or Inanna—Mother Earth—with rain. His rain, like sperm, fathers crop-children who rise like the dead from the body of their mother to stand straight and tall on the earth. The stories of Tammuz and Ishtar were the stories of the daily lives of the farmers at Arad, who, like midwives, tended their divine patrons during their annual ritual of giving birth.

The wall around the city followed the contour of the amphitheater. The inside and outside surfaces were made of two rows of carefully set stones. The space between these inside and outside walls was filled with rubble. The wall was over a mile long, twelve to fifteen feet high and six to eight feet thick. There were two main gates, several smaller gates, and some thirty-five to forty round and rectangular towers along the wall.

Private houses were built using a common blueprint called the *Arad House* design. Besides what they learned from the actual houses they excavated, Aharoni and Amiran also recovered a model of an Arad House from the site. The roof on the model was flat—something that could not be definitively established from the excavations of the houses themselves.

Wheat, barley, peas, lentils, and flax seeds for flour and cereals, and olive pits for oil also covered the courtyards of Arad houses. These seeds and pits had been carbonized in the fire that destroyed the Arad houses. There were also bones from sheep and goats that were herded for their wool, milk, and hides; bones of draft animals such as oxen, which were used to pull plows; and bones of the donkeys used to carry trade goods to and from the cities. Annales archaeologists use these material remains to reconstruct

slowly developing social institutions such as the economies of both daily life and foreign trade in the cities at Arad.

Besides the cartouche of Narmer, and the icons for the stories of Tammuz and Ishtar, Aharoni and Amiran recovered a third group of written artifacts: seals for notarizing commercial transactions. There are two styles of seals that were recovered by archaeologists working in the world of the Bible: stamp or scarab seals and cylinder seals. Scarab seals developed in Egypt; cylinder seals in Mesopotamia. Both were found at Arad. Thus, the people of Arad had economic ties as far away as Mesopotamia in the north and as far away as Egypt to the west.

A deep layer of ashes covered the first cities at Arad, indicating that they had been attacked and burned in 2800 B.C.E. Nevertheless, there were survivors, because the city was immediately resettled (Stratum III). Eventually, however, drought or economic competition forced people to abandon the site about 2650 B.C.E. Arad remained uninhabited for the next fifteen hundred years.

ARAD FROM 900 TO 586 B.C.E.

Because artifacts from the Chalcolithic and Bronze Age villages and cities at Arad reflect almost two thousand years of human activity, and because so few of the material remains there were written artifacts, Aharoni and Amiran studied the site primarily as Annales archaeologists. In contrast, there are abundant written artifacts from Arad during the Iron Age, and so the excavators studied these periods of the site as biblical archaeologists. The village and two Iron Age forts reflect only about four hundred years of human activity, and there were abundant written artifacts available on site and from elsewhere to interpret the other material remains.

Few architectural remains of the temple in Jerusalem, which was destroyed by the Babylonians in 586 B.C.E., have been recovered. Nonetheless, archaeologists are able to reconstruct the design of the temple from similar temples excavated elsewhere in the world of the Bible.

Curiously, the detailed descriptions of the temple, such as those in the books of Samuel–Kings (1 Kgs 6:1—7:51) and the book of Ezekiel (40:1—48:35), are not much help in reconstructing the temple. These traditions were not intended to be architectural blueprints. In traditional cultures, crafts such as those used in the construction of the temple were handed on through deliberately long and carefully guarded apprenticeships. Guilds did not develop how-to handbooks for their members. The description of the temple, like the description of the ark of Noah, affirms what was done, not how to do it. ■

Not all written artifacts are helpful in understanding the village and the two forts at Arad during the Iron Age. In the book of Numbers (Num 21:1; 33:40), the people of Arad prevent the Hebrews from entering Syria-Palestine from the south. In the book of Joshua (Josh 12:14), Arad is on a list of cities conquered by the Hebrews. In the book of Judges (Judg 1:16), the people at Negev Arad are called *Kenites*. There is a village that was founded after 1100 B.C.E. (Stratum XII) just beneath the first Fort Arad. Biblical archaeologists, however, have been unable to synchronize biblical traditions with the material remains in the village. Furthermore, there is no evidence that this village was destroyed. In time it was fortified with a casemate wall.

The people who finally resettled Arad were soldiers from Judah. They came to build a fort. They named their fort *Arad*, which archaeologists found cut into a broken piece of pottery at the site. Curiously, the soldiers wrote the name backwards four times.

What brought the soldiers of Judah to Arad was not only its watershed but also its location along the Edom highway. The highway was a lifeline for the economy and the military security of Judah. Forts such as Arad, Ramoth-negeb (Hebrew: *ḥorvat ʿuza*), and Kinah (Arabic: *khirbet taiyib*) guarded the Edom highway like stagecoach stops and cavalry forts in the American west (2 Kgs 3:8). This east–west trade route connected the coastal highway in the west (Josh 19:8; 1 Sam 30:27) with the royal highway in the east. From Arad, the Edom highway descends to the northern end of the Jebel Usdum Mountains and from there into the Arabah Valley.

The first Fort Arad was not large (Stratum XI). It was about 165 feet wide and 180 feet long and was surrounded by a casemate wall. The outer wall of the casemate is about five feet thick; the inner wall of the casemate is four and one-half feet thick. The casemates in the eastern wall were used as barracks for the soldiers assigned to the fort. Four towers reinforced the western wall.

In 925 B.C.E., Shoshenq I (ruled 945–924 B.C.E.) invaded Syria-Palestine from Egypt. His annals describe his march and the cities he conquered. Shoshenq's annals list Arad as one of his conquests. A destruction layer (Stratum X) containing pottery dated to the tenth century confirms that the first Fort Arad was destroyed sometime after 1000 B.C.E.

After the destruction of the first Fort Arad a second fort was built at the site (Strata VI–X). This fort was square—170 feet on a side—and surrounded by a solid wall. The outside surface of the wall has a saw-toothed pattern. This off-set, in-set design strengthened the wall in the same way that corrugation strengthens a steel plate. The design also gives the wall a more aesthetic appearance.

At the outside base of the wall there is a glacis—a slopping, layered, packed-earth ramp with a plastered surface. The glacis sheeted water away from the wall's foundations to prevent erosion.

A significant change inside the second Fort Arad was the construction of a broad-room sanctuary. Letters recovered at the fort make it clear that the Hebrew rulers of Judah were responsible for the garrison at Fort Arad, and that Yahweh was the divine patron of the garrison.

Biblical archaeologists also noted that the sanctuary at Arad followed the same design that was used to construct the temple for Yahweh in Jerusalem. The temple in Jerusalem was a rectangular building some 140 feet long and 85 feet wide. It was divided into three parts. The entrance was a courtyard about 35 feet long. The great room was about 70 feet long. The holy of holies was 35 feet long. The sanctuary at Arad also has a courtyard, a great room, and a holy of holies.

The annals of Solomon record his construction of a "House of Yahweh," a reference to which is found in one of the letters recovered at Arad. By building a temple for Yahweh, Solomon officially took possession of the land that Yahweh promised to Abraham and Sarah (Gen 11:27—12:8). Once Yahweh had a house, then Israel officially became a state. There is little reason to question that the sanctuary at Fort Arad, like the great temple in Jerusalem whose design the sanctuary imitated, was dedicated to Yahweh (Aharoni 1968).

In front of the sanctuary at Arad was a paved rectangular courtyard, which was almost forty feet long and twenty-five feet wide. There is a large altar on the east side of the courtyard that was built from undressed fieldstones. The base of the altar was a little over seven feet square and some five feet high. The top of the altar was covered by a single large stone. A groove had been carved along the edge of the stone to collect blood and juice from the sacrifices as they were prepared on the altar.

Again, as biblical archaeologists Aharoni and Amiran note, the altar in the courtyard at Fort Arad also corresponds to the building code in the book of Exodus. The code opens with a cluster of stipulations dealing with worship. The use of precious metals like gold and silver as well as sacred sculpture are prohibited (Exod 20:22–23). Altars were to be built of earth (Exod 20:24). Stone altars were permitted as long as the stone was uncut (Exod 20:25). Yahweh is the sculptor of uncut stone, humans the sculptors of dressed stone. The altars are to focus on the work of Yahweh, not human work.

Grain ostracon (potsherd) listing distribution of wheat, beginning with the heading wheat followed by a list of names and symbols. From Arad, Stratum VII. Israelite Iron Age II. Size 18.5 x 15.5 cm. Inv. R 694. Location: Dagon Agricultural Collection, Haifa, Israel. Photo Credit: Erich Lessing / Art Resource, NY.

Replica of incense altars in sanctuary dedicated to Yahweh at Arad. Location: Israel Museum (IDAM), Jerusalem, Israel. Photo Credit: Erich Lessing / Art Resource, NY.

Altars were not to be installed on a raised platform (Exod 20:26). Platforms would give the congregation a better view of the liturgy, but they would also give the congregation a view of the genitals of the priests around the altar. The stipulation is not to avoid scandalizing the congregation, but rather to avoid violating the protocol for a sanctuary of Yahweh. Yahweh is the creator of land and children. The Hebrews must be careful to acknowledge these prerogatives by never appearing before Yahweh with their feet covered or their genitals uncovered (Deut 28:57; 1 Kgs 15:23; 2 Chr 16:12; Isa 6:2; 7:20; Ruth 3:4–7). Only landowners wore sandals, and the fathers of households uncovered their genitals only when preparing to father a child.

A door in the long eastern wall of the sanctuary led into the great room. There was a low, plastered bench around the base of the wall. Four steps led from the great room into the holy of holies in the center of the western wall. A set of incense altars stood on either side of these steps.

Unlike the rest of Fort Arad, the sanctuary was decommissioned but not destroyed. The two standing stones in the holy of holies were laid on their sides. The walls were knocked down to fill in the courtyard, the great room, and the holy of holies, and then backfilled with earth. Biblical archaeologists note that the sanctuary at Arad may have been dismantled in obedience to the decree of Hezekiah of Judah in 715 B.C.E. that Yahweh should be worshiped only in the temple in Jerusalem, and that all other sanctuaries to Yahweh in Judah should be closed (2 Kgs 18:22).

ARAD OSTRACON 2
(Matthews and Benjamin 2006, 198–200)

To: Eliashib, commanding officer at Arad. From: . . . commanding officer at . . . . Issue the Kittim 2 *bat* rations of wine and 300 loaves of bread for the next four days, and another *homer*-ration of wine for the rest of the garrison. Deliver the rations tomorrow. Do not be late. Fill some of the jars with old wine, if there is any left.

More than two hundred artifacts with Hebrew and Aramaic writing on them were recovered from Fort Arad. Some are only 2.5 inches high. This is the largest collection of written artifacts excavated in any one place in Israel to date (Aharoni and Naveh 1981). Most of the writing is on broken pieces of pottery; some writing is on whole pots. There are also nineteen letters and seals recovered from the house of Eliashib, the commander of the fort. The majority of the letters date to 650–600 B.C.E., when Judah was continuously threatened by Babylon.

There are tax records for grain, olive oil, and wine delivered to Fort Arad from villages in Judah. There is a proclamation announcing the coronation of a new ruler in Judah. There are orders for Eliashib to issue rations to the Kittim, who were mercenaries from Crete and Cyprus. A four-day ration for seventy-five soldiers was three hundred loaves of bread and eighty-five quarts of wine. Therefore, each soldier received one loaf of bread per day (Jer 37:21) and eight ounces of wine. New wine was recently fermented (Deut 32:14). Old wine was stale—or at least past the date when it was best to drink it (Ps 69:21). There is an order to reinforce Ramoth-negeb, six miles southeast of Arad. Arad was the headquarters for its sector of the Negeb. Apparently, when Babylon invaded Judah from the north in 594 B.C.E., Edom invaded from the south (Ps 137:7-9; Lam 4:22). Whether the troops from Arad and Kinah, four miles northeast of Arad, were successfully deployed to Ramoth-negeb is unclear. Archaeologists found the broken piece of pottery on which the order was written lying in the ashes of the fire that destroyed the fort—a silent, desperate moment frozen in time.

CONCLUSION

The excavations at Arad are a good example of what archaeology can and cannot do. On the one hand, the Annales archaeology of the Chalcolithic and Bronze Age villages and cities at Arad can reconstruct the development of slowly evolving social institutions such as architecture and food production. There are so few written artifacts, however, that cultural history cannot connect these villages and cities with significant political or military events of the period. On the other hand, the biblical archaeology of the rich archive of written artifacts from the site of the forts at Arad, together with relevant traditions from the Bible, can reconstruct the role that Arad played in the political and military events of Judah during the Iron II period (900–586 B.C.E.). Nonetheless, biblical archaeology cannot yet synchronize the stones and stories for the Late Bronze or Early Iron Age periods at Arad. The stones tell one story; the Bible tells another. How to understand and appreciate both remains a work in progress.

WHAT YOU HAVE LEARNED

- Only two written artifacts were recovered from Chalcolithic and Early Bronze Arad. Annales archaeology interprets the social institutions such as architecture and trade represented by material artifacts without using written artifacts.
- Chalcolithic villagers selected the site for Arad for two reasons. A unique geological formation hardened when wet, which allowed water to run off. The fan-shaped natural amphitheater would sheet the runoff easily into a cistern at its base.
- Judah stationed troops at Arad to protect the strategic east–west highway.
- One Arad ostraca refers to the temple in Jerusalem as the "House of Yahweh"—an expression that also appears in the Bible.
- During the war between Babylon and Judah, the Edomites became partners with the Babylonians attacking and destroying Arad in 586 B.C.E.

STUDY QUESTIONS

1. During what periods was Arad inhabited?
2. What does archaeology reveal about the lifestyle of the inhabitants of Arad?
3. Are there any correspondences between the finds at Arad and the Bible?
4. What types of archaeology can be used to analyze remains from Arad?

PREVIEW: QUMRAN

Chapter 10 describes how the excavation at Qumran is an example of the school of cultural history or biblical archaeology. It also explains how the people of Judah survived in the non-Jewish worlds of Persia and Greece, why the community at Qumran considered the household of Hashmon to be no better than foreign rulers of Judah like the Persians and the Greeks. Then the chapter shows how Roland de Vaux, who excavated Qumran, used his personal experiences and cultural background to interpret the site as a Jewish monastic community preparing for the end time. The chapter also mentions other interpretations that have been suggested for the site. Finally, it tells why purity for the community at Qumran had little to do with hygiene, how purity guidelines were used at Qumran, and how de Vaux and other scholars interpret the elaborate water system at Qumran.

10

Qumran

Until the discovery of the Dead Sea Scrolls (1947–1956), the oldest manuscripts of the Bible were from around the year 1000 C.E. One scroll from Qumran containing the book of Isaiah was copied around 200 B.C.E. Consequently, the Dead Sea Scrolls contain copies of the Bible that were twelve hundred years older than any manuscripts previously available to scholars. It was now possible to see just what was happening during those turbulent years when Syria-Palestine was ruled by outsiders—first the Persians (538–332 B.C.E.), then the Greeks (332–168 B.C.E.), and then the Romans (63 B.C.E.–640 C.E.)—and by insiders, the Hasmoneans (170–63 B.C.E.), who, for some in Judah, ruled like outsiders.

PERSIAN YEHUD (538–332 B.C.E.)

Hormuzd Rassam (1826–1910) was a Christian from Mosul and the first Western-trained archaeologist in the British Mandate of Iraq. In 1852 he succeeded Austin H. Layard as the director of the British Museum's excavations at Nineveh and Kalhu. One of the most remarkable artifacts Rassam recovered from the Esagila, the temple of Marduk, the divine patron of Babylon, was a cylinder about nine inches long. It was inscribed with a decree of Cyrus II, Great King of Persia (559–530 B.C.E.). The decree was written in the Akkadian language using cuneiform script (http://www.kchanson.com/ancdocs/meso/cyrus.html). Few Persians understood Akkadian, but it was the official language in which all formal documents were published. Cyrus promulgated the decree shortly after his conquest of Babylon in 539 B.C.E. The promulgation of the decree inaugurated the Persian period (538–332 B.C.E.) in Syria-Palestine (E. M. Meyers 1994, 25–32).

In this decree, Cyrus indicts Nabonidus, Great King of Babylon (555–539 B.C.E.), for failing to protect and provide for the land and people of Babylon. He then orders the repatriation of the hostages in Babylon, whom Nebuchadnezzar and Nabonidus had deported from the lands that they had conquered. Households from Judah had been deported between 597 and 586 B.C.E., following their failed revolts against Babylon (2 Kgs 24:1—25:21; Jer 34:1-7).

The Cyrus Cylinder, preserved today at the British Museum in London, is one of Iran's most revered artifacts. There is even a replica of the cylinder at United Nations headquarters in New York City. The decree is a charter of human rights two thousand years older than the Magna Carta of England. It is a call for religious and ethnic freedom. It banned slavery and oppression and the confiscation of property by force or without compensation; and it gave states the freedom to choose whether or not they wanted to join the Persian Empire. ∎

Cyrus Cylinder, inscribed with the Decree of Cyrus II, ruler of Persia (559–530 B.C.E.). Recovered by Hormuzd Rassam from the library founded by Ashurbanipal (668–627 B.C.E.), ruler of Assyria, in Nineveh (Iraq). ANE, 90920. Location: British Museum, London, Great Britain. Photo Credit: Erich Lessing / Art Resource, NY.

THE DECREE OF CYRUS
(Matthews and Benjamin 2006, 207–9)

I entered Babylon as a friend of Marduk and took my seat in the palace. Every day I offered sacrifice to Marduk, who made the people love and obey me. Therefore, I ordered my soldiers not to loot the streets of Babylon, nor to molest the people of Sumer and Akkad. I no longer enslaved the people of Babylon to work for the state, and I helped them to rebuild their sanctuaries, which had fallen into ruin. . . . Every ruler from the Mediterranean Sea to the Persian Gulf, rulers who dwell in palaces in the east and rulers who live in tents in the west, came to Babylon to bring me tribute and to kiss my feet.

I returned the statues of the divine patrons of Ashur, Susa, Agade, Eshnunna, Zamban, Meturnu, Der, and Gutium to their own sanctuaries. When I found the sanctuaries across the Tigris in ruins, I rebuilt them. I also repatriated the people of these lands and rebuilt their houses. Finally, at Marduk's command, I allowed statues of the divine patrons of Sumer and Akkad, which Nabonidus had moved to Babylon, to be returned to their own sanctuaries, . . . which I rebuilt.

May all the members of the divine assembly whose statues I have returned to their sanctuaries ask Bel and Nebo for a long life for me every day. May they remember me to Marduk, my divine patron, with the prayer: *Remember Cyrus, the ruler who reveres you, and his son, Cambyses.*

The Decree of Cyrus also provides subsidies to emancipated peoples so that they can rebuild their cities and the sanctuaries of their divine patrons (Ezra 1:1-4; 6:3-5). The Second Temple in Jerusalem was not actually completed until 516 B.C.E. during the reign of Darius I (522–486 B.C.E.). The book of Ezra (Ezra 6:1-15) describes how Darius searched the royal archives for the Decree of Cyrus. The book of Isaiah (Isa 44:28; 45:1) celebrates the Decree of Cyrus and bestows the title of *Anointed* or *Messiah* on Cyrus. He is the only non-Israelite to be given such an honor.

Thus, the beginning of the Persian period in Syria-Palestine was marked by hope and renewal. The Persians appointed local leaders as governors to oversee daily life in the province. Zerubbabel, Nehemiah, and Ezra are governors mentioned in the Bible. The names of others, for example, Elnathan and his wife Shelomith, who was Zerubbabel's daughter, have been identified from their seal impressions (Latin: *bulla*; plural *bullae*) recovered by archaeologists (Avigad 1976; E. M. Meyers 1985).

> A **bulla** is a seal formed when a lump of wet clay is stamped with the impression of, for example, the sender of a letter. A papyrus scroll would be rolled up, tied with a string, and secured with a bulla.

As the people of Judah were being resettled in the province of Yehud a series of wars between Persia and Greece began. In 512 B.C.E. the army of Darius I crossed the Bosporus Straits and marched up the Danube River. Soon, however, Ionia and Cyprus started a revolt against Persia (499 B.C.E.), and the ships of Athens defeated the Persian fleet at the Battle of Marathon (490 B.C.E.). Because Persia had its military resources deployed against the Greeks, Egypt and Babylon also declared their own independence.

Greece was not only winning military wars against Persia, but was winning cultural wars as well (Stern 1982). Persia's colonies in Syria-Palestine used Greek coins—such as tetradrachmas—to buy and sell. They bought Greek goods, for example, black-glazed Attic wares, at trading posts along the coast of the Mediterranean Sea. Even the Persians themselves hired Greek soldiers to fight for them. The Persian Empire in Egypt and Syria-Palestine became increasingly Greek.

Hellenism

The Hebrews of Yehud assimilated Greek culture. Consequently, the signature rituals of Hebrew life began to disappear as more and more people in Judah ate and worked and married as if they were Greeks.

Attic terracotta drinking cup, 540 B.C.E. Location: The Metropolitan Museum of Art, New York, NY. Photo Credit: Image copyright © The Metropolitan Museum of Art / Art Resource, NY.

The desire for reform is reflected in the books of Zechariah and Ezra. The Judaism in the stories began to challenge the Hellenism in the stones of Yehud. Reformers placed their hope in the creation of a new and divine world governed by biblical principles (Zech 5:1-4). They looked at their leaders—Ezra and Nehemiah—as the new Moses and the new Aaron (Meyers and Meyers 1987, 277–92).

The traditions in the books of Zechariah, Ezra, and Nehemiah are set not in the time of Alexander, when the signature rituals of Hebrew life were challenged by the Greeks, but in the time when Cyrus emancipated the people of Judah from exile in Babylon and allowed them to return home. In this period, the Hebrew lifestyle was challenged by the Persians. The books of Ezra and Nehemiah, for example, are set in the time when Jews began to return from Babylon. Ezra returned to Jerusalem in 458 B.C.E. (Ezra 7:7-8) and Nehemiah returned in 445 B.C.E. (Neh 1:1). The time when these traditions developed and were told, however, is later. Ezra and Nehemiah are portrayed as the new Moses and the new Aaron in the time of the Persians in order to inspire the people of Judah in the time of the Greeks. The books want their audiences to consider: *How did we preserve our identity in the time of the Persians? How should we preserve our identity in the time of the Greeks?*

The people of Yehud were also swept up into the wars of liberation that broke out in Egypt, Cyprus, and Syria-Palestine. By 350 B.C.E. Hazor, Megiddo, Ein Gedi, and Jericho had been destroyed by one side or the other. Consequently, when Alexander actually invaded Syria-Palestine in 332 B.C.E. the transfer of power from Persia to Greece occurred peacefully. The people of Egypt welcomed him as a new pharaoh. The people of Jerusalem decorated the city with wreaths, put on white linen garments, and marched out of the city behind the priests in their hyacinth blue and gold vestments to welcome Alexander (Josephus, *Antiquities* 11:326–39). Only Tyre, Gaza, and Samaria mounted a military defense against Alexander. Assimilation and civil strife had already conquered the land (E. M. Meyers 1994, 32–42). Syria-Palestine was now Hellenistic by law, not just in fact.

GREEK JUDAH (332–168 B.C.E.)

When Alexander died, his generals subdivided the empire. Ptolemy ruled Egypt; Seleucus ruled Persia, Mesopotamia, and Syria. Judah would be claimed first by Ptolemy, and then by Seleucus. The west had come to the east, and the stones in Judah and the stories in Ecclesiastes and Daniel offer a window into this painful struggle for survival and cultural identity.

The book of Daniel is composed of two kinds of stories. It begins (Dan 1:1—6:29) and ends (Dan 13:1—14:42) with *teaching stories*. The core of the book (Dan 7:1—12:13) is a series of *apocalypse stories*. Today, apocalypse stories threaten the powerful in an impending end-of-the-world battle between God and Satan, after which an elite will govern a one-thousand-year empire in God's name. In the world of the Bible, apocalypse stories console the powerless by assuring them that their suffering will end soon and that in the end good, not evil, will prevail. The core of the book of Daniel is thus made up of apocalypse stories consoling the people of Judah.

During the first Hellenistic period (332–168 B.C.E.), the relationship between the people of Judah and the Greeks deteriorated. In the beginning, the people of Judah were welcomed in the Hellenistic world as teachers, as advisors, and as interpreters of dreams. The teaching stories with which the book of Daniel opens view the role of the people of Judah in this new Hellenistic world positively. These stories are told in Aramaic, which was the common language used by both Jews and Greeks. The stories encourage the people of Judah to live as Daniel lived by making themselves useful to their foreign rulers without losing their cultural identity (Benjamin 2004, 404–27).

Slowly, conditions in Syria-Palestine began to change. Greeks began to discriminate against the people of Judah. According to the apocalypse story in Dan 7:1-28, this Hellenistic world was about to be destroyed by the Ancient One (7:9). Like Daniel, the people of Judah must now prepare to follow the Son of Man (7:13) into a new world where all the peoples of the earth will be welcome and equal. But the status of the people of Judah in the Hellenistic world continued to deteriorate. Greeks began to consider the Semitic lifestyle of the people of Judah to be barbaric, their way of doing business to be primitive, and their worldview to be treasonous. Consequently, Antiochus IV Epiphanes, the Seleucid ruler of Syria-Palestine (175–164 B.C.E.), mounted a campaign to Hellenize the people of Judah.

Hellenism was a worldview that developed in western Mediterranean cultures like Greece and Rome, and it is the worldview of western European cultures like the United States and Canada today. Hellenism was the official worldview of the empire of Alexander, and it was radically different from the Semitic worldview of the people of Judah.

The language of Hellenism was Greek, an Indo-European language. Although Greeks in the world of the Bible spoke Aramaic because it was the diplomatic language used by peoples in Semitic cultures, they did not consider it to be comparable to their native Greek language. The traditions of Hellenism were handed on in the *Iliad* and the *Odyssey* of Homer. Hellenists considered traditions like the Enuma Elish flood stories and the Bible to be crude and barbaric.

The base community in Hellenism was the city (Greek: *polis*), whose hundreds, and sometimes thousands, of citizens created a centralized and surplus economy with vast trade networks bringing luxury goods from the ends of the earth. The base community in ancient Israel was the household (Hebrew: *bêt ʾāb*, literally, "house of father"), whose thirty to fifty members created a decentralized and subsistence economy with little trade and virtually no luxury goods.

The teachers who developed the book of Daniel and its audiences in Judah spoke Greek, Aramaic, and Hebrew. The Hebrew (Dan 1:1—2:4a + 8:1—12:13 NRSV), Aramaic (Dan 2:4b—7:28 NRSV), and Greek—Susanna (Dan 13:1-64 NRSV) and Bel and the Dragon (Dan 14:1-42 NRSV)—traditions in the book of Daniel testify not only to their language skills, but also to their assessment of the political climate for the people of Judah after Alexander's invasion. ∎

Tetradrachma of Antiochus IV Epiphanes (175–164 B.C.E.), Greek ruler of Syria-Palestine whose campaign to Hellenize the people of Judah led to the Revolt of the Maccabees (167 B.C.E.). Location: Israel Museum (IDAM), Jerusalem, Israel. Photo Credit: Erich Lessing / Art Resource, NY.

Pigs had been domesticated during the Neolithic period (8000–3800 B.C.E.) in the world of the Bible. Initially, pigs were moved out of the mainstream food chain for economic reasons. They competed too strongly with humans for water and grain. By the Bronze Age (3400–1200 B.C.E.), however, they were again herded in villages with good rainfall, which could produce enough grain for both the pigs and the villagers. Furthermore, centralized urban economies could not easily store, transport, and divide pork for redistribution. Pigs were also reintroduced into Syria-Palestine by the Philistines (1200–1000 B.C.E.), and by the Greeks (332 B.C.E.–640). ■

Hellenism considered the human body to be the most exquisite divine creation. Consequently, Hellenistic piety expected everyone to exercise and groom their bodies with devotion. The baths and the games were rituals in which Greeks exercised stewardship of this divine gift. Likewise, the Greeks developed a high-energy diet based on pork.

The people of Judah were not prudish. They did not hate their bodies. For them, however, Yahweh's greatest creation was not the human body but the cosmos, of which the human body was only a part. Consequently, the people of Judah cared for their bodies just as they cared for their lands and for their herds. They pruned their vines to increase their fertility, and they circumcised their sons so that they might father more children. Circumcision outraged the Greeks. They considered it a mutilation of a divine work.

The diet of the people of Judah was ascetic. They did not eat pork (Leviticus 11; Deuteronomy 14; Isaiah 65–66; Tob 1:10-11; Jdt 10:5; 12:1-2; 1 Macc 1:62-63; 2 Macc 5:27; 6:8-31; 7:10). Eating modestly and fasting regularly reminded the people that the physical power to bring in a harvest or to parent a child was a divine gift, and not a human achievement. The people of Judah believed that those who arrogantly overfed themselves in due time would starve (Deut 8:2-16; Ps 55:19; Prov 3:34; 15:33; 18:12). Only those who fasted would thrive (2 Sam 22:28; Ps 18:27).

Some Hellenists understood and appreciated the Semitic worldview and converted to a Semitic way of life as *God-fearers*. Even more people of Judah, however, converted to Hellenism and embraced a Greek lifestyle. Most Hellenists, and many people of Judah, considered the worldview of the other to be foolish.

To continue its dialogue with these changing political conditions, the book of Daniel added more apocalypse stories (Dan 1:1—2:4 + 8:1—12:13). These stories were told in Hebrew, the ancient language of the people of Judah, in order to encourage the people to withdraw from the Aramaic-speaking world of their Greek rulers. Both Aramaic and Hebrew traditions appear together today in the book of Daniel to recall the painful evolution of the people of Judah from full participation to radical alienation from the Greek world. The pairing tradition in Aramaic and Hebrew is not a call for Greek speakers and Hebrew speakers to reconcile their differences, but emphasizes that the people of Judah had done their best to fit in, but for their own survival they needed now to segregate themselves from the conquerors they once admired.

The culmination of the campaign of Antiochus Epiphanes to Hellenize the people Judah was granting Jerusalem the status of a *polis* and celebrating the event by erecting a statue of Zeus (for which Antiochus had posed) in the House of Yahweh. He also sacrificed hogs to Zeus in the temple during the dedication ceremonies in December 167 B.C.E. This was the "abomination that makes desolate" or the "abomination of desolation" (Dan 11:31; 12:11; 1 Macc 1:54; 2 Macc 6:1-50). The act by which Antiochus Epiphanes had intended to inaugurate a Hellenistic state in Judah that would live forever would, in fact, destroy it.

The book of Daniel sentenced Antiochus Epiphanes to death in "two thousand three hundred evenings and mornings" (Dan 8:14). He would be dead in some three and one-half years. Other traditions in the book of Daniel such as an ordination of a Son of Man (Dan 7:25) and the resurrection of the dead (Dan 12:7) place similar limits on his reign. The book of Daniel is emphatic: the end of the reign of Antiochus Epiphanes has already been determined by Yahweh and the divine assembly. The people of Judah have only to be patient.

HASMONEAN JUDAH (167–63 B.C.E.)

The book of Daniel is critical not only of Antiochus Epiphanes but also of any human solution to the crisis created by the Seleucid ruler. From its perspective, the matter will be settled on the divine plane, not on the human plane. The book of Daniel does not support revolutionaries. It refers to them as a "human hand" (Dan 8:25) or "little help" (Dan 11:34). It encourages the people of Judah to see the immediate crisis surrounding the administration of Syria-Palestine by Antiochus Epiphanes on the larger scale. By putting it in perspective, they may better survive the persecution. It wants them to let Antiochus self-destruct rather than taking any direct action against him. His vaunting ambition will destroy him. Resistance will only postpone his inevitable collapse.

But the people of Judah did not wait patiently for Yahweh and the divine assembly to deal with Antiochus Epiphanes. They fought for their own independence and created their own independent state. The books of the Maccabees, Josephus, and the stones in the land of Judah tell the stories of this war of independence and the dawn of the second Hellenistic period (167–63 B.C.E.).

The household of Hashmon (Greek: Hasmoneus) led the successful revolt against Antiochus Epiphanes. These Hasmoneans founded a state that they governed until the Roman general Pompey (106–48 B.C.E.) occupied Judah in 63 B.C.E. to end the civil war between John Hyrcanus II and Aristobulus II. The brothers both claimed the right to follow their mother, Salome Alexandra, onto the throne of Judah. Pompey arrested Aristobulus and appointed John Hyrcanus as the religious leader of the new Roman province of Judea.

QUMRAN

The founding of an independent state of Judah did not bring an end to the conflict between Hellenistic and Semitic worldviews. The Hasmoneans opposed the Hellenism of Antiochus Epiphanes, but, in turn, they were opposed by other communities in Judah that considered them to be too Hellenistic.

One community that opposed the household of Hashmon made an exodus from Jerusalem about 100 B.C.E. They traveled down the Jericho road and into the desert along the western shore of the Dead Sea. On the site of an earlier fortress (630–580 B.C.E.) along the Wadi Qumran they built a settlement. The ruins today are seven miles south of Jericho and twenty miles north of Ein Gedi. The settlement was built on a marl clay

The caves of Qumran, where the Dead Sea Scrolls were found in 1947. Location: Qumran, Israel. Photo Credit: Erich Lessing / Art Resource, NY.

terrace more than eleven hundred feet below sea level at the foot of the cliffs where the caves containing the Dead Sea Scrolls were found (Magness 2002, 32–38).

Qumran Interpreted as a Jewish Monastery

The first excavations at Qumran (1951–1958) were directed by Roland de Vaux. De Vaux's interpretation of the stones at Qumran was primarily dependent on written artifacts like Josephus, Pliny, Philo, and the Dead Sea Scrolls. He was a cultural historian and a biblical archaeologist.

Two important assumptions guided de Vaux's interpretation of the site. First, he assumed that the scrolls recovered from eleven caves in the area around the ruins were stored there by the Qumran community. Second, he assumed that the Qumran community was a Jewish monastic order similar to the Essenes described by Flavius Josephus (38–93) in

Jewish War (2.119–61), by Pliny the Elder (23–79) in *Natural History* (5–73), and by Philo (30 B.C.E.–45) in *Every Good Man Is Free* (75–91). De Vaux established the parallel between the Essenes and the community at Qumran despite the fact that none of these ancient writings mention Qumran by name, nor attribute to the Essenes the unorthodox use of a solar calendar to date religious feast days or a belief in predestination—all of which characterize the community of the Dead Sea Scrolls.

De Vaux's critics have pointed out that his reconstruction of community life at Qumran are more a reflection of his personal life experience as a Dominican friar and the cultural ideals of his native France than a sober assessment of the artifacts recovered from Qumran itself. The pattern of daily life that de Vaux proposes for the members of the Qumran is not much different from the community life of the Catholic Order of Preachers founded by Dominic de Guzman (1170–1221) to which de Vaux himself belonged. He even labeled artifacts at Qumran with terms uniquely monastic like *refectory* and *scriptorium*. Likewise his critics consider his interpretation of Qumran to be modeled on the ideals of the French intellectualism of his day, reflected in A. C. Sertillanges, *The Intellectual Life: Its Spirit, Conditions, and Methods* (1923) and the *Petit Larousse Illustré* (1959). The ideal life for French intellectuals like de Vaux was a combination of asceticism and learning.

Scholars like Norman Golb, Yizhar Hirschfeld, Yitzhak Magen, and Yuval Peleg challenge de Vaux's Qumran-Essene hypothesis; scholars like Hanan Eshel, Magen Broshi, Edna Ullmann-Margalit, and Jodi Magness defend it. Unfortunately, until the final report of de Vaux's excavation is published, and all the artifacts and records from Qumran now at the Ecole Biblique in Jerusalem (http://ebaf.edu) are available to scholars, little

consensus on the interpretation of Qumran and the Dead Sea Scrolls can be established (Atkinson 2008).

Alternative Interpretations of Qumran

Norman Golb challenges both of de Vaux's assumptions. He argues that the Dead Sea Scrolls were not copied or kept by the community at Qumran but were from the libraries of various communities in Jerusalem, who hid them when the first war between Judah and Rome (66–70) was imminent (Golb 1980, 1995). Golb also argues that the community members were not peace-loving ascetics but fighters who, like the militant Sicarii at Masada, fought the Romans to their deaths.

From 1993 to 2004 Yitzhak Magen and Yuval Peleg directed new excavations at Qumran. They also challenged de Vaux's assumption that the structures were used by a community that developed an elaborate water system used for ritual bathing (Hebrew: *miqva'ot*). Magen and Peleg argue that the water system at Qumran was part of a pottery factory. The cisterns were used to wash the clay before using it to make pots (Magen and Peleg 2006).

From 1996 to 2002, Yizhar Hirschfeld directed a large-scale excavation at Ein Gedi and a regional study of both shores of the Dead Sea (Hirschfeld 2004). The similarity between Ein Gedi and other settlements contemporaneous with Qumran also convinced him that de Vaux's Qumran-Essene hypothesis was wrong, and that the Dead Sea Scrolls were not copied and stored by a Jewish monastic community at Qumran. Qumran, Hirschfeld concluded, would have had no attraction for Jewish monks seeking to flee the world, because it was a thriving center of commerce owned by a wealthy Herodian household. Qumran was just one of many plantations (Latin:

When the household of Hashmon (170–63 B.C.E.) and subsequently Herod (63–4 B.C.E.) ruled Judah, there was an economic renaissance in the communities along the shores of the Dead Sea. Jericho, Qumran, Ein Gedi, Masada, En Boqeq on the west; Callirrhoe and Macherus on the east were all centers for the production of farm products and the mining of salt and bitumen (Hirschfeld 2004, 11–12). A network of routes and harbors connected all these settlements to one another, to the regional capital at Jericho, and to the state capital of Jerusalem, and the network linked the entire region with settlements in the hills of Judah to the west and the mountains of Moab to the east. ∎

villa rustica) that formed a sophisticated commercial complex exporting its products to Syria-Palestine, the Sinai, Egypt, and Rome.

Agriculture along the Dead Sea was diversified. There were plantations of tree crops that produced dates, balsam, incense, grapes, citrus, and other fruit. Farmers also raised plant crops like wheat, barley, and vegetables. Date palms are indigenous to the Dead Sea Valley. They cope well with the extreme climate and brackish water. Dates were processed into date honey, which was a staple in Mediterranean diets. Date palms also filter salt from the ground water, and their branches provide shade from the sun. Farmers used them to create microclimates, where they planted wheat, barley, and vegetables. Finally, date palms are an abundant source of raw materials used in the construction of buildings, furniture, tools, and other commodities. They were the most important cash crop in the region.

Farmers also harvested resin from balsam trees. Factories converted the resin into luxury cosmetics. Grape vines and citrus trees also thrived in the soil and climate along the Dead Sea as well as a wide variety of vegetables.

Plantations also mined salt and bitumen from the Dead Sea. Salt and asphalt production are the primary industries by which the peoples of the Dead Sea valley traditionally have made their living. Today, potash is taken from the Dead Sea for fertilizers and explosives. In the world of the Bible, these salt blocks were used to start fires (Pilch 1999, 4–5). Asphalt was used as an adhesive to haft stone blades to wooden handles, and as caulking for boat hulls.

In 2001–2002 Hanan Eshel and Magen Broshi directed excavations focused on finding where the members of the Qumran community lived. They found three artificial caves used as dwellings and a circle of stones used as a tent site. The trails between these caves and Qumran were littered with first-century Common Era coins and sandal nails (Broshi and Eshel 2004). Their conclusions supported those of de Vaux that Qumran and the caves are related to one another.

Similarly Jodi Magness and Edna Ullmann-Margalit also support de Vaux's conclusion that Qumran was a Jewish monastery, and that the community there copied and cared for the scrolls found in the caves (Magness 2002; Ullmann-Margalit 2008). For Magness, the ritual baths, the common dining room, and the ritual disposal of meal bones point to a religious community, not a pottery factory or a commercial plantation. Likewise, for her, the three inkwells recovered at Qumran link the site with the Dead Sea Scrolls recovered from the caves.

Roland de Vaux

> **JODI MAGNESS**
> *The Archaeology of Qumran and the Dead Sea Scrolls*
> (2002, 15–16)
>
> I find myself—an American Jewish woman—in the curious position of defending the interpretation proposed by de Vaux who was a French Dominican priest! But this book is not about my personal beliefs and background or about de Vaux's. It is about the archaeological evidence. Obviously, de Vaux's interpretation of Qumran was influenced by his background (who isn't?). De Vaux's bias is evident in his use of monastic terms to describe some of the rooms and installations at Qumran (such as "refectory" and "scriptorium"). But the objections that have been raised by de Vaux's critics have obscured the fact that his interpretation of the site is basically correct.

The Dead Sea Scrolls and the Bible

Among the Dead Sea Scrolls are the earliest copies of sections from almost all twenty-four books of the Bible. Only Esther and Nehemiah are missing. Before the discovery of the Dead Sea Scrolls in 1947, the earliest existing scrolls of the Bible were copied around 1000. The Dead Sea Scrolls were copied between 200 B.C.E. and 68, more than one thousand years earlier. By comparing the text of the Bible today with the Dead Sea Scrolls, biblical scholars have learned much about how the Bible developed. Since the year 100 there has been only one official Hebrew text. The Dead Sea Scrolls, for example, include more than one version of the Hebrew text, which indicates that there was not a single authoritative version of the Bible between 200 B.C.E. and 100. Some of these alternative versions have been preserved in Greek, Latin, and Syriac translations.

There was no established canon at the time of the Dead Sea Scrolls—no official list identifying which books belonged to the Bible and which did not. Clearly some books of the Bible were more popular than others during the period. There are eight or more copies of Genesis, Exodus, Leviticus, Numbers, Deuteronomy, Isaiah, Hosea, Joel, Amos, Obadiah, Jonah, Micah, Nahum, Habakkuk, Zephaniah, Haggai, Zechariah, Malachi, Psalms, and Daniel. Deuteronomy, Isaiah, and Psalms were the most popular, and most copied, books among the Dead Sea Scrolls.

After the end of the first war between Judah and Rome (70) a school of Jewish scholars developed at Jabneh on the coast of the Mediterranean Sea. These scholars edited a fixed text of the Hebrew Bible that would be the standard or model for copyists. Their work is known as the *Masoretic Text*. Prior to the Masoretic Text different copies of the same passage might differ from each other in spelling and wording. ∎

Pieces of an Isaiah Scroll from Qumran. Location: Archaeological Museum, Amman, Jordan, Kingdom. Photo Credit: Erich Lessing / Art Resource, NY.

The Teachings of the Community

The Dead Sea Scrolls also include books containing the teachings of the community, which scholars have named, for example, the *Damascus Document*, the *Community Rule* or *Manual of Discipline*, and the *War Scroll*. The teachings and traditions in the scrolls do not mention Essenes. They simply refer to "the Community" (Hebrew: *yaḥad*). The founder of the community was the "Teacher of Righteousness" and its leaders were the "Heirs of Zadok," the high priest during the reigns of David and Solomon (900–925 B.C.E.).

The ritual of initiation for candidates who wanted to become members of the community lasted more than two years. They forfeited their personal property to the community and took vows to obey the heirs of Zadok. Some members were married and lived active lives in the villages and cities of Judah. Others lived contemplative lives of celibacy and simplicity in the desert.

The Dead Sea Scrolls demonstrate how the community understood the Bible and applied it to their daily life. The community distinguished itself especially by its theology of forgiveness, its liturgical calendar, and its belief that the Hasmonean state of Judah was about to end.

The community did not believe that the sacrifices offered at the Jerusalem temple by the Hasmonean priests forgave sins. The members of the community atoned for their sins by prayer and by living a simple life.

The community also followed a solar calendar rather than a lunar calendar, which meant that their feast days did not coincide with those celebrated throughout the Hasmonean state of Judah.

When the household of Hashmon won its war of independence from the Greek rulers of Syria-Palestine in 170 B.C.E., it celebrated the victory by rededicating the temple in Jerusalem. Jews today remember the event in the celebration of Hanukkah. The community in the Dead Sea Scrolls, however, considered the Hasmonean temple to be as heretical as the "abomination of desolation" in the book of Daniel (Dan 11:31). Therefore, just as the "Ancient of Days" had brought down the temple of Antiochus IV Epiphanes, the Greek ruler of Syria-Palestine, the temple dedicated by the household of Hashmon would also be destroyed.

The daily life of the community in the Dead Sea Scrolls imitated the daily life of the Hebrews during their forty-year exodus from Egypt into the desert. They waited in the desert for two messiahs. The *Messiah of Israel* would rule a new state; the *Messiah of Aaron* would rule a new temple. When these two messiahs appeared, the community would serve as a cadre for the *Sons of Light*. They would be the key officers and personnel who would train these divine warriors and lead them in a forty-year war against the Hasmonean *Sons of Darkness* and their allies.

In *The Sacred and the Profane: The Nature of Religion* (1959), Mircea Eliade assigns religion the role of synchronizing the human or profane plane with the divine or sacred plane. A spiritual person (Latin: *homo religiosus*) follows a way of life that harmonizes these two dimensions of human experience—the human and the divine. The guidelines for synchronizing the human and the divine in the Dead Sea Scrolls and other commu-

nities in Judah were called *laws of purity* (Neusner 1994). The biblical inspiration for these lifestyle guidelines (Hebrew: *halakah*) are preserved in teachings on things clean and unclean in biblical books such as Exodus, Leviticus (Lev 11:1—16:34), and Numbers.

"Clean," "pure," "wise," "unclean," "impure," and "foolish" were labels that taught people in the world of the Bible a specific way of looking at life. Some formal education did take place in schools, whose teachers explained why certain ways of doing things were clean, and others were unclean, for example, but most education was informal. Labeling was the principal means of informal education (Benjamin 2004, 105–13).

The labels "clean" or "pure" in the books of Exodus, Leviticus, and Numbers, and "wise" in the books of Proverbs, Ecclesiastes, and Job, are parallel. They describe acceptable, honorable, or spiritual human behavior. The clean, the pure, and the wise successfully harmonize their lives on the human plane with the lives of their divine patrons on the divine plane. Everything they do here imitates something that their divine patrons are doing there. The labels "unclean," "impure," and "foolish" describe unacceptable or shameful behavior. Unclean or impure behavior had little or nothing to do with attitudes toward hygiene. They defined status and were analogous to credit ratings today. The unclean, the impure, and the foolish did not harmonize the human plane with the divine plane—the sacred with the profane. Consequently, they put their households and villages at risk socially and economically.

Clean behavior entitled households to life. The clean ate moderately, did not get drunk, worked hard, made good friends, sought advice before acting, held their temper, paid their taxes, and imposed fair legal judgments. The clean were careful in dealing with one another during menstruation, sexual intercourse, childbirth,

A water channel carried water to this reservoir at Qumran. Location: Qumran, Israel. Photo Credit: Erich Lessing / Art Resource, NY.

and death. The clean were equally conscientious about what food they ate, what clothes they wore, what animals they herded, and what crops they planted in their fields. "Clean" was the label for a household in good standing, licensed to make a living in the village, and entitled to the support of other households in the village. Clean households cared for their own members and were prepared to help their neighbors. Only the clean were entitled to buy, sell, trade, arrange marriages, serve in assemblies, and send warriors to the tribe. Only the clean were entitled to make wills, appoint heirs, and serve as legal guardians for households endangered by drought, war, and epidemic. The clean were in place and functioning well because they harmonized the sacred and the profane in their daily lives.

"Unclean" was a label for households sentenced to death by placing its land and children at risk. The unclean ate too much, drank too much, were lazy, quarrelsome, selfish, and thought nothing about lying to the village assembly. They were thoughtless in their sexual relationships and disrespectful of the newborn and the dead. The herds of the unclean were mangy and their farms run-down. Unclean households did not fulfill their responsibilities to their own members or their neighbors. The unclean were on probation. The unclean were out of place and not functioning properly. Consequently, both their contributions to the village and their eligibility for its support were suspended. The "unclean" label downgraded the status of a household until the household demonstrated that it was once again contributing to the village.

The material remains at Qumran reveal that not only the community in the Dead Sea Scrolls, but also the community at Qumran, were both seriously committed to harmonizing their lives on the human plane with the actions of Yahweh on the divine plane. Purity guidelines defined all their actions.

The Water System at Qumran

The water system at Qumran is the clearest record in the stones of the community's commitment to harmonize their daily lives with the actions on the divine plane. Water installations at the site catch and store far more water than would be needed for the members' survival.

An aqueduct diverted water from the Wadi Qumran into the northwest corner of the site and filled pools throughout the site. In front of each pool there was a settling basin, which slowed the flow of the water until the silt in it had slowly dropped to the bottom of the pool (Magness 2002, 54). The first settling basin just inside the settlement was broad and shallow, adjoined by a small stepped pool. From this settling pool the water flowed south through a channel, filling the round Iron Age cistern and the two rectangular pools nearby.

At the end of the water system was a large ritual bath (Hebrew: *mikveh*). The stairs leading into the pool are divided by a floor-level banister. One side of the stairs was used for entering the bath, the other side for leaving it. The stairs into the pool led members away from their old lives; the stairs out of the pool led them to renewed lives.

Communal Life

The material remains at Qumran show how important it was for the community to be self-sufficient if its members were to avoid contact with outsiders. For example, they manufactured their own pottery. There are remains at the site of the vats the members used to cure their clay before

Earthquakes were common in Syria-Palestine. In 31 B.C.E., a violent earthquake severely damaged the settlement at Qumran. Huge cracks appeared in the walls of the water system, but the community did not abandon the site (Magness 2002, 63–69). They repaired and remodeled the structures. ∎

Pottery lidded jar of the sort used to store the Dead Sea Scrolls. From Qumran, Israel. H. 56 cm. Inv. 131444. Location: British Museum, London, Great Britain. Photo Credit: © British Museum / Art Resource, NY.

using it to make pots. There are remains of the fast wheel they used to throw their pots and of the kilns where they fired them.

Potters also developed a unique type of pot that was found both at Qumran and in the caves around the site. The large mouth of the pot and the shape of its lid allowed members of the community to handle liquids according to the ritual guidelines they had established for themselves. At some point, the pots were also used to store the scrolls found in the caves.

Common life was also a value for the community at Qumran. To provide space for assemblies of the community they built a large room, which was used also for eating. A pantry containing the remains of some one thousand bowls adjoined the large room. One of the water channels at the site was able to be diverted to flood the floor of the large room to clean or to purify it.

There is also a cemetery at Qumran that contained as many as eleven hundred graves. Most of the dead are male and were buried with their heads to the north, their feet to the south. Each grave is covered with stones.

THE BOOK OF EZEKIEL AT QUMRAN

The belief of some today that the world will come to an abrupt end, and then eternity will begin, would have been foreign to the Hebrews in general and to the Hebrews who were members of the Qumran community. They expected every old world to be replaced by a new world.

Another significant difference between the worldview in the world of the Bible and today's worldview is how to solve problems. Today problems are solved by looking into the future. In the world of the Bible problems were solved by looking into the past. Today, it is assumed that the future development of wind and solar energy

will control the overuse of fossil fuels. In the world of the Bible it was assumed that the Creator endowed humans not only with the cosmos but also with all they needed to know to live in it. Problems arise when humans forget. So when the community at Qumran faced the problem of surviving in a Judah ruled by the household of Hashmon, they reflect on their past for models, and the most significant models for them were preserved in the Bible.

The book of Ezekiel, for example, surveys a new land, designs a new temple, promulgates a new code of law, and establishes a new liturgy for a new world (Ezek 40:1—48:35). Like the child celebrated in the book of Isaiah (Isa 7:14), the city described in the book of Ezekiel is named *Immanuel* (Ezek 48:35). The end-time community at Qumran may have been inspired by traditions like those preserved in the book of Ezekiel. Their inspiration motivated them to build at Qumran a microcosm—a model of a new world that would replace the old world created by the household of Hashmon in Jerusalem.

In more than one way, the stones of Qumran imitate the characteristics of the stories in the book of Ezekiel (Magness 2002, 50). In both the city of Immanuel and the settlement at Qumran there was an abundance of water. Likewise, the city of Immanuel and the settlement at Qumran were not simply where people lived; they were sacred centers (Greek: *omphaloi*) where people prayed. Finally, the lives of the people of Immanuel and the lives of the community at Qumran were lives of radical simplicity, thoroughly synchronized with the divine plane.

During the first war between Babylon and Judah (597–586 B.C.E.), the Babylonians deported the members of the household of David—anyone connected officially with the government in Jerusalem. Then the Babylonians redistributed their land in Judah to households who had not participated in the revolt (Hebrew: ʿam hāʾāreṣ, literally, "the people of the land").

The book of Ezekiel was an attempt to assess the reasons for the collapse of the Judah ruled by the household of David (Benjamin 2004, 400–403). The book of Ezekiel also proposes a vision for a new world for the people of Judah—a world without monarchs and without royal policies like those pursued by the household of David, which were responsible for the wars between Babylon and Judah that took away the land and children that Yahweh had bestowed upon the people of Judah. The book of Ezekiel also attempted to reeducate the members of the household of David so that when they returned from exile they would commit themselves to lives of radical simplicity and lives thoroughly synchronized with the divine plane.

The Hasmonean kings and queens who ruled Judah from 170 to 64 B.C.E. were no more successful than the household of David who had ruled Judah from 1000 to 586 B.C.E. Instead of providing for the people of Judah, both administrations taxed them into starvation. Instead of protecting the people, the rulers plunged them repeatedly into wars they could not win.

Just as the book of Ezekiel was an effort to reeducate the household of David, the daily life of the community at Qumran was an effort to reeducate the household of Hashmon. There are some significant parallels between the traditions in the book of Ezekiel and practices at Qumran in the way both understood human behavior and divine blessing in the new worlds they were trying to create.

In the dedication of the city of Immanuel, Ezekiel is taken away from the Jerusalem built by the household of David to a mountain on the divine plane, where Yahweh—described as "one, whose appearance was like bronze, with an architect's line of flax and measuring reed in his

hand"—is prefabricating a city (Ezek 40:3). When the armies of Babylon have destroyed the old Jerusalem, Yahweh will move the city of Immanuel—the New Jerusalem—from the divine plane to the human plane. Similarly, Qumran is set apart from the old Jerusalem build by the household of Hashmon. Qumran is a prototype for the new Jerusalem built by Yahweh in the desert.

The book of Ezekiel proposes a code of honor for the household of David in the city of Immanuel (Ezek 46:1–24) that is similar to the purity guidelines for the community in the Dead Sea Scrolls. According to Ezekiel, the fathers of the households in the New Jerusalem will be not monarchs but priests. These fathers have only limited authority. They are to live modestly and deed their land only to children born inside the household. No member of the household can serve as a priest for more than seven years, and no other household is to be evicted from its land to support the household of David. In this New Jerusalem, the household of David is to ponder and to celebrate the great stories of how Yahweh delivered the Hebrews from slavery and endowed them with land. They do not live in the temple compound, but enter Yahweh's sacred space only to offer the morning sacrifice and to lead pilgrims in procession to the temple.

Once Yahweh officially takes possession of the city, the *Hand of Yahweh*, Ezekiel's guide, escorts him to the dedication of the city's spectacular new water system (Ezek 47:1-12). The first stop on the tour is the Gihon Spring in the Kidron Valley. Early in the Iron Age, Jerusalem was located on a low, fifteen-acre ridge of land called Mount Ophel, cut out of the central hills by the Kidron Valley on the east and the Central Valley on the west. Today, this spur juts out to the south of the Temple Mount constructed by Herod on Mount Moriah, and is outside the Old City walls built by Suleiman (1494–1566). The Gihon Spring is

Jerusalem's principal water source and is located at the foot of the Mount Ophel ridge in the Kidron Valley (1 Kgs 1:33). In antiquity, the Gihon Spring was a siphon spring that pumped intermittently for about thirty minutes every four or five hours.

The provisions at Qumran for large quantities of water stored throughout the settlement may be an attempt to actualize the vision in the book of Ezekiel. Ezekiel watches the Gihon Spring pump enough water to turn the Kidron Valley into a massive reservoir, which then overflows and runs down the road from Jerusalem to Jericho. Even when the freshwater from the spring reaches the saltwater in the Dead Sea, the Gihon continues to pump. In this new city, the Gihon Spring pumps enough freshwater to sweeten the saltwater of the Dead Sea, from the spring at Qumran to the oasis of Ein Gedi just north of the fortress of Masada. "When the freshwater enters the Dead Sea it becomes fresh. Wherever the river goes, every living creature that swarms will live, and there will be very many fish, once these waters reach there. It will become fresh, and everything will live where the river goes" (Ezek 47:8-10).

Nonetheless, Yahweh is environmentally sensitive. Enough salt marshes will be preserved that the communities that historically have depended on the salt marshes in this forbidding terrain are protected. "Its swamps and marshes will not become fresh. They are to be left salt" (Ezek 47:11).

When Ezekiel's great time voyage ends, he has seen what Yahweh sees. The war and the exile brought the old world built by the household of David to an end, but those same events set the new world built by Yahweh into existence. The time voyage puts the tragic events of his world into perspective. Despite the elaborate detail with which Ezekiel recounts his experience of the city of Immanuel, the voyage has a single and simple message for the people of Judah: "Yahweh, not the household of David, and not the Great King of Babylon, is the architect of all human events. It is Yahweh, and only Yahweh, who protects the land and feeds the people." The community in the Dead Sea Scrolls and the stones at Qumran may have had much the same idea about the household of Hashmon in Jerusalem.

WHAT YOU HAVE LEARNED

- As a cultural historian and biblical archaeologist, Roland de Vaux used written artifacts like the Dead Sea Scrolls to interpret the material artifacts from Qumran.
- Initially, the people of Judah assimilated both Persian and Greek lifestyles to survive, but ultimately returned to their historic lifestyle set down in the Bible.
- The community at Qumran withdrew its endorsement of the household of Hashmon even though this family was native to Judah and responsible for liberating Judah from its Greek conquerors. Once in power, however, the Hasmoneans abandoned the traditional liturgical calendar and began celebrating feasts at different times of the year. They also expelled the family that historically had served as priests for the temple in Jerusalem and appointed priests from another household. The Hasmoneans arrested and tortured the priest who was the Teacher of the community at Qumran.

- De Vaux used his personal experience in a Catholic monastery to describe the daily life of the community at Qumran as that of a Jewish monastery. He also used the ideals of his native French intellectualism to describe the ideals of the community at Qumran as a commitment to simplicity and a life of learning.
- Other scholars have interpreted the remains at Qumran as reflecting a pottery factory or an agricultural plantation.
- For de Vaux, the elaborate water system at Qumran was used for ritual bathing to renew the members' commitment to their covenant. According to the theory of Qumran as a pottery factory, the water and cisterns would have been used to wash clay. According to the theory of Qumran as an agricultural planation, the water would have been used to irrigate crops.

STUDY QUESTIONS

1. What is the significance of the Cyrus Cylinder?
2. What were the effects of Hellenism on the people of Judah?
3. What does the book of Daniel reveal about conditions in Syria-Palestine?
4. What are the principal theories about the lifestyle of the community that inhabited Qumran?
5. How does the book of Ezekiel illuminate some aspects of the life and teachings of the Qumran community?

Part 3

Annales Archaeology

- Part 3 is an introduction to the School of Annales Archaeology.
- Chapter 11 describes how the School of Annales Aarchaeology, founded by Marc Bloch (1886–1944) and Lucien Febvre (1878–1956), studies slowly developing and long-lasting social institutions (French: *la longue durée*) such as farming, herding, pottery making, and architecture.
- Chapters 12, 13, and 14 examine agriculture, pottery, and architecture as models of the long-lasting institutions reconstructed by Annales archaeologists.

PREVIEW: ANNALES ARCHAEOLOGY

- Annales School
  - Foundation by Bloch and Febvre
  - *La Longue Durée*
  - Economics and Geography
  - Microhistory
  - Annales Archaeologists and the Bible
  - Processes

Chapter 11 describes important differences between the School of Cultural History and the School of Annales Archaeology and identifies some important figures in the development of Annales archaeology. It also explains three kinds of processes that are going on simultaneously in any culture.

11

Annales Archaeology

According to R. G. Collingwood in *The Idea of History* (1946), cultural historians want to understand why events happened and to reconstruct what the great figures who caused these events were thinking. Cultural historians chronicle the ideas and events of the rich and famous reflected in unique political, diplomatic, or military events (French: *événements*).

The Annales school was founded by Marc Bloch and Lucien Febvre while they were teaching at the University of Strasbourg in 1929. Bloch studied the history of France; Febvre studied the history of Spain. The School of Annales Archaeology was named after the journal *Annales d'histoire économique et sociale,* founded by Febvre and Bloch in 1929. The mission of the journal was to promote a new approach to the study of history.

Marc Bloch

Bloch and Febvre were more interested in the daily lives of ordinary people and the more slowly developing and long-lasting institutions of society (French: *la longue durée*) such as farming, herding, architecture, and ways of thinking about birth and death (Knapp 1992). For Annales archaeologists, only by reconstructing these long-term and slowly changing ways of looking at life is it possible to interpret accurately the material remains of past cultures. The key to the past is not in rapidly changing events such as military conquests, but rather in social institutions that evolve over time, remaining largely the same for generations. To understand the past it is more important to understand how people farmed than whom they fought.

Febvre's most famous student was Fernand Braudel (1902–1985). His most important work is *The Mediterranean and the Mediterranean World in the Age of Philip II* (1949). Braudel began composing this study from memory while he was a prisoner of war during World War II! He emphasized the contribution of economics and geography to the interpretation of any period of history and inaugurated a second trajectory of the Annales school (1960–1980).

Emmanuel Le Roy Ladurie was a student of Braudel. Le Roy Ladurie pioneered a third trajectory of the Annales school called *microhistory*.

Thomas E. Levy assembled thirty archaeologists to use the Annales method to report on the state of the archaeology of society in Syria-Palestine (Levy 1998). These essays all use some form of the interdisciplinary school of Annales archaeology. ∎

Lucien Febvre

Microhistorians study an event, locality, family, or individual to reveal the underlying structures of daily life in a particular period. In *The Peasants of Languedoc* (1974) Le Roy Ladurie reconstructed daily life in Languedoc (France) from 1500 to 1900 by analyzing records of tithes, wages, taxes, rents, and profits. The focus of microhistory is not on the powerful who were collecting tithes, taxes, rents, and profits but on the powerless who were paying them. Le Roy Ladurie described the worldviews of ordinary people—worldviews that developed slowly and changed little over time.

Annales archaeologists working in the world of the Bible today excavate society as a whole, not a specific site. They focus on broad sweeps of time and create generalizations. They try to determine when humans began to farm, herd, and make pots, and how long it took for these activities to develop and then to change. To construct these grand cultural visions, Annales archaeologists collaborate with their colleagues in economics, linguistics, sociology, anthropology, psychology, and the natural sciences.

For Annales archaeologists, every stratum in an excavation is layered. A layer of occupation is not a snapshot of a single moment in the life of a village or city but a mix of short-, medium-, and long-term processes all paused at very different points in their development.

Some processes like wars develop quickly and last only a short time. But whether a war lasts a year, like the war between Assyria and Judah that destroyed the city of Lachish (701 B.C.E.), or ten years, like the war between Judah and Babylon that destroyed the city of Jerusalem (597–586 B.C.E.), it is a short-term process or *event* (French: *événement*).

Other processes such as village life or climate change evolve more slowly and last longer. Grain recovered from a destruction layer at Jericho reflects some two hundred years of climate change at the site between 1750 and 1560 B.C.E. Annales archaeologists call these medium-term processes *crossroads* institutions (French: *conjunctures*).

Processes such as architecture, farming, herding, and burial customs develop very slowly and remain virtually unchanged for long periods of time. From 100 B.C.E. to 68 C.E. the people of Qumran buried their dead to emphasize their ongoing relationship with the living, just as in 8000 B.C.E. the people of Jericho just a few miles north buried their dead. What each culture did with the dead bodies was different, but the burials reflected a slowly developing and long-lived worldview that the living and the dead are still in touch with one another. Annales archaeologists call these processes *long-lasting* (French: *la longue durée*) social institutions.

WHAT YOU HAVE LEARNED

- Cultural historians reconstruct the short-term processes (French: *événements*) like wars and building projects at a site. Annales archaeologists reconstruct long-term processes such as the development of pottery and farming techniques at a site.
- The Annales school was founded by Marc Bloch and Lucien Febvre. Febvre's most famous student was Fernand Braudel, whose seminal work is *The Mediterranean and the Mediterranean World in the Age of Philip II* (1949).
- For Annales archaeologists, every stratum in an excavation is a mix of short-, medium-, and long-term processes all paused at very different points in their development.

Emmanuel Le Roy Ladurie

STUDY QUESTIONS

1. How does the school of Annales archaeology differ from the school of cultural history?
2. What are some of the social institutions in the world of the Bible that would be important for Annales archaeologists?

PREVIEW: AGRICULTURE

- Neolithic Period
  - Natufians
  - Natufian Implements
  - Art
- Iron Age
  - Farming
  - Tools
  - Water Management
  - Herding
  - Land Ownership

Chapter 12 describes agriculture, the first example of a long-lasting institution reconstructed by Annales archaeologists. It shows how Neolithic peoples changed the course of human history, how Neolithic people hunted gazelle, and how Neolithic people prepared for and then celebrated their hunt. It also explains what it means to say that the economy of Hebrew and other Iron Age villages in the world of the Bible was dimorphic. Finally it looks at the inventions that allowed the Hebrews to farm hillsides and to build villages in locations without natural water sources.

12

Agriculture

THE NEOLITHIC PERIOD (8000–3800 B.C.E.)

The Natufian (10,300–8500 B.C.E.) and Neolithic (8000–3800 B.C.E.) periods in the world of the Bible were characterized by discovery and creativity. Slowly developing, but long-lasting ways to farm, to herd, to build houses, to make tools, to make pottery, and to bury the dead appear for the first time in the settlements of these remarkable cultures. The practical inventions of Natufian and Neolithic peoples not only produced radical changes in their daily life; they also inspired dramatic changes in the way that people understood life (McCarter 2007).

Natufian culture developed at the eastern end of the Mediterranean Sea just before the end of the Pleistocene era. It was a unique Stone Age culture whose villages, farming, and hunting techniques were the prototypes of both the cities of the Neolithic period and the agriculture that supported them. ∎

The Natufians

Dorothy Annie Elizabeth Garrod (1892–1968) was the first woman professor at Cambridge University (Cohen and Joukowsky, 2004). After excavating the Wadi en Natuf at Shukba between Jerusalem and Tel Aviv (Garrod 1957), she named these resourceful people *Natufians*. No written traditions from Natufian cultures have been recovered. Their stories are told only in stones.

Dorothy Annie Elizabeth Garrod

The Younger Dryas

At the end of the Ice Age, according to landscape archaeologists (see chapter 5), global temperatures rose and the glaciers covering Europe began to melt, causing the Mediterranean Sea to rise to its present level. Around 12,500 B.C.E., this gradual warming suddenly reversed. The Younger Dryas geological period—named for an alpine wildflower (Latin: *dryas*)—brought much colder temperatures, between fifty degrees above zero Fahrenheit and five degrees below zero, for some thirteen hundred years.

The Younger Dryas destroyed the wild cereals, legumes, almonds, acorns, pistachios, and cereals gathered by the Natufians, who reacted by clearing scrub and planting seeds. Gordon Hillman spent over twenty years investigating the remains of ancient food plants at a unique site at Abu Hureyra (Iraq). Seeds survived at Abu Hureyra because they had been accidentally charred in house fires before they were buried. They are the oldest cultivated seeds recovered by archaeologists. Wild seed varieties gathered as food gradually vanished at Abu Hureyra, before the cultivated varieties appeared. Those wild seeds most dependent on water were the first to die out, followed by the hardier ones. This was a clue to why the Natufian hunter-gatherer people turned to cultivating some of the foods they had previously collected from the wild. The wild grasses and seeds on which the people relied for food died out, and they were forced to start cultivating the most easily grown plants in order to survive (Simmons 2007).

The Natufians did not irrigate their crops. They took the wild seeds and sowed them where natural soil moisture would allow them to germinate and grow. Wild stands of these cereals, however, could not have continued to grow unaided in such locations because they would have been overgrown by native scrub. Therefore, these first farmers had to clear out the competing vegetation.

Natufian Implements

To harvest and process their crops the Natufians developed a technique to produce short blades, or microliths, by carefully knapping flint or obsidian. Microliths are geometric in shape—triangles, crescents, or trapezoids. The shape of a microlith can be used to date it.

Archaeologists recovered a sickle from one of the houses at Yiftahel (Israel). The handle was made from a cow's rib and the blade was flint. The blade shows no signs of having been used to harvest grain. Abrasives such as silica in the stems of plants generally create wear patterns on blades used by farmers (Howard 1999). But the sort of silica gloss charac-

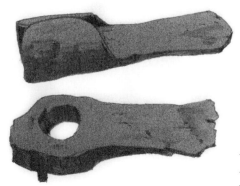

Iron plow point (top) and tool head, recovered at Beth Shemesh, 701–586 B.C.E. Drawing based on a photo by the author. University of Pennsylvania Museum.

164

teristic of sickles used in early agriculture is missing from this Natufian sickle blade. Natufian and Neolithic peoples also made stone mortars, grinders, and storage pits.

The Younger Dryas period also killed the great animals of the Pleistocene era—mammoths, mastodons, giant bison, and ground sloths. The Natufians therefore began to hunt smaller game. Archaeologists have recovered stone shaft straighteners or planes. These grooved stones were heated and then used in bending and straightening arrow shafts, which indicates that the Natufians had bows and arrows.

Hunting Gazelle

Two types of gazelle were popular with the Natufians, as well as deer, wild cattle, boar, asses, and ibex. They also hunted birds and fished in the Jordan River Valley (Firmage 1992).

The Natufians at Nahal Oren (Israel) seemed to have domesticated gazelles. Gazelle bones, including many immature animals, were numerous at the site. At some point, the Natufians changed from herding gazelles to herding goats. Goats graze more diverse plants than gazelles, and so were, no doubt, easier to herd. At most Natufian sites gazelles were hunted, not herded.

The quantity of gazelle, deer, or antelope bones at a site is a measure of the role that hunting played in ancient economies. Before animals were domesticated at Jericho (Palestine) between 8500 and 7500 B.C.E., for example, 37 percent of the meat consumed was gazelle. Between 7500 and 6000 B.C.E., after animals had been domesticated, less than 18 percent of the meat consumed at Jericho was gazelle. Between 2000 and 1550 B.C.E. only about 3.5 percent of meat consumed was gazelle.

The principal method of hunting gazelle in Syria, Jordan, the Negev (Israel), the Sinai (Egypt), and Saudi Arabia involved the use of large, triangle-shaped corrals into which the gazelle would be driven. During the 1920s airmail pilots named these structures *kites*. Natufians built one large kite around the Azraq Oasis (Jordan), on the boundary between the bush steppe and the black basalt desert, just west of the village of Azraq ad Duruz.

The kite head was a pit several hundred yards in circumference enclosed by a stone wall. Low walls one or two miles long formed the tails of the kite (T. J. Wilkinson 2003, 175–76). These tail walls were often only one or two stones high. Although these walls were far too low to serve as real barriers, gazelle avoided these rows of stones rather than jump them.

Natufians built their kites along the migration routes followed by gazelle. Key locations were around watering holes, or where natural

Paleontologists, who study human development, refer to early humans (or *hominids*) who stood upright rather than walking on all fours as *Homo erectus*. Louis and Mary Leakey recovered remains of these early humans, who lived five million years ago, in Kenya and Tanzania in Africa. Donald Johanson recovered the skeleton of "Lucy," who lived 3.2 million years ago, in Ethiopia.

The earliest human tools were also discovered in East Africa. These hand axes had round handles—shaped to fit comfortably into the palm of a human hand—and blades chipped or knapped to a cutting edge. Outside Africa, the earliest hand axes—manufactured about 1.5 million years ago—were recovered at Ubeidiya (Israel) at the site of an ancient lake just south of the Sea of Galilee. Early humans migrating out of Africa into Syria-Palestine brought the technology with them. ■

obstacles forced the gazelle off course. The gazelle would be herded between the widely separated tails, and then driven toward the head of the kite corral usually situated just beyond a slight rise and out of sight. Around the corral and along the tails were blinds where hunters waited. Trapped in the head of the corral the gazelle would be killed (Helms and Betts 1987).

> In a lament in the book of Psalms mourners beg Yahweh to hunt their enemies like gazelle into a kite corral (Hebrew: *madḥēpâ*; Ps 140:1-11 [Hebrew 140:1-12])
>
> *Complaint*
>
> ⁹Those who surround me wag their heads;
>
> *Petition*
>
> Let their lies overwhelm them!
> ¹⁰Let burning coals fall on them!
> Let them be flung into pits like gazelle, no more to rise!
> Do not let liars rule the land;
> Let death hunt down the violent like gazelle into a kite trap.

Sketch of a gazelle in limestone. 2-7/8" x 5-7/8". 10,000 B.C.E. Recovered from Umm Ez-Zuwetina Cave in Israel. Israel Museum.

The Natufians used animal bones and stones to make harpoons, fishhooks, and jewelry. Ostrich egg shells were turned into containers. There are a few human figurines made of limestone, but the favorite subject was the gazelle.

Neolithic Art

Neolithic people decorated the inside walls of their houses with spectacular paintings of their divine patrons, their human ancestors, people dying and rising from the dead, flowers, geometric patterns, imprints of hands, stars, erupting volcanoes, and hunts of wild animals. To pray for success before hunts and to celebrate success after them, Neolithic hunters shaped and then *hunted* small statues of gazelle and other animals and made elaborate wall paintings of successful hunts. In one large wall painting at Çatal Höyük (Turkey)—the *River Fork Tell*—a wild bull over six feet long is surrounded by hunters. The horns of such a great bull have been recovered at Ubeidiya (Israel). The span between the tips of the two horns is over five feet.

Ubeidiya is in the north of the Jordan River Valley southeast of the Sea of Galilee, a remnant of the prehistoric Lake Ubeidiya. Excavations at the site have revealed over sixty settlement layers from between 1,500,000 and 700,000 B.C.E. As a result of later earthquake activity these archaeological layers are now not horizontal, but almost vertical. ∎

Sketch of a Neolithic Bull Hunt. Wall painting recovered at Çatal Höyük, Turkey. 6500 B.C.E. The bull is six feet long.

Besides painting animals on walls and sketching them on stones, Neolithic artists also learned to shape animals in both clay and stone. A wonderful collection has been uncovered at a sanctuary in the Uvda Valley (Israel), a rich alluvial valley in the mountains northwest of Eilat. Abundant rainfall created a savannah where Neolithic people gathered grain and hunted deer, gazelle, asses, and birds (http://www.jewishvirtual library.org/jsource/Archaeology/eilat.html).

One open-air sanctuary in the Uvda Valley has a courtyard forty feet on a side surrounded by a low stone wall (http://mfa.gov.il/mfa/go.asp?MFAH00v30). Its corners are oriented to the four points of the compass. There were three cone-shaped jars full of ashes in the court-yard, and in the holy of holies there were sixteen upright stones each eight to twelve inches tall. Outside the courtyard, Natufian artists created a mosaic of sixteen life-size animals by pressing small, rectangular pieces of limestone into the ground. Fifteen leopards with square heads, huge eyes, four legs, and raised tails face east. One antelope with twisted horns faces west. These animal sculptures were not simply works of art or a record of a hunt. The stylized designed and geographical installation of these figures indicates that they were icons that channeled power from the divine plane to the human plane allowing Neolithic people to manage their daily life.

THE IRON AGE (1200–586 B.C.E.)

Neolithic culture ended when humans began to replace their flint tools and weapons with tools and weapons molded from copper. This marked the beginning of the Chalcolithic Age. *Chalcos* is the Greek word for "copper," and *lithos* is the Greek word for "stone" or "flint." During the Chalcolithic Age copper and flint were the raw materials used to manufactures tools and weapons. Agriculture, farming, and herding in the world of the Bible remained remarkably stable throughout the Chalcolithic and Bronze Ages. Political and economic change brought the Late Bronze Age (1500–1200 B.C.E.) to an end, and the Iron Age (1200–586 B.C.E.) began. When the Egyptians lost both military and economic control of Syria-Palestine, villagers there stopped farming and herding for them. They revolted against the surplus state culture that the Egyptians had imposed on them. After the cities along the coast that governed the villages were destroyed, villagers moved east toward the Jordan River and established a decentralized subsistence culture in the hills north of Jerusalem. Among these villagers were the Hebrews who become the ancestors of ancient Israel.

There is little artifact evidence that the villages in the hills of Judah were founded by outsiders or warriors; they were natives of Syria-Palestine and were farmers and herders. The economy of their villages was agricultural, not military. They left almost no weapons. They built few fortifications or monumental buildings. Their writing, language, and material culture link them to cultures found throughout Syria-Palestine. Archaeology suggests also that these villagers in the hills west of the Jordan River Valley were from cities along the coast, not nomads from the desert. They were social survivors who fled the famine, plague, and war that brought the Bronze Age to an end (Faust 2006).

Farming

The words for both the oak (Hebrew: *ʾallon, ʾelon*) and the terebinth (Hebrew: *ʾēlâ, ʾallâ*) are built on *ʾēl*, a word meaning "powerful," "divine," or "Creator." These great trees were divine gifts or divine images (Isa 44:14-17). ■

Farmers and herders were remarkably successful at maximizing their labor and spreading their risks. They cleared new areas of *maquis* brush and cultivated the land, using wooden or iron blades. They farmed a combination of wheat and barley, depending on the quality of the soil, the temperature, and the amount of rainfall. They tended fig and olive trees and skillfully managed grape vines on terraced hillside plots.

To feed a growing population required more farmland, and landscape archaeologists have determined that Iron Age villagers cleared the land of brush and trees—oak (Latin: *quercus ithaburensis, quercus calliprinos*), cypress, pine (Latin: *pinus halepensis*), and terebinth (Latin: *pistacia palestina*)—so they could plant grapes, olives, and cereal crops (Josh 17:16-18). This deforestation dramatically changed the appearance of the region.

The fertile red topsoil (Latin: *terra rossa*) in the hills was just over eighteen inches deep. *Terra rossa* is a Mediterranean soil containing red iron-rich clay usually deposited on top of limestone bedrock. The clay content of this soil allows it to hold moisture well, but it also erodes easily. ■

To convert the cleared slopes into level fields and to slow the process of erosion, villagers built retaining walls to create terraces (Hebrew:

mĕrômê śādeh [Judg 5:18]; *śĕdê tĕrûmōt* [2 Sam 1:21]), which were benches built on the slopes of hills. Walls were constructed parallel to the contours of the slopes. Infill or slope wash created deep, fertile soil beds behind the walls, and villagers used these for farming.

Tools

Iron Age villagers also learned to quarry ore and to forge iron. Although they continued to use bronze tools and weapons, iron required much less time and fuel to produce. They cast iron into axe heads to clear the land more easily. They shaped tips for their picks to dig canals more easily and cisterns for collecting rainwater. They molded iron tips for their plows to loosen the soil more easily for farming.

Water Management

Villagers without natural springs and wells depended on good water management to survive. Cenomanian limestone was formed one hundred million years ago at the bottom of seas more than four hundred feet deeper than they are today. Some villagers dug cisterns into the Cenomanian limestone bedrock because when moisture wets this kind of limestone it becomes water tight. Others lined their cisterns with plaster. To make plaster villagers dug large kilns into hillsides. They filled the kilns with firewood and limestone chunks. They had to keep these kilns fired for some three to six days at over 1600 degrees Fahrenheit to turn limestone into lime. Two tons of limestone and two tons of wood were needed to produce one ton of lime (Herr and Clark 2001). When lime is soaked in water before it is mixed with plaster and used to line cisterns, it becomes *slaked*, or water tight.

Herding

Village economy in the world of the Bible was *dimorphic*—a combination of farming and herding (King and Stager 2001, 112–22). Some villagers farmed, some herded. Herds included both black goats and fat-tailed Awassi sheep (Borowski 2003, 25–34). Sheep and goats are acclimated to the hot, dry climate of Syria-Palestine. They graze on grass during the wet season and on stubble left in the fields during the dry season. Herders

Goats are good companion grazers for sheep. Their grazing habits complement one another. Sheep, for example, pull up grass—roots and all—as they graze. Goats, however, simply browse the leaves of grass, and move quickly through a pasture without overgrazing it. In a mixed herd, sheep will follow the goats as they browse doing less damage to pasture (Gong, Hodgson, Lambert, and Gordon 1996). Likewise, goats eat weeds and other plants that sheep cannot digest. ■

also kept bulls, cows, oxen, and asses. Farmers used oxen to pull plows; they rode asses.

Sheep and goats were herded for milk, meat, hides, and wool. Herders sheared their sheep at the end of the wet season. After the sheep were shorn, herders paid their debts. Mesha, the ruler of Moab, paid his taxes to Israel in wool (2 Kgs 3:4). After Nabal's herds had been safely shorn, David asked him to pay him and his warriors for protecting the herders (1 Sam 25:2).

Land Ownership

Land ownership was governed by a theology common throughout the world of the Bible. Many cultures believed that all farmlands and pastures belonged to their divine patrons. These divine patrons then assigned farms and pastures (Hebrew: *nāḥălâ*) to each household. These lands could be inherited but not sold. Households could mortgage their farms and pastures, but only if they were able to repay the mortgage in less than seven years. At the end of that period, the land would revert to the original owner (Lev 25:8-55).

In the stories of Elisha in the books of Samuel–Kings (2 Kgs 8:1-6), Elisha tells a woman from Shunam to mortgage her land during a drought and to migrate to Philistia. Seven years later when she returned to Shunam, her creditor returned the land to her. Jeremiah uses the statute of limitations on mortgages as a pantomime or symbolic action. When the Babylonians invaded Judah, he went through enemy lines to reclaim land in Anathoth that his household had mortgaged even though it was about to be overrun (Jer 32:6-44). His pantomime challenged audiences to believe that despite the sense of impending doom settling over Judah as the Babylonians advanced, the people needed to have hope that Yahweh would restore their land and children.

CONCLUSION

Farming and herding practices in the world of the Bible were already centuries old when the first Hebrew villages appeared in Syria-Palestine. Although their worldview was a radical departure from worldviews reflected in the great cities of the Late Bronze Age, farming and herding in early Israel remained remarkably consistent with farming and herding in the Bronze Age and the Neolithic period before it. Farming and herding were long-lasting social institutions that developed very slowly and changed very little regardless of the shifts taking place in the short-term events and crossroads processes developing around them.

WHAT YOU HAVE LEARNED

- With their inventions of agriculture and pottery, Neolithic peoples changed the course of human history.
- Neolithic hunters invented a blind called a *kite* to hunt gazelle. They stampeded herds between narrowing lines of rocks leading to a deep pit surrounded by a wall.
- To pray for success before hunts and to celebrate success after hunts Neolithic hunters shaped small statues of gazelle and other animals and made elaborate wall paintings of successful hunts.
- The economy of Hebrew villages was *dimorphic* because villagers both farmed and herded to support their households.
- To farm steep hillsides more easily Hebrew villagers built terraces to level the soil.
- To build villages in locations without natural water resources the Hebrews learned to seal the walls of their cisterns with waterproof plaster.

STUDY QUESTIONS

1. What types of discoveries enable archaeologists to describe the people known as Natufians?
2. What effect did the Younger Dryas period have on the environment and inhabitants of Syria-Palestine?
3. What information in the Bible finds corroboration in the archaeology of Syria-Palestine concerning herding, farming, and land ownership?
4. How does the study of agriculture fare under the purview of Annales archaeology?
5. How does Neolithic art reflect the lifestyle and worldview of the people of that period?

PREVIEW: POTTERY

- Neolithic Pottery
  - Potter's Wheel
  - Godmother Figures
  - Cave Art
  - Skulls
  - Statues
- Creator as Potter
- Body and Soul
  - Greek Philosophy
  - Hebrew Concepts
  - Egyptian Traditions

Chapter 13 describes the development of pottery, a second example of a long-lasting institution studied by Annales archaeologists. It shows how the invention of the potter's wheel improved the quality of pots, and what, besides decoration, a slip or glaze did for pots. It also explains why pottery statues of Godmothers portray them with large breasts, distended abdomens, and heavy legs and hips; why Neolithic potters shaped images of their households from sticks and clay. The chapter also shows why the stories of Adam and Eve describe Yahweh creating as a potter, but what Yahweh uses that a human potter does not. It tells how the Bible thinks about the soul, in contrast to Greek philosophers, who considered the soul (Greek: psychē) to be the unique spiritual component of every human being. Finally, the chapter demonstrates what the ba *soul and the* ka *soul reflect in Egyptian psychology.*

13

Pottery

NEOLITHIC POTTERY

Natufian peoples shaped vessels, tools, baskets, and statues from wood, reeds, stone, and bone. As early as 5500 B.C.E., Neolithic peoples in Syria-Palestine discovered how to throw pottery (Wood 1992, 5:427–28; Franken 1992, 5:428–33). ("Throwing" derives from the Old Saxon term for "twist.") These potters knew how to distinguish between clay and other soils. They also knew how to mix and knead their clay so that it could be shaped into coils that they twisted on woven mats.

The handles or spouts of some pots were decorated with notches or incisions. After pots were shaped, they were carefully dried to a leather-hard consistency without cracking or shrinking. Some dried pots were painted with simple lines or geometric designs. A slip or glaze was applied to the outside surface of some pots to help waterproof the pot and make it more attractive. These coatings of colored, opaque, or transparent material were made from fine grained clays or sand containing trace elements of metals such as copper, iron, or lapis lazuli. The glaze on some pots was polished or burnished into the clay with a stone to give pots a lustrous sheen and to prevent the glaze from flaking off when the pots were fired.

Neolithic potters originally fired on open hearths. Later pottery was fired in enclosed kilns or ovens. Neolithic pottery from Jericho, for example, was fired in kilns, not in open fires (Franken 1992). Animal dung was used as a fuel to raise temperatures in the kiln to 1300–1700 degrees Fahrenheit to create a dark red glow in the clay.

The potter's wheel developed gradually. Neolithic potters probably graduated from coiling their pots on a mat to using a shallow bowl to build a coiled pot. The slow wheel was a simple turntable. Potters attached a wooden platform where potters shaped the clay to a stone bearing that fit into a stone socket. These wheels did not turn easily, and were only used for easier coiling. The speed of the slow wheel could be increased if one potter turned the table,

Kneading clay; after a wall painting from ancient Egypt, about 2500 B.C.E. See Victor Bryant's discussion of "The Origins of the Potter's Wheel" at http://www.ceramicstoday.com/articles/potters_wheel2.htm.

Lighting a kiln.

Emptying the kiln.

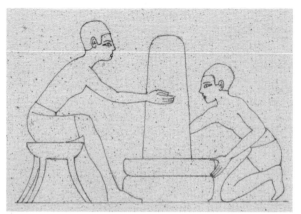

Slow wheel. One potter turns the wheel while another shapes the clay.

Fast wheel, with shaft, stabilizing bar, flywheel, and thrust-bearing assembly.

Kenamun, mayor of Thebes during the Eighteenth Dynasty (1550–1070 B.C.E.), was also in charge of the granaries of Karnak temple. The potters are part of a larger painting in his tomb showing the arrival at Thebes of a fleet of seagoing ships from Syria and the Aegean. ■

Çatal Höyük is a Neolithic city built between 6500 and 5700 B.C.E. along the edge of a small river south of the great salt depression in central Turkey and north of the fertile Konya Plain. The plain stretches from Çatal Höyük to the Hasan Dag volcanoes. It lies three thousand feet above sea level. The village was built in two areas, leaving two tells. The largest is thirty-two acres. The water in nearby crater lakes is brackish, but springs fed by rain in the hills north of the city provided fresh water. The city traded salt mined from Tuz Golu, a great salt lake; obsidian mined at Hasan Dag and Karaca Dag; and flint. ■

while another potter shaped the clay. A wall painting in the tomb of Kenamun at Thebes (Egypt) shows two potters working together on a slow wheel.

The fast wheel developed around 2000 B.C.E. (http://www.ceramics today.com/articles/potters_wheel2.htm). Two wheels were connected to a shaft. Potters turned the lower wheel with their feet and shaped their pots on the top wheel with their hands.

Pottery came in many shapes and sizes: dipping jugs, drinking cups, round pilgrim flasks, broad open bowls, cooking pots, and strainers for beer and wine. Enormous storage jars preserved grain. Smaller jars stored and shipped wine and olive oil.

Godmother Figures

Like herding, farming, and architecture, pottery making not only gave Neolithic people a reliable means of cooking, transporting, and storing food, but also changed the way they thought about human creation. An example of how Neolithic artists viewed pottery as a sacred science can be seen in their creation of a range of ceramics with human features.

Neolithic statues of the Godmother shaped from clay were common. Most are seated on a birthing chair. The only complete statue of a Godmother was recovered at Horvat Minha (Israel), where the Yarmuk River flows into the Jordan River from the east. The Godmother is seated, although the chair itself is missing. Like similar statues, she is steatopygous, or large-hipped. Her breasts are pendulous, her abdomen is

Far left. *Godmother figurine with hips and thighs representing a child bearer and wearing a pointed cap. She holds her left breast to nurse all the humans to whom she has given birth. Munhata, Jordan Valley. Clay (6th millennium B.C.E.). Stone Age. Location: Israel Museum (IDAM), Jerusalem, Israel. Photo Credit: Erich Lessing / Art Resource, NY.*

Near left. *Godmother represented on a birthing chair; original: clay, 6000–5500 B.C.E. From Çatal Höyük.*

distended, and her legs are heavy. She is a child-bearer, with her left hand lifting her breast to nurse her children.

The most famous ceramic statue of a Godmother was recovered from Çatal Höyük (Turkey). She is giving birth seated on a birthing chair and using two leopards to support herself in the squatting position. Her hips are wide from child-bearing. Her breasts are full from nursing. She is the Mother of All Living (Gen 3:20).

Archaeologists sometimes refer to statues of women birthing or nursing as fertility figurines. Women especially honor the Godmothers of their cultures for their fertility—the ability to conceive and give birth to humans. The statues not only honor the Godmothers, but are used by women to petition their Godmother for fertility.

Cave Art

The earliest painting of a leopard was made in Chauvet Cave in the Ardeche Gorge (France) (http://www.culture.gouv.fr/culture/arcnat/chauvet/en/). The cave was discovered in 1994, and explored by Jean Clottes, a science adviser to France's Ministry of Culture, in 1998. The leopard is one of 416 paintings of predators such as rhinos, lions, cave bears, and mammoths in a string of three chambers, seventeen hundred feet long, as well as one connecting gallery and three vestibules.

Most cave art depicts hunted animals. These animals, however, are not eaten. They are predatory, dangerous animals, whose strength and power Stone Age artists were trying to capture. At least one-third of

By reenacting both the creation of the world and human creation, traditional cultures remind themselves of their role as co-creators with their divine patrons (Eliade 1959, 68–113). Creation is never a past event but an ongoing, present event in which every generation participates. Humans and their world are annually re-created. Each year they return to that first moment of creation. All the failures of the preceding year are destroyed, and everything starts over in perfect condition. These celebrations of the New Year are acts of hope. Failure exists, but it is not permanent. ∎

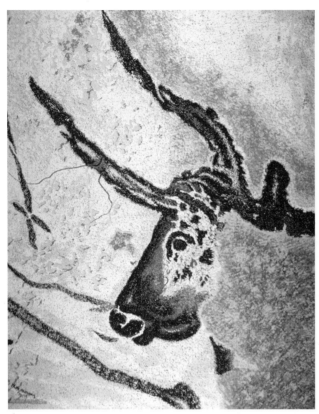

Bull. Serigraphic transcription of cave painting. Location: Lascaux Caves, Perigord, Dordogne, France. Photo Credit: Douglas Mazonowicz / Art Resource, NY.

the buildings in Strata VII–VIII at Çatal Höyük are sanctuaries. The walls and floors of these sanctuaries were repeatedly refinished with white plaster. Some sanctuary walls were covered with paintings that were annually painted and repainted. In Stratum VII there is a pair of painted leopards. These leopards have been repeatedly replastered and repainted. The repeated plastering and repainting is an indication that this artwork is not simply record keeping. The repetition is a form of storytelling that reenacts divine events like the ritual of bull jumping in Minoa or bullfighting in Spain (Roaf 1990, 45).

Skulls

Neolithic artists also plastered human skulls and shaped life-size human bodies from reeds and clay. These works of art are not portraits; they are powerful representations of the incarnation of the divine in human form, and they linked the living and the dead. They reconstructed the features on skulls with plaster. Many lower jaws and the teeth have been removed from the skulls. The eye sockets are inlayed with cowrie shells or pellets of clay. Carefully shaped bases angle the skulls in a particular direction. Some of the skulls are painted with red or brown iron oxide. The top and back of the skulls were usually left untouched, but occasionally they were painted. Most of the plastered skulls were found below the floors of houses.

The dead of the Neolithic village of Jericho were buried beneath the floors of houses or in the fill of abandoned buildings (http://ancientnear east.tripod.com/86.html). The graves frequently contained more than one burial. Some of the skeletons in these multiple burials were articulated, that is, each bone was in its correct anatomical position; some were not. The skulls had been removed from many of the skeletons.

The practice of separating skulls from skeletons and reburying the disordered skeletal remains in collective graves was widespread during the Neolithic period, but only the skulls recovered at Jericho, Tall Ramad (Syria), and Beisamun (Israel) were plastered.

Seven skulls were found buried together under the floor of one room of a house and two more in another room of the same house at Jericho. No other detached skulls were excavated anywhere else at Jericho. The jaws of these skulls had been removed from all but one, and the face and base of the skulls were covered with plaster. The features were reconstructed to give the appearance of a living human being. One other plastered skull was found at the north end of the mound, making a total of ten. Five of these skulls were adult males.

Plastered skull buried under the floor of a house in Beisamun, Upper Jordan Valley. Neolithic. Location: Israel Museum (IDAM), Jerusalem, Israel. Photo Credit: Erich Lessing / Art Resource, NY.

Statues

In addition to the plastered skulls recovered at Jericho, statues from the Neolithic period were also recovered in 1983 at ʿAin Ghazal (Jordan). The site was initially discovered during the building of a new road in the 1970s on the northeast outskirts of Amman (Jordan) (http://www.ucl.ac.uk/archaeology/). ʿAin Ghazal is almost thirty acres and was occupied from 7250 to 5000 B.C.E. Radiocarbon tests date charcoal in the pit with the statues to 6000 B.C.E.

There are two kinds of statues: dumpies and figures. Dumpies are about a foot high; figures, three feet high. Dumpies have solid, roughly shaped and unpainted bodies. Figures have well-defined arms and legs. The bodies of the statues were painted with red iron oxide, black carbon, and white lime. The heads of both dumpies and figures have detailed eyes, noses, mouths, and ears. Their eyes were painted with black tar and blue copper oxide. They are elliptical and have round irises. Their noses turn up at the ends and the nostrils are simply two narrow cuts. Their mouths are also just narrow cuts. Their ears are small, unshaped knobs.

The statues are shaped from plaster over a core of branches tied with string. Although this organic material has decayed, it left impressions in the plaster. The cores in the dumpies were one bundle of branches. The cores of the figures were several bundles tied together. The heads and necks of the cores were also reinforced with string. The branches in the cores stuck out from the bases of the statues so that they could be mounted into plaster floors. Some figures were arranged in groups: father, mother, and child surrounded by dumpies.

The statues were carefully buried in a building inside the village. Below the pit were two plastered floors, but there is no evidence that the statues were used in the building where they were buried, or in any of the surrounding buildings.

THE CREATOR AS POTTER

The stories of Adam and Eve (Gen 2:4—4:2) describe the epoch primeval with metaphors of pottery making, farming, and herding drawn from the Neolithic period when Stone Age humans took two momentous steps toward civilization. They learned to farm and they learned to make pottery. When Neolithic people invented farming and pottery, they created a new world. Consequently, creation stories told during the subsequent Bronze Age (3400–1200 B.C.E.) often describe divine patrons as farmers when they create the world and as potters when they create humans.

The metaphor of the creator as a potter is modified, however, so that the techniques of the divine and human potters are similar but not identical. For example, all potters work with two ingredients: one is firm and the other fluid. Human potters mix clay with water. Divine potters use a variety of thinners. In the stories of Atrahasis, the divine midwife, Nintu-Mami, thins her clay with blood (Atrahasis 1:229–34). In the stories of Gilgamesh, the Godmother, Aruru, uses saliva (Gilg. 1:30–40). In the stories of Adam and Eve, Yahweh wets the clay with only the condensation created by breathing on it.

A STORY OF THE ʾĀDĀM AS A FARMER
(Gen 2:4-17)

Sterility affidavit (Gen 2:4-6)

When Yahweh, Our Creator,
    Began to create the heavens and the
        earth,
There were no orchards,
    There were no fields of grain.
There were no planting rains,
    There were no harvesting rains.
There was no one to work the soil,
    There was no soil to work.

There was only water pouring through
    dikes of clay,
    There was only water flooding the
      earth.

Cosmogony (Gen 2:7-14)

Then Yahweh sculpted an *ʾādām* from
    clay,
    Made it live by breathing moisture
      onto the clay.
Yahweh, Our Creator, built a plantation,
    Yahweh installed the *ʾādām* in Eden.
There were trees delightful to see,
    Fruit good to eat.
The Tree of Life was in the middle of
    Eden,
    And the Tree of the Knowledge of
      Good and Evil.
There were rivers,
    Abundant water for the garden.
The Pishon flowing through the desert of
    Havilah in Arabia,
    The Gihon running through the land
      of Cush in Ethiopia.
The Tigris rolling east of Asshur in Iraq,
    The Euphrates.
There was gold,
    Twenty-four carat gold.
There was the gemstone bdellium.
    There was lapis lazuli.

Covenant (Gen 2:15-17)

Finally Yahweh, Our Creator, gave Eden
    to the *ʾādām* to cultivate,
    The *ʾādām* was to care for the planta-
      tion of Yahweh.
Yahweh decreed: *You shall eat from any*
    tree in Eden,
    Except the Tree of Knowledge of Good
      and Evil.
Anyone who eats from this tree shall die.

(*translations by the author*)

In the Bible the living are moist. Blood, sperm, tears, and saliva distinguish the living from the dead, the moist from the dry. In the stories of Adam and Eve, Yahweh is a divine potter who shapes the ʾādām from clay and then gently moistens and polishes the ʾādām with the saliva that condenses on the surface of the ʾādām when Yahweh breathes on it.

BODY AND SOUL

Pottery making revolutionized human life. Comparing the body to clay did not degrade it, but elevated it. Comparing the soul to the saliva carried in human breath did not shame it, but honored it.

Greek Philosophy

Greek philosophers—and subsequently Christian teachers—thought of the soul as completely independent of the body. For example, once the body died, the soul went on living. In the world of the Bible, the soul and body are completely integrated. One cannot live without the other. Even in death, body and soul remain joined together.

Greek philosophers considered the soul to be good and noble, but the body to be bad and ignoble. Consequently, Christian teachers stressed that it was important to subdue the body by punishing it with forms of physical torture like wearing uncomfortable clothes and whipping the body until it bled. In the world of the Bible, the body and soul are equally good and noble. They are best friends, not rivals. Finally, Greek philosophers considered the body to be material and the soul to be spiritual. Consequently, Christian teachers used only the unseen wind or human breath as metaphors for the soul; they avoided any metaphors connected with matter or the human body.

Hebrew Concepts

There are two important words for soul in Hebrew: *rûaḥ* and *nephesh*. Both words are connected with the throat (Schroer and Staubli 2001, 56–67). The soul is not only something that can be seen, the human throat; it can also be heard when a human trills (Psalms 103–104). Of all the things that pass through the throat, the most important is breath and the saliva it carries. Life comes into the body on the air humans breathe and in the saliva it contains. Life leaves with the last breath and the last drop of moisture in the body (Ps 69:1; 1 Kgs 17:21-22; Gen 35:18). Where there is no breath and where there is no saliva or blood or tears or sperm, there is no life.

The Hebrew word *nephesh* occurs more than 750 times in the Bible with a rainbow of very concrete and observable meanings (B. E. Reid 1996). For example, the *nephesh* soul reacts emotionally to each human experience, and its reaction is observable in the way breathing patterns change (Exod 6:9; Prov 14:29; Judg 8:3; Mic 2:7). The *nephesh* soul is also a synonym for the human personality. Some *nephesh* souls are unfaithful (Hos 4:12); some are faithful (Isa 28:6); some are arrogant (Dan 5:20); some are jealous (Num 5:14); some are despairing (Job 7:11).

The very limited understanding of the soul as the immaterial and personal part of a human being emerges in the world of the Bible only after the Hebrews were conquered by Persia and then by Greece. When the Bible was translated from Hebrew into Greek, for example, *nephesh* was translated by the Greek word: *psychē*—over six hundred times, virtually erasing all the rich and diverse understandings of soul in the world of the Bible.

Khnum (R), the divine potter wearing a ram's mask, creates Hatshepsut (L) and her ka soul (R) on his potter's wheel. Heqet (L), the divine midwife, brings Hatshepsut to life by touching her with the ankh sign.

Egyptian Traditions

Some of the most fascinating insights into understanding the richness of soul theology in the world of the Bible come from Egypt. In the birth story of Pharaoh Hatshepsut (1473–1458 B.C.E.) written on the walls of her funeral chapel at Deir el Bahri (Egypt), Hatshepsut's Godfather, Amen, orders the divine potter, Khnum, to shape both the human body and the *ka* soul of his daughter.

CREATION OF HATSHEPSUT

Amen-Re summoned Khnum, the divine potter, who shaped human bodies. Fashion for me the body of my daughter and a *ka* soul . . . worthy of her dignity and glory.

O Amen-Re, answered Khnum, it shall be done as you have said. The beauty of your daughter shall surpass that of the members of the divine assembly and shall be worthy of her dignity and glory.

So Khnum fashioned the body of Hatshepsut and her *ka* soul. They were identical twins, and more beautiful than any other woman on the face of the earth. Khnum fashioned them from clay on his potter's wheel. Heqet, the divine midwife, knelt by his side holding the *ankh* sign of life toward the clay to bring Hatshepsut to life.

The main constituents of a human being in Egypt were the body (Egyptian: *khat*), its *ka* soul, and its *ren* name, which remained always in close proximity to each other even in the tomb, and the *shut*, the *ba* soul, the *sahu*, and the *akh*, which were more mobile and independent. The connotations of *ba* soul, *ka* soul, *sahu* and *akh* overlap and evolve. There are no exact English equivalents for these Egyptian terms.

Body (Egyptian: *Khat*)

As the representative of the divine assembly, Khnum shaped the *khat* body and its *ka* soul on a potter's wheel and then used the sperm to insert them into the mother's womb. The Egyptians viewed the body as spiritual, not physical, from its conception to its death. The biological aspects of the body's functions were of little interest. Instead, Egyptians studied the helpful and threatening invisible spirits that lived in the human body. They conceived of life on the human plane continuing on the divine plane after death. Everything people used on the human plane was buried with them for their use in the afterlife. Therefore, Egyptians preserved the bodies of their pharaohs and other wealthy people as mummies (Egyptian: *saH*) so that they could be raised from the dead in the afterlife. They also buried small statues of the field and household slaves (Egyptian: *ushabtis*) of the dead. They too were raised from the dead in the afterlife to continue to serve their masters.

Khnum is the divine potter with the head of a ram. The Egyptian word *khnum* means to create or to create all things that are and all things that shall be. Khnum, the divine potter, represented the divine assembly of Egypt when shaping humans on his potter's wheel.

Khnum, husband of Satis and father of Satis, was the divine patron of Elephantine Island and the rapids it created in the Nile River. Egyptians believed that the annual Nile floods began in a cavern beneath the island. ■

Page from the Book of the Dead of Hunefer, from Thebes, Egypt, 19th Dynasty, ca. 1275 B.C.E. To the left, Anubis brings Hunefer into the judgment area. Anubis is also shown supervising the judgment scales. Hunefer's heart, represented as a pot, is being weighed against a feather, the symbol of Maat or "what is right." Location: British Museum, London, Great Britain. Photo Credit: © British Museum / Art Resource, NY.

Ammit was portrayed with the head of crocodile, the torso of a leopard, and the hindquarters of a hippopotamus. Ammit sat beside the Scales of Justice in front of the throne of Osiris while Anubis weighed the souls of the dead. ∎

Before moving bodies to their tombs, priests celebrated the ritual of Opening of the Mouth. This enabled the deceased to testify to the virtues of the dead they met the members of the divine assembly during their twelve-hour journey from the human plane to the divine plane.

The most important part of the body was the heart (Egyptian: *jb*). Intelligence and conscience resided in the heart. The heart gave human life direction. Following one's heart meant living a full life. When the heart got tired, the body died. When a dead person began the journey into the underworld, the heart, as a record of a person's moral past, was weighed by Anubis against a feather representing Maat. If the heart was too heavy, Anubis fed the soul to Ammit, which prevented the dead from ever entering the afterlife. Priests did not remove the hearts of the dead from their bodies. They simply place a scarab over the heart so that it would not testify against the dead during the journey to the afterlife.

Status (Egyptian: *Ren*)

The name (Egyptian: *ren*) gave humans their social status. Only when humans had *ren* names could they have relations with others. Without a name, a human was not alive. Every status required a separate name. Osiris, the divine patron of the afterlife, for example, had one hundred different names. Names had divine power. Knowing a person's names gave one power over that person. Divine patrons bestowed names on their human clients that were kept secret even from their human mothers. Egyptians carved their names into the walls of their tombs so that they would last forever. Saying the names of the dead kept them alive. Erasing these names prevented the dead from entering the afterlife.

Personality (Egyptian: *Ba*)

The *ba* soul was associated with divinity and power. This *ba* was the immortal force inherent in human beings that made up human personalities. Each *ba* soul was unique. It entered a person's body with the breath of life, and it left at the time of death.

The *ba* soul was generally represented in the form of a bird with a human head perched on trees planted by the tomb, but it could assume any shape it wished. It had the ability to take on different forms. Like human imagination and human dreams, the *ba* soul could go virtually anywhere. The *ba* soul of the deceased was able to move freely between the underworld and the physical world, but it always returned to its body to share the stories of its experiences. Some members of the divine assembly had many *ba* personalities. Originally, members of Egypt's divine assembly who manifested themselves anonymously to humans were called *ba* revelations. Later, the visible forms that these divines assumed were called the *ba* of Re.

Soul (Egyptian: *Ka*)

The *ka* is usually translated as "soul" or "double"—an invisible friend. *Ka* is pronounced like the Egyptian word for "bull," a symbol of fertility. Therefore, the *ka* soul was a powerful life-creating force. A *ka* would live on after the physical body had died. When people died, they met their *ka*.

During the life of the body, the House of the *ka* was the body's tomb. Like the *khat* body, the *ka* soul ate and drank. Egyptians left offerings of food, drink, and worldly possessions in tombs for the *ka* to use.

The *ka* soul was a constant companion of the body. Paintings of pharaohs and Horus always show their *ka* soul written behind their names.

Shadow (Egyptian: *Shut*)

The body and its shadow soul were inseparable. This pitch-black shadow (Egyptian: *shut*) was not an ordinary shadow. The *ba* soul and the shadow soul are depicted leaving the tomb of the dead together. *Shut* shadows were a blessing for those who could rest in them in a hot country like Egypt. The shadows of divine patrons protect their human clients. Egyptians considered their pharaohs to be the shadows of Horus, and they referred to Amarna as "the shadow of Re."

Star (Egyptian: *Akh*)

The *akh* star belongs to the afterlife; the *khat* body belongs to this life. The *khat* body is buried, while the *akh* star, the Shining One, ascends into the night sky. It is the part of the body least bound to the others, but it is just as important as the others for assuring the immortality of the deceased.

The members of the divine assembly are *akh* stars. Pharaohs, having a divine nature, became *akh* stars and joined the stars after the demise of their mortal bodies, but later ordinary mortals too attained this status when they became transfigured dead.

Psyche (Egyptian: *Sahu*)

The *sahu* soul is immortal. It is a personification of the human psyche, which motivates humans to take action.

The Hymn to the Atum tells the story of the birth of the first nine members of Egypt's divine assembly (Matthews and Benjamin 2006, 7–9). In the story, the Sun (Egyptian: *Re Atum*) creates Father Wind (Egyptian: *Shu*) by sneezing, and Mother Rain (Egyptian: *Tefnut*) by spitting. They give birth

183

to Father Earth (Egyptian: *Geb*) and Mother Sky (Egyptian: *Nut*). Father Earth and Mother Sky are the parents of four: Father Osiris, Mother Isis, Father Seth, and Mother Nephthys. Horus is the son of Father Osiris and Mother Isis, who are both brother and sister and husband and wife. The story ends with these nine (Greek: *ennead*) giving birth to all the multitude of the land. ■

CONCLUSION

Like farming and herding, pottery making was a process that developed slowly and changed little in contrast to the rapidly changing short-term events and the crossroads processes. In addition, like farming and herding, pottery making was not simply a technical skill; it was a genuine reflection of how peoples in the world of the Bible looked at their lives and understood their relationship to their divine patrons. Pottery not only made their lives more humane; pottery enriched their ways of thinking about themselves and about their divine patrons. Pottery making was at once a simple and yet profound lesson about both creatures and their Creator.

WHAT YOU HAVE LEARNED

- Wheels allowed potters to work more quickly and to throw pots with thinner walls.
- Slips and glazes not only added decoration to the outside walls of pots; they also waterproofed them.
- Statues of Godmothers portrayed them with large breasts, distended abdomens, and heavy hips and legs to emphasize that they are the mothers of all humans.
- Neolithic potters shaped images of their households from sticks and clay to reenact their creation.
- The stories of Adam and Eve describe Yahweh as a potter who creates humans from clay and saliva. Human potters use clay and water.
- Unlike Greek philosophy, which considers the soul to be exclusively spiritual, the Bible gives the concept of the soul a whole range of meanings most of which are very physical.
- Like human imagination and dreams, *ba* souls in Egyptian psychology are birds who can fly anywhere, but they always return to their bodies with their stories. *Ka* souls are the best friends to their human bodies and remain with them throughout life and death.

STUDY QUESTIONS

1. What kinds of objects did Neolithic peoples make from clay?
2. Give some examples of the Creator being depicted as a potter.
3. What were the Greek ideas about the soul and the body?
4. How did Hebrew concepts about the soul differ from those of the Greeks?
5. How was the Egyptian view of the afterlife reflected in their practices relating to death?

PREVIEW: ARCHITECTURE

- Natufian Architecture
  - Crannogs
- Bronze Age Architecture
  - Arad House
- Iron Age Architecture
  - Landscape Archaeologists
  - Pillared Houses
  - Households
  - Work of Lawrence Stager

Chapter 14 describes a third example of a long-lasting institution reconstructed by Annales archaeologists. The chapter explains how humans in the Neolithic, Bronze, and Iron Ages each had unique styles of domestic architecture, and how the pillared house common in the villages of ancient Israel and throughout Syria-Palestine during the Iron Age is not only a practical and efficient dwelling but also a reflection of the social structure of marriage and daily life in the household.

14

Architecture

During the Neolithic period (8,000–3800 B.C.E.) the Natufians and other Neolithic peoples colonized the Negeb at Gebel Maghara and Har Harif in the Sinai, at Nahal Oren and Megiddo in the Carmel Mountains, at Kefar Giladi and Banias in the Galilee, at Beisamun near Lake Hula, at Yiftahel and Horvat Minha on the Jordan River, at Shaʿar ha-Golan on the Yarmuk River, at Jericho and Gilgal in the Jordan Valley, at Abu Ghosh near Jerusalem, and at Nahal Hemar on the Dead Sea.

Natufian villages and camps have been excavated at Tell Abu Hureira, Mureybat, and Yabrud III in Syria; Hayonim Terrace, Ain Mallaha, Beidha, Ein Gev, Hayonim Nahal Oren, Mugharet el Wad, Shuqba, and Salibiya I in Israel; Jericho on the West Bank; and Jiita III, Borj el-Barajné, Saaidé, and Aamiq II in Lebanon. From this homeland in Syria-Palestine, the Natufians traded abroad for obsidian from Turkey, shellfish from the Nile River Valley, and malachite beads.

Smaller camps were used for hunting and foraging. For example, the Valley Cave (Arabic: *Mugharet el Wad*) is the largest of the Mount Carmel caves. Natufian households used both the Valley Cave and the broad terrace in front of it as a camp.

The first excavations at Nahal Oren, six miles south of Haifa, in 1941 identified remains of Natufian culture. Nahal Oren was repeatedly occupied and then abandoned. Curiously, most humans who occupied the site lived outside rather than inside the cave. There were few natural resources at Nahal Oren. Not only was there little to support permanent settlements of farmers and herders, but there was also little to support hunters and gatherers. Little grain was recovered at the site, and there is little soil around the cave suitable for growing grain. Consequently, it is hard to explain where the wheat recovered at the site was grown.

Natufians dug their houses into the ground on a stone foundation with a roof made of branches. No trace of the mud brick characteristic of the later Neolithic period has been found. These round houses were nine to eighteen feet in diameter with a round or rectangular fire pit in the center.

Natufian villages covered about two-tenths of an acre, or an area of thirty yards square. These villages housed some one hundred to one hundred fifty people. Above the ground, Natufian houses may have looked like crannogs—dwellings built along lakesides in Scotland, Ireland, and Wales after 3000 B.C.E. Crannogs were roundhouses of wood and branches supported on stilts driven into the lake bed. Sometimes, in place of stilts, tons of rocks were piled onto the lake bed to make an island foundation for the crannog. Several hundred crannog sites have been identified, but only a few have been excavated.

Neolithic peoples settled Beisamun (Israel) on the west shore of Lake Hula around 7000 B.C.E. The village covers some thirty acres. Nonetheless, there is less than two and one-half feet of human settlement debris.

Crannog

There are rectangular stone-walled houses with plaster floors which were widely spaced along the lakeside. One of these had two rooms with a hearth and the remains of two plastered skulls and several secondary burials beneath its floor. One of the skulls belonged to an adult female.

Yiftahel (Israel) was settled on the northern coast after 6500 B.C.E. The site was abandoned about 6000 B.C.E. shortly before the invention of pottery. Large rectangular houses found at the site show that these Neolithic people knew how to make and use lime-based plaster.

At Çatal Höyük, Neolithic peoples built single-story, rectangular houses with roofs supported by wooden beams. Most were built with a flat roof, which provided working space for food preparation.

Houses did not have a door but were entered through openings in the roofs that were reached using ladders. After entering their houses, villagers pulled the ladder down into their houses to keep the inhabitants safe. Inside the houses were benches of firmly packed soil running along the walls for sleeping. Villagers were buried in the benches where they slept.

BRONZE AGE ARCHITECTURE

During the Bronze Age, houses were built using the Arad House blueprint. The outside walls formed a rectangle. The door was in one of the long sides. A rectangular building with a door in its long side is called a *broad room* floor plan. There were low benches running along the inside walls of Arad Houses. During the night, benches were used for sleeping. During the day, they were used for storage. None of the benches at Arad was used for burial. Floors of Arad Houses were some two feet below ground level. People had to step down from the street into their houses. The floors were not paved but were covered with packed soil. The flat roofs of Arad Houses were supported by a single wooden pillar that was set on a single stone base. The base kept the pillar from drilling into the soil and allowing the roof to sag or collapse.

Doors in an Arad House were either carved from a single shaped stone or built with wood. The top post fit into a socket in the lintel (Hebrew: *mašqôp*) above the door, and the bottom post into a socket in the threshold (Hebrew: *sap, miptān*). The lintel was supported by two doorposts (Hebrew: *mězûzôt*).

Walled courtyards surrounded the doors of Arad Houses. There were stone work tables in the courtyards, which archaeologists found littered with flint, bone, and copper tools. Women used stone mortars and pestles for grinding grains, spindle whorls for spinning thread, shuttles for weaving, and needles for sewing. Men used sickles with toothed flint blades for harvesting grain, flint scrapers for cleaning hides, drills for making jewelry from shells and beads, and awls for leatherwork. Two jars of jewelry were also recovered from the site.

Model of a shrine, shaped like a house, from Arad. Pottery. Early Bronze period (3400–2000 B.C.E.). Location: Israel Museum (IDAM), Jerusalem, Israel. Photo Credit: Erich Lessing / Art Resource, NY.

IRON AGE ARCHITECTURE

Landscape archaeologists walked the surface of the some sixteen hundred square miles in the hills north of Jerusalem and west of the Jordan River recording the number of village sites and the size of these sites. Using these calculations they discovered that, at the beginning of the Iron Age, the population there was growing about two percent a year. Some twenty twelve-acre, Late Bronze villages cramped into less than thirty square miles were relaced by more than one hundred one-acre, Iron Age villages sprawling over seventy-six square miles. The population expanded from some forty thousand people in 1200 B.C.E. to some eighty thousand people by 1000 B.C.E.

Landscape archaeologists study the development of the land itself, including the impact that humans have on its development. Landscape archaeologists study the way humans who live on the land describe their land and the way humans modify and idealize their land. Landscape archaeologists reconstruct the dynamic relationship between the land as

An isotope is a variation of a standard element. For example, oxygen (O^2) is the standard element; ozone (O^3) is an isotope. Over time some elements convert into isotopes. The rate of conversion is standard. For example the conversion of the standard element of Carbon (C^{12}) into the isotope Carbon 14 (C^{14}) is used to date once living material such as leather or wood. ∎

a whole and the humans who use it (T. J. Wilkinson 2003). They use climate; vegetation; isotopes recovered from lakes, caves, and the sea bottom; pollen from lakes; and coastline movement to chart landscape changes. They also use aerial photography and satellite imagery to reconstruct the development of the land. Once the changes in a particular environment have been reconstructed, Landscape archaeologists look for causes. Some causes are natural; some are human. Natural disasters are events such as earthquakes, floods, or drought. Human impact on the land includes terracing the hillsides for farms, cutting down trees to plant crops, diverting rivers for irrigation, mining, and the development of sanctuaries.

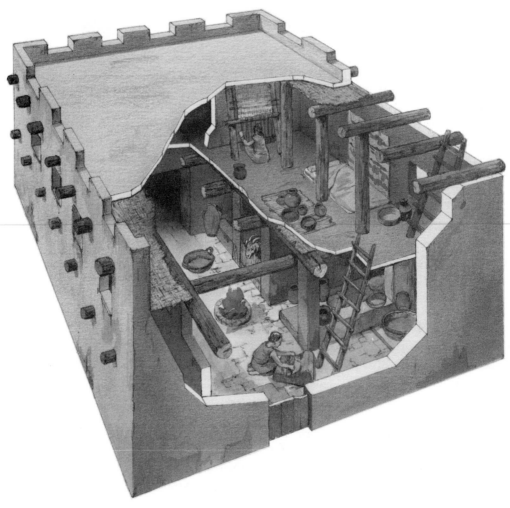

Cut-away of pillared house.

Houses

Pillared or four-room houses were the signature domestic architecture during the Iron Age. They were also a model of the worldview of the villagers who built them. The pillared house is a prime example of a long-lasting institution studied by Annales archaeologists. For example, the Romans (37 B.C.E.–324) installed the same style stone door in their fortress at Araq (Jordan) as was used in pillared houses during the Iron Age (1200–586 B.C.E.). Similarly, villagers around Antioch (Turkey) today still roof their houses with brush and adobe and reseal these roofs with stone rollers just as Iron Age villagers did.

Pillared houses were rectangular with five hundred to eight hundred square feet of living space (King and Stager 2001, 21–84). There was enough room for two adults and two children; each would have about ninety to one hundred square feet of living space.

Several houses grouped together around a shared courtyard formed a household (Hebrew: *bêt ʾāb, bayit*: Arabic: *zaʿila*). There were as many as thirty people from four generations in a household (Judges 17–18). Villages (Hebrew: *mišpāḥôt*) were made up of as many households as the natural resources (Hebrew: *naḥălâ*) at the site could support (1 Kings 21). The seven villages in the tribe of Manasseh, for example, each had some forty square miles of resources.

Iron Age villagers secured themselves by forming tribes (Hebrew: *šēbeṭ, maṭṭeh*) to spread work and to distribute risk (Josh 7:14-18; Jer 32:6-15). Villagers helped one another clear land and build terraces and breed and herd livestock. They sent warriors to rescue one another when they were attacked and legal guardians (Hebrew: *gōʾēl*) to restore households at risk from the untimely death of their fathers. They sent deputies (Hebrew: *gōʾēl haddām*) to arrest and execute murderers.

Iron Age villagers built their pillared houses on foundations of two or three courses of field stones. The outside walls were about three feet thick. They were framed with large limestone blocks stacked into piers or pillars. The windows (1 Kgs 6:4; Ezek 41:26) or spaces between the pillars were filled with rubble (Isa 33:15; Prov 17:28). Alternating solid pillars with loose stone fill allowed the walls to bend without breaking during earthquakes.

The main door (Hebrew: *delet, petaḥ*) in a pillared house was built into the narrow end of the outside wall. Like doors in Arad Houses, doors in pillared houses were either carved from a single shaped stone or built with wood. Pivot posts extended from the top and bottom on one side of the door.

There were two kinds of ovens—the *tabun* oven and the *tannur* oven. Both were made from *terra cotta*, which was like clay hardened to make bricks today. Each oven was shaped like a haystack. Both had a chimney hole at the top.

Both *tabun* and *tannur* ovens were used for baking bread. In the *tabun*, loaves were placed on pebbles scattered inside the oven. The opening at the base of the oven and the chimney were sealed. The oven was heated from the outside by stacking wood, charcoal, or manure chips against the oven. In contrast, in the *tannur*, the fire was kindled inside. Dough was slapped against the walls of the oven to bake just as the people of South Asia do today to bake Naan bread. ■

Carved ivory depicting a woman at a window. Ninth–eighth century B.C.E. From Nimrud. Once part of a piece of furniture. Ivory, 11 x 8.85 cm. Inv. AN 118159. Location: British Museum, London, Great Britain. Photo Credit: © British Museum / Art Resource, NY.

The door opened into a rectangular workroom in the center of the house. Workrooms were ten to twelve feet wide. Here villagers pressed olives and grapes and ground grain. Material remains from workrooms include silos dug into the floor and stone hand mills for grinding grain into flour. There were also ovens for baking bread and fireplaces for cooking vegetables, olives, grain, figs, beans, lentils, lamb, and goat.

Some workroom floors were packed earth (French: *terre pisé*), layers of ash, and clay; some were plastered. Ceilings were five to six feet above the floors and supported by beams of stone or wood running from the outside walls and supported by pillars on either side of the work room. These two rows of pillars created side rooms some five to ten feet wide. At least one side room was a stable.

Most animals grazed outside during the day and were brought inside at night. The fatted calf (Ps 50:9; Amos 6:4; Jer 46:21; Mal 4:2) was an exception. The veal from this calf was a delicacy. The calf never left the stable, so that its diet and weight could be monitored. When guests came to the house, villagers slaughtered their stable-fed calf (1 Sam 28:24).

Villagers dug a shallow cesspit into the floor of the stable, which was then paved with flagstones. Urine from the livestock that was not absorbed by the straw bedding trickled through the cracks between the flagstones, and drained into the cesspit. Mangers for fodder or cribs for grain were cut into large blocks of stone and installed on the floor between the pillars. In the New Testament there is no room for Mary and Joseph to sleep on the second floor with the members of the household, so they sleep in the stable with the animals. When Mary gives birth to Jesus, she places him in one of the stone mangers between the pillars (Luke 2:7).

No windows have been recovered from pillared houses, but windows do appear in the pillared houses carved on ivory inlays for furniture. These skylights (Hebrew: *ḥallônîm*) through the outside walls of the side rooms admitted light and ventilated the smoke from the ovens and hearths inside.

Across the back of the house was a broad storeroom (Hebrew: *yarkâ* [Amos 6:10]; *yarkātayim* [Ps 128:3]) for food and supplies. Some of these storerooms could be entered only through the roof. Provisions were kept in large storage jars and stone-lined silos.

Early in the Iron Age (1200–1000 B.C.E.) pillared houses were built with only one floor. Later (1000–586 B.C.E.) they were built with two floors. Villagers used inside ladders or outside stairs to reach the second floor (Hebrew: *ʿălîyâ*). In some houses wooden steps were attached to a stone pillar. The second floor was a large loft used for eating meals and for sleeping (1 Kgs 17; 2 Kgs 4:10; 2 Kgs 17:1-6). Women wove cloth on the second floor and created shrines there for the divine patrons of the household (Hebrew: *tĕrāpîm*).

Open beamed ceilings (Hebrew: *mĕqāreh* [Judg 3:24; 2 Kgs 6:2-5; Eccl 10:18]) supported the second floor and the roof (Hebrew: *gāg*). The beams (Hebrew: *qôrôt, rāhîtîm*) on both floors were fourteen to sixteen feet long. Villagers laid branches across the beams above the second story to create flat roofs. They sealed their roofs with an adobe of clay, straw, sand, charcoal, and ash (Ps 129:7). The finished roof was about fifteen inches thick (Herr and Clark 2001). After rains these flat roofs needed to be patched and flattened with a stone roller to remain water-tight (King and Stager 2001, 23–24).

During the dry season, villagers like Saul and Samuel slept on their roofs (1 Sam 9:25-26). Elijah carried his host's son to the roof where he slept (1 Kgs 17:19). David first saw Bathsheba bathing on the roof of her house while he was walking on the roof of the palace (2 Sam 11:2).

Villagers also went to the roof to pray (Jer 19:13; 32:29; 2 Kgs 23:12). Because it was sacred space, Bathsheba bathed on the roof of her house at the end of her menstrual period (2 Sam 11:2). Jeremiah indicted the people of Jerusalem for praying to the *hosts of heaven* and to *other gods* on their roofs (Jer 19:13; 32:29; 2 Kgs 23:12).

The second floor (Hebrew: *ʿălîyâ*) of a pillared house became a metaphor for the divine plane. The Hebrews called their creator *El*—a second-floor resident (Ps 104:3, 13). ∎

Woman bathing, 900-700 B.C.E. Terracotta figurine. Israelite with Egyptian influence. From Achziv. Location: Israel Museum (IDAM), Jerusalem, Israel. Photo Credit: Erich Lessing / Art Resource, NY.

HOUSEHOLDS

Households were the base communities in the world of the Bible. The pillared house common throughout Syria-Palestine during the Iron Age (1200–586 B.C.E.) is an artifact whose architecture reflects the way a household was organized, and how a household worked (Meyers 2003b, 34–36). Pillared houses are the material remains of households.

In "The Archaeology of the Family" (1985) and in *Life in Biblical Israel* (2001) with Philip J. King, Lawrence E. Stager demonstrated how

Households are social institutions with four generations. Some members of households are blood kin, some are not. Households are communities of covenant or choice. Even members of households that are blood relatives must ratify their kinship by covenant. ∎

Annales archaeology can be used to reconstruct the social world of ancient Israel reflected in the pillared-house floor plan. The result is a seminal study of long-lasting trends among the people of ancient Israel.

Households exercised political, economic, diplomatic, legal, and educational authority in ancient Israel. Stable households exercised this authority not only for their own members but also for the common good of the other households in their village and for their tribe.

Marriage

On average, Iron Age men lived to the age of forty; women to the age of thirty-five. Women married when they were twelve to fourteen years old. Men married when they were twenty to thirty years old. There was romance in the world of the Bible, just as there is romance in every other world, but not every sexual relationship in the world of the Bible was an affair of the heart. Marriage was a carefully negotiated covenant, sealing a significant political or economic relationship between households. It was designed to bring together two households willing to exchange substantial goods and services with each other over a significant period of time (Matthews and Benjamin 1993, 13–17).

Codes of sexuality determined whether a man or a woman was eligible for marriage. There were different criteria for men and women. *Virginity* (Hebrew: *bĕtûlîm*; Arabic: *ird*) was the technical term for the legal eligibility for a woman to enter a marriage. *Chastity* was the technical term for the legal compliance of a woman with the terms of her marriage covenant.

To propose marriage, the father of the household of the groom sent an expensive gift to the father of the household of the bride (Gen 34:12; Exod 22:16; Deut 22:9; 1 Sam 18:25; Mal 2:14). When the marriage covenant was ratified, households exchanged a bride-price (Hebrew: *mōhar*) or a dowry (Hebrew: *zēbed*). The bride-price was the investment of the household of the groom in the household of the bride. The dowry was the investment of the household of the bride in the household of the groom.

Males were polygamous; one man had two or more wives. A marriage was ratified when a groom spread his cloak over a bride and conferred on her either the title *primary wife* (Hebrew: *ʾiššâ*) or *secondary wife* (Hebrew: *pilegeš*). In English translations of the Bible, words such as "prostitute," "mistress," or "concubine" are not always the titles of shamed women who were promiscuous or were sexual partners for hire. They were often titles of honor identifying secondary wives and distinguishing them from the primary wife who was the mother of the household (1 Kgs 11:1-8).

Most marriages were endogamous. Marriage covenants were negotiated between households in the same village. Endogamous marriages were financially conservative, and they strengthened already existing and proven relationships between households. The financial risks were small but so were the financial rewards. Endogamous marriages were designed to keep the resources of a village intact. They were common in subsistence cultures like early Israel, whose material resources were scarce. The most common endogamous marriage was a cross-cousin marriage between the households of two brothers. The bride and groom were *cousins*, but not necessarily blood relatives. The words "uncle" or "father's brother" in many kinship systems refers to a covenant or business partner, not necessarily a sibling. In the world of the Bible, the relationship between a man and his uncles was as important as the relationship between a man and his father.

Marriages were also patrilocal. Newly married couples were members of the household of the father of the groom and lived with him. Marriages were patrilineal. That is, eligibility for inheriting the resources of a household was determined by relationships between men and the fathers of their households. Although kinship and birth order contributed to a man's eligibility, covenant was more important than kinship in identifying which male would inherit, and how much he would inherit (Hebrew: *bĕkōrâ*).

Roles within a Household

Members of a household described their relationship to one another as a line of descent or lineage. A lineage (Hebrew: *pĕrāzôt*) is an organizational flow chart beginning with a single couple and their children. Lineages vary in size or generational depth. Some are shallow lineages made up of the descendants of only one set of grandparents or great-grandparents. Some are deep lineages with several dozen generations subdivided or segmented into smaller households. A segmented lineage is a deep lineage subdivided into two or more households. The households are each linked to a son or daughter in the parent lineage. Some parent lineages in the world of the Bible are subdivided into as many as twenty households or generations (http://umanitoba.ca/faculties/arts/anthropology/tutor/descent/unilineal/segments.html).

The father of a household protected and provided for its land and children. He adopted or exiled sons and daughters, recruited workers and warriors, negotiated marriages and other covenants, hosted strangers, and designated heirs. The mother of a household also protected and provided for its land and children. She bore children and arranged for the other wives in the household to bear children. Despite regular pregnancies, women carried only four children to term, and only two of those four would survive to become adults (Gruber 1989). The mother of a household also supervised the processing and storing of grain,

beer, and vegetables. She rationed and prepared food (Hebrew: *leḥem*), taught clan traditions to the children and to the women, and mediated domestic disputes. She was the primary advocate in choosing which young warrior (Hebrew: *na^car*) would become the heir (Hebrew: *bĕkōr*), or *firstborn* (Gen 27:29; Deut 21:15-17), of the household (Matthews and Benjamin 1993, 22–36).

Competition among the young men to become the next father of the household was intense. They competed in one of three areas of public life: as warriors, as priests, or as tribal officials.

Young men who became tribal officials served as stewards or business managers—literally *slaves*—for households with deep lineages. Their names often appear on scarab seals with which they notarized covenants for their households. Young men who became warriors (Hebrew: *gebārîm*) fought as special forces. Here they had the opportunity to distinguish themselves. Their acts of heroism would recommend them to the elders of their households when the time came to appoint an heir. Young men who became priests served at tribal sanctuaries dedicated to Yahweh. Micah, for example, hired a young man to serve at the sanctuary on Mount Ephraim for his household (Judges 17). Samuel was a young man who served Eli at Yahweh's sanctuary at Shiloh.

Members of a household were buried together so they could "sleep with their ancestors." The most important responsibility that members of a household had to one another was "to honor [Hebrew: *kibbēd*] their father and mother" (Exod 20:12)—to see that they were properly buried. Households dug their tombs as caves outside, but adjacent to, their villages. A proper burial included not only the interment of a body in a household tomb but also remembering the dead at thanksgiving meals (Hebrew: *marzēaḥ* [Amos 6:7; Jer 16:5]).

CONCLUSION

Stager's work has been widely recognized for its presentation of ancient Israel. His work has had equal impact in demonstrating how important theory is to good fieldwork, and how important it is for biblical archaeologists to apply a range of disciplines to their work. Using an enriched relationship between stones and stories, Stager demonstrates how much the use of written artifacts like the Bible can bring to the material remains of the pillared house. He also demonstrates that by the integration of archaeology with anthropology and sociology the stories in the stones can be enriched and can bring to life not simply a building technique but an entire social structure that first appeared in the Iron Age and continues to be reflected in the daily life of traditional peoples in the world of the Bible today.

WHAT YOU HAVE LEARNED

- Neolithic humans (8000–3800 B.C.E.) invented freestanding houses to replace caves.
- Architectural styles included partially subterranean round houses with thatched roofs and retangular houses with flat roofs, with a door either in the roof or in the long wall, and sleeping benches along the inside walls.
- Iron Age houses (1200–586 B.C.E.) in Israelite villages and throughout Syria-Palestine were not only practical dwellings but blueprints for marriage and daily life in ancient Israel.

STUDY QUESTIONS

1. What were Natufian houses like?
2. What is the role of a landscape archaeologist?
3. How did a pillared house differ from the Arad model?
4. What was a "household" in Iron Age Israel?
5. What was the mother's role in the household?

Part 4

Processual Archaeology

- Part 4 is an introduction to the School of Processual Archaeology.
- Chapter 15 describes how processual archaeologists reconstruct the way in which cultures at a site adapted to changes in their natural and human environment.
- Chapter 16 describes a specific kind of processual archaeology called *Ethnoarchaeology*. Ethnoarchaeologists live with and observe still-existing cultures in order to understand extinct cultures. For example, what ethnoarchaeologists have learned about childbirth in traditional cultures today contributes to the understanding of childbirth and its use as a metaphor in the Bible.
- Chapters 17 and 18 look at Gezer and Tel Miqne, two important sites excavated by processual archaeologists, and what those sites have contributed to the understanding of the stories of Solomon and Samson in the Bible.

PREVIEW: PROCESSUAL ARCHAEOLOGY

- Processual, or New, Archaeology
  - Medieval Worldview
  - Renaissance
  - General Systems Theory
  - Stones Telling Stories

Chapter 15 describes how processual archaeologists reconstruct the way in which cultures at a site adapted to changes in their natural and human environment. It also explains basic differences between cultural history and processual archaeology; for example, cultural history is an adaptation of history to archaeology, and processual archaeology is an adaptation of anthropology to archaeology.

15

Processual Archaeology

Philip Phillips (1900–1994) crafted a sentence that became the motto of the School of Processual, or *New*, Archaeology: "New World archaeology is anthropology or it is nothing" (Phillips 1955, 246–47). With Gordon R. Willey (1913–2002), Phillips pioneered the processual archaeology that is still widely used today (Willey and Phillips 1958). Processual archeologists emphasize the dynamic relationship between cultures and their environments. Change occurs when cultures adapt to shifts in their environment (T. J. Wilkinson 2003, 226).

Like most of the disciplines studied and taught at universities today, cultural history and processual archaeology are both developments of the Enlightenment. The ideas of the Enlightenment became prominent in the eighteenth century in the Renaissance cultures of Europe that flourished at the end of the medieval period.

THE MEDIEVAL WORLDVIEW

The medieval worldview considered human experience, and especially human religious experience, to be mysterious. Medieval people had little confidence in their ability to understand either the world in which they lived or the divine world. The world was a mystery that defied human understanding. They respected the world; they did not try to understand it.

Like people in the world of the Bible, medieval people viewed their world as a home to the divine. Trees, rocks, and water, for example, were all manifestations of the divine (Eliade 1959, 116–59). Medieval cultures, therefore, taught humans to acknowledge the divine continually in their daily lives. Every action was carefully and reverently undertaken. Medieval people not only prayed before they ate; they prayed before they did anything. Medieval cultures relied on the Bible and tradition to interpret their experience. As the guardians and interpreters of the Bible and tradition, Jewish, Christian, and Muslim religious authorities dominated medieval cultures.

In ordinary speech "modern" often means *scientific*; "medieval" means *superstitious*. Technically, however, "modern" and "medieval" simply identify two different ways of looking at the world. One is not more accurate than the other. ∎

CHRONOLOGY

Middle Ages	500–
Early Middle Ages	500–1000
High Middle Ages	1000–1300
	(1250)
Late Middle Ages	1300–1450
Renaissance	1300–1700

As difficult as it is for the peoples of Europe, North America, and Japan today to understand, medieval people did not trust the human mind. For them, the human mind was not a very reliable guide to life. More often than not, the human mind tricked rather than tutored human beings. The weakness of the human mind was in how it collected information. The mind used the five senses—hearing, seeing, feeling, smelling, and tasting—to collect the data it needed to make decisions. But these senses are easily deceived. Therefore, decisions based on such faulty sensual data could not be trusted. The Middle Ages are sometimes referred to as the *Dark Ages* because of the distrust of the human mind—the *light*.

THE RENAISSANCE

The Renaissance (1300–1700) began in Italy and spread throughout Europe. It had wide-ranging consequences in all intellectual pursuits but is perhaps best known for its impact on art, reflected in the work of Leonardo da Vinci and Michelangelo (1475–1564). The Renaissance introduced critical thinking and the scientific method into European education. Students read and discussed Greek and Roman classics and studied the world in which they lived through the physical sciences.

An important legacy of the Renaissance is modernism, a worldview that assumes that human experience, even human religious experience, makes sense. Modernism has an almost absolute confidence in the human mind and its ability to understand human experience. Today Enlightenment cultures rely on the human mind to solve problems. These cultures have confidence that humans can use their minds to face challenges and resolve those challenges. If the senses could be trained to collect data accurately, then the interpretations of this data by the human mind would be trustworthy.

PROCESSUAL ARCHAEOLOGISTS AND GENERAL SYSTEMS THEORY

Like anthropologists, processual archaeologists use material remains to reconstruct not only the physical but also the cultural processes that brought the material remains into existence and governed their use. Using sample artifacts to reconstruct a process is a technique developed by General Systems Theory, which assumes that all life is controlled by systems or processes (Bertalanffy 1968). Some processes are simple; some are complex. A simple process is how to make pottery—where to find the clay, how to prepare it, shape it, harden it, fire it, and decorate it. A complex process is politics—how to feed the people in a community and how to protect their land.

By using General Systems Theory, processual archaeologists assume that every artifact they recover has a clear and essential purpose in the daily life of the human community at the site. There is a purpose in the stones. Nothing recovered at a site is meaningless or even whimsical. There are no unexplainable or chaotic artifacts. General Systems Theory also assumes not only that the process reflected in any given artifact can be reconstructed, but also that this reconstruction can be used to reconstruct all the other processes operating in a culture. The part is a model of the whole. Finally, General Systems Theory assumes that the process of adaptation in a culture is predictable. Once a process has been reconstructed from an artifact for any given point in its evolution, then processual archaeologists can use the reconstruction to chart how the process will evolve as it faces new changes.

General Systems Theory *is the interdisciplinary study of complex entities and the models which can be used to describe them. It was proposed in the 1940s by biologist Ludwig von Bertalanffy (1901–1972: Bertalanffy 1968). Rather than reducing an entity to the sum of its parts, General Systems Theory focuses on the relations that connect the parts into a whole system (http://pespmc1.vub.ac.be/systheor.html).*

PROCESSUAL ARCHAEOLOGISTS AND CULTURAL HISTORIANS

Cultural history and processual archaeology both study the human past. Both consider the human mind a reliable tool for understanding the past, and both use the Wheeler-Kenyon method to collect material remains from the past. They are two different schools or theories of archaeology. The difference between cultural history and processual archaeology is not that one is objective and the other is subjective. Each has its own strategy for reconstructing the story in the stones.

Cultural historians reconstruct the past by describing the past—dating and cataloguing artifacts (Trigger 2006). They ask: *Who made these artifacts? When were these artifacts made?* (Renfrew and Bahn 1996, 36–39). For cultural historians, the most important partner for interpreting the material remains is written artifacts from the site or from elsewhere. They use stories to interpret the stones—hence the name cultural *history*. Processual archaeologists use artifact samples from the site to reconstruct anthropological *processes* or ways of adapting to change. They use these processes to interpret the stones—hence the name *processual* archaeology.

For cultural historians, cultures are basically stable. Consequently, they interpret any radical change at a site as evidence that new people have conquered the site or immigrated to the site. New people arrive; the old people do not evolve.

For processual archaeologists, in contrast, cultures are basically dynamic. They evolve. The same population at a site can be responsible for even dramatic changes in the material remains there. Dramatic changes in material remains are not necessarily evidence for the arrival of new populations at a site, but rather of significant adaptations by the established population to changes in the environment, for example, the buildup of salts in the soil of a site or a shortage of cooking fuel or a drought. The material remains of past cultures tell how cultures survived. Artifacts are not actions; they are reactions. Change is adaptation. It is part of the human evolutionary process.

During the Late Bronze Age, for example, the Mycenaean, Egyptian, and Hittite trade empires delivered tin and copper, which the peoples of Syria-Palestine used to make bronze tools and weapons. Then the trade empires collapsed. Tin and copper were no longer available. Sources of fuel—wood and charcoal—were also being exhausted. Material remains at sites reflect creative adaptation to these changes. Iron tools and weapons began to replace bronze tools and weapons. Iron ore did not have to be imported, as did tin and copper. Much less wood and charcoal were needed to refine iron. Thus, iron working was a creative adaptation to changes in the environment of cultures in the world of the Bible.

Cultural historians let the stones tell their own stories. These researchers are not looking for something; they are listening to something. They want to know what happened at a site, when it happened, and why it happened. They reconstruct a material history of the site by letting the story in the stones unfold on its own. They dig and listen.

Processual archaeologists question the stones. They have a story when they begin to excavate and want to determine whether that story is true. They want to know if there is artifact evidence for what they think happened at the site. They want to know if there are stones to support their stories.

Processual archaeologists are positivists. Nothing about the world of the Bible can be taken for granted. Everything must be supported by evidence and experiment. They develop concrete theories or questions about a site and then go into

the field to test their theories. They talk and then dig. Theories, however, are not only developed before an excavation begins. As the excavation progresses, processual archaeologists create new theories and ask new questions. Then they modify their dig strategies from season to season in order to test those theories.

During excavations under the direction of Chang-Ho Ji at Khirbat ʿAtaruz (Jordan), workers recovered a plaque with two male figures standing side by side. One holds a lion; the other holds a bull. There is no inscription. Both figures could be humans such as Gilgamesh and Enkidu in the stories of Gilgamesh from Mesopotamia (Matthews and Benjamin 2006, 21–32). One figure could be human, one divine. The male holding the lion could be a ruler of Israel such as Ahab; the male holding the bull could be his divine patron, Yahweh. Lions are a symbol of royal authority; bulls are a symbol of divine authority. Both images could be divine. Other material remains at the sanctuary are also twinned. Thus, the plaque from one season created new questions and new theories for upcoming seasons. So the team decided to clear a courtyard outside an entrance to the sanctuary flanked by twin towers to answer the question, *Is Khirbat ʿAtaruz a sanctuary dedicated to two divine patrons?*

Cultural historians assume that eventually the stones will tell only one, coherent story—a *metahistory*. They assume that when the excavation has been completed all the stones will become part of a single story. Therefore, cultural historians need to recover every stone to tell the story of a site. Processual archaeologists, in contrast, assume that they will never recover a complete archaeological record, even if they excavate the entire site. Therefore, they reconstruct the systems that the artifacts reflect. Then, using those reconstructions, they hypothetically fill in the gaps in the artifact record. Processual archaeologists can tell a lot about human life at a site by doing just a little.

CONCLUSION

For processual archaeologists, human life is a dynamic process. By looking carefully at any part of the process it is possible to understand the entire process. More than one worldview drives the process. The process is pluralistic, not monolithic. There is only one set of stones, but they reflect a variety of stories. The School of Processual Archaeology is committed to using stones to reconstruct the dynamic of human life at a site and the diversity of stories that those stones represent.

WHAT YOU HAVE LEARNED

- Processual archaeologists reconstruct the way in which cultures at a site adapt to changes in their natural and human environment.
- Culural historians describe artifacts; processual archaeologists explain them.
- Processual archaeologists assume that every artifact is a meaningful part of a social process, and that they can reconstruct the entire process from the artifacts.
- Cultural historians assume that a culture at a site is stable. For cultural historians, change at a site is a always a sign of conquest by outsiders or the arrival of new peoples. Processual archaeologists assume that cultures at a site are dynamic; they continue to change and adapt.
- Cultural historians assume that a single metahistory of a site can eventually be reconstructed from the artifacts recovered there. Processual archaeologists assume that the story of a site will always be incomplete, and they reconstruct the systems that the artifacts reflect. Then, using those reconstructions, they hypothetically fill in the gaps in the artifact record.

STUDY QUESTIONS

1. How did the worldview of the Middle Ages differ from that of the Renaissance?
2. How is General Systems Theory applied to archaeology?
3. Compare the approaches of cultural historians and processual archaeologists.

PREVIEW: ETHNOARCHAEOLOGY

- Middle Range Theory
- Jewish, Bedouin, and Arab Peoples
- Birthing Practices in Traditional Cultures

Chapter 16 describes a specific kind of processual archaeology called ethnoarchaeology. Ethnoarchaeologists live with and observe still-existing cultures to better understand extinct cultures. For example, what ethnoarchaeologists have learned about childbirth in traditional cultures today contributes to the understanding of childbirth and its use as a metaphor in the Bible.

16

Ethnoarchaeology

In "Archaeology as Anthropology," Lewis R. Binford outlined the method of processual archaeology called *Ethnoarchaeology* (Binford 1962; Binford and Binford 1968). In studying living cultures for the light they shed on extinct cultures, ethnoarchaeologists observe not only how the peoples in these cultures create material things but also why they create them. Ethnoarchaeologists want to learn not only how people use material things but also why they use them. These observations, or ethnographies, become the basis for interpreting the artifacts and the worldviews of cultures of extinct peoples. For example, Binford wanted to prove that the Mousterian artifacts from Ice Age France were adapted to their environment. Therefore, he spent time with the Nunamiut people of Alaska, who lived in an Ice Age climate. He observed how and why artifacts were created in his host cultures.

Lewis R. Binford

In 1949 Robert K. Merton used the work of Emile Durkheim and Max Weber (1864–1920) to develop Middle Range Theory (Merton 1949). This sociology was a balanced application of theory and method to the study of human behavior and social organization. Merton criticized sociologists for collecting data without any effort to reconstruct a theory for understanding the data. He also criticized sociologists for constructing grand theories of human behavior and social organization without doing any fieldwork. Merton did not want to explain the whole world, but he concentrated on data that were transparent enough to provide a limited understanding of human behavior and social organization. Universal theories were unreliable. Only Middle Range Theories were reliable tools for understanding human behavior and social organization.

Binford refined Middle Range Theory for use in archaeology. Middle Range Theory in archaeology, as in sociology, is an artful blend of theory and practice. Here Middle Range Theory identifes and measures a few specific properties of extinct cultures by both collecting artifacts carefully and reconstructing a theory for understanding the function of these artifacts, why they survived, and what they can contribute to understanding the worldview of the maker culture.

Binford's work earned him the title the "Father of the New Archaeology." He published his legacy as *Constructing Frames of Reference: An Analytical Method for Archaeological Theory Building Using Hunter-Gatherer and Environmental Data Sets* (2001).

LAMENT
(Ps 139:1-24)

Yahweh, you know when I sit down
    You know when I stand up;
    You know my thoughts from far
        away.
You track my path and find my den,
    You know all my ways. . . .
Where can I go from your spirit?
    Where can I flee from your presence?
If I ascend to heaven, you are there;
    If I am buried in Sheol, you are there.
If I take the wings of the morning,
    If I settle at the farthest limits of the
        sea,
Even there your hand shall lead me;
    Your right hand shall hold me fast.
If I say, "Surely the darkness shall cover
    me;
    Surely, the light around me will
        become night,"
Even the darkness is not dark to you;
    The night is as bright as the day;
    Darkness is as light to you.
For it was you who formed my inward
    parts;
    You *massaged* me in my mother's
        womb.
I praise you, for I am fearfully and won-
    derfully made.
    I know well how wonderful are your
        works.
My frame was not hidden from you,
    When I was being made in secret,
    When I was incubating deep in the earth
        . . . .

ETHNOARCHAEOLOGY OF JEWISH, BEDOUIN, AND ARAB PEOPLES

Ethnoarchaeology in the world of the Bible has focused on both Arab and Bedouin peoples. Raphael Patai (1910–1996) was an anthropologist who studied Jewish life in Hungary and went on to use ethnoarchaeology to study Bedouin culture as a way of understanding the culture of the biblical Hebrews. He taught at the Technion (Haifa) and the Hebrew University (Jerusalem) and founded the Palestine Institute of Folklore and Ethnology. In 1952, he was asked by the United Nations to direct a research project on Syria, Lebanon, and Jordan for the Human Relations Area Files (http://www.yale.edu/hraf/).

Patai's work was wide-ranging but focused primarily on the anthropology of traditional cultures surviving in the Middle East today as a tool for understanding the culture of ancient Israel. Among his works on the ethnoarchaeology of the world of the Bible are *The Arab Mind* (1973) and *Sex and Family in the Bible and the Middle East* (1959). The ethnoarchaeology of Bedouin peoples focuses on cultures that live in the part of the world today where the Hebrews lived yesterday. Thus, they are separated in time but not in place. The most important criterion for ethnoarchaeology, however, is not geography but rather similar environmental challenges (Eilberg-Schwartz 1990, 87–102).

ETHNOARCHAEOLOGY OF CHILDBIRTH

Ethnoarcharologists have lived for longer or shorter periods of time in traditional cultures around the world to observe how midwives work with parents and children. Their patient observations have created an invaluable archive of materials for better understanding and appreciating the role of midwives in the world of the Bible. The ethnoarchaeology of childbearing focuses not on cultures related to the Hebrews geographically but on the common experience of childbirth among women in traditional cultures in general. Studies of midwives in most traditional cultures show that they provide both clinical and legal services to households. Clinically, midwives see that women who are going to give birth are physically prepared (Delaney 1988, 264). Legally, they are responsible for seeing that the women are officially designated and financially compensated.

Menstruation (Latin: *menses*) played a key role in the preparation of child-bearers. Intercourse during menstruation was strictly prohibited (Lev 15:19-24; Delaney 1988, 89; Buckley and Gottlieb 1988, 19–20). By observing when a woman had finished her menstrual period, midwives determined the appropriate time for the couple to have sexual intercourse (Jensen, Benson, and Bobak 1977, 733). Before couples had intercourse, midwives monitored women's nutrition and prescribed special foods or aphrodisiacs considered to increase fertility. For example, the mandrake, which is a Mediterranean herb with egg-shaped leaves, white or purple flowers, and a large forked root (Latin: *mandragora officinarum*), was used by midwives as an aphrodisiac in ancient Israel (Song 7:13; Gen 30:14-20). Aphrodisiacs are often shaped like or smelled like the reproductive organs they are expected to stimulate. Midwives certified that

Two female figures, Halaf culture and Late Chalcolithic, around 5000–4500 B.C.E. The figurine on the left comes from north-east Syria, the one on the right probably from south-east Turkey. Both Godmother figures have large breasts and wide hips. Necklace, loincloth, body-paint and jewelry are painted on them. ANE, 125381. Location: British Museum, London, Great Britain. Photo Credit: Erich Lessing / Art Resource, NY.

mothers were pregnant by palpating or massaging their uterus (Ps 139:1-24; see sidebar p. 206). Another definitive sign of a healthy pregnancy was the movement or kick of the fetus in the uterus (Gen 16:4). This physical contact between midwives and unborn children created an enduring bond between them and the children. The fetus not only grew accustomed to the touch of its midwife but also responded to her gentle hands.

In some cultures, midwives construct birthing huts. They use music to exorcise any members of the divine assembly who are not welcome at birth, and they prevent their return by caulking any openings in the walls of the birth hut and carefully sweeping the dirt floor or scattering flour on it so that any invisible member of the divine assembly who tries to enter and harm the mother or her child can easily be detected. Pioneer mothers in the American West used similar tactics to protect their families from rattlesnakes. They removed all the shrubs and grass from around their houses, which were built off the ground on pilings of brick or stones. Every day they swept the dirt smooth so that any snake that crawled up into the cool shade under the house would leave a clear trail to its hiding place.

BIRTHING IN TRADITIONAL SOCIETIES

In traditional cultures, mothers deliver kneeling, squatting, sitting, or standing. Their midwives used birthing stools, music, and massage to control pain (Donegan 1978, 141–63; Jordan 1983). Paleolithic (9000 B.C.E.) rock drawings from Europe and a Neolithic (6000–4000 B.C.E.) clay figurine of the Godmother of Çatal Höyük portray a steatopygous or large-hipped woman giving birth sitting (Towler and Bramall 1986, 1–5; Anati 1987, 125). Birthing stools were used to support the

mother's weight and position her hips for delivery. The Cuna in Panama use hammocks during labor (Severin 1973, 124). The mother sits over a hole in the hammock through which the midwife delivers her baby.

Azteca mothers in Mexico announced their pregnancy by wrapping a long black sash (Spanish: *cinta*) around their waists. During pregnancy it helped support their uterus. During labor, midwives tied the sash over a beam in the hut to create a sling to support the mother's hips.

On the American frontier, midwives used milking stools as birthing stools (Wertz and Wertz 1977, 13–14). Birthing chairs have reappeared in delivery rooms in the United States in response to the increasing demand of healthy mothers who intend to deliver their babies without drugs and in an upright position (Roberts and Van Lier 1984).

In the world of the Bible, the birthing stool was simply two rocks or bricks pushed close enough together to support the mother's hips (J. A. Thompson 1986, 267). At Abydos, archaeologists recovered a birth brick decorated with a mother giving birth with the help of her midwife (Wegner 2002; McGeough 2006). Mothers may have knelt on these bricks while giving birth, or midwives may have laid the newborn on a cushion framed by the bricks during its adoption, or official acceptance.

Just as the midwives used music to prepare the rooms where intercourse would take place, they also used music during labor and delivery. The rhythm or melody was as important as the words. Midwives, however, were not simply entertainers. Music was a sympathetic ritual (C. L. Meyers 1991, 24–25). The rhythm of the voice or the drum set a healthy pace for respiration and heartbeat and tuned newborns to the rhythm of the culture with which they were joined during these creative moments.

Greco-Roman women giving birth on low stools. Relief from the Ptolemaic period (332–37 B.C.E.) Location: Temple of Sobek and Horus, Kom Ombo, Egypt. Photo Credit: Erich Lessing / Art Resource, NY.

To clear the newborn's airway in some traditional cultures, midwives set newborns down firmly on the ground. The Cuna splashed the newborn in a stream or a water-filled canoe (Severin 1973, 124). Clinically, these techniques closed a valve so that the newborns could begin to breathe. It also jolted them out of primary apnea, which sometimes arrests their respiration.

By earthing newborns, that is, placing newborns on the ground and then removing them, midwives also reenacted with Mother Earth the parturition they had just completed with their human mothers. Earthing also affirmed the widespread belief that before entering the womb of its human mother, the newborn gestated in the soil, rocks, trees, plants, flowers, rivers, and springs (Ps 139:15; Wis 7:1-6; McKenzie 1907). For traditional cultures in Germany, Australia (van Gennep 1974), Africa (Burton 1961, 115), and Japan (Batchelor 1892, 225), the soil is the primary mother of all humans (van Gennep 1909/1960, 52).

After delivery, midwives held up the newborns, inviting their adoption. The first cry of newborns as they inflated their lungs and began to breathe was considered a legal petition to join their households and become members of the village community. Legally to adopt their

Midwives are depicted assisting Cleopatra in childbirth in this sketch, based on an ancient drawing on papyrus.

children parents would answer the primal scream of the newborn with a hymn inviting the household to praise their divine patron and accept this child (Job 3:7). Formulas such as "a . . . child is conceived" (Job 3:3) introduced newborns to their households (Gen 21:6-7). Eve celebrated the successful birth of Cain and Abel with the hymn "I have gotten a son with the help of the Lord" (Gen 4:1). If no one adopted a newborn, the midwife left it, just as it came from the womb—unwashed and unclothed—in an open field, where it could be adopted by another household (Stager and Wolff 1984, 50). In the world of the Bible, life began not with the physical process of birth but rather with the legal process of adoption.

Once parents spoke for their newborn, midwives rinsed off the placental fluid with saltwater in order to clean and sterilize the child. Then the midwife gently massaged the newborn's body with oil to protect the skin from drying and cracking. Washing conferred legal standing on newborns.

Midwives further defined the social status of their newborns by clothing them. Receiving blankets were not simply a practical necessity but uniforms that identified newborns as members entitled to all the rights and privileges of their households. The Mbuti of Australia strengthen the bond between the newborn and Mother Earth by swaddling it in a carefully prepared bark blanket (Severin 1973, 85–87).

Finally, the midwife placed the newborn in the nursing position on the lap of the mother. Again, the Mbuti further strengthen the bond between newborns and their Earth Mother by nursing them with catch water from the pulp of trees before offering them human breast milk.

Midwives carefully dispose of the umbilical cords of the newborn (Jensen, Benson, and Bobak 1977). They treat umbilical cords the way they wish the newborn to be treated in later life. For example, they do not allow animals that are the totems of any member of the divine assembly who could harm the newborn to eat the cord. Among the Swahili, the cord is placed around the child's neck and then later buried where the child was born so that the child will always be welcome in the house of its parents.

With the child safely born and legally adopted, midwives continue to serve as pediatricians, teaching child-bearers how to care for themselves and child-rearers how to care for their children (Gruber 1989; Habicht 1985). Mothers sought their advice on ordinary matters such as birth control. Breast-feeding was common and also provided a natural spacing of the children, since women who are breast-feeding several times a day are less likely to ovulate or conceive. Female infants would be weaned in eighteen months; male infants in thirty, in order for the mother to resume ovulating (1 Sam 1:21-24; Granqvist 1947, 108; Gruber 1989, 68).

Mothers also looked to their midwives for support in extraordinary crises such as stillbirth or crib death. Birth and death mirror each other in traditional societies. Midwives and mourners assist at each threshold. High infant mortality rates and the need to provide an adequate labor supply would have required couples to have more than one child. Even with an average of four births per couple, only two children generally survived to adulthood (Hopkins 1985, 156; Angel 1972, 94–95).

For the Hebrews, Yahweh was neither male nor female but both male and female (Mollenkott 1983, 1–35). Humans were gendered; Yahweh was integral. Among its rich archive of metaphors for Yahweh, the Bible regularly portrays Yahweh as a mother (Latin: *dea mater*), as a midwife (Latin: *dea obstetrix*), and as a nurse (Latin: *dea nutrix*). As a mother, Yahweh carries a child in her womb, labors to give birth (Deut 32:18; Job 38:28-29; Isa 42:14), teaches her child to walk (Hos 11:3-4), and wipes tears from its eyes (Isa 66:13-14). As a midwife, Yahweh delivers a newborn (Job 38:8; Isa 66:9), clothes it (Gen 3:21; Job 10:10-12; 38:8-9), and places it in its mother's arms (Ps 22:9-10). As a nurse, Yahweh cradles her child (Hos 11:3-4; Isa 46:3-4), nurses it (Ps 34:8; Isa 49:15; Hos 11:4; 2 Esd 1:28), and weans it (Ps 131:1-2; Wis 16:20-21).

The book of Isaiah identifies Yahweh as a true midwife who is Judah's companion in labor (Isa 26:16-18). The book of Psalms also describes Yahweh as the midwife who aspirates newborns and protects them from crib death (Ps 8:1-10). Some of the same imagery appears in the book of Wisdom (Wis 7:1-6), where Yahweh delivers the Wise Woman and then sets her down firmly on the ground until she begins to breathe (Wis 7:3).

A PARENT'S DUTIES NOT DONE
(Ezek 16:4-5)

As for your birth,
    On the day of your birth
Your umbilical cord was not cut,
    You were not washed with fresh
        water . . . ,
You were not rinsed with saltwater,
    You were not wrapped in swaddling
        clothes.
No one pitied you,
    No one loved you enough to do these
        things for you . . .
You were abandoned in an open field,
You were abhorred on the day you were
    born.

The prophetic rebuke of Jerusalem in Ezekiel 16:2-5 gives us, as if in a negative, the most complete list of a midwife's postpartum services in the Bible. It expects midwives to cut and tie off the umbilical cord, to rinse newborns with saltwater, and then wrap them in a receiving blanket. Because no one in the account in Ezekiel adopts the child, the midwife takes the newborn from the birthing room and leaves it covered with blood in an open field. Here human jurisdiction ends. In this field, the midwife transfers the newborn from human jurisdiction to the jurisdiction of the divine assembly, over which Yahweh presides. By placing it here in the same condition in which it left the womb, the household waives its own right to adopt the child and declares that it is eligible for another to claim.

CONCLUSION

Ethnoarchaeologists living with still-existing traditional cultures today have observed and reconstructed the clinical and legal services of midwives (Jordan 1983). Their reconstructions allow biblical scholars to better understand why midwives were so highly regarded in ancient Israel. Midwives in the world of the Bible were important not only to the parents whom they helped conceive, birth, and rear children, but also to the whole community, which learned from their work how to understand their divine patrons. The Hebrews' gratitude to these women remains enshrined in the powerful metaphors of birth and birthing with which they described their Creator and creation in the Bible.

WHAT YOU HAVE LEARNED

- Ethnoarchaeology is a specific kind of processual archaeology.
- Ethnoarchaeologists live with and observe still-existing cultures in order to better understand extinct cultures and to test their reconstructions of social institutions in the field.
- Theories about how social institutions in early Israel worked are often tested by studying Bedouin peoples.
- Ethnoarchaeologists use the research of anthropologists on midwives and child-bearing in traditional cultures to interpret material artifacts from the world of the Bible.
- The description of post-partum practices in the book of Ezekiel (Ezek 16:2-5) preserves the most complete list of a midwife's postpartum services in the Bible. It expects midwives to cut and tie off the umbilical cord, to rinse newborns with saltwater, and then to wrap them in a receiving blanket.

STUDY QUESTIONS

1. How does ethnoarchaeology follow the methods of processual archaeology?
2. What is Middle Range Theory?
3. What is the method of ethnoarchaeology?
4. What is the significance of depicting Yahweh as a midwife?

PREVIEW: GEZER

- Middle Bronze Culture
- Sanctuary
- Standing Stones
- Cities and Villages
- Monumental Architecture
- Writing

Chapter 17 describes the excavations at Gezer, an important site excavated by processual archaeologists, and indicates what those excavations contributed to the understanding of the stories of Solomon in the Bible.

17

Gezer

Tel Rehov (Israel), Megiddo (Israel), Ashkelon (Israel), Tall Al-'Umayri (Jordan), Gezer (Israel), Ekron (Israel), and the underwater sites at Uluburun (Turkey) and Cape Gelidonya (Turkey) were all excavated by processual archaeologists. The researchers were committed to using the scientific method and went into the field with clearly defined goals for their excavations. They were especially conscious of how the material remains demonstrated the flexibility of the maker cultures to changes in their environment, whether these changes occurred in nature or as the result of human activity. If the Bible and other written artifacts were relevant for their excavation, they made use of them, but only after a full model of interpretation for the sites had been reconstructed on the basis of the material remains alone.

Tel Gezer is about halfway between Jerusalem and Tel Aviv today, five miles south-southeast of Ramleh. It guards the western entrance to Jerusalem from the coastal highway. The thirty-three-acre site was occupied from the Bronze Age (3400–1200 B.C.E.) to the Hellenistic Period (323–37 B.C.E.). Boundary markers from the Hellenistic period (Stratum I) reading "The Boundary of Gezer" definitively identify the site.

R. A. S. Macalister directed the first major excavations at Gezer (1902–1905, 1907–1909). Following techniques common at the time, Macalister dug thirty trenches and then refilled them. He identified eight of the twenty-six settlement layers.

The second major excavations at Gezer (1964–1974 + 1984, 1990) were directed by G. Ernest Wright, Nelson Glueck, William G. Dever, and Joe D. Seger. Dever wanted the Gezer excavations to be a field school for applying processual archaeology and General Systems Theory to excavations in Syria-Palestine (Dever 1993).

To some extent, Dever focused the excavations at Gezer on specific historical questions. For example: *Was the restoration of Gezer part of a state resettlement program during the reign of Solomon? Were villagers forcibly moved from the hills into cities like Gezer to more rapidly convert the decentralized and subsistence culture of early Israel into a centralized and surplus culture of Israel as a state?* (Faust 2003). But as a processual

Many of the most accomplished archaeologists in the United States and Canada today learned their craft together at Gezer. Among them are Dever, Seger, Lawrence Stager, Seymour Gitin, John S. Holladay, Eric M. Meyers, Carol L. Meyers, Dan P. Cole, Oded Borowski, H. Darrell Lance, Anita M. Walker, and Robert B. Wright.

A consortium of institutions under the direction of Steven M. Ortiz and Sam Wolff resumed work at Tel Gezer in 2006 (http://www.gezerproject.org/). The project is reinvestigating the Iron Age levels of occupation (Strata V–XIII). ∎

215

archaeologist he also concentrated on more general questions of human evolution and social change in Syria-Palestine. He excavated to test various theories about how cultures adapt to change. He described not only evolutionary patterns of development at Gezer but also the impact of inventions such as metalworking on development. He took an interdisciplinary approach to excavating Gezer, analyzing the contribution of seeds, bones, and geology to understanding human settlement at the site.

Changes in theory at Gezer led to changes in practice. In contrast to the trenching techniques used by Macalister, Kathleen Kenyon had rigorously focused her excavations at Jericho and Jerusalem on opening very small squares. Influenced by Israeli archaeologists like Yohanan Aharoni, however, Dever widened the Wheeler-Kenyon method to include excavations of entire architectural structures such as the main gate and its wall. As the work progressed at Gezer, field supervisors faithfully kept diaries, drew top plans, and recorded each find on locus sheets.

A sanctuary of standing stones constructed by the Middle Bronze community that lived at Gezer between 1650 and 1468 B.C.E. (Strata XVIII–XIX). Location: Gezer, Israel. Photo Credit: Erich Lessing / Art Resource, NY.

GEZER (1650–1468 B.C.E.)

Humans settled at Gezer during the Chalcolithic Age (Stratum XXVI), inaugurating some twenty-six periods of occupation at the site. Three human communities used the site during the Early Bronze period (Strata XXIII–XXV), five during the Middle Bronze period (Strata XVIII–XXII), four during the Late Bronze period (Strata XIV–XVII), nine during the Iron Age (Strata V–XIII), one during the Persian period (Stratum IV), and three during the Hellenistic period (Strata I–III).

A sanctuary constructed by the Middle Bronze community that lived at Gezer between 1650 and 1468 B.C.E. (Strata XVIII–XIX) and the main gate constructed by the Iron Age community that lived at Gezer between 1000 and 920 B.C.E. have made particular contributions to understanding the world of the Bible.

The Middle Bronze period (2000–1500 B.C.E.) was a remarkable time in the world of the Bible. Refugees from the Early Bronze period (3400–2000 B.C.E.) returned from the hills and deserts to rebuild their cities. Early Bronze culture in Syria-Palestine had collapsed abruptly between 2300 and 2000 B.C.E. Natural disasters such as drought and epidemics set off food wars between cities that had crops and those that did not. Egypt delivered the final blow to Early Bronze culture as its armies campaigned throughout Syria-Palestine, creating a wasteland in its attempt to defend against peoples from the borders of Mesopotamia who were moving south (Mazar 1990a, 141–43).

Middle Bronze cities were magnificent. Throughout the Bronze Age, there were none larger or more heavily fortified. Walls twenty-five feet thick and a mile long were built with stones weighing over two thousand pounds. City people in the Middle Bronze period were merchants. Villagers were herders and farmers. Some were rich and some were poor. The wealthy were served by warriors, bureaucrats, artists, tradespeople, and slaves. They were masters of the planning, organization, production, distribution, and enforcement that the construction and operation of great cities demand.

Middle Bronze cultures in Syria-Palestine invented the alphabet. Hundreds of word pictures in Mesopotamian cuneiform and Egyptian hieroglyphics were reduced to thirty hieroglyphics in Ugaritic and twenty-two letters in Hebrew. Ordinary people, not just an elite corps of scribes, could now read and write (Daniels and Bright, 1996, 21–32). Middle Bronze cultures manufactured bronze tools and weapons with tin imported from Afghanistan. They crafted jewelry with alabaster and faience from Egypt. They turned exquisite pottery on new high-speed

The earliest standing stones in the world of the Bible were erected during the Neolithic period around 5000 B.C.E. Although the sanctuary at Gezer was built in the Middle Bronze period (1650–1500 B.C.E.), it continued to be used by communities at Gezer until the end of the Late Bronze period (1500–1200 B.C.E.). ■

wheels. They carved fine wooden furniture inlaid with ivory from Syria. They exported grain, olive oil, wine, cattle, timber, and slaves.

During the Middle Bronze period, colonists and warriors from Syria-Palestine, whom native Egyptians despised as *Hyksos* or *northerners*, occupied the delta where the Nile River flows into the Mediterranean Sea. The Hyksos ruled Egypt (1630–1539 B.C.E.) from the Nile delta to Thebes, three hundred miles to the south. Middle Bronze culture thrived in Egypt until 1540 B.C.E., when Kamose (1555–1550 B.C.E.) declared Egypt's independence from the Hyksos. For the next 150 years, pharaohs systematically razed Hyksos cities and exterminated their culture from Avaris in the delta of Egypt north to Megiddo in the valley of Jezreel in Syria-Palestine.

To create the Middle Bronze sanctuary at Gezer, ten large stones were erected (Hebrew: *maṣṣēbôt*) in the soil along a straight line running north-south. Some of the stones are ten feet high. The sacred space around the stones is plastered and edged with a low stone curb. In front of the line of standing stones there is a large stone into which a basin or socket has been carved (Dever 1993; 1997).

Sometimes communities erected simply a single stone, but generally there are two, three, five, seven, nine, or twelve stones. Sometimes the stones are arranged in a straight line as they were at Gezer; sometimes the arrangement is curved, as it is at Gilgal. Standing stones were not images of members of the divine assembly, but rather dwellings for them. Therefore, the covenant between Yahweh and Israel did not outlaw them (Exod 20:4-5; Deut 5:8-9). Likewise, the Bible does not consider the standing stones of other cultures in Syria-Palestine to be idols. The Bible orders the Hebrews to smash the standing stones of strangers because as long as those stones stand, the divine patrons of the strangers have places to stay (Exod 23:24; 34:13; Deut 7:5; 12:5). If the Hebrews destroy the standing stones, then the divine patrons of their enemies are homeless. Because they have no place to stay, they cannot defend their peoples against the Hebrews.

At Bethel, Jacob erects the stone from which Yahweh appeared to him in a dream (Gen 28:10-22; Isa 19:19). The tradition never explicitly says that the stone is an image of Yahweh. Jacob anoints the stone to acknowledge the presence of Yahweh in the stone. Similarly, the standing stones that the Hebrews erected at Arad, the bull site in Samaria, Lachish, Dan, Tirzah, and Hazor were not images of Yahweh but places for Yahweh to stay with them. The stones are ongoing reminders that the covenant between Yahweh and Israel is still in effect (Zevit 2001, 256–66).

The inscription on this piece of a pithos storage jar from Kuntillet ʿAjrud reads: "For YHWH and his Asherah." Despite the biblical understanding that YHWH was not married, popular piety may have considered YHWH and Asherah to have been a divine couple.

Most standing stones have been shaped. The dwellings for Godfathers are represented by tall and thin stones; the dwellings for Godmothers, by short and squat stones. The two standing stones in the Hebrew sanctuary at Arad roughly conform to these canons of style. The theology of the divine patron of ancient Israel as a couple, rather than as a single divine male, appears also in the prayers of Hebrew pilgrims who visited the sanctuaries at Kuntillet ʿAjrud and Khirbet el-Qom. On broken pieces of pottery, they wrote their prayers to both Yahweh, their Godfather, and Asherah, their Godmother (Zevit 2001, 350–438).

Biblical traditions connect the erection of stones with the cutting of a covenant between the Hebrews and Yahweh. As long as the stone stood, the covenant remained in effect. If the stones were broken, as happened in the story of Moses, the covenant was abrogated (Exod 23:24; 34:13; Deut 7:5; 12:3). The list of witnesses to the covenant between Yahweh and Israel at Sinai in the book of Exodus (Exod 24:1-18) describes the stones as tablets on which the covenant is inscribed. The list of witnesses for the covenant between Yahweh and Israel at Gilgal in the book of Joshua (Josh 3:1—5:12) describes the stones as representations of the twelve tribes of Israel. Yet in most sanctuaries, including those erected by the Hebrews, standing stones housed the divine patrons of the community that erected them. This architecture created a visual image of the divine plane, from which the divine assembly watched over the people for whom the sanctuary was a sacred center.

Stones were erected also to commemorate human events. Shoshenq I erected a standing stone at Megiddo as a memorial of his conquest of the city. Jacob erected a stone as a memorial to the covenant between Jacob and Laban at Gilead on the border between their lands (Gen 31:43-54). Standing stones were also erected over graves. These tombstones reflect the expectation of the living that where the dead are buried divine intercourse will take place and the community will be recreated. For example, a stone was erected on the grave of Rachel (Gen 35:16-20).

The magnificent Middle Bronze city at Gezer and its impressive sanctuary of standing stones were destroyed in 1468 B.C.E. The annals of Tuthmosis III (ruled 1479–1425 B.C.E.) report that he waged sixteen campaigns in Syria-Palestine. Gezer was one of his victories.

GEZER (1000–920 B.C.E.)

The Hebrews' most important natural resource was their geographical location. Two trade routes passed through their land: the coastal highway (Latin: *Via Maris*) and the royal highway. The coastal highway was a north–south trade lane that ran along the Mediterranean Sea from Egypt to the Carmel Mountains. The royal highway ran along the eastern ridge of the Dead Sea Valley between the Red Sea and Damascus. Income

from transit trade and outright piracy from these two routes was significant (1 Kgs 10:14-15).

The two most important social institutions in the world of the Bible were the village and the state (Matthews and Benjamin 1993, 155–58). Villages are decentralized and subsistence economies; states are centralized and surplus economies. One of Dever's questions was: *Is Gezer (Stratum VIII) evidence that the decentralized and subsistence villages of early Israel had developed into a centralized and surplus state ruled by David and Solomon?* Hebrew villages appeared in the hills or highlands of Judah, west of the Jordan River and north of Jerusalem, around 1200 B.C.E. Just when these villages develop into a centralized, surplus state economy is not so clear.

State economies in the world of the Bible were composed of a *mother* city and its villages or *daughters*. Architecturally, a city was a complex of domestic and public buildings surrounded by a wall. This walled community maintained a successful trade network with smaller, unfortified surrounding villages. Cities were governed by a monarch and a city assembly. Monarchs (Akkadian: *hazannu*) leased the land to households (Akkadian: *hupsu*). Cities controlled more land and produced more goods than they needed simply for survival. The surplus was traded to outsiders for luxury goods.

The Hebrews founded villages in the hills as a strategy for protecting themselves from the wars raging along the coastal highway. In time, however, they exhausted the scant natural resources in these hills and began migrating back to the foothills and plains along the coast. In some areas the Hebrews negotiated with their new neighbors in the foothills and on the plains, establishing covenants for goods and services that were mutually beneficial. In other areas, however, the Hebrews and their new neighbors became bitter enemies. The Hebrews and their Philistine, Midianite,

Ammonite, Moabite, and Amalekite neighbors raided one another's herds and farms.

The Hebrews finally broke out of their villages and began to occupy, purchase, or conquer new land (Edelman 1988). David is generally considered the last chief—a temporary warlord elected to lead the tribe of warriors into battle. Solomon is the first monarch—a permanent ruler and commander of a full-time professional army of soldiers. From the reign of Solomon on, the monarchs of ancient Israel all constructed monumental public works and fortifications such as the gates and casemate walls at Gezer, Hazor, and Megiddo. By the end of Solomon's reign around 930 B.C.E., the evolution from Israel as villages to Israel as a state was generally considered to have been complete.

A closer look at the material remains along the coastal highway, however, reveals that neither David (ruled 1000–970 B.C.E.) nor Solomon (ruled 970–930 B.C.E.) had much political or economic control over the Philistines. The Philistines were clearly dominant (Bierling 2002). As their threat to Egyptian trade along the coastal highway increased, Pharaoh Siamun (ruled 978–959 B.C.E.) attacked Gaza, Gath, Ekron (Stratum IV), Ashdod (Stratum X), and Tel Qasile (Stratum X). Siamun published the annals of his campaign in Syria-Palestine on the sanctuary walls at Tanis. In his annals, Siamun is pictured attacking a Philistine warrior armed with a double-bladed axe characteristic of the Sea Peoples. The warrior is holding the axe by the blade, not the handle, reflecting his incompetence as a fighter. The blade itself is drawn at an angle, indicating that the handle has cracked just at the point where it slides into the blade, so it is useless as a weapon. Neither the warrior nor his weapon is a threat to Siamun (Kitchen 2003, 108–10).

Midway up the coastal highway, an east–west cutoff connected that highway to Jerusalem. Gezer guarded the intersection. During his campaign against the Philistines in 967 B.C.E., Siamun also attacked the Canaanite city of Gezer to keep the Philistines from expanding farther inland (Stratum IX). He ceded the city to the Hebrews to clearly identify the border of Philistia and to guard the coastal highway for Egypt.

Following Siamun's campaign, palaces, sanctuaries, and fortifications were constructed at Gezer, Beth-Shemesh, Megiddo, Taanach, Beth-Shean, Yokneam, and Hazor to secure trade routes against Philistine interference. These building programs transformed the landscape along the coast highway, which was important to both Israel and Tyre. Fortifying Gezer gave Israel a secure border. The actual reconstruction of Gezer may have been done by Hiram of Tyre (1 Kgs 5:1). Both David and Solomon took advantage of Tyre's skill in business and building

The need to protect land and people was a common stimulus for the formation of a state. Villages were defended by militias of part-time warriors who were farmers and herders commanded by charismatic leaders. States had standing armies of full-time professional soldiers commanded by trained military officers. Ongoing military crises generally prompted villagers to forgo their self-determination in exchange for strongman rule in a state. In order to protect their land and children, village households were willing to relinquish a portion of their authority. ∎

(1 Kgs 9:10–25). Solomon may have paid Hiram by ceding land north of the Carmel Mountains to Tyre (Miller and Hayes 2006, 208–9; Kitchen 2003: 112–15).

The main gate at Gezer is one example of the monumental architecture identifying the strategic importance of the city (Stratum VIII). It is also a test case for determining whether Gezer is evidence for state formation in Israel. The gate at Gezer followed the same pattern as the gates of Hazor and Megiddo (Yadin 1958). The main gate of Gezer is the best preserved of the three. The space on either side of the main gate of Gezer was subdivided into three smaller rooms or "bays." Low stone benches ran along the base of the walls. The gate was repeatedly redesigned and repaired until it was destroyed by Shoshenq I (Stratum VIII). This destruction layer was dated by red-slipped pottery polished by hand and manufactured prior to Shoshenq's campaign (Dever 2001b, 131–38; Holladay 1990).

In 925 B.C.E., Shoshenq I invaded Syria-Palestine. His annals describe his march and the cities he conquered. These annals are a geography for Syria-Palestine at the end of the Iron I period (1200–900 B.C.E.) and the beginning of the Iron II period (900–586 B.C.E.). The conquest of Gezer (Stratum VIII) in 925 B.C.E. was one of his victories (1 Kgs 11:40; 2 Chr 12:2–4) along with Tirzah, Rehob, Beth-Shean, and Megiddo.

Writing is also a signature of state formation. Education or wisdom was an important skill for good government. As villages evolved into states, instruction in tradition by mothers of households to integrate women and children into the community evolved into schools taught by male scribes (Jamieson-Drake 1991). Wise men such as Ptah-hotep and Amen-em-ope taught the men who would be rulers of states in Mesopotamia, Syria-Palestine, and Egypt. The recovery of several clay inkwells (Stratum VII) and the Gezer Almanac (Stratum VIII) suggest that Gezer may have been home to a school for scribes.

Sometime between 950 and 925 B.C.E. a student at Gezer practiced writing Hebrew on a limestone tablet four inches long and four inches wide (Albright 1942). The student copied an almanac identifying the specific chores for each season of the farmer's year. Macalister recovered the artifact during his excavation at Gezer in 1908. In Syria-Palestine the agricultural year began in the fall, when olives were harvested and the October rains softened the sun-dried soil enough so that planting could start (Matthews and Benjamin 2006, 155–56).

GEZER ALMANAC

(Matthews and Benjamin 2006, 155–56)

August and September to pick olives;
    October to sow barley;
December and January to weed;
    February to cut flax;
March to harvest barley;
    April to harvest wheat and pay tithes;
May and June to prune vines;
    July to pick the fruit of summer.

Stratum VIII (967–925 B.C.E.) at Gezer became a battlefield not just for invading pharaohs but for twentieth-century scholars as well. Archaeologists who identified the material remains at Gezer as evidence for a powerful, centralized state ruled by Solomon are called *maximalists*. Dever and K. A. Kitchen, for example, are maximalists who argue that Stratum VIII clearly shows that Gezer was a provincial capital in the state of Israel ruled by Solomon (Dever 2001b; 2005; Kitchen 2003).

Biblical scholars who find no evidence in Stratum VIII that Solomon built the gates, walls, and other buildings at Gezer are called *minimalists*. Niels Peter Lemche, Thomas L. Thompson, and Keith W. Whitelam, for example, are minimalists who strongly disagree with Dever and Kitchen (Lemche 1997; T. L. Thompson 1996; Whitelam 1996). They argue that no archaeological evidence from Gezer supports the historical reliability of the biblical tradition that Israel was a state ruled by Solomon between 1000 and 900 B.C.E. The Israel of the period was still no more than a scattered federation of villages in the hills north of Jerusalem.

The Gezer Calendar, seven horizontal lines of Hebrew inscription, one vertical line at left. Wood and gypsum (Iron Period II), from Gezer, Israel. This is the first known agricultural calendar. Height 7.2 cm. Location: Archaeological Museum, Istanbul, Turkey. Photo Credit: Erich Lessing / Art Resource, NY.

CONCLUSION

The debate between the archaeologists and the biblical scholars frequently lacked civility but has, nonetheless, contributed to a more nuanced understanding of what was happening in Syria-Palestine between 1000 and 900 B.C.E. If Tyre built the walls and gates and other buildings of Gezer for the Egyptians, who then gave the city to Solomon to create a border that the Philistines were not to cross, then the evidence for a centralized state of Israel ruled by Solomon still remains to be found. If the renewed excavations at Gezer by a consortium of institutions under the direction of Steven M. Ortiz and Sam Wolff cannot connect the construction of the city with Solomon, then what Solomon may have brought to Israel was not so much political power and economic wealth as the genius of knowing how to negotiate successfully the survival of the Hebrews in a world dominated by powerful and often hostile neighbors.

The power brokers in the world of Solomon were the Philistines, the Egyptians, and the people of Tyre. They were the wagers of wars, the barons of trade, the builders, and the bankers. The Hebrews had emerged from their asylum in the hills north of Jerusalem onto the military, political, and economic playing field of Syria-Palestine. Ancestor stories in the Bible (Gen 11:27—25:18) celebrate Abraham and Sarah not for building great cities but for negotiating good covenants. Abraham and Sarah were the patrons of the household of David and Solomon, who is probably responsible for telling those stories preserved today in the Bible. David and Solomon remembered Abraham and Sarah for their skill in negotiating with their divine patron (Gen 11:27—12:8), with their enemies (Gen 12:9—13:1), and with their friends (Gen 13:5—14:24). Perhaps Solomon remembered Abraham the way he himself wanted to be remembered at Gezer—not so much as a builder but as a covenant maker. Whether they were dealing with Yahweh, their divine patron; with the Egyptians and the Philistines, their ancient enemies; or with the people of Tyre, their friends, covenants were the Hebrews' strategy of choice for establishing the life-supporting conditions for land and children. The Hebrews may have survived their entry into the Iron Age not because they were rich and powerful, but because they knew how to negotiate covenants with the rich and powerful. And the material remains at Gezer, not built by Solomon but rather given to him by Shoshenq I, may be a prime example of what such successful covenant making can accomplish.

WHAT YOU HAVE LEARNED

- Gezer is an important site excavated by processual archaeologists.
- Processual archaeologists wanted to know if material artifacts at Gezer would demonstrate that Israel was a central, surplus state by 1000 B.C.E. The evidence is still inconclusive.
- Standing stones (*maṣṣēbôt*) like those at Gezer were dwellings for members of a culture's divine assembly, not images of their divine patrons.
- The Gezer Almanac identifying specific chores for each season of the farmer's year, may indicate that there was a royal school for scribes there.
- The gates, walls, and public buildings at Gezer may have been built by Tyre for Egypt, which then turned the city over to Israel to prevent the Philistines from blocking the coastal highway.

STUDY QUESTIONS

1. What do the excavations at Gezer suggest about the reign of Solomon?
2. What do we know about cities in Syria-Palestine in the Middle Bronze Age?
3. What are "standing stones"?
4. What was the importance of the geographical location of Gezer?
5. What are the differences between a village economy and a state economy?

PREVIEW: TEL MIQNE

- Tel Miqne
  - Transition from Late Bronze to Iron Age
  - Early Artifacts
  - Philistines at Ekron
  - Megaron
  - Ekron Fortress
- Olive Oil Industry
- Weaving
- Saga of Samson

Chapter 18 describes the excavations at Tel Miqne, an important site excavated by processual archaeologists. Three significant questions were used to interpret the artifacts, producing the following results. Excavators demonstrated that the transition from the Bronze Age to the Iron Age in Syria-Palestine was complex, not uniform, and gradual, not spontaneous. They also reconstructed the shifting political conditions between Philistines, Israelites, Phoenicians, Assyrians, and Egyptians; the interaction of these diverse cultures; and their economic development. Finally, they clearly described the development and then decline of Philistine culture in Syria-Palestine, providing an important corrective for the generally barbaric and hostile portrayal of the Philistines in the Bible.

18

Tel Miqne
(1550–603 B.C.E.)

Processual archaeologists begin with a question. Trude Dothan and Seymour Gitin wanted to know if the transition from the Late Bronze Age (1500–1200 B.C.E.) to the early Iron Age (1200–1000 B.C.E.) in Syria-Palestine was uniform and simultaneous (Dothan 1990). Fourteen seasons of excavating at Tel Miqne (1981–1996) clearly show that the transition was complex, not uniform, and gradual, not spontaneous. Egyptian, Sea People, and native cultures in Syria-Palestine began to show Iron Age characteristics and to develop Iron Age technologies in different ways and at different times (http://www.aiar.org/miqneekron.html).

Tel Miqne is some twenty miles southwest of Jerusalem on the western edge of the foothills (Hebrew: šĕpēlâ) in the Sorek Valley. The site is some 350 feet above sea level. Tel Miqne is on the biblical border between Judah and Philistia. Political and economic conditions change more quickly in border cities than in cities in the heartland. Dothan and Gitin also wanted to clarify the relationship between Philistines, Israelites, Phoenicians, Assyrians, and Egyptians from 1200 to 586 B.C.E. The excavations at Tel Miqne are important for understanding the culture of the Sea Peoples in Syria-Palestine, particularly the Philistines. Therefore, Tel Miqne was a prime site for reconstructing the shifting political conditions, the interaction of diverse cultures, and economic development between 1200 and 586 B.C.E.

Artifacts from Tel Miqne also provide a fresh context for reconstructing a calendar for both Philistia in particular and Syria-Palestine in general. The Philistines who conquered Tel Miqne in 1175 B.C.E. imposed their western Mediterranean culture on the native peoples who survived the war. As a Philistine city, Tel Miqne rose and fell. The culture of the Philistines was influenced by contact with the cultures of Canaan, Egypt, Israel, Judah, and Assyria but was never completely assimilated by any of them. After Judah ceded Tel Miqne to Assyria in 701 B.C.E., the city flourished until Babylon destroyed it in 603 B.C.E. and relocated the survivors.

TEL MIQNE 1550–1175 B.C.E.

Artifacts indicate that there were human settlements at Tel Miqne from 4000 to 3000 B.C.E. and from 1700 to 603 B.C.E. Less-enduring settlements were built on the site between 64 B.C.E. and 640. From 4000 to 1550 B.C.E., Tel Miqne was used by various peoples. They left pottery and bricks at the site, but their settlements were completely destroyed by the inhabitants who came after them. The people who lived at Tel Miqne between 1550 and 1175 B.C.E. left a clear record of their presence (Strata VIII-X). They were Canaanites—peoples native to Syria-Palestine—but they traded with people from all over the world of the Bible. They

Vases from Tomb IV at Mycenae (Greece), 1500–1400 B.C.E. Location: National Archaeological Museum, Athens, Greece. Photo Credit: Vanni / Art Resource, NY.

The Philistines were a Sea People. Gaston Maspero (1846–1916), founder of the Institut français d'archéologie orientale and director of the Egyptian Museum (Cairo), coined the name *Sea Peoples* (French: *les peuples de la mer*) in 1881. Reference to these groups first appears in the Annals of Merneptah (ruled 1224–1214 B.C.E.). The Egyptians and the Hittites identified at least nine groups of Sea Peoples: Karkisa, Labu, Lukka, Meshwesh, Shardana, Shekelesh, Tjakkar, and Philistines (http://www.courses.psu.edu/cams/cams400w_aek11/www/index.htm).

The Sea Peoples had been uprooted from their homelands by the collapse of the great empires of Egypt, Hatti (Turkey), and Mycenae (Greece). They migrated left behind imports from Egypt, Cyprus, Troy (Turkey), and Mycenae (Greece).

The pottery imported from Mycenae, called *Monochrome Mycenaean III C: 1b*, was decorated with only one color. Potters used dark brown or red paints to create spirals and lines on their wares. The pottery imported from Troy, called *Minyan* or *Trojan Grey Ware*, was grey or tan (S. H. Allen 1994). Potters decorated their wares with alternating straight and wavy horizontal lines.

Also recovered from this period was a seal shaped like a beetle that was imported from Egypt during the reign of Amenophis III (ruled 1391–1353 B.C.E.). The inscription on the seal commemorates the dedication of a sanctuary to his divine patron, Hathor, known as the Lady of the Sycamore Tree.

TEL MIQNE 1175–975 B.C.E.

Between 1300 and 1175, Tel Miqne was protected by a mud-brick wall some ten feet thick (Stratum VIII). Shortly after 1200 B.C.E., Tel Miqne was conquered by Philistines. The last Canaanite city was totally destroyed by a fire that left its storerooms full of jars containing carbonized grains, lentils, and figs. The Philistines developed Tel Miqne into a large city called "Ekron" with a rich material culture. As a member of an urban league with Ashdod, Ashkelon, Gath, and Gaza, Ekron had significant economic and political influence in the region. From 1175 to 1000 B.C.E., the residential neighborhoods of Ekron covered about forty acres; the administrative district covered ten acres (Dothan and Gitin 1992).

Between 1175 and 1125 B.C.E., the Philistines imported less pottery from Mycenae and began to manufacture their own Mycenaean pottery at Ekron (Stratum VII). Neutron Activation Analysis identified the chemical compounds in the clay used to make the pottery. These compounds are found only in soils around Ekron, not in Mycenae. Philistine potters made large mixing bowls with horizontal handles, called *kraters*, and pitchers with strainer spouts for decanting wine into cups. Like the imported pottery, Mycenaean ware manufactured at Ekron was decorated with only one color of paint.

Between 1125 and 1050 B.C.E., the Philistines at Ekron began to manufacture a new style of pottery, called *Philistine Bichrome Ware* (Strata V–VI). The ware was made from local clay, but, unlike the locally made Mycenaean pottery, it was decorated with two colors of paint instead of one. Potters used red and black paint to draw fish and birds on their ware.

Philistine culture closely integrated work and worship. In the northeast section of Ekron, the people built their kilns—ovens for firing pottery. Along with industrial artifacts around the kilns, archaeologists recovered liturgical artifacts that have nothing directly to do with firing pottery. Among the liturgical artifacts around the kilns were small painted statues of animals and a small statue of the Godmother of the Sea Peoples. She is wearing a feather headdress and a bird mask. Her body and the throne on which she is sitting meld into one.

The close association of work and worship reflects a belief that crafts such as pottery making are not human inventions; they are divine gifts. Potters believed that they were taught their craft by their divine patrons not only so that they could make a living, but also so that they could make a difference in their cultures. Their divine patrons gave them their skill and also their raw materials. The Godmother of the Sea Peoples taught them not only how to throw pots but also where to find the water and the clay. To acknowledge their debt to their divine patrons the Philistines arranged their work space to reflect sacred space, and they punctuated their workdays with worship.

from Mycenae, Troy (Turkey), and Crete through Cyprus and then on to Syria-Palestine and Egypt. After a fierce battle on Egypt's Mediterranean coast, Ramesses III (ruled 1194–1163 B.C.E.) ceded control of much of the southern coast of Syria-Palestine, including Tel Miqne, to the Sea Peoples. ∎

Archaeologists use Neutron Activation Analysis to identify chemical compounds in pottery. There are some fifty compounds occurring in nature whose stable isotopes can be converted into radioactive isotopes with one extra neutron. To convert these isotopes from stable to radioactive, archaeologists place a pottery sample in a nuclear reactor and bombard it with neutrons. During the process the compounds capture an extra neutron and become radioactive. These radioactive isotopes are like bar codes—a unique signature for a particular chemical compound. The particles not only identify the compounds in the pottery, but also how much of the compound is found in the clay formula (http://www.lbl.gov/nsd/education/ABC/wallchart/chapters/13/5.html). ∎

In addition to the work-place sanctuaries, the Philistines built a huge hearth sanctuary, called a *megaron*, at Ekron between 1125 and 1100 B.C.E. (Stratum VI). This public building was some sixty-five feet long and forty-five feet wide. The brick walls were four feet thick, plastered and painted blue. The floor in the great room of the sanctuary was compacted soil (French: *terre pisé*). The roof over the great room was supported by two pillars some seven and one-half feet apart. This construction style is similar to that of the great room of the sanctuary at Tel Qasile, whose roof also is supported by twin pillars.

The first Philistine city at Tel Miqne continued to thrive until its destruction after 975 B.C.E. (Stratum IV). Pharaoh Siamun (ruled 978–959 B.C.E.) may have destroyed Ekron, Ashdod (Stratum X), and Tel Qasile (Stratum X) during his campaign against Gezer (1 Kgs 3:1; 9:16).

TEL MIQNE 975–701 B.C.E.

The Philistines who survived the destruction of their first city in 975 B.C.E. did not rebuild their neighborhoods. Instead they moved into the ten-acre administrative district at Ekron's city center (Stratum III). Ekron was no longer a city. It was simply a fortress. The survivors built a new brick wall to protect their fortress. This wall was further fortified by a brick tower covered by large, smooth blocks of limestone called *ashlars*. One block was laid with the narrow end facing out; the adjoining block was laid with the wide side facing out. This alternating *header*, or narrow, and *stretcher*, or wide, construction technique created a building flexible enough to ride out the shocks of an earthquake.

Sometime between 750 and 700 B.C.E., Judah gained control of the fortress at Ekron (Stratum IIA). As part of his preparation for an invasion by Assyria, Hezekiah of Judah (ruled 715–687 B.C.E.) imposed a war tax on Ekron. The Philistines were to send grain, wine, and olive oil to the governor of Hebron. Archaeologists have recovered some of the *lmlk* (*lemelek*, meaning "belonging to the king") seals that were attached to storage jars (http://www.lmlk.com/research/index.html). More than one thousand *lmlk* seals have been found at forty-three different sites, mostly in Judah.

Philistine Godmother figure shaped like a four-legged chair. From Ashdod. Clay figurine. Location: Israel Museum (IDAM), Jerusalem, Israel. Photo Credit: Erich Lessing / Art Resource, NY.

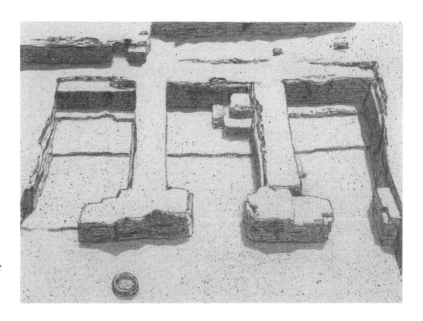

Sanctuary (identified by archaeologists as Building 350) at Tel Miqne; drawing based on a photograph in Dothan 1990.

TEL MIQNE 701–603 B.C.E.

In 701 B.C.E., Sennacherib, Great King of Assyria (ruled 704–681 B.C.E.), attacked Judah (2 Kgs 18:13-15). He destroyed Lachish and attacked Jerusalem. Ekron was not destroyed but was part of the ransom that Hezekiah paid for Jerusalem. Under Assyrian rule, Ekron once again became a thriving independent state (Stratum IC). Assyria established a seventy-year period of peace in Syria-Palestine, which allowed its covenant partners such as Padi, and then Ikausu, at Ekron to flourish.

THE THIRD YEAR OF THE REIGN OF SENNACHERIB
(Matthews and Benjamin 2006, 190–92)

The official and ranking citizens of Ekron deposed Padi, their king, and put this loyal covenant partner of Assyria in chains. They placed him in the custody of Hezekiah, the king of Judah. Once they realized what they had done, they called on the pharaohs of Egypt for assistance.

Although the Egyptians marshaled a large army against me, I inflicted a great defeat upon them in the Plains of Eltekeh with the help of Ashur, my divine patron (2 Kgs 19:9). I personally captured the Egyptian and Ethiopian chariots and their commanders, and then laid siege, conquered and looted the cities of Eltekeh and Timnah.

231

Advancing to Ekron, I slew its rebellious officials and ranking citizens and impaled their bodies on the towers of the city (1 Sam 31:10). All the rest of the people who had raised a hand against me were taken captive. The innocent were spared. King Padi was released from prison in Jerusalem and once again placed on his throne and his tribute payments were reinstated.

Because Hezekiah of Judah did not submit to my yoke, I laid siege to forty-six of his fortified cities, walled forts, and to the countless villages in their vicinity. I conquered them using earthen ramps and battering rams. These siege engines were supported by infantry who tunneled under the walls. I took 200,150 prisoners of war, young and old, male and female, from these places. I also plundered more horses, mules, donkeys, camels, large and small cattle than we could count. I imprisoned Hezekiah in Jerusalem like a bird in a cage. I erected siege works to prevent anyone escaping through the city gates. The cities in Judah which I captured I gave to Mitinti, king of Ashdod, and to Padi, king of Ekron, and to Sillibel, king of Gaza. Thus I reduced the land of Hezekiah in this campaign, and I also increased Hezekiah's annual tribute payments.

Hezekiah, who was overwhelmed by my terror-inspiring splendor, was deserted by his elite troops, which he had brought into Jerusalem. He was forced to send me four-hundred twenty pounds [Akkadian: thirty talents] of gold, eleven-thousand two-hundred pounds [Akkadian: eight-hundred talents] of silver, precious stones, couches and chairs inlaid with ivory, elephant hides, ebony wood, box wood, and all kinds of valuable treasures, his daughters, wives, and male and female musicians. He sent his personal messenger to deliver this tribute and bow down to me (2 Kgs 18:14-16).

The fortifications, the industrial districts, the residential neighborhoods, and the administrative district of the new Ekron were well planned. Buildings were constructed on a system of terraces that sloped from the outer walls to the city center. The Philistines rebuilt the walls around Ekron and added a new battle tower at the southeast corner of the city. The main gate on the south side of Ekron had a tower and three piers that created two bays. This pattern is parallel to that used to construct the gates of Ashdod, Gezer, and Lachish.

Incense altars with raised corners, or *horns*, were common in the northern Hebrew state of Israel but not in Philistia or Judah. The presence of ten such altars in Ekron may indicate that after Assyria conquered Israel (721 B.C.E.), some Israelite workers were deported to Ekron.

The old residential neighborhoods inside the walls were rebuilt, and a new ten-acre suburb northwest of the walls was constructed. The limestone needed for all this urban development was imported from Judah, as were the stonemasons needed to shape and install it. In contrast to the hostility between the Hebrews and the Philistines that is reflected in the Bible, Hebrews and Philistines were trade partners during 701–603 B.C.E.

Olive Oil

More than one hundred olive oil presses were installed along the inside of the walls near the gate along a street complete with drains and curbs, and in an industrial district in the northeastern section of the city. The workshops were rectangular buildings with three rooms: one room for production, one for storage, and an outer room that opened to the street. The room that opened to the street was used for both devotion and for dining. Incense altars for worship and pottery for preparing and serving food were found in these rooms.

Olive oil press, Ekron, 701–603 B.C.E.

Farmers produced at least 290 gallons of olive oil during a good harvest year. This made Ekron the largest olive oil producer in the world of the Bible. The city was near the foothills, where the soil and climate for growing olives were excellent. Ekron was also close to the coastal highway running from Egypt to Damascus and to ports like Ashkelon, from which the olive oil could be shipped to the western Mediterranean.

Pressing or milling olives was a four- or five-step process. First, olives were washed and then crushed in a rectangular vat with a heavy stone roller to create a paste. Second, the paste was loaded into loosely woven baskets. The baskets were stacked on top of one another over a vat. Each mill had two pressing vats, one on each side of the crushing vat. Third, pressure was applied to the baskets using a lever. One end of the lever was set into a socket in the wall; the other end was weighted with stones. Each stone had been drilled and threaded with a rope that was then looped over the end of the lever. Four stones were used to weight each lever. The baskets trapped the skins and pits, and the oil flowed through the weave of the baskets into collection vats.

Fourth, the oil was ladled from the vat into larger ceramic separation jars to separate the water from the oil pressed from the olives. These separation jars had two holes halfway down their side walls. These holes were sealed with bungs or plugs until the water and oil had settled. The oil rose to the top of the krater; the water settled to the bottom. Fifth, by unplugging the holes, the water could be drained off, leaving the olive oil. The oil was then collected and stored.

Weaving

At Ekron, olives were harvested and milled during four months of the year. During the rest of the year, the Philistines at Ekron used the workshops to weave cloth. Looms had two uprights, a horizontal warp beam, a shed rod, a heddle rod, and weights. The warp-weighted loom held the warp threads parallel under tension by tying them in small bunches to stone or pottery weights. Loom weights have been recovered from many of the workshops, and similar weights have been found from 7000 B.C.E. at Çatal Höyük (Turkey).

About 630 B.C.E., Babylon destroyed the Assyrian empire, and Egypt seized Ekron (Stratum IB). Ekron lost its access to the world markets for its olive oil that Assyria had guaranteed and that Egypt could no longer provide. Ekron's economy softened, and by 603 B.C.E. Nebuchadnezzar, Great King of Babylon, had conquered Ekron. Archaeologists found a sad souvenir from those last days at Ekron. Buried in the storeroom of one of Ekron's workshops was a stash of iron farm tools: plows, a knife, and sickle blades. The farmers who hid them never returned to resume

their peacetime lives at Ekron. Six hundred years of Philistine presence at Ekron had come to an end.

THE SAGA OF SAMSON (JUDGES 13:1—16:31)

In the traditions of Egypt and of ancient Israel, the Sea Peoples, and especially the Philistines, are barbarians. The demonization of the Philistines is particularly brutal in the saga of Samson (Judg 13:1—16:31), in which the Philistines burn Samson's wife and her household to death and blind and torture Samson. The same caricatures of the Philistines appear in the stories of the ark of the covenant (1 Sam 4:1—7:1), in which Philistines desecrate the ark; in the stories of David's rise to power (1 Sam 8:4—2 Sam 8:13), in which Goliath taunts the Hebrews and David for not having a man among them; and in the stories of Saul (1 Sam 8:4—31:13), whose dead body the Philistines behead and hang on the walls of Beth-Shean.

Archaeology reveals the Philistines as survivors, artists, merchants, and political and economic power brokers, qualities that are reflected also in the Bible. In the stories of David's rise to power, Achish, the Philistine ruler of Gath, grants David asylum when Saul wants to assassinate him. And in the stories of David's successor (2 Sam 9:1—20:26 + 1 Kgs 1:1—11:43), when Absalom revolts against David, only Cherethites and Pelethites—Sea Peoples like the Philistines—come to his support.

The Philistines came to the Near East through Cyprus from the western Mediterranean. In ordinary speech today, the word "Philistine" is often derogatory. The word identifies people who are outsiders, who are uncultured, or whose interests are material and commonplace. In the world of the Bible, however, the Philistines and Hebrews were neighboring cultures that appeared in Syria-Palestine for the first time at the end of the Late Bronze Age (1400–1200 B.C.E.), when the empires of Mycenae, Hattusas, and Egypt collapsed. The Philistines and the Hebrews were peoples brought together in the same land, at the same time, by Egypt, their common enemy.

The Philistines were part of the federation of Sea Peoples. Ramesses III fought against them, and some of the Sea Peoples subsequently settled on the southern coastal plain of Syria-Palestine, which became known as *Philistia* or *Palestine*. Ramesses III built his funeral chapel (Arabic: *Medinet Habu*) in the Valley of the Pharaohs at the site where Ameno- phis I (ruled 1525–1504 B.C.E.) and Hatshepsut (ruled 1473–1458 B.C.E.) had built a sanctuary celebrating the primeval hill that emerged from the waters of chaos, the place where Atum stood to create the cosmos. The Sea Peoples were looting the coast of Syria-Palestine and Egypt. Like Atum, who stood on a mound of soil in the Valley of the Pharaohs and drove chaos from Egypt, Ramesses pictured himself standing on the shores of Egypt and driving the Sea Peoples from Egypt. Ramesses' battle against the Sea Peoples was the first day of creation.

At Medinet Habu a high pylon gate opens into a broad courtyard with another pylon gate ninety feet high leading to the holy of holies. Emphatically carved on both sides of the entrance pylon, more than eight inches deep into the walls, are the annals of a pharaoh conquering his enemies. In 1829, Jean François Champollion conclusively identified the pharaoh of Medinet Habu as Ramesses III (ruled 1194–1163 B.C.E.) and translated his annals describing the defense of Egypt under attack by the Sea Peoples (Matthews and Benjamin 2006, 151–54).

Annunciation to the Wife of Manoah (Judges 13:1-25)

Storytellers set the saga of Samson in the land of Ekron and its sister city, Timnah. Timnah (Hebrew: *Tel Batash*) is located in the Sorek Valley between Beth Shemesh and Ekron (Josh 15:10-11). Although the popu- lation of Ekron was Philistine, quarry workers and stonemasons from Judah came and went to work on building projects. The population of Timnah was more culturally diverse than that of Ekron. Philistines, Canaanites, and Israelites lived side by side in Timnah (Panitz-Cohen and Mazar 2006). Only 30 or 40 percent of the pottery artifacts from the period in Timnah were manufactured in the traditions of the Sea Peo- ples. Both the geographical and the social settings of the saga of Samson are consistent with the settings reconstructed by archaeology for Ekron and Timnah. These hero stories are a fascinating profile of daily life on the border between Ekron and Judah.

In the beginning of the story of Samson (Judg 13:1-25), Samson's parents, Manoah and his wife, have no children. A diving messenger brings the news of Yahweh's intervention and they have a son. The wife of Manoah is wise. Because the message involves childbirth, and because women have a greater role in childbirth than men, the messenger deals with the wife of Manoah, rather than with Manoah. The wife of Manoah respects the messenger, pays close attention to the directions, and conscientiously tells Manoah what the messenger tells her to do for their son.

In contrast, Manoah is a fool who not only knows little or nothing about child-bearing, but also does not listen to his wife, who does. In addition, Manoah violates the protocol of a host by asking the messenger for his name. The foolishness of fathers in annunciation stories emphasizes the powerlessness of human beings in contrast to the power of Yahweh to give birth to children even from infertile couples. The wife of Manoah is infertile, yet Yahweh allows her to give birth to the hero Samson, who will free the Hebrews from Ekron and their other Philistine enemies. Birth is a divine gift, not a human accomplishment. Infertile women are liminal women, who, like Israel itself, are without status. But infertile women, like Israel itself, are chosen by Yahweh to free the slaves. Samson will deliver the people of Judah who live along the border with Ekron from Philistine domination.

Samson Courts the Woman of Timnah (Judg 14:1-20)

Samson grows up to become a fearless hunter. He is undaunted by animals, but he is defeated by women. The saga of Samson characterizes him as a womanizer who seduces the Philistine woman of Timnah and the woman of Gaza, but Delilah, also a Philistine woman, outwits Samson and seduces him. In the story, Samson's mother is a Hebrew; she is the mother of a household in Israel. The other three women in the saga are Philistines; they are strangers. The wife of Manoah is the insider whom Yahweh protects. The woman of Timnah, the woman of Gaza, and Delilah are the outsiders from whom Yahweh protects the Hebrews.

Samson goes down to Timnah, a daughter city of Ekron. He crosses back and forth over the frontier that separates Judah and Philistia. Samson is a fool for seeking to have intercourse with strange women. Samson married the woman from Timnah, and during the first six days of the wedding, the household of the groom displayed the bride-price that it was investing in the household of the bride. Likewise, the household of the bride displayed the dowry that it was investing in the household of the groom. The guests looked over the bride-price and the dowry to be sure that they met the stipulations of the covenant that the two households had negotiated. On the seventh day of the wedding feast, the bride and groom were expected to consummate their marriage.

Riddles were part of wedding rituals. Riddles are word games that men used at weddings to determine their new status in the household created by the wedding. According to the hero story, Samson put a riddle to the people at the wedding feast (Judg 14:11-20). Samson lost the riddle contest, because his wife coaxed the answer from him and revealed it to her people. This rendered Samson impotent and therefore unable to consummate the marriage. To redeem the honor of his household, Samson killed and stripped thirty Philistine warriors to shame them. Exposing the genitals of a warrior was comparable to castration. Only children played naked. Clothing was the uniform of a sexually active adult. To remove the clothing of sexually active adults returned them to the status of children.

In the world of the Bible, marriage was almost always patrilocal. Women left the households of their fathers and moved to the households of their husbands. In this story there is no marriage. Samson leaves the wedding feast unable to consummate his marriage, so the woman of Timnah returns to the household of her father unmarried.

Samson Massacres the Garrison of Lehi (Judges 15:9-17)

The stories of how Samson massacred the garrison of Lehi (Judg 15:9-17) and raided the spring at Hakkore (Judg 15:18–20) use mnemonics to help their audiences remember the cry that Samson let out, where he cried out, and the unorthodox weapon with which he massacred the Philistines.

The name Lehi, or "Jawbone Springs," reminds the Hebrews where Yahweh began their deliverance from the Philistines. Here Samson cried out for independence. Both the Hebrew words for "spring of water" and "cry out" have one letter in common: ʿayin. The ʿayin is shaped like a fork with two tines. As a word picture, these prongs represent the crack in the face of a rock through which the water, here portrayed as the handle of the fork, trickles like tears from a human eye. By drinking water from the spring shaped like the sound of a cry for help, Samson cries out. The shape gives birth to a sound.

The letter ʿayin and the jawbone of an ass also have the same shape. Again, the association with the shape of the spring led Samson to the

Samson's weapons in these stories are his bare hands. The Hebrews considered Philistine weapons to be state-of-the-art. The Philistines had the best available arsenal of military hardware, yet the best iron weapons (like the tools hidden by the farmers at Ekron) that the Philistines could forge were no match for the hands of Samson—or the jawbone of an ass—when these unorthodox weapons were wielded by heroes lifted up by Yahweh to deliver the Hebrews from slavery. Samson would deliver the Hebrews living along the border with Ekron from Philistine oppression just as Moses had delivered the Hebrews from slavery in Egypt. ∎

shape of his unorthodox weapon. Traditional people strongly believe in the desire of creation to harmonize. Nothing likes to stand out or create discord. Therefore, Samson chose a weapon that harmonized with the place where he would deliver Israel.

Samson Terrorizes the Wadi Sorek (Judges 16:4-22)

In the story of Samson terrorizing the Wadi Sorek (Judg 16:4–22), Samson delivers Israel from Philistia three times, before Delilah delivers Philistia from Israel by shaving Samson's head. A man's hair and his beard were comparable to his pubic hair because both appear during puberty. By shaving Samson's head, Delilah castrates him and leaves him as weak as a child. When Delilah lets Samson fall asleep on her lap, she also transforms him from powerful to powerless. Samson tries to fall between the legs of Delilah and have intercourse with her as an adult, but instead falls asleep on her lap like a child.

When the Philistines took Samson prisoner, they gouged out his eyes. This tactic rendered warriors powerless. Blinding was equivalent to castration because the eyes of warriors were equivalent to their testicles. To be blind was to be impotent. Mutilating prisoners of war also prevented them from bearing arms. They were powerless to protect their land and their children. Mutilated warriors could work, but they could not fight. Mutilation also clearly identified convicts and served as a warning to others. The Philistines sentenced Samson to grind at a mill—the great warrior was forced to do the work of a woman.

Samson Destroys the House of Dagon (Judges 16:23-31)

Prisoners of war were brought back from the battlefield as evidence to the people at home that the warriors had fulfilled their obligation to protect them from their enemies. Some prisoners were sold as slaves. Others, like Samson, were publicly tortured and executed in mock battles. The Philistines tortured Samson during the festival of Dagon, their divine patron.

Samson retaliated and put out the *eyes*, or twin pillars, of the Philistine sanctuary in retaliation for the loss of his eyes. The pillars marked the place where the divine patrons of the community enter and leave the human plane. The Philistine sanctuaries at both Ekron and Tel Qasile likewise rested on two pillars. Through these eyes of the Philistine temple, Dagon entered Philistia. Blindness closed the vent, cutting Philistia off from its divine patron. The Philistines left Israel powerless by blinding Samson, and Samson left Philistia powerless by blinding Dagon.

CONCLUSION

The saga of Samson does not celebrate Samson. In all his glory Samson was a fool. Only blind and powerless did he become a hero. The saga of Samson teaches its audiences that Yahweh does not need great warriors to deliver Israel from its enemies, but can use a blind man like Samson. It is Yahweh, and Yahweh alone, who feeds and protects the land and its people—even from the great Philistines of Ekron, Gath, Gaza, Ashkelon, and Ashdod. The stones from the excavations at Ekron are the scenery against which the stories in the saga of Samson were told.

WHAT YOU HAVE LEARNED

- Tel Miqne is an important site excavated by processual archaeologists.
- Processual archaeologists demonstrated that the transition from the Bronze Age to the Iron Age in Syria-Palestine was complex, not uniform, and gradual, not spontaneous.
- They also reconstructed the shifting political conditions between Philistines, Israelites, Phoenicians, Assyrians, and Egyptians; the interaction of these diverse cultures; and their economic development.
- Finally, processual archaeologists clearly described the development and then decline of Philistine culture in Syria-Palestine, providing an important corrective for the generally barbaric and hostile portrayal of the Philistines in the Bible.

STUDY QUESTIONS

1. Does the picture of the Philistines in the Bible accurately reflect what is known about them from archaeology?
2. What does Neutron Activation Analysis tell about pottery?
3. How was olive oil pressed in Iron Age Ekron?
4. In the saga of Samson, what was his relationship with the Philistines?

PREVIEW: CAPE GELIDONYA
AND ULUBURUN

- Ancient Seafaring
- Nautical Archaeology
- Cape Gelidonya
- Uluburun
- Seafaring and the Bible
- Philistines as Sea Peoples
- David and Goliath

Chapter 19 looks at nautical archaeology and the artifacts that have been recovered from the sites of Cape Gelidonya and Uluburun. The chapter describes ancient ships and their cargo.

19

Cape Gelidonya and Uluburun

ANCIENT SEAFARING

Seafaring was a Stone Age technology in the world of the Bible. The peoples of Mesopotamia, Syria-Palestine, and Egypt developed boats for use on lakes and rivers, and ships for seagoing. Neolithic sailors and merchants carried obsidian, turquoise, cowrie shells, and bitumen to the communities in the Near East. Thousands of shipwrecks are like time capsules preserving artifacts of maritime trade (Bass 1975, 62). During the Bronze Age (3400–2000 B.C.E.) ships sailed from Mesopotamia to ports like Magan (Oman) and Dilmun (Bahrain) for products such as gold, copper, lapis lazuli, ivory, wool, leather, pearls, and timber (Bass 1991). Similarly, ships sailed from Egypt to Byblos (Lebanon), Ugarit (Syria), and Punt (Somalia) for products such as timber, ivory, copper, tin, turquoise, resin, ostrich shells, murex shells, hides, ointments, and fruit.

From the beginning, sailors and shipbuilders from Syria-Palestine were masters of the sea. Egyptians recruited them to man their ships and deliver goods. In 2900 B.C.E., a majority of the dockyard workers at Saqarra had Semitic names. In 1300 B.C.E., the city of Ugarit negotiated a contract to build a fleet of 150 ships. In 1200 B.C.E., Ugarit negotiated a contract to build a freighter to carry 450 tons of grain. In the story of Wen-Amun (1196–1070 B.C.E.), the economy of Egypt was completely dependent on sailors and ships from Syria-Palestine (Matthews and Benjamin 2006, 347–54).

On the walls of the tomb of Pharaoh Sahure (ruled 2458–2446 B.C.E.), there are paintings of an Egyptian fleet and its crew from Syria-Palestine. The main mast is an inverted V with a tall, narrow sail. When the mast was not in use, it was laid back on a support near the stern. There were three steering oars. Ships with crews from Syria-Palestine also appear in a relief carved during the reign of Pharaoh Unas. The main mast is an inverted W.

Since the Neolithic period (6000–3800 B.C.E.), divers, simply holding their breath, have collected food, raw materials, and lost artifacts from depths up to one hundred feet. In 2007, Herbert Nitsch dove to a record 702 feet simply holding his breath. Decompression sickness (DCS) is a dangerous and occasionally deadly condition caused by nitrogen bubbles that form in the blood and other tissues of divers who surface too quickly. According to the Divers Alert Network (DAN), fewer than 1 percent of divers fall victim to decompression sickness—one case in every 7,400 dives and one death in every 76,900 dives. ■

241

Nebamun was a wealthy Egyptian. Around 1400 B.C.E. he built his tomb near Thebes with a painting of a ship with a crew from Syria-Palestine arriving in Egypt. The yardarm on the main mast curves down toward the deck. Above the rail of the ship there is a wicker fence to protect the deck from waves.

Kenamun was a mayor of Thebes during the reign of Amenophis III (1391–1353 B.C.E.). The 18th dynasty (1540–1070 B.C.E.) founded the New Kingdom, during which noteworthy pharaohs such as Tutankhamun, Akhenaten, Hatshepsut, and Tuthmoses III reigned. There is a painting in the tomb of Kenamun showing a fleet of ships from Syria-Palestine unloading cargo at an Egyptian port. Each sailor wears a round medal around his neck. The ships have quarter rudders with tillers for steering and sails attached to both upper and lower yards. There are wicker fences along their rails of the ships to protect the deck from waves, and each ship had a crow's nest. In the painting, stevedores are carrying amphoras, pilgrim canteens, and spindle bottles down the gangplank. On the deck are storage jars almost six feet tall. Three of such pottery vessels were found in the Uluburun wreck (fourteenth century B.C.E.), which probably sailed from a Syro-Palestinian port.

NAUTICAL ARCHAEOLOGY

Nautical archaeologists study the design and construction of ships—merchant ships, war ships, fishing ships—and harbors. They also study settlements that were once on land but are now under water. The archaeological wealth on the floor of the Mediterranean is difficult to estimate.

Artifacts from shipwrecks are consistently better preserved than those from land excavations; consequently, there are more examples of any given artifact in an underwater site than at the sites of land excavations (Bass 1996b, 5:283–84). Most clay, glass, and metal artifacts recovered by land archaeologists have been damaged or recycled. Unlike in ships' cargoes, little raw material is recovered from land sites; whereas land sites are a puzzle of many times and cultures, shipwrecks are a moment frozen in time. Therefore, shipwrecks are easier to date than land sites and, once dated, can provide a reliable chronology for the cargo.

Nautical archaeologists adapt the Wheeler-Kenyon method to recover artifacts from the seabed (Bass 1970; Muckelroy 1978). One important difference, however, is the time factor. Time is a challenge for underwater archaeologists. Storms that uncover shipwrecks can return quickly to bury them again. Moreover, archaeologists working deep under water may be limited to as little as an hour's work on a single dive to avoid decompression sickness.

Land archaeologists typically excavate squares fifteen feet on a side. Underwater archaeologists excavate squares six feet on a side. The underwater square is a movable metal grid anchored over the site and used to map the location of artifacts. Underwater sites are generally recorded using a submersible with a camera that passes back and forth over site. The resulting images are then linked to create a composite picture of the entire site.

Metal detectors play an important role in the work of underwater archaeologists. They find nails and fittings from ships that are generally scattered across the seabed and also locate cargoes of raw metal. Metal objects such as knives that are exposed to salt water are rapidly coated with a crust that soon erodes the metal object completely. The process is called "concretion." The crust, however, preserves a perfect mold of the now lost object. Underwater archaeologists use x-rays to study these clumps in order to decide whether to rescue and open them.

Underwater soil is removed with a large air lift or siphon. The airlift is like a giant vacuum cleaner. The mouth of the siphon is covered with a mesh to catch any small artifacts. The remaining water and soil are carried up the hose, which is anchored on the surface to a raft. When the soil and water reach the surface, both are sprayed into the air and drop back into the water. Although the siphon quickly and effectively removes the soil covering artifacts, the soil and water that the siphon sprays back into the water at the surface pollutes the water and is toxic to sea life.

Once artifacts have been recorded, they are collected into plastic crates attached to balloons. When the crates are full, the balloons gently float them to the surface.

CAPE GELIDONYA

Pliny (*Natural History* 5.27.97) called Cape Gelidonya the "Chelidonian Promontory" of Lycia (Turkey) on the western end of the Bay of Antalya. Running south from the cape are five small Chelidoniae or Besadalar Islands. Strabo (14.2.1 and 14.3.8) mentioned only three of them, and Pliny (*Natural History* 5.35.1–31) only four.

About 1200 B.C.E., on the northeast coast of Devecitasi Abasi, the largest of the five islands, a rock near the surface cut through the hull of a merchant ship. Spilling its cargo as it sank, the ship settled with its stern facing north and resting on a large boulder almost 165 feet below the surface. The bow touched down on the seabed. In time the stern slipped off the boulder into a gully (Bass 1975: 1–10).

In 1954, Kemal Aras, a ship's captain and sponge diver from Bodrum, saw the cargo of a Late-Bronze-period shipwreck in over eighty-five feet of water. Four years later, he described it to Peter Throckmorton, an American journalist and amateur archaeologist who was cataloguing ancient wrecks along the southwest Turkish coast. Throckmorton located the site in 1959 and asked the University Museum at the University of Pennsylvania to excavate it.

In 1960, Rodney Young (1907–1974) convinced his graduate student George Fletcher Bass to direct the underwater excavation of Cape Gelidonya. The Cape Gelidonya shipwreck became the first underwater excavation carried out on the seabed, the first underwater excavation directed by an archaeologist who was also a diver, and the first underwater excavation conducted following the standards of excavations on land. Bass pioneered underwater archaeology at Cape Gelidonya and in 1973 founded the Institute of Nautical Archaeology (INA) at Texas A&M University—the world's first school for the archaeological study of humans and the sea (http://ina.tamu.edu/).

Visits to the site in the late 1980s by an INA team reconstructed how the ship had sunk between 1250 and 1150 B.C.E. The shape of the pottery on board, similar to two nearly intact Mycenaean IIIB stirrup jars, allowed archaeologists to date the wreck to the Late Bronze period (1500–1200 B.C.E.). Radiocarbon tests on brushwood from the wreck dated the wreck to 1250–1150 B.C.E. plus or minus fifty years.

Because of a lack of protective sediment, most of the ship's hull, held together with pegged mortise-and-tenon joints, had been eaten by *teredos* sea snails.

The brushwood dunnage used as packing around the ship's cargo explains why Homer describes Odysseus carpeting the inside hull of his ship with brush (*Odyssey* 5.257). The distribution of cargo on the seabed suggests that the ship was almost thirty-five feet long.

Most of the cargo was for bronze working. There were broken bronze tools from Cyprus to be recycled. This scrap was packed in baskets. There were also ingots of both copper and tin to be alloyed to create new bronze.

The copper was cast in thirty-four flat, four-handled ingots. These four-handled ingots were once thought to imitate tanned ox hides and were worth the value of an ox. Now, however, it is clear that the shape of these ingots simply made them easier to carry (Buchholz and Karageorghis 1973). The rough edges and surface of the ingots do not imitate tanned ox-hides but are simply the result of open casting. The ingot shape was cut into soil or sand and filled with molten copper. The exposed surfaces of the ingots dried rough. The weights of the ingots from Cape Gelidonya vary. Some weigh thirty-five pounds and some fifty-seven pounds. Therefore, they are not a form of currency. There were also copper bun-shaped or disc-shaped ingots. Each averaged about six pounds. In addition, there were eighteen much smaller, flat, oval-shaped ingots, at least one of them bronze, that seem to have been cast in multiples of one pound.

Copper ingot. From Enkomi, Cyprus. Ca. 1225-1150 B.C.E. 69.8 x 40.6 x 5 cm. W. 1306 oz (approx.). Inv. GR 1897,0401.1535. Location: British Museum, London, Great Britain. Photo Credit: © British Museum / Art Resource, NY.

The recovery of stone hammerheads, stone polishers, a whetstone, and a large flat stone anvil, suggest that a smith may have been on board the ship.

Many of the copper ingots and scrap bronze pieces were excavated in lumps covered and held together by a rock-hard covering of calcium carbonate or **concretion**. The four-handled ingots were cast in three basic shapes, all familiar from Egyptian tombs painted between 1400 and 1200 B.C.E. Such ingots are said to have been tribute from Syria-Palestine.

The merchant's cylinder seal was found in his cabin at the stern of the ship. The seal is from Syria-Palestine, not from the western Mediterranean. Not only the captain's seal but also the weights from the Cape Gelidonya wreck strongly suggest that the merchant on the ship was from Syria-Palestine, not Mycenae. About sixty pan-balance weights were discovered, manufactured from hematite stone and either domed or shaped like sling stones. The different weights included *qedets* from Egypt weighing .32 ounces and *nesefs* and *shekels* from Syria-Palestine weighing .36 ounces and .40 ounces respectively. Merchants used the standards of the places where they did business.

The pottery was a mixture of Mycenaean, Cypriot, and Syrian wares. Artifacts recovered from the stern of the wreck were not cargo but the personal possessions of the crew. There were four scarabs and a scarab-shaped plaque, an oil lamp, and stone mortars. There is also a razor from Egypt. The ship's cargo was from Cyprus; the ship, however, was from Syria-Palestine. Even its anchor was manufactured in a style used primarily in Syria-Palestine, not Mycenae.

The only foreign merchant ships depicted in Late Bronze Age art in Egypt are from Syria-Palestine. Some sixteen Egyptian paintings—some made more than two hundred years before the Cape Gelidonya shipwreck—show four-handled copper ingots, and tin ingots, with merchants from Syria-Palestine, not from Mycenae (Bass 1975, 56). A mold for casting four-handled copper ingots was recovered at Ras ibn Hani, the port of Ugarit (Syria). The Cape Gelidonya wreck has revealed much about the history of metalworking and seafaring during the Late Bronze period. We now know that the Mycenaeans from the western Mediterranean did not enjoy a monopoly in metalworking and seafaring in the eastern Mediterranean during the Late Bronze period (1500–1200 B.C.E.). Peoples from Syria-Palestine were working metal and seafaring in the eastern Mediterranean before the Iron Age (1200–586 B.C.E.) began.

Primary marks pressed into the copper before it cooled may be letters from the dialect of Greek spoken on Cyprus during the Late Bronze period, which still has not been deciphered. This alphabet may have developed from another dialect of Greek on Cyprus— Linear A Greek, which also has not been deciphered. Linear A Greek, similar to Semitic languages like Hebrew, is written from right to left, instead of from left to write like most Indo-European languages, and it does not leave spaces between words (Latin: *lectio continua*). Secondary marks were scratched onto some ingots after the metal cooled. The meanings of these marks, like that of the primary marks, are still unknown. ∎

> **Concretion** *is a technical term for a stone-like mass or clump created by minerals suspended in the water around a metal artifact. A concretion sometimes contains a hollow space after the artifact has rusted away. This hollow can be casted by filling it with epoxy, recovering the original shape of the metal object. http://www.abc.se/~pa/uwa/glossary.htm.*

ULUBURUN

From 1984 to 1994 the INA excavated a shipwreck at Uluburun near Kas (Turkey). The shipwreck lay on a steep rocky slope 140 to 170 feet below

MANIFEST FOR SHIP AT ULUBURUN

- Ten tons of copper from Cyprus
  - 354 ox hide-shaped ingots
  - 120 bun-shaped ingots
- One ton of bun-shaped and ox hide-shaped tin ingots
- One ton of terebinth resin for manufacturing incense in 150 jars made in Syria-Palestine
- 175 disc-shaped ingots of glass like those mentioned in tablets from Ugarit (Syria) and Amarna (Egypt)
  - cobalt blue
  - turquoise
  - a unique lavender ingot
- Logs of Egyptian ebony wood (Latin: *Dalbergia melanoxylon)*
- Ostrich eggs for manufacturing containers
- Elephant tusks
- Twelve hippopotamus teeth
- Murex shells
- Tortoise carapace shells for manufacturing the sound-boxes of stringed instruments
- Pottery made in Cyprus
  - Nine storage jars of pomegranates and olive oil
  - Rhyton drinking cups finished in faience: three shaped like the head of a ram, one shaped like the head of a woman
- Bronze and copper cooking pots and bowls
- Jewelry from Syria-Palestine
  - Bracelets
  - Gold pendants
- Scrap gold and silver
- Jewelry from Egypt
  - Gold jewelry
  - Electrum jewelry
  - Silver jewelry
  - Stone jewelry
- A unique scarab seal with the cartouche of Queen Nefertiti
- Thousands of beads
  - Glass beads
  - Agate beads
  - Carnelian beads
  - Quartz beads
  - Faience beads
  - Ostrich shell beads
  - Amber beads
- Two duck-shaped ivory cosmetics containers
- Trumpet carved from a hippopotamus incisor into the shape of a ram's horn
- Bronze tools
  - Awls
  - Drills
  - Chisels
  - Axes
  - Adzes
  - Saw
- Bronze weapons
  - Spearheads
  - Arrowheads
  - Daggers
  - Swords
- Fishing equipment—evidence the crew fished from the ship
- Lead net and line sinkers
  - Netting needles for repairing nets
  - Fishhooks
  - A harpoon
  - A bronze trident
- Two wooden writing boards with two leaves joined with an ivory hinge, and slightly recessed to receive wax writing surfaces
- A bronze- and gold-plated female figurine, similar to artifacts recovered from Syria-Palestine, which may have been the ship's divine patron
- Personal property of two passengers from Mycenae (Greece)
  - Two lens-shaped seals
  - Two swords
  - Two pectorals with glass relief beads

sea level. Tree ring analysis of a small piece of firewood or dunnage packing dates the sinking of the ship to 1306 B.C.E. The hull was constructed from fir. Its planks were fitted together with mortise-and-tenon joints and oak pegs. The anchors were rectangular blocks of stone. They had a single hole drilled for the rope. This style of anchor was used only in Syria-Palestine, not the western Mediterranean.

The quantity and quality of the ship's cargo of raw materials and manufactured goods indicates that it was a royal vessel. Manifests from royal freighters delivering copper from Alashiya (Cyprus) for Akhenaton were recovered during excavations at his capital city at Tel el Amarna. None of these manifests listed more than ten tons of copper. Therefore, we can conclude that the shipwreck at Uluburun was probably a royal freighter. It carried the largest known collection of Late Bronze Age artifacts found to date in the Mediterranean.

Among the artifacts were two wooden writing boards joined with an ivory hinge, slightly recessed to receive wax writing surfaces. One writing board was found in a large storage jar originally filled with pomegranates. This board is five hundred years older than a similar board recovered by archaeologists at Nimrud (Iraq), which had been the oldest recovered to date. To stiffen the wax enough to hold the shape of the symbols and letters pressed into it with a stylus, scribes mixed the wax with resin. If the one ton of resin found in 150 jars recovered from the shipwreck at Uluburun were intended for use by scribes, it would suggest that writing was widespread during the Late Bronze period in the world of the Bible.

Also among the artifacts were two medallions with glass relief beads. The sailors from Syria-Palestine painted on the walls of the tomb of Kenamun are wearing round gold medallions like these pectoral medallions recovered from the shipwreck at Uluburun.

The Uluburun and Cape Gelidonya wrecks are windows into the craft of metalworking and the metal trade and seafaring during the Late Bronze Age. These excavations have shown that metalworking, the metal trade, and seafaring were not limited to western Mediterranean cultures. Now it is clear that the people of Cyprus and Syria-Palestine worked and traded metals in the eastern Mediterranean.

SEAFARING AND THE BIBLE

The Philistines

Curiously, however, the Hebrews in the Bible associate metalworking with the Philistines and seafaring with Tyre. Almost nowhere in the

STORIES OF SAUL

(1 Sam 13:15-22)

Samuel and about six hundred warriors left Gilgal and went toward Gibeah of Benjamin. Saul, his son Jonathan, and the warriors who were with them camped in Geba of Benjamin; but the Philistines camped at Michmash. The Philistines sent out three detachments to forage for food and supplies. One raided from Ophrah to Shual; another Beth-horon; and another the mountain above the Valley of Zeboim.

Now there were no smiths anywhere in Israel because the Philistines ordered: "The Hebrews are not to make swords or spears for themselves."

Therefore, the Israelites went to the Philistine smiths to sharpen their plows, mattocks, axes, and sickles. The charge was .25 ounces of silver for plow points and mattocks; .10 ounces of silver for axes and goad points. So on the day of the battle not one of Saul's or Jonathan's warriors had a sword or a spear except Saul and his son Jonathan. ∎

Bible do the Hebrews celebrate their skill on the sea or with the forge. For example, the stories of Saul (1 Sam 13:15-22) seem to note, with embarrassment, that Hebrew farmers went to Philistine smiths to have their metal tools sharpened and repaired. Likewise, the story of how David delivered Israel from Goliath in the books of Samuel–Kings (1 Sam 17:1–58) describes the metal armor and weapons of this Philistine warrior with awe.

David and Goliath

The biblical story of how David delivered Israel from Goliath (1 Sam 17:1-58) characterizes David as the annals characterized Ramesses III, destroying the chaos of the Sea Peoples and creating the cosmos of Israel. Neither the Annals of Ramesses III nor the story of how David delivered Israel from Goliath are battle reports. They are assessments of how shifts of power in Egypt and Syria-Palestine will impact indigenous peoples there. Both admit that the newcomers are dominant. The question is: Will the Egyptians, or the Hebrews, survive? Both the annals and the hero story are optimistic. The technological superiority of the Sea Peoples cannot overcome the will of the Egyptians or of the Hebrews to survive.

In the Annals of Ramesses III, the Sea Peoples are masters of the sea; in the story of how David delivers Israel from Goliath, they are masters of metalwork. Both traditions emphasize the courage of the hero—Ramesses or David—in standing their ground against overwhelming odds.

David visits the front to bring gifts for his brothers' commander (1 Sam 17:17-18). In one tradition Saul meets David before his duel; in another he meets David only after watching him kill Goliath. Both traditions want to show that David did not revolt against Saul, his patron, but that Saul accepted David, his client, as his heir (Benjamin 2004, 194–95).

The crisis in the story begins when Goliath taunts the warriors of Israel. Taunts (2 Kgs 2:23-25) are a common strategy in making war in the world of the Bible. Tiamat taunts Marduk (Enuma 4:63-74). Gilgamesh taunts Ishtar (Gilg. 6:31-78). Aqhat and Anat taunt each other, taunt Yamm, or taunt Baal (Aqhat 6:35-49).

David is fearless. He has no question that Yahweh will deliver him from Goliath. David shames Goliath by calling him "uncircumcised" (1 Sam 17:26). Western Mediterranean cultures such as the Philistines did not circumcise their sons; Semitic and African cultures like the Hebrews did. Circumcision was originally a sign that males had reached puberty and that they were now sexually active adults. They were men.

ANNALS OF RAMESSES III
Year 8 of the Reign of Ramesses III

. . . Strangers from the Islands formed a federation with one another. Suddenly, their warriors were invading and destroying every land. No land could defend itself against them. In one campaign, they cut down Hatti, Kode and Arzawa in Turkey, Carchemish in Syria, and Alashiya in Cyprus. They pitched their battle camp at Amor, and began slaying the peoples of Syria-Palestine and devastating their lands as no one had ever done before. Then they turned toward Egypt, whose fire was preparing to devour them. In this federation were the Peleset, the Tjekker, the Shekelesh, the Dannuna and the Weshesh. They attacked every land on the face of the earth, confidently boasting: "We will be victorious!"

Now my divine heart was plotting how I was going to snare them like birds. . . .

I, ruler of the divine assembly, ordered my governors and commanders in Syria-Palestine to deploy their soldiers and maryanu chariots at Djahi on the coast. I ordered them to outfit every warship, freighter and transport from stem to stern with heavily-armed, handpicked troops, and to blockade the mouth of every river along the coast. These ships were the pride of Egypt, and they roared like lions in the mountains. Runners led the chariots manned by the best, hand-picked soldiers. The bodies of the horses quivered as they waited to crush these strangers under their hoofs. As Montu, the divine warrior, I led them into battle, so that they could see my outstretched hand. . . .

Those who reached the border of Egypt by land were annihilated. Their hearts and souls will never rise again. Those who attacked by sea were devoured at the mouths of the rivers, while the spears of the soldiers on shore tightened like the wall of a stockade around them. They were netted, beached, surrounded, put to death and stacked, head to foot, in piles. Their ships and cargo drifted aimlessly on the water. I decreed that no one in the lands of these strangers was to even say the word: "Egypt." Whoever pronounced the word was to be burned alive. Since the day I ascended to the throne of Re-Harakhti, the divine patron of pharaohs, since the first day the divine power of the uraeus serpent rode like Re upon my brow, I have not let a single stranger see the border of Egypt, or any of the Nine Bows even boast of having fought against it. I have seized their lands, and crossed their borders. Their rulers and their people all sing my praises, for I have walked in the ways of Re, ruler of all the earth, my incomparable Godfather, who rules the divine assembly.

David calls Goliath an impotent child and shames the warriors of Israel for being afraid of a *little boy*.

The story punctuates the fierceness of the Sea Peoples by describing the state-of-the-art metal armor worn by Goliath. They are masters not only of the old metal (bronze) but also of new metal (iron). There is little archaeological evidence that Philistine settlements produced more bronze or more iron than Hebrew settlements. Nonetheless, tradition used references to a monopoly in metalwork, particularly in ironwork, to identify dominant cultures. Like iron, the Philistines were virtually invincible (McNutt 1990).

Goliath's armor and his size contrast the power of surplus state economies like Philistia with the powerlessness of subsistence village economies like Israel. When Saul attempts to dress David in the same armor as

Goliath, he is trusting in the armor of his military policies for protection. But David trusts only in Yahweh. Saul and his soldiers go into battle fully armored, which demonstrates that they depend on themselves for victory. In contrast, David goes into battle unarmed, depending only on Yahweh for victory.

Now Goliath taunts David: "Am I a dog that you come to me with a stick?" (1 Sam 17:43). Although there is a long-standing tradition that David kills Goliath with a slingshot, he may have used an atlatl, or throwing stick. Yahweh protects the Hebrews from weapons of bronze and iron with weapons of wood. Goliath asks David if he thinks the Philistines are dogs ready to play fetch.

CONCLUSION

Underwater archaeology provides a unique and important tool for the study of shipbuilding, technology, and trade. Ships brought the Sea Peoples into the world of the Bible and changed that world forever. The Philistines were the single greatest threat to the Hebrews' survival. The Hebrews were no match for their ships, their metals, or their trade. Nonetheless, the Hebrews survived and the Philistines did not. The silent record of that irony between Ramesses and the Sea Peoples and David and Goliath is in the stones under the sea and on land.

WHAT YOU HAVE LEARNED

- Artifacts recovered from underwater sites are often better preserved than those found on land, and they can generally be dated more accurately.
- Artifacts pertaining to metalworking have revealed much about the metals that were available and where metalworking was done.
- The excavation at Cape Gelidonya has shown that sailors from Syria-Palestine were part of maritime commerce in the Late Bronze Age.
- The biblical stories of Saul and David depict the enmity that existed between the Hebrews and the Philistines.

STUDY QUESTIONS

1. What method is followed by nautical archaeologists?
2. What have artifacts recovered from underwater sites revealed about the cultures of Syria-Palestine?
3. What do the artifacts recovered from shipwrecks suggest about the lifestyle of cultures around the Mediterranean?

Part 5

Post-Processual Archaeology

Part 5 is an introduction to post-processual archaeology. Chapter 20 describes post-processual archaeology as a critique or revision of processual archaeology. Chapter 21 is a sample of post-processual archaeology applied to a remarkable hero story in the book of Judges (9:50-57). The story celebrates an unnamed woman for delivering her city from its enemy with an extraordinary weapon. The mill she uses to feed her household becomes the weapon she uses to defend it.

PREVIEW: POST-PROCESSUAL ARCHAEOLOGY

- Work of William Dever
- Post-processual Archaeology as Critique
- Artifacts and Worldviews
- Synchronic vs. Diachronic Approach
- Diversity of Interpretations
- Presuppositions
- Cultural Resource Management
- Critical Theory

Chapter 20 describes post-processual archaeology, which critiques processual archaeology for interpreting any change in the artifact record as an adaptation to a change in the natural or human environment. For post-processual archaeologists, changes in artifacts are reflections of a change in the worldview of a culture at a site. Post-processual archaeologists stress the importance of identifying the assumptions of the archaeologists and other stakeholders involved in a site that might prejudice their interpretation of artifacts. Finally, post-processual archaeologists are committed to working with cultural resource managers and other educational and tourist industries to publicize their sites.

20

Post-Processual Archaeology

The close relationship that had existed between archaeology and biblical studies in the United States since the time of William F. Albright (Albright 1942) was repeatedly challenged by William G. Dever (Dever 1973; 1985; 1992). Dever argued that biblical archaeologists in the Albright school were so committed to proving that the Bible was a historically accurate record of events that they completely ignored the developments that processual archaeologists brought to the discipline. Dever further alleged that biblical archaeologists ignored processual archaeology because they assumed that ancient Israel did not evolve in the same ways as other cultures in Syria-Palestine. For biblical archaeologists, ancient Israel was unique and could not be studied using the scientific method.

By the 1980s Dever had prevailed, and archaeology in Syria-Palestine came of age (Dever 2005, 80). It was no longer an amateur enterprise of biblical scholars but a separate, professional, processual discipline.

POST-PROCESSUAL ARCHAEOLOGY AS CRITIQUE

Curiously, however, archaeologists working in Syria-Palestine began using processual archaeology just as processual archaeologists working in other parts of the world were beginning to question and reevaluate their method. Ian R. Hodder described this critique, which has been ongoing since 1975, as *post-processual archaeology*. The critique embraces a variety of revisions. What they all have in common is their objection to the assumption of processual archaeology that cultural changes are always adaptations to changes in the human or natural environment. Post-processual archaeologists assume that the artifacts recovered at a site demonstrate how a culture adapted not only to changes in its environment but also to the evolution of its worldview.

Israeli archaeologists at the Tel Aviv Institute of Archaeology provided an important catalyst for the use of post-processual archaeology in Syria-Palestine. The surface surveys they conducted throughout Israel during the 1970s and 1980s profoundly changed the focus of Israeli archaeology. This environmentally oriented fieldwork created a new interest in the people without history (Bunimovitz 2007).

The emphasis on the rural backbone of Syria-Palestine countered the urban bias of processual archaeology and its reliance on elitist political history. The archaeology of the silent majority that emerged served as a healthy antidote to the preoccupation of processual archaeologists with great men and great deeds. In contrast, post-processual archaeologists were interested in what artifacts revealed about the dynamics of households in antiquity and the relationship of men and women

William G. Dever

in the household especially by identifying women's space, men's space, and shared space.

ARTIFACTS AND WORLDVIEWS

Post-processual archaeologists use artifacts to reconstruct the world-views of the maker cultures. Material remains are not only tools for survival; they reveal how people looked at their world and how they lived in that world. Artifacts reflect how maker cultures think and learn and communicate. They focus not only on how humans used their hands but also on how they used their minds. They are interested not only in what people did but also in what it meant to them. Changes in the material remains at a site reflect changes in a culture's worldview. When people begin to think differently about their experience, that change can be seen in their material remains.

Post-processual archaeologists assume a more dynamic balance between determinism and free will than processual archaeologists. They use artifacts not only to reconstruct how people in a particular culture interpreted their experiences but also how they shaped those experiences. Material remains reflect how people developed, maintained, and changed systems in their cultures. Post-processual archaeologists are interested not just in what people do, but in what people know and what they want to do. People creatively interpret their experiences and intentionally design experiences. For example, they not only experience starvation during times of famine, but they fast during times of plenty.

People cannot make their experience conform to their expectations, but their actions can transcend natural systems and human change. People are intelligent agents of social change (Bourdieu 1984; Giddens 1986).

For example, the sanctuaries of the original Early Bronze Age community at Megiddo were round. The sanctuaries of their successors, however, were rectangular. Post-processual archaeologists reconstruct not just the techniques necessary to build a round or a rectangular sanctuary but also what was going on in the culture at Megiddo that is reflected in the change in shape of its sanctuaries. Likewise, sanctuaries dedicated to Yahweh at Beersheba

Synchronic *schools of interpretation give a snapshot of a particular system at a particular moment in time. Synchronic methods focus on how something is at a given moment and how each part fits into the system*

The term **diachronic** *identifies schools of interpretation that, like a motion picture documentary, examine the origins, development history, and change that take place over time.*

and Arad were both decommissioned. At Beersheba the altar stones were recycled to repair a warehouse wall. At Arad the *maṣṣēbôt*, or standing stones, were laid carefully on their sides. They were not smashed or broken. Then the entire sanctuary was filled in with soil. It was buried, not vandalized or recycled. Post-processual archaeologists consider these changes in material remains to reflect a change in the way the people of Judah thought about Yahweh. When the sanctuaries at Beersheba and Arad were built, the people of Judah worshiped Yahweh throughout their land. When the sanctuaries were decommissioned, the people of Judah had decided to worship Yahweh only in Jerusalem, the sacred center of their land. Their worldview had changed, and the material remains preserved the transition.

POST-PROCESSUAL ARCHAEOLOGY AS A DIACHRONIC APPROACH

Processual archaeology is synchronic; it reconstructs a specific moment in the past. Synchronic methods give a snapshot of a particular system at a particular moment in time. Synchronic methods focus on how something is at a given moment and how each part fits into the system. In contrast, post-processual archaeology is diachronic; it emphasizes what happens over time. Diachronic methods examine the origins, development, history, and changes that take place over time, like a motion picture documentary.

Processual archaeologists use their interpretations of artifacts from any given site to develop generalizations or a metahistory about the development of such institutions as agriculture and states, and about the rise and fall of civilizations in a region or in an archaeological period. Post-processual archaeologists are much more site-specific. They limit their interpretations of artifacts from a particular site to that site and generalize much less about what that site says about the culture in the region or in a particular archaeological period. They consider generalizations about cultures in a particular region or in a particular archaeological period to be unreliable. Instead, post-processual archaeologists focus on a single site and its surroundings and assume that cultures in the same region or in the same period are more likely to be different than similar.

DIVERSITY OF INTERPRETATIONS

Processual archaeologists develop a single interpretation of their artifacts. Post-processual archaeologists consider diverse interpretations of a site to be more helpful in understanding ancient cultures than a single interpretation. Like other postmodernists, post-processual archaeologists emphasize the importance of diversity in explaining change and the need to realize that all explanations of change are relative, not absolute. No single interpretation definitively explains the culture at a site. The goal of modernism is to develop a single worldview or metahistory that explains how humans process their experience. Modernism is looking for *the* answer. Postmodernism is looking only for *an* answer. For modernism, there is a single worldview based on universally accepted values. For postmodernism, there are diverse worldviews based on valid but not universally accepted values.

For post-processual archaeologists the interpretation of artifacts is a discourse or conversation. Artifacts are dynamic. They are not symbols with a single, fixed meaning but symbols with a subtle range of meanings in both their cultures of origin and in the hands of the archaeologists who recover and interpret them. Artifacts are icons manufactured to communicate a specific message.

No site can be adequately interpreted without a staff that is interdisciplinary. There are not only academic professionals like archaeologists, ceramicists, and paleobotanists on a staff, but also religious leaders, government officials, and local people on the staff. For example, any excavation team that uncovers human remains in Israel will immediately add religious representatives to the staff. Imams and rabbis are not archaeologists, but they guarantee that the remains are dealt with appropriately. ∎

Archaeologists work to reconstruct the grammar of both the worldview of the artifacts' culture of origin and a dictionary of symbols appearing in artifacts. Graves, houses, and pottery, for example, are not only conversations between their makers and the people of their time but also conversations with the archaeologists who interpret them.

Post-processual archaeologists assume that there is no such thing as an objective interpretation of the material remains of a culture. Since 1993, for example, Hodder has continued to survey the interpretations of all the stakeholders involved in his excavation of a nine-thousand-year-old Neolithic site at Çatal Höyük (http://www.catalhoyuk.com/). He surveys his own interpretation as the dig director, and also those of the professional staff, of the student volunteers, of the local Turkish villagers, of the Turkish departments of antiquities and of tourism, and of women's groups and other visitors to the site. Each group brings it own assumptions and experiences to the excavation. Allowing each group to speak makes it less likely that any one group can dominate or distort the interpretation of the material remains from the site.

As dig director, Hodder interprets the artifacts from Çatal Höyük from a university perspective. He uses them to reconstruct both the lives of the rich and famous during the Neolithic period and the lives of the poor and anonymous at the site. Ceramics specialists on the team at Çatal Höyük interpret the artifacts from the perspective of potters. They are interested in where the people got their clay, how they prepared it, and how they shaped it. Paleobontanists on the team interpret the material remains from the perspective of farmers. They want to identify the kinds of crops grown and to determine just how successful the people of Çatal Höyük were at herding.

Student volunteers on the team interpret the artifacts from the perspective of their educational goals. Graduate students are looking for ways to use their fieldwork in their dissertations. They are also thinking about how their field experience will contribute to their careers in archaeology. Turkish villagers interpret the artifacts from the perspective of descendants of this long-extinct people. They wonder how the people of Çatal Höyük are like the people of Turkey today and also how they are different.

Feminists who visit Çatal Höyük interpret its material remains from the perspective of women. They feel a strong sisterhood with this ancient people, whose divine patron was a Godmother rather than a Godfather. They want to know if cultures having a Godmother as a divine patron create a more equitable environment for ordinary women. Socialists who study Çatal Höyük interpret its material remains using the sociol-

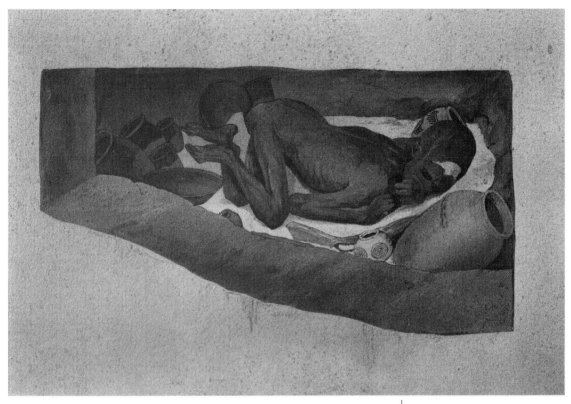

Replica of a cist burial, about 3400 B.C.E., from Nagada, Egypt. British Museum.

ogy of Karl Marx (1818–1883) in his *Communist Manifesto* (1848). They are sensitive to artifacts that reflect a primitive democracy among these Neolithic peoples. They are looking for ancient prototypes of classless societies today.

PRESUPPOSITIONS OF ARCHAEOLOGISTS

Post-processual archaeologists are interested in defining the relationship of politics and archaeology. Interpretations are unavoidably influenced by what is happening in the world while archaeologists are excavating. For example, how do the attacks on the World Trade Center on September 11, 2001, impact the interpretation of a massive destruction layer at a site in Syria-Palestine? This is why archaeologists are expected to clearly identify their assumptions and experiences in order to limit the distortions that these preconditions might create in their interpretations. Post-processual archaeologists also study the impact of cultural developments today, such as postmodernism and feminism, on the interpretation of the material

257

remains of past cultures. Their goal is to understand how such issues and interests influence the way people today think about the past and, consequently, how these issues and interests influence their interpretation of artifacts from past cultures. Post-processual archaeologists catalogue the values of those recovering and interpreting artifacts and the influence of contemporary movements on the interpretation of material remains of past cultures to reduce the possibility that these presuppositions will distort the interpretations of the artifacts, or that researchers will use artifacts to promote destructive value systems like sexism, Nazism, colonialism, imperialism, and racism.

ARCHAEOLOGY AND CULTURAL RESOURCE MANAGEMENT

Post-processual archaeologists are concerned with the ethics of archaeology. They do not, for example, assume that professors are better interpreters of the material remains of past cultures than politicians or local religious leaders. Before they go into the field, post-processual archaeologists ask probing questions about how best to distribute responsibilities for an excavation (Silberman 2003, 10). They carefully negotiate the legal status of the material remains from the excavation. International law provides that artifacts are the property of the states where they are recovered. Nonetheless, humanity in general and ethnic communities with strong emotional ties to ancient sites are also entitled to have their rights respected by archaeologists.

Post-processual archaeologists also negotiate a power-sharing process to develop the excavation strategy. They do not assume that the director of the excavation alone should decide what portions of a site should be excavated and what portions of the site should be left buried. Nor do they take for granted that well-funded teams from universities abroad who view antiquities as educational resources for their students should have more control over these decisions than local departments of antiquities, which view ancient sites as an economic resource for attracting tourists.

Post-processual archaeologists also negotiate how to publicize the findings and the interpretations of the artifacts from a site. They do not assume that articles in professional journals are a more appropriate medium than school textbooks or television programming. They work collaboratively with the industries of cultural resource management, tourism, and entertainment to package the past for pleasure and profit.

Cultural Resource Management (CRM) refers to the protection of archaeological sites. Although some states and cities in the United States have passed laws requiring Cultural Resource Management, Congress has been the most proactive in passing laws to protect sites on federal lands. Cultural resource management is the largest employer in the field of archaeology, yet there is often little dialogue between cultural resource managers and archaeologists about what should be preserved and how it should be preserved. Cultural resource management is still largely a service sector for the development of public parks and monuments.

Cultural heritage is articulated in different ways by universities, the media, and the entertainment industry. Until the emergence of post-processual archaeology, cultural resource management did not involve academic archaeology to any degree. Processual archaeologists make a clear distinction between their field- and laboratory-based research, on one hand, and the interpretation of artifacts for the general public by cultural resource managers on the other. They also distinguish between their work in reconstructing ancient cultures and the use that educational and entertainment media make of their work. Post-processual archaeologists, however, consider archaeology as the mediation of that past in the present not only by university-based scholars but also by cultural resource managers, media journalists, and the general public, for example, on the Internet.

Both processual and post-processual archaeologists agree that it would be impossible to continue their work without the willingness of governments to protect ancient sites and public interest in antiquity. Post-processual archaeologists, however, are more committed to bridging the gap between the worlds of academic research and Cultural Resource Management. They take a serious interest in contributing to the conversation about how cultural heritage should be preserved and interpreted in a world that is postcolonial and intensely global.

ARCHAEOLOGY AND CRITICAL THEORY

Post-processual archaeologists follow the principles of critical theory, which assigns a shelf life to the assumptions of all disciplines. Interpreting a site is an ongoing, open-ended conversation between the archaeologists and their artifacts, between the culture of the artifacts and the culture of the archaeologists. The assumptions of any discipline such as archaeology should, according to critical theory, be regularly reviewed and evaluated to certify that the way the discipline goes about the business of learning, or of speaking and of making use of its findings, are still valid. Critical theory is particularly suspicious of any discipline that exercises a monopoly in its field. Critical theory is also suspicious of any discipline whose methods of learning, ways of speaking, or applications are too simple. Human life is seldom simple, and the cultures that people create reflect complexity.

CONCLUSION

Post-processual archaeology emphasizes that archaeologists do not discover the past; they tell stories about the past (Shanks 1996). The interpretation of a site reflects the questions that its archaeologists and other stakeholders who are affected by the interpretation of an archaeological site ask about artifacts from the site. The values and interests of the excavators and these stakeholders are embedded in their work; these values and interests determine what researchers keep and what they study.

Post-processual archaeologists are also advocates of a rainbow of stories about the stones. They assume that there is at least as much diversity at the site they are studying as there is among those who are interested in and working at the site. To the extent possible, that diversity needs to be given expression in their interpretations of the artifacts.

Like Annales archaeologists, post-processual archaeologists tell stories about ordinary men and women (Ackerman 2003; C. L. Meyers 2003b; 2003c; 2003d). They are students of the little people in the world of the Bible. They focus on the less dramatic but no less significant roles of ordinary men and women—mothers, fathers, midwives, widows, elders, teachers, slaves, herders, and farmers who live in households and villages.

WHAT YOU HAVE LEARNED

- Post-processual archaeology is a critique of processual archaeology.
- Change in the artifact record is not only an adaptation to a change in the natural or human environment but also a reflection of a change in the worldview of a culture at a site.
- Post-processual archaeologists also stress the importance of identifying assumptions of the archaeologists and other stakeholders involved in the site that might prejudice their interpretation of artifacts from a site.
- Post-processual archaeologists are committed to working with cultural resource managers and other educational and tourist industries to publicize their sites.

STUDY QUESTIONS

1. In what ways is post-processual archaeology a critique of processual archaeology?
2. What is the difference between synchronic and diachronic approaches in archaeology?
3. What is the importance in diversity in interpretations of material remains?
4. How can the presuppositions of archaeologists affect the interpretation of material remains?
5. Why is it important to publicize archaeological finds?

PREVIEW: HOUSEHOLD ARCHAEOLOGY

- Archaeology and the Feminine Mystique
- Daily Life
- Gender
- Group-work Tradition
- Beer and Bread

Chapter 21 describes two specific kinds of post-processual archaeology called gender archaeology and household archaeology, which can be used to interpret a hero story in the book of Judges. Gender archaeology is interested, for example, in how the work of men and that of women in the world of the Bible are valued. Women who bake bread for their men and their children are not seen as powerless, but their authority to feed gives them remarkable control over those whom they feed. Household archaeology is interested, for example, in space in a house; some is shared by men and women, while some space is women's space, and some space is men's space. The woman who saves Thebez from Abimelech uses the flour mill with which she feeds her household to defend it. Likewise, she defends her household not by trespassing on men's space but by remaining within women's space on the roof of the house.

21

Household Archaeology

In 1963, Betty Friedan (1921–2006) published *The Feminine Mystique*, which launched the second wave of the women's movement and became the charter for a national debate about the roles of women in the workplace. Friedan began her five years of research at her fifteenth college reunion. She asked two hundred alumnae from Smith College to fill out a questionnaire. The results confirmed what she had already suspected—many American women were unhappy and did not know why.

Friedan concluded that women in her generation were victims of a *feminine mystique*—unrealistic expectations that men have of women. Women felt worthless because they were defined by this feminine mystique as financially, intellectually, and emotionally dependent on the men and the children in their lives. The mystique programmed them to believe that they would be happy only if they were married and had children.

For Friedan, the feminine mystique developed in the middle-class suburban communities built for veterans of World War II and their families. It was a response, in part, to the need that veterans had for women to mother them—to help them recover from the trauma of war. Similarly, technology—dishwashers, toasters, washing machines, dryers, electric irons—was moving into the home. New appliances were marketed as simplifying homemaking, but in reality many of these new machines made women's work less meaningful and less valuable.

The impact of the women's movement was, initially, most evident in departments of literature and in the literary and historical-critical study of the Bible. Phyllis Trible and Phyllis A. Bird pioneered the study of gender in biblical studies during the 1970s (Trible 1973; Bird 1974). Bird used historical criticism to reconstruct the lives of Hebrew women. Historical criticism reconstructs the community of origin where a biblical tradition developed in order to better understand how the tradition was understood in that context. Trible used literary criticism to learn from female characters in the Bible about men's attitudes toward women in ancient Israel. Literary criticism focuses on how a biblical tradition casts characters, develops its plots, and uses motifs and techniques in order to recover the worldview of the narrators.

First wave feminism addresses how politics defines women. Second wave feminism addresses how work defines women. Third wave feminism addresses how race defines women. ■

Carol Meyers

At that time, literary and historical criticism of the Bible, however, revealed little about the lives of ordinary men and women, because the Bible is interested primarily in how women affect the lives of elite males (Fuchs 1985; Exum 1983). Historical and literary criticism of the Bible could not provide an accurate, systematic, or complete record of the daily lives of ordinary people. For example, the ancestor story of the two shrewd midwives in Exod 1:12-21 celebrates women, but the story celebrates them for using their power and authority to the advantage of Hebrew males (Bal 1988).

In 1984, Margaret W. Conkey and Janet D. Spector argued that archaeology had its own feminine mystique (Conkey and Spector 1984). They found that their fellow archaeologists were seldom objective or inclusive in reconstructing the role of gender at their excavations. Too many simply assumed that the roles of men and women were the same in ancient cultures as in their own. In response to Conkey and Spector, archaeologists working in the prehistoric periods of Europe and the Americas began to develop an archaeology of gender based on the artifacts themselves (Conkey and Gero 1991).

Carol Meyers expanded the study of gender from literary and historical criticism of the Bible to the social-scientific study of gender based on household archaeology (C. L. Meyers 2003a–d). Meyers challenged archaeologists not just to pay more attention to what artifacts reveal about the lives of women in ancient Israel but also to rethink the goals of archaeology in the world of the Bible altogether. She encouraged archaeologists to use a more creative mix of disciplines and reliable social-scientific models to understand both the biblical traditions and the material remains of ancient Israel. Consequently, archaeologists today working in the world of the Bible study not only the lives of the powerful but also the lives of the powerless—not only cities but also villages; not only palaces but also households; not only men but also women.

During most of the twentieth century, archaeologists working in the world of the Bible preferred to excavate cities, the domain of men, rather than to excavate households, the domain of women. Urban excavations focused on male palaces, forts, and sanctuaries. Even archaeologists who do excavate households often interpret their artifacts only in light of what they could reveal about the development of patriarchal culture in ancient Israel. For example: Were Hebrews insiders or outsiders? How did settlement take place—by conquest, by immigration, or by revolution?

Excavations reconstructed the great events in the lives of the rich and famous of ancient Israel, Egypt, and Mesopotamia. Archaeologists looked for artifacts connected with the lives of great men and their conquests, expeditions, cities, palaces, temples, walls, water systems, libraries, correspondence, famines, earthquakes, and, ultimately, their deaths and burials. Finding Abraham, Moses, Joshua, David, and Solomon was important. Reconstructing the plagues, the exodus, the conquest, the temple, and the destruction of Jerusalem was important.

Egypt and Mesopotamia were more careful to tell the stories of their great men in stone than ancient Israel. Therefore, much has been learned about Sargon, Tiglath-Pileser III, Hammurabi, Sennacherib, Nebuchadnezzar, Akhenaton, Thutmosis III, Amenhotep, Ramesses II, Merneptah, Ramesses III, and Amen-em-ope. Few of the great men of ancient Israel who are celebrated in stories have comparable stones to speak for them.

Archaeology in the twenty-first century may still find material remains to document the presence of Hebrew slaves in Egypt during the New Kingdom, to explain the origins of early Israelite villages in Syria-Palestine, and to unlock the secrets of the Israel of David and Solomon. Ongoing excavations at Tel Rehov (http://www.rehov.org/), Hazor (http://unix ware.mscc.huji.ac.il/~hatsor/hazor.html), and Megiddo (http://megiddo .tau.ac.il/) may yet tell the stories of Israel's great men.

HOUSEHOLD ARCHAEOLOGY

Post-processual archaeologists realize that, although during the twentieth century cultural historians and biblical archaeologists focused on the rich and the powerful, they actually recovered a remarkable amount of material about the poor and the powerless. Consequently, gender and household archaeologists have turned their attention to this archive of material remains from completed excavations and now pay more attention to what the material remains reveal about the daily life of ordinary men, women, mothers, fathers, herders, farmers, midwives, slaves, teachers, elders, bakers, brewers, priests, prophets, and elders (Nakhai 2005). Household archaeology reveals much about how women, who bake bread for their men and their children, have a remarkable authority over them.

Household archaeology shows that throughout Syria-Palestine during the Iron Age (1200–586 B.C.E.) material remains were socially and economically similar, and that material development was consistent (C. L. Meyers 2002). Even when Israel developed from a decentralized, subsistence and village culture to a centralized, surplus city culture around 1000 B.C.E., the economics of households were not significantly changed, and the volatile politics of Israel and Judah between 925 and 586

Model of an Egyptian man making bread. Nelson-Atkins Museum of Art, Kansas City.

Millstone for grain. Hellenistic, 6th century B.C.E. Location: Haaretz Museum, Tel Aviv, Israel. Photo Credit: Erich Lessing / Art Resource, NY.

B.C.E. did not seriously interrupt the need for households to farm and herd.

Gender is an important factor in the distribution of power in the households of Syria-Palestine. The authority of women and men in households was comparable but not identical. One task of household archaeology is to observe and record what artifacts reveal about the gender of the spaces in a house. Usually men, women, and children worked separately, but sometimes they worked together. Women map their space in a house differently from men, and archaeologists can use artifacts to identify the common and gendered specifics in a house.

Men and women of households in ancient Israel ate together and slept together, so space for eating and sleeping was common space. Women, however, were the only ones in the households of ancient Israel who were responsible for weaving and baking, so areas for those activities were women's space. Space defined by women's work (Gen 24:28; Ruth 1:8; Song 3:4; 8:2) was called the "household of the mother" (Hebrew: *bêt ʾēm*), and space defined by men's work was called the "household of the father" (Hebrew: *bêt ʾāb*). When Naomi says to her daughters-in-law, Ruth and Orpah, "Go back to your mother's house" (Ruth 1:8), she is telling them to rejoin the women who weave and bake in the households where they were born.

The Woman from Thebez

Gender-specific work was also group work. Group work not only accomplished its task but also created important social relationships among the men or the women doing it. While grinding flour, older women would teach younger women not just how to bake bread but also how to deal with the men and the children they fed. The story of the woman delivering Thebez from Abimelech (Judg 9:50-56) may have been a group-work tradition told by either men or women (Halpern 1978; 1992).

> ## A WOMAN DELIVERS THEBEZ FROM ABIMELECH (JUDG 9:50-57)
>
> Abimelech attacked Thebez (Hebrew: *Tirzah*), northeast of Shechem and breached the wall of the lower city.
>
> All the men and women of Thebez fled with their leaders behind the walls of the upper city. They locked the gate, and prepared to defend the city.
>
> Abimelech attacked the upper city, and was preparing to set fire to its gate.
>
> When Abimelech was close to the wall, a woman threw her grinding stone at him and crushed his skull.
>
> Immediately Abimelech gave his shield bearer the order "Draw your sword and kill me, so people will not say: 'A woman killed him.'"
>
> So the shield bearer thrust his sword into Abimelech's chest.
>
> When the Israelites fighting with Abimelech saw that he was dead, they all fled from Thebez to their villages. Thus Elohim, Israel's divine patron, punished Abimelech for murdering his seventy covenant partners.

The signature of a hero in the Bible is an unorthodox weapon. During the Iron I period the Philistines set the standard for military weapons forged from iron. Yet these state-of-the-art weapons wielded by warriors like Abimelech were no match for the unorthodox weapons wielded by the heroes lifted up by Yahweh to deliver the Hebrews from slavery to their enemies. Ehud uses a two-edged knife (Judg 3:16); Jael, a mallet and a tent peg (Judg 4:21); Shamgar, an ox-goad (Judg 4:31); Samson, the jawbone of an ass (Judg 15:15); and the woman of Thebez, her grinding stone (Judg 9:53). Hebrew heroes use the tools with which they feed their households to protect them. The same skills and strength that the woman of Thebez used to grind flour every day for her household, she used to defend it. She crushed the head of Abimelech as she crushed the heads of grain. The man who crushed the gate of her city was crushed by the woman he threatened. Abimelech's shame-filled death became a taunt: "Who killed Abimelech son of Jerubbaal? Did not a woman throw

Grinding stone. http://upload.
wikimedia.org/wikipedia/
*commons/9/90/Metate_et_*
mano.jpg

a *grinding stone* at him from the wall of Thebez and kill him?" (2 Sam 11:21).

The tools of peace become the weapons of war. Ordinary people "beat their plowshares into swords" (Joel 3:10). The same things that women used to make their homes, they also used to defend them. They were not professional warriors; they were citizen soldiers. They fought in support of Yahweh the divine warrior. Their powerlessness made it clear to audiences that it was Yahweh, and not the woman from Thebez or Jael, who delivered the people from their enemies. Yahweh did not lift up professional soldiers to lead the Hebrews from slavery to freedom. The heroes in the books of Joshua, Judges, Samuel, and Kings were ordinary men and women who use the tools of their trade to deliver the Hebrews from their enemies.

Men would have told the story of the woman from Thebez to shame Abimelech, and any other man who would be king, for the heresy of forgetting that in ancient Israel only *Yahweh is Lord!* (M. S. Smith 1990, 46). Jews who became Christians continued this faith tradition by professing that *Jesus is Lord!* And later Muslims would pray *Allahu Akbar!* or *Allah is Great!* The profession of faith affirms that no human may wield divine power. Abimelech had ignored Israel's profession of faith: *Yahweh is Lord!* (Ps 29; 47:2; Deut 10:17; 1 Chr 12:6) Therefore, Abimelech was sentenced to the shameful death of being killed by a woman.

Women would have told the story to teach one another that when men fail to feed and protect their households, women can and must fill the void. Older women would teach younger women that Yahweh can use even a woman to protect and provide for their households. Household archaeology enriches the understanding of the story of the woman from Thebez by reconstructing how bread was made, by identifying where bread was made, and by deducing the authority that bread making gave to the women of a household and what it would mean for a woman to destroy her mill, even to defend her household from its enemies.

Bread and Beer

Cereals are used as food in African countries today more widely than anywhere in the developed world. They make up more than 75 percent of the calories in the average diet in Africa. Most of these cereals are naturally fermented. Fermenta-

Bread and beer were staples for households in the world of the Bible. Egypt's poor ate bread and drank beer. Egypt's rich drank beer and wine and ate pigeon, duck, oxen, and some forty kinds of bread and pastry. Egypt's dead prayed that the living members of their households would bring bread and beer to their tombs. The Egyptians had fifteen different words for bread. Post-processual archaeology and ethnoarchaeology both play important roles in reconstructing how people in the world of the Bible brewed beer and baked bread. Archaeologists have recovered models placed in tombs that illustrate how ancient Egyptians ground the grain, kneaded the dough, and strained the mash for beer and bread. Baking bread and brewing beer used substantially the same ingredients and, to the point of fermentation, the same procedure. Grain was the main ingredient of both bread and beer (Quirke and Spencer 1992: 17–18). The most common type of beer was brewed by straining the mash from fermented bread into a vat. Dates were used as sugar to feed the yeast.

tion is one of the oldest methods for preparing and preserving foods. Different methods of fermentation are used to make alcoholic beverages, lactic acid, leavened breads, and protein substitutes. (Lee 2003) ■

Bouza beer is a thick, pasty yellow brew (*Journal of Food Technology in Africa* 2002, 59–64). Brewers begin by coarsely grinding wheat, placing some of it in a wooden basin and kneading it with water into dough. The dough is cut into thick loaves, which are very lightly baked. Meanwhile, the remaining wheat is moistened with water, germinated for three to five days, sun-dried, ground, and mixed with the loaves of bread, which are soaked in water in a wooden barrel. *Bouza* beer from a previous brewing is added to serve as a starter. The mixture is allowed to ferment at room temperature for twenty-four hours, following which, the wort is sieved to remove large particles and diluted with water to a desired consistency.

Bouza beer has a very short shelf-life and is expected to be drunk within a day. Its pH increases to between 3.9 and 4.0 and its alcoholic content to between 3.8 and 4.2% within a twenty-four hour period (Ishida 2002: 81–88). (The people of Sudan today still brew *bouza* beer the way it was brewed in ancient Egypt [http://www.fao.org/docrep/x2184e/x2184e07.htm].) ■

A Hymn to Ninkasi describes how Sumerians brewed beer. They baked a bread (Akkadian: *bappir*) from barley or emmer wheat that was sweetened with date honey. The dried bread was crumbled and cooked with water and sprouted barley. This mash was spread on a large mat to cool. The mash was seasoned with date honey and fermented. Finally, it was filtered through a strainer into a storage jar. This beer was then drunk from a common bowl through long reeds or metal straws.

HYMN TO NINKASI
(Matthews and Benjamin 2006: 256–57)

You, Ninkasi, were born at the source of the rivers,
    You were nursed by Ninhursag. . . .
She laid the foundations of your great city on the sacred lake,
    She finished its walls for you. . . .
Your father was Enki-Nudimmud,
    Your mother was Ninti, Queen of the Underworld. . . .

You, who soothe the mouth, knead the dough with a great paddle,
    You sweeten the bread bowl with dates.
You bake the bread in a great oven;
    You stack the barley in piles to sprout. . . .

You, who slake thirst, dampen the piles of barley malt,
    While your great dogs guard them from thieves. . . .
You ferment the bread and malt in a jar,
    Waves of foam rise and fall. . . .

You, divine patron of brewers, spread the mash on great reed mats,
    You cool the wort. . . .
You press the mash with both hands,
    You filter the honey sweet brew. . . .

> Your strainer, Ninkasi, makes sweet music,
>> As you skillfully drain the wort into a storage jar....
> When you serve the filtered beer from the jar;
>> It gushes out like the Tigris and Euphrates....

Woman grinding grain to prepare bread. Painted wood. Egypt, Old Kingdom, 5th dynasty (2565–2420 B.C.E.). Location: Museo Archeologico, Florence, Italy. Photo Credit: Nimatallah / Art Resource, NY.

Beer is mentioned frequently in the Bible (Deut 29:6; 1 Sam 1:15; Isa 29:9; 28:7; 24:9). It was offered to Yahweh as a sacrifice (Num 28:7; Deut 14:26). Wise rulers (Prov 31:4), Nazirites (Num 6:3; Judg 13:4-14), and priests did not drink beer on days they were scheduled to enter the sanctuary (Lev 10:9). The poor drank beer to forget their suffering (Prov 31:6). Fools who drank too much beer became drunks (Ps 69:12; Isa 5:11 + 22; 56:12), started fights (Prov 20:1), and became false prophets (Mic 2:11).

The taste of the bread baked by the Egyptians would have depended on the grain used to make the bread. Archaeobotanists such as Mary Anne Murray excavating the workers' village at the pyramids on the Giza Plain in Egypt recover seeds using a flotation tank (Murray 2008; Davies and Friedman 1998, 83). The flotation tank is a vat full of flowing water. The seeds of barley and emmer wheat float to the top of the water. Dirt and stones sink to the bottom. These ancient seeds contained little of the gluten that makes bread light and crispy today.

The large, cake-like loaves baked by the Egyptians, were high in calories and starch. They were baked over open fires in large, bell-shaped pots. Each loaf fed several people at one meal more economically than baking flat bread. By baking bread in pots, the Egyptians could feed several hundred or even several thousand people quickly and efficiently. Bread pots (Egyptian: *bedja*) were made upside down over a cone, leaving a smooth and regular interior that was lined with finer clay so the loaf would not stick to the sides (http://www.fas.harvard.edu/~semitic/hsm/GizaBuilt Egypt.htm). The thick walls were formed of coarse Nile mud mixed with chopped grass and sand. The grass chaff burned out when the pot was fired, leaving a highly porous wall that retained and regulated heat so that the outer crust would not burn before the interior of the loaf was baked. Bread pots came in all sizes for baking conical loaves that ranged in size from small buns to medium loaves and large cakes.

The woman of Thebez crushed Abimelech's skull with a grinding stone. This stone was the upper half of her grain mill. The physical strength of the woman of Thebez is remarkable. During the Iron I period, every day women hauled water, toted fuel, milked goats, spun wool, weaved cloth, ground grain, and baked bread for themselves and their households (Herr and Boyd 2002, 34–37, 62). The average weight of a grinding stone at Tall Al-'Umayri (Jordan), for example, is six pounds thirteen ounces. In the 1998 excavation season alone, some eighteen saddle stones and some forty-five grinding stones were recovered. The woman of Thebez undoubtedly would have been strong enough to throw a grinding stone. Her strength won the battle for Thebez and for Israel. She was an ordinary woman who used the ordinary resources at hand to achieve heroic results.

Throwing her grinding stone was not only an act of strength but also an act of desperation for the women for Thebez. Once the grinding stone was gone, she could no longer bake bread for her household, which women did every day. There were no local quarries for basalt, so it would have been difficult for her to replace the grinding stone. Mills were so critical to the survival of a household that they could not be used as collateral for a loan. "No one shall take a mill or even the grinding stone as collateral, for that would be holding every member of the household hostage" (Deut 24:6).

The story of the woman from Thebez is not just a celebration of the physical strength of women in the Iron I period. This not just a human accomplishment; it is a divine action. These traditions celebrate Yahweh, who uses the powerless—such as a woman grinding grain—to shame the powerful—such as a man attacking a city.

The punishments of the powerful are proportionate (Latin: *talis*) to their crimes. Abimelech wanted to rule Shechem single-handedly as its head (Judg 9:37), and so he executed his seventy covenant partners upon a single stone. Therefore, he is executed by a single woman (Hebrew: *ʾiššâ ʾaḥat*) who drops a single stone upon his head (Janzen 1987, 35).

Most grain was ground in the first-floor courtyard of pillared houses, but there is some evidence for grinding grain on the second floor of a house. In 1994, a three-hundred-pound mill was recovered at Tall Al-'Umayri (Jordan) on top of mud brick rubble that once had been the upper story of a pillared house. Although it would have been difficult to carry such a heavy mill to the roof of the house, once it was

In 1991 a backhoe gouged a huge trench to the east of the building on the Giza Plain where priests embalmed the body of Menkaure, the pharaoh who built the third pyramid. Out of that trench came thousands of pieces of broken pottery. When Mark Lehner examined the trench, he found two intact bakeries. The large, bell-shaped pots in which the bread was baked littered the floor. Ancient tomb scenes show offering bearers carrying large conical loaves of exactly the shape that these pots would have produced (Lehner 1997). ∎

Phoenician model of a baker. Clay (900–800 B.C.E.). Iron Age. Location: Israel Museum (IDAM), Jerusalem, Israel. Photo Credit : Erich Lessing / Art Resource, NY.

In the world of the Bible, women used mills (Hebrew: *pelaḥ taḥtît*) to make flour. These mills had two parts. The lower part was the saddle—a concave stone that was about one and one-half feet long and one-half to one and one-half feet wide. The upper part was the grinding stone—a loaf-shaped stone (Hebrew: *pelaḥ rekeb*; Spanish: *mano*). The grinding stone could be grasped easily with one hand. It was about as long as the saddle stone was wide. Both parts of these mills, whole or broken, have been found in Bronze and Iron Age sites throughout Syria-Palestine.

Typically, grain mills were made of black basalt because the hard yet porous stone provides a rough surface and many cutting edges. Basalt stone was a luxury in the Thebez region of Syria-Palestine. ■

Official spellings of all sites in Jordan now correspond to the Arabic spellings of the written words, not the Arabic pronunciations of the spoken words; thus, the word for an ancient mound, *tell*, has become *tall*; it is, however, pronounced exactly the same as *tell*. *ʾUmayri's* spelling has changed from *ʾUmeiri*. ■

there, women could grind grain more comfortably in the breeze under the shade of reed canopies. In the story of the woman from Thebez, the "strong tower" (Judg 9:51 NRSV) may have been simply the roof of one of the pillared houses whose outer walls ringed the village, like the house of Rahab in the story of Rahab as a host (Josh 2:15). Because of the labor involved in building pillared houses, they often served more than one purpose. From here, defenders could easily throw rocks, sling stones, shoot arrows, and throw spears at invaders. The traditions also celebrate the woman from Thebez for being wise and shame Abimelech for being a fool. Only fools come close enough to the wall of a city and put themselves at risk of being killed by stones thrown at them by defenders. The strategy of the wise was to force the defenders of a city to waste their ammunition by firing it at the attackers who remained at a distance and safely out of harm's way.

CONCLUSION

Household archaeology reveals much about how women who bake bread for their men and their children have a remarkable authority over them. Archaeology also suggests that the woman of Thebez is not Joan of Arc. She is not a woman in a man's world. She is not on the ramparts of the inner city with men but on the roof of her own house adjoining the wall of the inner city. She is in women's space. On the roof of her house, she grinds her grain with the other women of the household. By throwing her mill at Abimelech she is an unlikely hero with an unorthodox weapon who identifies this struggle as the end-time duel between cosmos and chaos. The old world where she used the mill to grind flour for her household has come to an end. She will no longer be able without the mill to provide for her household. The food of the new world will be divine, not human. In the new world the Godmother, not the mother of the household, will provide for the people.

WHAT YOU HAVE LEARNED

- Two specific kinds of post-processual archaeology, *gender archaeology* and *household archaeology*, can be used to interpret a hero story in the book of Judges.
- Gender archaeology is interested in how the work of men and the work of women in the world of the Bible are valued. Women who bake bread for their men and their children are not seen as

powerless, but their authority to feed gives them remarkable control over those whom they feed.

- Household archaeology is interested, for example, in how space in a house is shared by men and women. Some space is women's space, and some space is men's space.

- The woman who delivers Thebez from Abimelech (Judg 9:50-57) uses the flour mill with which she feeds her household to defend her community. Likewise, she defends her household not by trespassing on men's space, but by remaining within women's space on the roof of the house.

STUDY QUESTIONS

1. What is the meaning of "feminine mystique"?
2. How does the approach of post-processual archaeology affect the interpretation of gendered material remains and sites?
3. How did group work enrich ancient societies?
4. What was the significance of baking bread?
5. What does the story of the woman from Thebez reveal about Yahweh's place in the lives of the people?

PREVIEW: BIBLICAL ARCHAEOLOGY TODAY

- Effects of War and Political Instability on Archaeology
- Collaborative Archaeological Work
- Archaeologists and Cultural Resource Managers

This afterword describes developing trends that will characterize archaeology in the world of the Bible in the near future. War and political instability in Mesopotamia will move more projects into Turkey, Saudi Arabia, Syria, or Kuwait. Assyriologists, Egyptologists, and biblical archaeologists will work more together than in isolation on projects. Archaeologists from faith-based universities will work alongside colleagues from religiously unaffiliated schools without being suspected of excavating to prove the Bible. Archaeologists will continue to develop working relationships with cultural resource managers, the industry of tourism, and even good antiquities dealers to educate the public about their work and its interpretation.

Afterword

Biblical Archaeology Today

Promising and ongoing work by archaeologists like James K. Hoffmeier along the coastal highway between Egypt and Syria-Palestine (Hoffmeier 1997; 2005; 2006); by Amihai Mazar at Tel Rehov in the Jordan Valley; by Israel Finkelstein, David Ussishkin, and Eric H. Cline at Megiddo (http://megiddo.tau.ac.il/); and by Amon Ben-Tor at Hazor are almost certain to produce finds that will completely change the paradigms currently in place for understanding the culture of ancient Israel. The next generation will inherit much from the painstaking and professional work of these and other excavators.

The Gulf Wars in Kuwait, Iraq, and Afghanistan destroyed much of the material heritage of these venerable cultures. The instability that these wars created also brought the work of foreign archaeologists there to a halt. Because of these tragedies, archaeological resources were shifted away from Kuwait, Iraq, and Afghanistan to Syria and Turkey with the result that new and important finds in these countries will occupy the next generation of archaeologists for decades.

Technology continues to improve the ability of archaeologists to assemble material and to do research. Computers provide more access to more artifacts more quickly. They also allow sophisticated models for comparison to be developed and applied. Projects such as the Chicago *Assyrian Dictionary* are coming to completion, and technology will allow the meticulous work of a century to be accessed and applied for a better understanding of the world of the Bible.

Archaeology in the world of the Bible during the twentieth century has repeatedly been divided and separated. Assyriologists specialized in the study of Mesopotamian cultures, and many had little or no interest in the relationship of those cultures with ancient Israel. Egyptologists specialized in the study of Egypt and its neighbors in Africa, and many likewise ignored the implications of their work for understanding the Bible. Even biblical archaeologists began referring to their field as Levantine studies, Middle Eastern archaeology, Syro-Palestinian archaeology, or archaeology of Palestine in the Iron Age. Now, however, there is a growing realization that the problem was not with the term "biblical archaeology" but with the way in which archaeologists working in Syria-Palestine were designing their excavations and using their material remains. Consequently, biblical archaeology is being reinstated as the title for the field (Zevit 2002).

The isolation of Assyriology, Egyptology, and even biblical archaeology from biblical studies may have been necessary for each discipline to define better its own identity and to achieve adequate confidence in its own area. The competition and the hostility are not gone, but there is likely to be less fragmentation in the community of learning where new graduates will be pursuing their careers. The field of biblical studies now increasingly recognizes that it needs the resources and the enrichment that Assyriology, Egyptology, and archaeology bring to it. Fortunately, the number of scholars who actively participate in multiple specialties is increasing and will continue to increase during the twenty-first century.

William Foxwell Albright used all the traditions and artifacts that archaeologists had recovered in his day to understand the world of the Bible. Today, that archaeological archive has multiplied again and again. There are more artifacts and better tools to sort, analyze, compare, and interpret them. The work of Rainer Albertz (1994), Ziony Zevit (2001), and Mark S. Smith (2001; 2002) are only a few examples of how productive the results of this new détente will be (J. E. Wright 2002, 67). These scholars will certainly inspire the next generation of archaeologists to be more inclusive in their own work.

In the golden age of biblical archaeology, fieldwork was both inspired and funded by people of faith. As biblical archaeology came under more and more scrutiny, a consensus began to develop that faith contaminates learning. Archaeologists and biblical scholars did not become atheists, but they often assumed that secular, or at least non-sectarian, archaeology and biblical studies were to be preferred. Nonetheless, some schools such as the Seventh-day Adventist universities continued to field a distinguished group of archaeologists whose work during the twentieth century has been academically sound (Younker 2004). Their ongoing work in the world of the Bible, in the academic community, and in professional organizations now stands out as an example of how faith-based schools, and denominations as a whole, can successfully engage in scientifically based field archaeology and yet remain active in biblical and religious studies. The next generation of archaeologists will certainly benefit from their

example. Faith, even in archaeology and biblical studies, is not only compatible with learning but can inspire and motivate learning.

Material remains from the world of the Bible have always had a profound impact on both the archaeologists who recover them and the public who view them. Today, technology distributes images and interpretations of the artifacts on a scale almost unimaginable for most of the twentieth century. Artifacts become an immediate stimulus for community identities and social and political claims of all kinds. Biblical archaeology will play a new social role as a partner, not a patron, in the study of the world of the Bible (Silberman 2003, 7–9).

The archaeology of emperors projected the worldviews of Western Europe onto the material remains recovered by archaeologists to validate their own cultures. The worldview of one nation challenged the worldview of another. It was a dangerous game, but there were few players. Then biblical archaeology brought the worldview of Christians from the Reformation tradition in the United States into play. The material remains of the past were used to demonstrate that Judaism, Christianity, and Islam were worldviews rooted in history, not in myth celebrating the recurring cycles of nature.

Today Britain, France, Germany, and the United States are not the only nations who define themselves by the material remains of the past. More and more states and ethnic communities in the world of the Bible are demanding not only political recognition but also cultural endorsement for their worldviews on the basis of the material remains of the past (J. L. King 1987; Silberman 2003, 9–10).

Archaeologists can no longer enjoy private pleasure and undisturbed isolation in recovering and interpreting the material remains of the past. They must now interact immediately with all those institutions and organizations who manage, maintain, interpret, present, and negotiate the social significance of the cultural heritage in the world of the Bible. Today's archaeologists are dialogue partners with governments, departments of antiquities, museums, ethnic groups, local residents, landowners, academic colleagues, religious leaders, financial backers, educators in local schools, and the media. Archaeologists no longer control the interpretation of the artifacts they recover but must negotiate with a wide variety of stakeholders to understand what they have unearthed. Archaeologists are no longer just recovering, restoring, and interpreting the material remains of the past. They are partners with those who use computer modeling to visualize what the site looks like today, and what it looked like yesterday. They work with museums to develop techniques to display and interpret their artifacts. They work with print, radio, television, and Internet media responsibly to popularize both the material remains and the stories that media requires to go with the artifacts.

The *Gospel of Judas* developed in Egypt among Coptic Christians. The papyrus fragments on which the *Gospel of Judas* was written had changed hands a number of times following its discovery in 1983. The Maecenas Foundation for Ancient Art in Switzerland approached National Geographic to authenticate and conserve the codex. In 2000 the National Geographic Society assembled a small group of scholars to work on the project (http://www.nationalgeographic .com/lostgospel/?fs=www9). When the project and the exhibitions are complete, the codex will be returned to Egypt, where it will be housed in Cairo's Coptic Museum. The project is a model for the demands that will be placed on archaeologists in the future.

Marvin W. Meyer, who worked on the translation of the *Gospel of Judas*, reported informally in 2007 at the annual meeting of the Pacific Coast Region of the Society of Biblical Literature at the Pacific School of Religion that his experience with the National Geographic project was generally positive, even if unorthodox by academic standards. The Geographic, for example, before even talking with Meyer about the project required him to sign an order of suppression restricting him from making public any information about the project. Nonetheless, the academic grapevine was already alive with rumors that the *Gospel of Judas* project was under way, so Meyer was not surprised after signing the order to hear what the Geographic had to propose. The physical resources that the Geographic made available to project members were all state-of-the-art. Nonetheless, security screeners searched Meyer coming and going from his work space as if he were working for the Los Alamos National Laboratory.

Academic translation projects like the New Revised Standard Version are collaborative. The work is done by committee. Drafts are made, then discussed, then revised. Only when the entire committee votes to accept a translation does it go to press. The Geographic project segregated Meyer from the other translators. Their work became collaborative only after it was completed. The Geographic model was not without precedent for an Egyptian text. According to the *Letter of Aristeas* (second century B.C.E.), arrangements not unlike those provided to Meyer and his colleagues by the Geographic were provided by Ptolemy II Philadephus (ruled 285–246 B.C.E.) to the seventy-two Jewish scholars who translated the Bible from Hebrew into Greek.

Afterword

When the *Gospel of Judas* project was complete, the National Geographic orchestrated a
grand debut for the project in Washington, D.C.
On the same day, the Geographic opened the
exhibition of the codex itself; released the *Gospel of Judas* (Ehrman et al. 2006) edited in part
by Meyer; and launched a Web site with a high-
quality copy of the Coptic text and its English
translation.

The next generation of archaeologists will be
much more comfortable working with corpora-
tions such as the National Geographic Society.
Academics will no longer segregate themselves
from the media or from cultural resource managers. They will become active participants in the
work of the preservation and publication of the
material heritage of the past. As Eric H. Cline,
another National Geographic Society collabora-
tor, enthusiastically proclaims:

> It is high time that professional archaeolo-
> gists, ancient historians, and mainstream
> biblical scholars take back their fields from
> the amateur enthusiasts, pseudoscientists,
> uninformed documentary filmmakers, and
> overzealous biblical maximalists and mini-
> malists who have had, for the most part, free
> rein to do what they wish, without any regard
> to scientific method or an unbiased investi-
> gation for the truth. . . . we as academics owe
> it to the general public. (Cline 2007, xi)

Albright defined biblical archaeology. His
work as an excavator, a ceramicist, a linguist, and
a cultural historian continues to be a beacon in
the best of times and the worst of times for the
discipline or, as Dever would label it, the *dialogue*
between archaeologists working in the Near East
and biblical scholars (Dever 1982, 103). At the
time of his death, colleagues hailed Albright as
a twentieth-century genius (Running and Freedman 1975). Today he is honored more modestly as
a twentieth-century, *American, Protestant* genius.
Albright was not the scholar of all time but a
scholar of his time (J. E. Wright 2002, 68).

As the director of the American School of
Oriental Research at Johns Hopkins University (1929–1959), Albright pioneered the biblical
archaeology movement. Anticipating the canons of processual archaeology, Albright brought

remarkable scientific skills to the discipline. He knew the pottery chronology; he knew ancient languages; and he knew the cultures of Israel's neighbors. Albright professionalized biblical archaeology. In the details of excavation and interpretation he was a master. The genius of Albright was admirable but isolating. The academic virtue of the next generation is not isolated genius but collegial collaboration. Genius today is assembling a good team, not enjoying uncontested control of all the evidence.

CONCLUSION

The beginning of the twenty-first century is a significant moment for archaeology and for the Bible. For perhaps for the first time since the traditions that the Bible preserves were written, but no longer told; perhaps for the first time since the world where those traditions developed came to an end, there is a possibility to hear those traditions again, and to return to that ancient and fascinating world. The extraordinary achievements of archaeologists and biblical scholars working together continue to reveal the world of the Bible, and the Bible itself, in ways that are not only intriguing but also inspiring. Archaeologists and biblical scholars have created a way back that will define a new way forward in understanding what these ancient and remarkable people had to say, and why they said it.

WHAT YOU HAVE LEARNED

- For the near future, war and political instability in Iraq and Afghanistan will move more archaeologists into Jordan, Cyprus, Turkey, Saudi Arabia, Syria, or Kuwait.
- Assyriologists, Egyptologists, and biblical archaeologists will work more together than in isolation on projects.
- Biblical archaeologists from faith-based universities will work alongside colleagues from religiously unaffiliated schools without being suspected of excavating to prove the Bible.
- Archaeologists will continue to develop working relationships with cultural resource managers, the industry of tourism, and even good antiquities dealers to educate the public about their work and its interpretation.

STUDY QUESTIONS

1. Describe the interdisciplinary nature of contemporary archaeology.
2. Can biblical archaeology be described as having come of age?
3. How does technology serve archaeology?

Appendix

The Next Generation

The descriptions in this appendix are drawn from the Web sites of the universities and programs surveyed. For more information, visit the Web sites indicated.

Outstanding universities in the United States and Canada train students in the archaeology of the Near East. Among their promising graduates a significant number will focus their careers on the world of the Bible.

University of Chicago

Department of Near Eastern Languages and Civilizations

http://humanities.uchicago.edu/depts/nelc/

The languages and civilizations of the Near East have always been a major part of the graduate degree programs in the Department of Near Eastern Languages and Civilizations at the University of Chicago.

William Rainey Harper, the University's founder and first president, was a specialist in Semitic languages and author of a Hebrew grammar that was widely used at universities and seminaries for more than seventy-five years.

Faculty members at the University of Chicago pioneered the disciplines of Assyriology, Egyptology, and ancient Near Eastern archaeology in the United States. The first program in Islamic civilization was also developed at the University of Chicago.

An interdisciplinary approach to learning is a characteristic of the Chicago intellectual tradition. The Department of Near Eastern Languages and Civilizations collaborates with the departments of anthropology, art history, classics, comparative literature, history, law, linguistics, political science, and religious studies. Many of the students and faculty also work at the Oriental Institute and the Center for Middle Eastern Studies.

The department also publishes the *Journal of Near Eastern Studies*, which is one of the leading journals in Near Eastern and Islamic studies.

Columbia University

Department of Art History and Archaeology

http://www.columbia.edu/cu/arthistory/

Graduate degrees in the Department of Art History and Archaeology at Columbia University are offered in a wide range of fields including Near Eastern art and archaeology. Students and faculty study urbanism, architectural space, and the context of visual images. Archaeology students here have access not only to programs in the department itself, but also to the Program in Archaeology, which is a coalition of six departments at Columbia University, as well as the network of archaeologists, archaeological sites, and museum collections in New York City as a whole.

Students intern at the Lamont-Doherty Earth Observatory, New York University, the City University of New York, the New York Botanical Garden, the American Museum of Natural

Appendix

History, the Metropolitan Museum of Art, the Brooklyn Museum of Art, the National Museum of the American Indian, the South Street Seaport Museum, and the Museum of the City of New York.

At Columbia University, archaeology is a multidisciplinary field practiced by faculty and students in the social sciences, natural sciences, and humanities. Faculty in the departments of anthropology, art history and archaeology, classics, historic preservation, history, Middle Eastern languages and cultures, and the Center for Environmental Research and Conservation conduct research on prehistory, ancient society, or historical archaeology. There are also researchers at Lamont-Doherty in fields such as dendro-chronology, paleo-climatology, and remote sensing.

Some faculty members in the Department of Art History and Archaeology participate in the interdepartmental program in the archaeology of pre-Columbian, medieval, and Mediterranean cultures. Others work at the Center for the Ancient Mediterranean focusing on Bronze Age cultures, Greek and Roman cultures, Byzantine cultures, and Near Eastern art and archaeology (http://www.columbia.edu/cu/cam/).

The Center for the Ancient Mediterranean at Columbia University links together faculty and students from various departments with an interest in the ancient Mediterranean cultures. The Center coordinates courses, organizes conferences, and accesses resources such as the Columbia's Art Properties Collections, the Wallach Art Gallery, and the artifacts from the excavations at Phlamoudhi (Cyprus). Ongoing fieldwork by faculty in New York City, upstate New York, the southwest United States, Mexico, Belize, Honduras, Peru, Argentina, Italy, Egypt, Greece, Syria, Yemen, Sicily, France, Cyprus, and the Andes offer students opportunities to learn the craft of field archaeology.

Harvard University

Department of Near Eastern Languages and Civilizations

http://www.fas.harvard.edu/~nelc/

The Department of Near Eastern Languages and Civilizations at Harvard University offers eleven graduate programs in different fields of study, all of which are concerned in some way with the cultures of the Near East.

The Widener Library has extensive holdings in Arabic, Armenian, Hebrew, Persian, Turkish, and Yiddish literature (http://hcl.harvard.edu/libraries/widener/history.html). Faculty and students also have access to the Andover-Harvard Theological Library of the Harvard Divinity School and the Center for Jewish Studies.

The Harvard Semitic Museum has a unique collection of ancient and medieval artifacts representing many of the cultures of the Near East. For students interested in biblical or other ancient Near Eastern studies, or in the archaeology of the Near East, a variety of opportunities for archaeological fieldwork in the world of the Bible are available.

Johns Hopkins University

Department of Near Eastern Studies

http://neareast.jhu.edu/

Founded in 1883, the Department of Near Eastern Studies of the Johns Hopkins University was the first in the United States to offer a doctorate in Near Eastern studies. The department now offers programs in Northwest Semitic languages and literatures including biblical studies, Egyptology, Assyriology, ancient law, and Near Eastern archaeology.

Students study the literary traditions and material artifacts of Near Eastern civilizations using literary criticism, legal studies, anthropology, and archaeology. The study of language and literature forms a major part of the program, with an emphasis on accessing traditions in their original languages. Consequently, even the archaeology program has a substantial language requirement.

University of Michigan

Department of Near Eastern Studies

http://www.umich.edu/~neareast/

The Department of Near Eastern Studies at the University of Michigan offers programs in Near Eastern languages, literatures, civilizations, linguistics, history, ancient studies, biblical studies, Egyptology, Mesopotamian and ancient Near Eastern studies, ancient Israel, the Hebrew Bible, and Judaism and Christianity in the Greco-Roman world.

The Department of Near Eastern Studies partners with the departments of anthropology, classical art and archaeology, classical studies, economics, history, history of art, Judaic studies, linguistics, political science, and sociology.

University of Toronto

Department of Ancient Near Eastern, Middle Eastern, and Islamic Studies

http://www.gradschool.utoronto.ca/programs/masters/Ancient-Near-Eastern-Studies-and-Middle-Eastern-and-Islamic-Studies.htm

The Department of Near Eastern, Middle Eastern and Islamic Studies at the University of Toronto studies the languages and literature, history, and material culture of the societies of the Near and Middle East, from prehistoric times to the present. The department has faculty with specialties in the art, archaeology, languages, and literatures of Egypt, Syria-Palestine, and western Asia.

The programs are rooted within the broad tradition of the humanities, and facilitate the study of the complex non-Western cultures and societies that constitute the cultural legacy of the ancient Near East, in order to provide greater understanding of their contribution to the historical development of Western civilization and the contemporary cultures and societies of the Middle East.

The Near Eastern department partners with the departments of classical studies and history of art to offer an interdisciplinary program in Ancient Studies.

University of Pennsylvania

Department of Near Eastern Languages and Civilizations

http://www.sas.upenn.edu/nelc/
http://www.arthistory.upenn.edu/aamw/

The Department of Near Eastern Languages and Civilization at the University of Pennsylvania and the Graduate Group in the Art and Archaeology of the Mediterranean World train students in the art and archaeology of classical and Near Eastern civilizations. Drawing on the resources of the University of Pennsylvania Museum of Archaeology and Anthropology, the program incorporates fieldwork, museum internships, and university instruction.

Members of the faculty of the Art and Archaeology of the Mediterranean World Graduate Group are from classical studies, history of art, anthropology and Near Eastern languages and civilizations, the Graduate School of Design, the University Museum's Applied Science Center for Archaeology and the Center for Ancient Studies, and the Center for Advanced Judaic Studies.

Students also have the opportunity to take courses at Bryn Mawr, Princeton, and Temple universities, which form part of a regional academic consortium with the University of Pennsylvania.

The program engages in the interdisciplinary humanistic study and teaching of the cultures of the Near East as they express themselves in languages and traditions, as well as art, architecture, archaeology, and material culture. These cultures encompass the geographic region that includes Mesopotamia, Egypt, Israel, Syria, Arabia, Anatolia, and Persia. Faculty members teach Sumerian, Akkadian, Hittite, Egyptian, Hebrew, Aramaic, Arabic, Persian, Turkish, and other languages of the region.

The deepest understanding of any Near Eastern culture and its impact on the cultures of the world in areas as diverse as writing, literature, religion, science, and politics requires a profound knowledge of its languages. The department's approach to languages and traditions is interdisciplinary. It places primary sources in their historical, cultural, and intellectual contexts and studies them using philology, literary criticism, history, archaeology, history of art and architecture, comparative law, religion, philosophy and ethics, psychology, gender studies, anthropology, and theater, cinema, and other performance studies. For example, the program studies the Hebrew Bible in the light of the Near East; the origins of monumental architecture in Egypt in comparison with that of Mesopotamia; and the origins of writing in Egypt, Mesopotamia, and Syria-Palestine.

Important assets for Near Eastern studies at the University of Pennsylvania are the University of Pennsylvania Museum, which provides hands-on contact with many of the texts and artifacts that are the primary sources of study. The Museum's Babylonian Section houses the second largest collection of cuneiform tablets in the United States and the most important collection of Sumerian literature in the world. The museum also houses the files of the Pennsylvania *Sumerian Dictionary* project. Faculty and graduate students are involved in translation and publication of the tablets and the preparation of the dictionary. In the Tablet Room, students can study original copies of the Sumerian Flood Story and part of the Gilgamesh Epic. The Egyptian Section houses approximately forty thousand Egyptian artifacts, by far the largest university collection in the United States and among the largest in the world. The section continues more than a century of ongoing fieldwork in Egypt. The Near East Section also has the largest collection of artifacts from Syria-Palestine outside of Israel.

University of North Carolina at Chapel Hill and Duke University
Consortium for Classical and Mediterranean Archaeology
http://www.aas.duke.edu/ccma/

Duke University and the University of North Carolina at Chapel Hill employ one of the largest concentrations of archaeologists in the United States, distributed in departments of classics or classical studies, art history, religious studies, and anthropology. The Consortium for Classical and Mediterranean Archaeology brings these faculties together to enhance the archaeology programs in the respective departments. The Consortium fosters an interdisciplinary dialogue on methods, theory, and practice in classical archaeology and material culture; provides students access to seminars, excavations, other research opportunities, and academic advising; and develops avenues for curricular and extracurricular interaction.

Graduate students at the University of North Carolina in Chapel Hill and at Duke University follow separate degree tracks in their respective departments, but as members of the Consortium graduate group, students may take any number of courses and seminars outside of their department and institution. They may choose thesis and dissertation under the direction of another department or at another university. Students are encouraged to develop their program of study and research to integrate appropriate fields of study and areas of specialization not represented in their home department.

University of California, Los Angeles
Cotsen Institute of Archaeology
http://www.ioa.ucla.edu/

The Cotsen Institute of Archaeology at the University of California in Los Angeles offers interdisciplinary research programs, bringing together faculty from eleven departments. The Cotsen Institute houses fifteen research laboratories, a computer laboratory, a reading room, a seminar room, and teaching facilities. Visiting scholars also contribute to seminars.

The Institute partners with other institutions such as the J. Paul Getty Museum, where students can acquire more advanced training in specialized components of archaeological method and theory. For example, there are programs in archaeological and ethnographic conservation with the Getty Museum.

Graduate programs train students in the interdisciplinary practices and techniques of archaeological investigation. They provide students with a strong background in archaeological interpretation and theory to enable them to undertake independent study, interpretation, and preservation of the archaeological heritage worldwide. Graduate programs are designed to provide broad training in theoretical perspective combined with in-depth study of specific areas. These programs

are interdisciplinary and draw on faculty from anthropology, art history, classics, East Asian languages and cultures, Germanic languages, history and Near Eastern languages and cultures.

The Institute provides a series of core courses for first-year students that provides training in archaeological theory and grounds the formation of a yearly cohort of students. There is also training in a diverse range of laboratory methods, enabling students to select the methods and techniques best suited to their interest, geographic region, and time period of study. Students work alongside their faculty to develop new technologies for demonstrating, analyzing, and communicating the past to a variety of professional and public audiences.

University of California, San Diego
Levantine Archaeology Laboratory
http://www.anthro.ucsd.edu/~tlevy/index.htm

The Levantine Archaeology Laboratory at the University of California in San Diego promotes archaeological field and laboratory research conducted by archaeologists and related specialists. Archaeology at the UCSD is an interdisciplinary and collaborative endeavor practiced by scholars who hold faculty or research positions in a variety of departments, ranging from anthropology to the Scripps Institute of Oceanography.

The mission of the laboratory is to disseminate Levantine research by making available resources, including laboratory facilities and study collections, to students and affiliated researchers; to develop resources that benefit archaeologists, academics, and students, while being able to expand the support—laboratory, equipment, funding—for Levantine archaeological research.

Artifacts and samples recovered by the Edom Lowland Project (http://www.anthro.ucsd.edu/

~tlevy/index_files/Edom.htm) in Jordan are analyzed and prepared for long-term storage at the laboratory. There is also a Levantine Zoo-archaeology laboratory.

Pennsylvania State University
Classics and Ancient Mediterranean Studies
http://www.cams.psu.edu/index.shtml

At Pennsylvania State University faculty in the Department of History and the Department of Classics and Ancient Mediterranean Studies hold joint appointments. Consequently, programs cover not only ancient Greece and Rome but also the ancient Near East—Egypt, Israel, Mesopotamia, and North Africa. The faculty also directs ongoing excavations in Egypt, Israel, and Greece.

Yale University
Department of Near Eastern Languages &
Civilizations
http://www.yale.edu.nelc/

Yale University offered the first formal program of study in Near Eastern languages in the United States. Faculty here pioneered in the language and literature of biblical Hebrew and the history of Judaism, Arabic and Islamic studies, cuneiform studies, Semitic epigraphy, philology, linguistics, and Sanskrit studies.

Yale publishes the *Journal of the American Oriental Society*, the first professional journal devoted to Oriental studies in the United States.

Charles Cutter Torrey, professor of Arabic and Semitic languages, directed the first American excavation in Syria-Palestine in 1900 and founded the American School of Archaeology at Jerusalem—today the Albright Institute—in

1901. The department sponsors archaeological field projects in Syria and Egypt.

Throughout its long history, the department's mission has expanded to include Assyriology, Egyptology, the archaeology of Western Asia, Northwest Semitic and Ugaritic studies, Hittitology, and the contemporary Near East. The Department of Near Eastern Languages & Civilizations today maintains its strong sense of traditional humanist values, as well as leadership in developing and evaluating new techniques, perspectives, and resources for study of the Near East.

The graduate program of the Department of Near Eastern Languages & Civilizations partners with the departments of anthropology, history, medieval studies, and religious studies to emphasize reflective scholarship based on sound knowledge of the languages, civilizations, and material cultures of the Near East.

The department founded the Yale Egyptological Institute in Egypt. The Institute provides instruction in the philology and cultures of ancient Egypt and Nubia. Egyptology courses at Yale present the history and archaeology of ancient Egypt and neighboring regions from the earliest predynastic through the Coptic period.

Texas A&M University
Institute of Nautical Archaeology
http://ina.tamu.edu/

The Institute of Nautical Archaeology at Texas A&M University studies the remains of boats and ships and the cultures that created and used them. The program therefore focuses on the history of wooden ship construction; seafaring through the ages; maritime commerce, cargoes, and ports; and the techniques used to record, analyze, and conserve the remains of these activities.

The Nautical Archaeology Program is part of the Department of Anthropology. Students and faculty conduct underwater archaeological research in various parts of the world, delving into time periods from prehistory to the recent past, and working with a plethora of societies and cultures.

Brown University
Artemis A. W. and Martha Sharp Joukowsky Institute for Archaeology and the Ancient World
http://brown.edu/Departments/Joukowsky_Institute

The Artemis A. W. and Martha Sharp Joukowsky Institute for Archaeology and the Ancient World studies complex societies of the premodern era. Its programs promote the investigation, understanding, and enjoyment of the archaeology and art of the ancient Mediterranean, Egypt, and Western Asia. The Institute's faculty and facilities provide a campus hub for research and teaching in this complex and compelling part of the world, including active fieldwork projects, diverse graduate and undergraduate curricula, and public outreach activities. The Artemis A. W. and Martha Sharp Joukowsky Institute for Archaeology and the Ancient World is dedicated to the academic study and public promotion of the archaeology and art of the ancient Mediterranean, Egypt, and Western Asia—extending from Anatolia and the Levant to the Caucasus, and including the territories of the ancient Near East.

The Program in Ancient Studies at Brown University is a collaboration of critical exploration and interdisciplinary scholarship that seeks to bring together all those at Brown (faculty, graduate students, undergraduates, and staff) who are interested in the cultures, religions, and histories of ancient civilizations. Geographically, the ancient world represented at Brown comprises early China and India, West Asia (Mesopotamia, Iran, Anatolia, and Israel), Egypt, the Mediterranean (especially Greece and Italy), the early Islamic and Byzantine worlds as well as the Pre-Columbian Mesoamerican civilizations.

CONCLUSION

Students who graduate from any of the rich variety of schools teaching archaeology will find that there is exciting work to be done in the area of archaeology and the Bible. Nonetheless, biblical archaeology will continue to be a craft of quiet perseverance rather than of high-profile discoveries. There are still languages to be learned, more and more books and journal articles to be read, and long physical seasons in the field. The material heritage of any culture does not reveal itself easily. Progress is made by those who are patient and hardworking, and they are rewarded by the gifted insights that such determination stimulates.

Glossary

Amphictyony. A league of twelve tribes whose lands surrounded a central sanctuary such as Shechem or Hebron. One tribe protected and provided for the sanctuary for one month each year.

***Annales* school of archaeology.** The school that takes its name from the French journal *Annales: économies, sociétés, civilisations*. Its approach to history is to study structures, including climate, agriculture, commerce, social groups, and the like.

Apologetics. The root of the word "apologetics" is the Greek word *apologia*. In a trial the prosecuting attorney delivered a *kategoria* or list of indictments; the defense attorney replied with an *apologia*. Apologetics is the study of how to reply and rebut charges of antisocial behavior.

Archaeology. The recovery, interpretation, and reconstruction of the cultural property of now-extinct cultures.

Ashlar. A large, smooth block of limestone.

Biblical archaeology. A subdiscipline of cultural history. William Foxwell Albright launched the Biblical Archaeology movement to demonstrate that the Bible was historically reliable. For example, in 1922 Leonard Woolley was directing an excavation of the royal tombs at Ur (Arabic: Tell al Muqayyar) north of Basra (Iraq), when he uncovered an eight-foot-thick layer of clean clay. He considered this layer unmistakable evidence that the flood stories in the book of Genesis (Gen 6:1—11:26) are historically reliable.

Body sherd. A broken piece of pottery valuable for identifying the composition of the clay and the technique used to make a pot.

Bulla. A seal formed when a lump of wet clay is stamped with the impression of, for example, the sender of a letter. A papyrus scroll would be rolled up, tied with a string, and secured with a bulla.

Burnish. A polish applied to seal and to shine the surface of a pot.

Calendars/archaeological calendar. Archaeologists working in the world of the Bible created a calendar using the raw materials used for tools and weapons, for example, Stone Age, Chalcolithic (Greek: *chalco* = copper; *lithic* = stone) Age, Bronze Age, Iron Age. The dates for these periods reflect the consensus of early archaeologists on when these materials first came into use. Subsequent research has made modifications in the dates, but the calendar dates have not been changed. Dates for the archaeological calendar in *Stones & Stories* follow *The Anchor Bible Dictionary* (1992) edited by David N. Freedman.

Calendars/ceramic calendars. Calendars based on political and economic events in written artifacts were replaced by ceramic calendars built around the raw material, the shape and the decoration used in pottery. Repeated careful excavations developed sequences for the evolution of pottery types from its first appearance in the Neolithic period (6000–3800 B.C.E.) to the pottery used in Syria-Palestine during the Crusades (1096–1291). Not only does pottery provide a chronology for a particular site, but the chronologies from more than one site can be used to recreate the chronology of an entire region.

Canon of the Bible. The list of books that are accepted as authoritative scripture. The enumeration of books included in the canon differs somewhat according to different traditions.

Concretion. A technical term for a stone-like mass or clump created by minerals suspended in the water around a metal artifact. A concretion sometimes contains a hollow space after the artifact has rusted away. This hollow can be casted by filling it with epoxy, recovering the original shape of the metal object. http://www.abc.se/~pa/uwa/glossary.htm.

Crannog. A dwelling built along the sides of lakes in Scotland, Ireland, and Wales after 3000 B.C.E. Crannogs are round houses of wood and branches supported on stilts driven into the lake bed. Sometimes, in place of stilts, tons of rocks were piled onto the lake bed to make an island foundation for the crannog. Several hundred crannogs have been identified, but only a few have been excavated.

Cuneiform. The earliest cuneiform inscriptions were pictographs or icons. These pictographs evolved into signs or patterns created by wedges. Originally, each cuneiform sign stood for one or more related words whose correct meaning was determined by the context. For example, a cuneiform star stood for both a star in the night sky and a member of the divine assembly. Cuneiform developed some six hundred signs that could represent either words or syllables. A few signs could also indicate that the sign following it referred to a particular category such as a city or a people. The remarkable thing about the cuneiform system is that, for all its complexity, it had sufficient flexibility to permit its adaptation to a large number of extremely different languages.

Demotic Egyptian. A cursive or longhand writing. It appeared about 650 B.C.E. and was used for business, legal, scientific, literary, and religious documents written on papyrus paper.

Diachronic. A term identifying schools of interpretation that, like a motion-picture documentary, examine the origins, development history, and change that take place over time.

Diagnostic sherd. A broken piece of pottery such as a rim, handle, or base from which the shape and decoration of the original pot can be reconstructed.

Dimorphic economy. Village economy in the world of the Bible was dimorphic—a combination of farming and herding. Some villagers farmed, some herded.

Druze. A minority faith tradition in Syria, Lebanon, and Israel. Historically the Druze are the disciples of al-Hakim bi-Amrih Alla, an Egyptian Muslim who in 1009 proclaimed himself to be divine—challenging both the Muslim belief in the uniqueness of Allah and the position of Muhammad as the last prophet of Allah. Although the Druze evolved from Shi'a Islam, Druze tradition today includes beliefs influenced by Persian Gnosticism and Hellenistic philosophy.

Dumpie. In 1983 two kinds of statues from the Neolithic period were recovered at 'Ain Ghazal (Jordan): dumpies and figures. Dumpies are about a foot high; figures are three feet high. Dumpies have solid, roughly shaped, unpainted bodies. Figures have well-defined arms and legs. The bodies of the statues were painted with red iron oxide, black carbon, and white lime. The heads of both dumpies and figures have detailed eyes, noses, mouths, and ears. The eyes, elliptical with round irises, were painted with black tar and blue copper oxide. Noses turn up at the ends, and the nostrils are simply two narrow cuts. Mouths are also just narrow cuts. Ears are small, unshaped knobs. The statues are shaped from plaster over a core of branches tied with string. The cores in the dumpies were one bundle of branches, while the cores of the figures were several bundles tied together. The heads and necks of the cores were also reinforced with string. The branches in the cores stuck out from the bases of the statues so that they could be mounted into plaster floors. Some figures were arranged in groups: father, mother, and child surrounded by dumpies.

Epigraphy. The science of copying and interpreting inscriptions and associated pictures.

Ethnography. Detailed descriptions by anthropologists of human behavior in a particular culture. Ethnographies are based on both the observations of the anthropologists as outsiders and interviews with members of the cultures they are studying as insiders.

Fast wheel. The fast wheel developed around 2000 B.C.E. Two wheels were connected to a shaft. Potters turned the lower wheel with their feet and shaped their pots on the top wheel with their hands.

Figures. *See* dumpies.

General Systems Theory. The interdisciplinary study of complex entities and the models which can be used to describe them. It was proposed in the 1940s by biologist Ludwig von Bertalanffy (1901–1972). Rather than reducing an entity to the sum of its parts, General Systems Theory focuses on the relations that connect the parts into a whole system (http://pespmc1.vub.ac.be/ systheor.html).

Glacis. A slopping, layered, packed earth ramp with a plastered surface. The glacis sheeted water off the wall and away from its foundations to prevent erosion.

Guffa. A bucket made from an automobile tire used to remove dirt and pottery from a square.

Hebrews. During the Late Bronze period (1500–1200 B.C.E.) Hebrews were displaced households (Akkadian: ʿapiru) whose common bond was not ethnic but social. War and famine were common causes of their social dislocation. These Hebrews often fought as mercenaries or supported their household by raiding. The Hebrews who founded the villages in the hills west of the Jordan River valley and north of Jerusalem at the beginning of the Iron Age (1200–1100 B.C.E.) were refugees from cities along the coast, not nomads from the desert. What these villagers had in common was that they were social survivors who fled the famine, plague, and war which brought the Bronze Age to an end. They were not warriors; they were farmers and herders. They left centralized, surplus states and created a decentralized, subsistence village federation called Israel. Politically these villagers were Israelites; culturally they were Hebrews.

Hieroglyphics. A writing system developed for a single language: Egyptian. There are as many as two thousand hieroglyphic characters. Each hieroglyph or stylized picture of a common object—a duck, a house, water, for example—represented the sound of the object or an idea associated with the object.

Horizontal excavations. Horizontal excavations remove one layer at a time across the entire surface of the site. Layers of occupation are peeled off an excavation site. While horizontal excavations give maximum exposure to a site, they destroy the chronology of the site's development.

Kiln. A brick-lined oven used to bake or fire pottery.

Krater. A wide-mouthed, two-handled bowl used for mixing wine and water. In the world of the Bible, wine was not stored ready to drink, but in a concentrated form. Hosts mixed the concentrated wine with an appropriate amount of water in a krater to make it drinkable.

Levigation. Soaking or slaking clay in water before mixing in order to remove contaminants.

Liminal women. Women in the world of the Bible who do not have a defining male to give them status. They are women temporarily without a household. Women of a household enjoy the status of daughter, wife, or widow. The defining male for a daughter is a father;

the defining male for a wife is a husband; the defining male for a widow is her son. Liminal women without status are the orphan without a father, the prostitute without a husband, and the widow without a son. Female characters such as Noami, Ruth (Ruth 1:1—4:22), or Tamar (Gen 38:1-30), portrayed in the Bible as liminal women, often exploit their lack of status for the good of others.

Martyrion. A shrine, usually octagonal, erected to contain the remains of a martyr, someone who "gives witness." The octagonal architectural style was used for other sacred sites as well: for example, the Dome of the Rock on the Haram esh Sharif ("Noble Sanctuary") in Jerusalem was erected to mark the site where Muhammad ascended from earth into heaven. It was intentionally built to rival Christian sites in Jerusalem like the Church of the Holy Sepulchre.

Maximalist/minimalist. Maximalist scholars—such as William G. Dever—regard the traditions in the Bible today as having developed over an extended period of time from at least 1200 B.C.E. as a reflection on the significance of the political experiences of the Hebrew peoples from the states of Israel and Judah during more than one-thousand years. Minimalist scholars—such as Niels P. Lemche—regard the traditions in the Bible today as having been created during a very short period of time after 300 B.C.E. in order to establish a cultural identity for Jews who were struggling to avoid assimilation into Greco-Roman culture. The traditions are not a reflection on political experiences but created models for the core values of Jewish identity.

Megaron. A Mycenaean or Greek style of architecture imported to the world of the Bible by the Philistines. The megaron is the main hall or central room of a palace with a pillared porch built around a central hearth.

Natufian culture. The Natufian (10,300–8500 B.C.E.) and Neolithic (8000–3800 B.C.E.) periods in the world of the Bible were characterized by discovery and creativity. Slowly developing, but long lasting, ways to farm, to herd, to build houses, to make tools, to make pottery and to bury the dead appear for the first time in the settlements of these remarkable cultures. The practical inventions of Natufian and Neolithic peoples not only produced radical changes in their daily life; they also inspired dramatic changes in the way that they understood life.

Orientalism. First, orientalism or Assyriology refers to the academic discipline that studies the Near Eastern cultures of Mesopotamia and its neighbors. William Foxwell Albright, for example, considered himself to be an orientalist, a student of Near Eastern cultures. Second, "orientalism" refers to a racial prejudice that developed after 1900 against cultures in the Middle East. This orientalism considers western European cultures to be intellectual, dynamic, and inclusive. In contrast, it considers cultures of the Middle East to be impulsive, stagnant, and intolerant. As a prejudice, orientalism influences not only public opinion but also scholarship and art.

Ostracon (*plural* **ostraca**). A broken piece of pottery used as a writing surface.

Pilgrimage. An ancient ritual for refreshing the connection between a household and the sacred center (Greek: *omphalos*) in its land. When the life of any household in the culture is at risk, pilgrims make their way to the sacred center to restore the flow of life from there to their households.

Post-processual archaeology. An umbrella term applied to a range of archaeological theories. What these schools have in common is their objection to the assumption of processual archaeology that cultural changes are always adaptations to changes in the human or natural environment.

Potsherd/sherd. A broken piece of pottery.

Probe trench. A trench, generally three feet wide and opened to test a site for a full square.

Processual archaeology. Method that examines human processes and systems that develop in response to the changes in the human or natural environment at a site. It applies the scientific method to archaeological data.

Rosetta Stone. While they were repairing the fortifications at Fort Julien near the Egyptian port city of Rosetta (Arabic: Rashid), French military engineers under the command of Captain Pierre-François Bouchard discovered the stone on July 15, 1799. It is dark grey and pink grano diorite. It weighs 1,600 pounds and is forty-five inches high, twenty-eight inches wide and ten inches thick. The Rosetta Stone was originally erected to call on Egyptians to worship their thirteen-year-old pharaoh, Ptolemy V Epiphanes (204–181 B.C.E.) on the first anniversary of his coronation in 196 B.C.E.

Sarcophagus. A coffin carved from stone.

Sea Peoples. The term first appears in the Annals of Merneptah (1224–1214 B.C.E.). The Egyptians and the Hittites identified at least nine groups of Sea Peoples: the Karkisa, Labu, Lukka, Meshwesh, Shardana, Shekelesh, Tjakkar, and Peleset or Philistines. The Sea Peoples had been uprooted from their homelands by the collapse of the great empires of Egypt, Hatti (Turkey), and Mycenae (Greece). They migrated from Mycenae, Troy (in Turkey), and Crete through Cyprus and then on to Syria-Palestine and Egypt. After a fierce battle on Egypt's Mediterranean coast, Ramesses III (1194–1163 B.C.E.) ceded control of much of the southern coast of Syria-Palestine, including Tel Miqne, to the Sea Peoples.

Shaman (Tungus: *šaman*). Shaman cultures first appear in South Asia and then migrate east through Siberia and into the Americas. Shaman cultures assume that there are both a divine plane populated by invisible spirits and a human plane populated by visible humans. Shamans are men and women who channel back and forth between these planes. They use drumming, dancing, chanting, and drugs to induce a state of ecstasy or trance in order to make the voyage. On their inaugural voyages unique spirits or totems appear to them as animals and serve as their guides. These guides teach shamans how to synchronize the human and divine planes so that life may thrive. For example, shaman cultures consider sickness to be the result of a collision between spirits and humans, which traps spirits inside humans. Guides teach shamans a variety of healing techniques for drawing out or freeing trapped spirits.

Slip. A thin finish coat of clay without additives applied to pottery.

Slow wheel. The potter's wheel developed gradually. Neolithic potters graduated from coiling their pots on a mat to using a shallow bowl to build a coiled pot. The slow wheel was a simple turntable. Potters attached a wooden platform where potters shaped the clay to a stone bearing that fit into a stone socket. These wheels did not turn easily and were used only for easier coiling. The speed of the slow wheel could be increased if one potter turned the table while another potter shaped the clay.

Sondage method. Sondage excavations cut a single trench across the entire site from the surface down to bedrock. Prior to the work of Petrie, Wheeler, and Kenyon some archaeologists used the sondage method. Petrie realized that these vertical trenches prevented archaeologists from accurately drawing top plans of the strata cut by the trenches.

Steatopygous. In the world of the Bible, Godmothers are often portrayed as steatopygous or full-hipped. Their breasts are pendulous; their abdomens are distended; their hips and legs are heavy. The characterization emphasizes that they are the mothers of all humans.

Subsistence culture. Subsistence cultures produce only enough goods and services to survive. There is no surplus left to trade for luxuries.

Surplus culture. Surplus cultures produce more goods and services than they need to survive. This excess or surplus is used to trade for luxuries—goods and services that are not needed for survival, but enrich the quality of life.

Glossary

Synchronic. A term identifying schools of interpretation that give a snapshot of a particular system at a particular moment in time. Synchronic methods focus on how something is at a given moment and how each part fits into the system.

Tabun oven. The tabun oven was made from terra cotta, was shaped like a haystack and had a chimney hole in the top. Loaves of bread dough were placed on pebbles scattered inside the oven. The opening at the base of the oven and the chimney were sealed. The oven was heated from the outside by stacking wood, charcoal, or manure chips against the oven.

Tannur oven. The tannur oven was made from terra cotta, was shaped like a haystack, and had a chimney hole at the top. The fire was kindled inside the tannur. Dough was slapped against the walls of the oven to bake, just as the people of South Asia do today to bake Naan bread.

Tell (Hebrew: *tel;* Arabic: *tell, tall*). An artificial hill or mound formed by the eroded debris from an ancient settlement.

Temper. To temper clay, potters add straw, dung, sand, salt, or beer to harden the clay and keep it from cracking and shrinking.

Terra sigillata. Bright red, polished pottery impressed with designs (Latin: *sigillata*) used throughout the Roman Empire from 100 B.C.E. until 300 C.E. The body of the ware was cast in a mold. Relief designs taken from a wide repertory of patterns were then applied to the ware. The style changes in these patterns and the potters' marks stamped on the vessels make terra sigillata pieces an important tool for dating other artifacts found with them. The quality of the pottery was high, considering that it was mass-produced.

Terraces. Terraces (Hebrew: *měrômê śādeh*, Judg 5:18; *śědê těrûmōt*, 2 Sam 1:21) in ancient Israel were benches built on the slopes of hills. Walls were constructed parallel to the contours of the slopes. Infill or slope wash created deep, fertile soil beds behind the walls, and villagers used these for farming.

Theodicy. An attempt to reconcile the idea of a good deity with the reality of evil in the world. Both the book of Job and the book of Jonah are theodicies. The book of Job asks, Why do good people suffer? The book of Jonah asks, Why do bad people go unpunished?

Theodolite. A surveying instrument used by archaeologists to create a grid for a tell. The theodolite has a telescope and a level mounted on a tripod.

Totem animal. In shaman cultures a totem animal is a godparent who teaches its people a signature skill needed to survive. For example, the raven is clever. In nature ravens are attracted by anything shiny, and can cleverly steal coins or jewels from humans. The raven became the totem of the Tlingit people in the Pacific Northwest, who tell the story about how the raven stole a shiny piece of the sun and gave it to them so that they could have fire. The Tlingit considered themselves clever because the raven taught them how to kindle a fire.

Tumulus. A convex dome of soil over a grave.

Ware. Pots made from clay combined with mineral and fossil additives.

Wash. A thin, almost transparent, coat of paint applied to pottery.

Wheeler-Kenyon method. The Wheeler-Kenyon method vertically excavates squares. A square is fifteen feet on each side and dug from the surface to bedrock. A balk is a three-foot-wide wall left between squares to provide a record of the strata excavated.

Bibliography

Aarons, L.

1982   "The Dayan Saga: The Man and His Collection." *Biblical Archaeology Review* 8:26–30, 36.

> Dayan's "collection transcended avarice or possessiveness. It was his poetry, his romance with history."

Abu El-Haj, Nadia

2001   *Facts on the Ground: Archaeological Practice and Territorial Self-fashioning in Israeli Society.* Chicago: University of Chicago Press.

> Abu El-Haj demonstrates the role that archaeology has played in Israeli society, examining how it emerged as a pervasive force that has shaped the region's social and political imaginations and has inspired violently contested territorial and national-cultural struggles. Based on archival research and ethnographic work among archaeologists, her work is the first critical account of Israeli archaeological practice. It traces the dynamic relationships among science, colonization, nation-state building, and territorial expansion.

Abusch, Tzvi

2001   "The Development and Meaning of the Epic of Gilgamesh: An Interpretive Essay." *Journal of the American Oriental Society* 121:614–22.

2002   *Mesopotamian Witchcraft: Toward a History and Understanding of Babylonian Witchcraft Beliefs and Literature.* Ancient Magic and Divination 5. Leiden: Brill/Styx.

Ackerman, Susan

1998   *Warrior, Dancer, Seductress, Queen: Women in Judges and Biblical Israel.* Anchor Bible Reference Library. Garden City, N.Y.: Doubleday.

2003   "Digging Up Deborah: Recent Hebrew Bible Scholarship on Gender and the Contribution of Archaeology." *Near Eastern Archaeology* 66:173–84.

2008   "Rocks of Unevangelized Lands." *Biblical Archaeology Review* 34:28, 74.

Aharoni, Yohanan

1968   "Arad: Its Inscriptions and Temple." *Biblical Archaeologist* 31:2–32.

1974   "The Horned Altar of Beer-sheba." *Biblical Archaeologist* 37:2–6.

1979   *The Land of the Bible: A Historical Geography.* 3rd ed. Translated by Anson F. Rainey. Philadelphia: Westminster.

1982   *The Archaeology of the Land of Israel: From the Prehistoric Beginnings to the End of the First Temple Period.* Edited by Miriam Aharoni. Translated by Anson F. Rainey. Philadelphia: Westminster.

Aharoni, Yohanan, and Michael Avi-Yonah

1993   *The Macmillan Bible Atlas.* Edited by Anson F. Rainey and Ze'ev Safrai. Completely rev. 3rd ed. Designed and prepared by Carta, Jerusalem. New York: Macmillan.

Aharoni, Yohanan, and Joseph Naveh

1981   *Arad Inscriptions.* Translated by Judith Ben-Or. Judean Desert Studies. Jerusalem: Israel Exploration Society.

295

Bibliography

Ahlström, Gösta W.
1986   *Who Were the Israelites?* Winona Lake, Ind.: Eisenbrauns.

1991   "The Origin of Israel in Palestine." *Scandinavian Journal of Theology* 2:19–34.

1993   *The History of Ancient Palestine from the Palaeolithic Period to Alexander's Conquest.* Edited by Diana Edelman. Journal for the Study of the Old Testament Supplement Series 146. Sheffield: JSOT Press.

Ahlström, Gösta W., and Diana Edelman
1985   "Merneptah's Israel." *Journal of Near Eastern Studies* 44:59–61.

Albertz, Rainer
1994   *A History of Israelite Religion in the Old Testament Period.* Volume 1, *From the Beginnings to the End of the Monarchy.* Volume 2, *From the Exile to the Maccabees.* Translated by John Bowden. Old Testament Library. Louisville, Ky.: Westminster John Knox.

Albright, William Foxwell
1940   *From the Stone Age to Christianity: Monotheism and the Historical Process.* Baltimore: Johns Hopkins University Press.

1941   *Archaeology and the Religion of Israel.* Baltimore: Johns Hopkins University Press.

1942   "The Gezer Calendar." *Bulletin of the American Schools of Oriental Research* 92:16–26.

1949   *The Archaeology of Palestine.* Baltimore: Penguin.

1963   *The Biblical Period from Abraham to Ezra.* New York: Harper & Row.

1966a   *Archaeology, Historical Analogy & Early Biblical Tradition.* Rockwell Lectures. Baton Rouge: Louisiana State University Press.

1966b   "The Historical Interpretation of Early Hebrew Literature." In idem, *Archaeology, Historical Analogy & Early Biblical Tradition*, 3–21. Rockwell Lectures. Baton Rouge: Louisiana State University Press.

1966c   "The Story of Abraham in the Light of New Archaeological Data." In idem, *Archaeology, Historical Analogy & Early Biblical Tradition*, 22–41. Rockwell Lectures. Baton Rouge: Louisiana State University Press.

1968   *Yahweh and the Gods of Canaan: A Historical Analysis of Two Contrasting Faiths.* Jordan Lectures in Comparative Religion 7. Garden City, N.Y.: Doubleday.

    Albright's classic definition of biblical archaeology is the study of "all biblical lands from India to Spain and from southern Russia to south Arabia, and the whole history of those lands from about 10,000 B.C., or even earlier, to the present time" (Albright 1966, 13).

1969   "The Impact of Archaeology on Biblical Research—1966." In *New Directions in Biblical Archaeology,* edited by David Noel Freedman and Jonas C. Greenfield, 1–14. Garden City, N.Y.: Doubleday.

    Despite Albright's observation that "writing without artifacts is like flesh without a skeleton, and artifacts without writing are a skeleton without flesh," he considered the primary impact of archaeology on the understanding of the Bible prior to 1966 to be the understanding of Northwest Semitic languages and the traditions of Egypt and Mesopotamia.

Alexander, Brian
1990   "Archaeology and Looting Make a Volatile Mix." *Science* New Series 250:1074–75.

Ali, Ahmed
1993   *Al-Qur'an: A Contemporary Translation.* Princeton, N.J.: Princeton University Press.

    Ali (1910–1994), a distinguished Pakistani novelist, poet, critic, and diplomat, began this translation project in 1988. His English translation faithfully reflects the Arabic poetry of the Qur'an and accurately renders the most important Islamic concepts.

Allen, Susan Heuck
1994 "Trojan Grey Ware at Tel Miqne-Ekron." *Bulletin of the American Schools of Oriental Research* 293:39–51.

Allen, Mitch
2007 "Think Small!" *Near Eastern Archaeology* 70:196–97.

Allen discusses copyright and fair use, the need to provide incentives for archaeologists to share their data, and the best methods for achieving uniformity in data archiving.

Allison, Penelope Mary, ed.
1999 *The Archaeology of Household Activities.* London/New York: Routledge.

Alred, Cyril
1987 *The Egyptians.* Rev. and enl. ed. London: Thames & Hudson.

Amiran, Ruth
1970 *Ancient Pottery of the Holy Land from Its Beginnings in the Neolithic Period to the End of the Iron Age.* New Brunswick, N.J.: Rutgers University Press.

Synthesizing the pioneering work of Petrie, Albright, and Wright, Amiran has written a detailed study of pottery chronology from prehistoric times through the Iron Age that is still the gold standard for dating pottery in Syria-Palestine.

Anati, Emmanuel
1987 *I siti a plaza di Har Karkom.* Capo di Ponte: Edizioni del Centro.

1993 *Har Karkom: In the Light of New Discoveries.* Capo di Ponte: Edizioni del Centro.

Andrews, Carol
1981 *The Rosetta Stone.* London: British Museum.

Andrews tells the story of the Rosetta Stone from its discovery and arrival in the British Museum to its eventual translation, which is included.

Angel, J. L.
1972 "Ecology and Population in the Eastern Mediterranean." *World Archaeology* 4:88–105.

Arav, Rami, ed.
2008 *Cities through the Looking Glass: Essays on the History and Archaeology of Biblical Urbanism.* Winona Lake, Ind.: Eisenbrauns.

Arav edits an anthology of articles on cities like Dan, Hazor, Kinneret, and Tzer in Iron Age Galilee.

Arnold, Philip P.
1991 "Eating Landscape: Human Sacrifice and Sustenance in Aztec Mexico." In *To Change Place: Aztec Ceremonial Landscapes,* edited by David Carrasco, 219–32. Niwot: University of Colorado Press.

Arnold translated "Atl Caualo," a ritual for ending drought, from Nahuatl as the basis for his study. See Bernardino de Sahagun, *Florentine Codex: General History of the Things of New Spain.* Translated and edited by A. J. O. Anderson and C. Dibble, book 2, chap. 20:42–46. 13 books. Santa Fe: School of American Research and the University of Utah.

Ascalone, Enrico
2007 *Mesopotamia: Assyrians, Sumerians, Babylonians.* Translated by R. Giammanco Frongia. Berkeley: University of California Press.

Brief overview of Mesopotamian civilization.

Asher-Greve, Julia M.
2004 "Gertrude L Bell, 1868–1926." In *Breaking Ground: Pioneering Women Archaeologists,* edited by Getzel M. Cohen and Martha Sharp Joukowsky, 142–97. Ann Arbor: University of Michigan Press.

With the publication of *The Thousand and One Churches* (1909) and a chapter in *Amida* (1910), Bell gained considerable recognition as an archaeologist. No other women worked in field archaeology before World War I in such remote areas and under such hazardous conditions. Bell conducted all her excavations alone, accompanied only by her cook, Fatuh, and other servants. Male archaeologists

Bibliography

worked with teams of specialists. In spite of her experience, Bell was never invited to participate in an excavation. Excavation teams in the Near East were all male and were not prepared to accept women.

Atkinson, Kenneth
2008   Review of Katharina Galor, Jean-Baptiste Humber, and Jurgen Zangenberg, eds., *Qumran, The Site of the Dead Sea Scrolls: Archaeological Interpretations and Debates. Proceedings of a Conference Held at Brown University, November 17–19, 2002.* Leiden: Brill, 2006. *Review of Biblical Literature* http://www.bookreviews.org

Atkinson provides an update of relevant publications and their relationship to the interpretation of Qumran.

Averbeck, Richard E., Mark W. Chavalas, and David B. Weisberg
2003   *Life and Culture in the Ancient Near East.* Bethesda, Md.: CDL.

Avigad, Nahman.
1976   *Bullae and Seals from a Post-Exilic Archive.* Qedem 4. Jerusalem: Hebrew University.

Avi-Yonah, Michael
2002   *The Holy Land: A Historical Geography from the Persian to the Arab Conquest, 536 B.C.–A.D. 640.* Jerusalem: Carta.

Avni, Gideon
2007   "From Standing Stones to Open Mosques in the Negev Desert: The Archaeology of Religious Transformation on the Fringes." *Near Eastern Archaeology* 70:124–38.

Badone, Ellen, and Sharon R. Roseman
2004   *Intersecting Journeys: The Anthropology of Pilgrimage and Tourism.* Chicago: University of Illinois Press.

Bailly, Antoine, Robert Ferras, and Denise Pumain, eds.
1995   *Encyclopedie de Geographie.* Paris: Economica.

Baines, John, and Jaromir Malek
1980   *Atlas of Ancient Egypt.* New York: Facts on File.

Bakir, A. M.
1978   *Notes on Middle Egyptian Grammar.* Oxford: Aris & Phillips.

Bal, Mieke
1988   *Death and Dissymmetry: The Politics of Coherence in the Book of Judges.* Chicago Studies in the History of Judaism. Chicago: University of Chicago Press.

Balter, Michael
2005   *The Goddess and the Bull: Catalhoyuk, An Archaeological Journey to the Dawn of Civilization.* New York: Free Press.

Barth, F., ed.
1969   *Ethnic Groups and Boundaries.* Boston: Little, Brown.

Bar-Yosef, Ofer
1998   "The Natufian Culture in the Levant: Threshold to the Origins of Agriculture." *Evolutionary Anthropology* 6:159–77.

Bar-Yosef describes the archaeological evidence for the origins of agriculture in the ancient Near East. He addresses the question of why the emergence of farming communities was an inevitable outcome of a series of social and economic circumstances that caused the Natufian culture to be considered the threshold for this major evolutionary change. Currently, archaeology points to two other centers of early cultivation that led to the emergence of complex civilizations, central Mexico and the middle Yangtze River in China. The best-recorded sequence from foraging to farming, however, is found in the world of the Bible. The record warns against viewing all three evolutionary sequences as identical in terms of primary conditions, economic and social motivations and activities, and the resulting cultural, social, and ideological changes.

Bar-Yosef, Ofer, and F. R. Valla, eds.
1991   *The Natufian Culture in the Levant.* Ann Arbor: International Monographs in Prehistory.

Basola, Moses
1999   *In Zion and Jerusalem: The Itinerary of Rabbi Moses Basola (1521–1523).* Edited with notes and an introduction by Abraham David. Translated by Dena Ordan. Jerusalem: Bar-Ilan University Press.

The Ottoman sultan Salem I (ruled 1516–1520) defeated the Persians (Iran) and then invaded Greater Syria. Salem destroyed Mamluk resistance in 1516 at Marj Dabaq, north of Aleppo, taking control of present-day Lebanon, Syria, Jordan, and Israel. In the wake of the Ottoman conquest, Jews began to visit the world of the Bible. Moses Basola, an Italian, made a pilgrimage from 1521 to 1523. His journal describes details of his sea and land journey and of his visits to sites connected with the Bible and Jewish life, especially in Safed and Jerusalem.

Bass, George F.
1966   *Archaeology Under Water.* New York: Frederick A. Praeger.

Bass summarizes the history and techniques of underwater archaeology.

1967,   "Cape Gelidonya: A Bronze Age
ed.   Shipwreck." *Transactions of the American Philosophical Society* 57, 8:1–177.

Bass publishes the full excavation report for Cape Gelidonya west of the Bay of Antalya (Turkey). About 1200 B.C.E. a ship smashed its hull on a rock near the surface northeast of the largest of the islands. The personal possessions of the crew and its stone anchor link the ship to Late Bronze Age Syria-Palestine or Cyprus. Furthermore, Egyptian art associated with the ship's cargo of four-handled copper ingots and tin ingots points to merchants from Syria-Palestine. Therefore, Homer's "Phoenicians" or merchants from Syria-Palestine in the *Iliad* are not an anachronism.

1970   *Archaeology Under Water.* 2nd ed. Harmondsworth: Penguin.

1973   "Cape Gelidonya and Bronze Age Maritime Trade." In *Orient and Occident: Essays Presented to Cyrus H. Gordon on the Occasion of His Sixty-fifth Birthday,* edited by Harry A. Hoffner, 29–38. Neukirchen-Vluyn: Neukirchener Verlag; Kevelaer: Butzon & Bercker.

Bass refines the original excavation report.

1975   *Archaeology Beneath the Sea.* New York: Walker.

Bass writes a popular account of the excavation.

1988   "Return to Cape Gelidonya." *Institute of Nautical Archaeology Newsletter* 15, 2 (June):2–5.

Bass interprets the wreck at Gelidonya in light of discoveries made at the wreck at Uluburun.

1991   "Evidence of Trade from Bronze Age Shipwrecks." In *Bronze Age Trade in the Mediterranean: Papers Presented at the Conference Held at Rawley House, Oxford, in December 1989,* edited by N. H. Gale, 69–82. Studies in Mediterranean Archaeology 90. Jonsered: Paul Åströms Forlag.

1995   "Sea and River Craft in the Ancient Near East." In *Civilizations of the Ancient Near East,* edited by Jack M. Sasson, 3:1421–31. New York: Charles Scribner's Sons.

1996   "Cape Gelidonya." In *Shipwrecks in the Bodrum Museum of Underwater Archaeology,* edited by George F. Bass, 25–35. Bodrum: Bodrum Museum of Underwater Archaeology.

1997   "Cape Gelidonya." In *Oxford Encyclopedia of Archaeology in the Near East,* edited by Eric M. Meyers, 1:414–16. New York: Oxford University Press.

Batchelor, J.
1892   "Specimens of Ainu Folklore." *Transactions of the Asiatic Society of Japan* 20:216–27.

Bibliography

Batto, Bernard F.

1992   *Slaying the Dragon: Mythmaking in the Biblical Tradition*. Louisville: Westminster John Knox.

Batto argues that the "Sea of Reeds" is—as the Septuagint translates it—the Red Sea, a geographical metaphor for the "Sea at the End of the Earth" or Chaos. At the Red Sea, Yahweh, the Creator, confronts Chaos to bring the new world of Israel to birth.

Beitzel, Barry, ed.

2006   *Biblica: The Bible Atlas. A Social and Historical Journey through the Lands of the Bible*. Lane Cove, New South Wales: Global.

Biblica is an atlas written for general readers rather than for students, which brings the world of the Bible to life and enables readers to visualize and appreciate the incidents and narratives in the Bible.

Bell, Gertrude

1909   *A Thousand and One Churches*. London: Hodder & Stoughton.

2001/ *The Desert and the Sown: The Syrian*
1907   *Adventures of the Female Lawrence of Arabia*. New York: Cooper Square.

2005/ *Persian Pictures*. New York: Anthem.
1894

Gertrude Bell Archive

http://www.gerty.ncl.ac.uk/

The Gertrude Bell papers consist of about 1,600 detailed and lively letters to her parents, her sixteen diaries, which she kept while she was traveling, and some forty packets of miscellaneous items. There are also about 7,000 photographs, taken by her from 1900-1918. Those of Middle Eastern archaeological sites are of great value because they record structures which have since been eroded or, in some cases, have disappeared altogether, while those of the desert tribes are of considerable anthropological and ethnographical interest.

Belzoni, Giovanni Battista

1820   *Narrative of the Operations and Recent Discoveries Within the Pyramids, Temples, Tombs and Excavations in Egypt and Nubia*. London: John Murray.

Ben-Ezer, Ehud

1997   *Courage: The Story of Moshe Dayan*. Tel Aviv: Ministry of Defence.

Ben-Ezer describes Dayan as a shrewd and intuitive explorer of ancient sites who collected antiquities that were ignored or abandoned by archaeologists or state agencies—antiquities that would otherwise have been destroyed.

Benjamin, Don C.

1983   "Legal Instruction concerning Charges of Premarital Promiscuity against a Daughter from an Urban Family." In idem, *Deuteronomy and City Life: A Form Criticism of Texts with the Word City ('ir) in Deuteronomy 4:41—26:19*, 222-36, 300-301. Lanham, Md.: University Press of America.

The city played an important role in Israel's understanding of itself and of its divine patron. The urban traditions in Deuteronomy are key to Israel's theology of the city. They were developed by Israelites who encountered Yahweh in the city and fulfilled their obligations to Yahweh through urban institutions such as the gate court. Here Yahweh freed the oppressed—defendants charged with unwitnessed murders, victims in unsolved crimes, parents of incorrigible children, wives accused of promiscuity, women victims of sexual assault, and widows without heirs.

2004   *The Old Testament Story, An Introduction*. Minneapolis: Fortress.

Bentley, R. Alexander, and Herbert D. G. Maschner

2008   "Introduction: On Archaeological Theories." In *Handbook of Archaeological Theories*, edited by R. Alexander Bentley, Herbert D. G. Maschner and Christopher Chippindale, 1-10. Lanham, Md.: Rowman & Littlefield.

Bentley, R. Alexander, Herbert D. G. Maschner, and Christopher Chippindale, eds.

2008   *Handbook of Archaeological Theories*. Lanham, Md.: Rowman & Littlefield.

Bentley, Maschner, and Chippindale gather original, authoritative articles on the theories of archaeology. These archaeologists provide a comprehensive picture of the theoretical foundations by which archaeologists contextualize and analyze artifacts. This anthology demonstrates the immense power that theory has for building interpretations of the past, while recognizing the wonderful archaeological traditions that created it. An extensive bibliography is included.

Ben-Tor, Amnon, ed.

1992   *The Archaeology of Ancient Israel.* Translated by R. Greenberg. New Haven: Yale University Press.

Amnon Ben-Tor uses the archaeological calendar as an overall outline for the book, which covers the Neolithic period to Iron Age III. Some chapters also follow the archaeological calendar, for example, Gabriel Barkay subdivides "The Iron Age II-III" into chronological periods: "The Iron Age IIa—the Tenth–Ninth centuries B.C.E.," "The Iron Age IIb—the Eighth Century B.C.E.," "The Iron Age IIIa—the Seventh Century B.C.E.," "Archaeology of Jerusalem in the Iron Age II–III," and "The Iron Age IIIb—the Sixth Century B.C.E." Other chapters, however, are outlined thematically. For example, Amihai Mazar subdivides "The Iron Age I" into themes: "The Decline of Egyptian Domination in Canaan," "The Settlement of the Philistines and Other Sea Peoples in Canaan," "Material Culture of the Israelite Tribes during the Period of the Judges," "Canaanite Culture and the Rise of Phoenician Culture," "Transjordan," "The Development of Metallurgy," "Art," "Writing and Literacy," "Trade Relations," and "Transition to the Monarchy."

Ben-Tor, Amnon, and M. T. Rubiato

1999   "Excavating Hazor—Did the Israelites Destroy the Canaanite City? *Biblical Archaeology Review* 25:22–39.

Ben Yehuda, Eliezer

1948   *A Complete Dictionary of Ancient and Modern Hebrew.* Tel Aviv: La'am.

Bertman, Stephen

2005   *Handbook to Life in Ancient Mesopotamia.* New York: Oxford University Press.

Betrò, Maria Carmela

1996   *Hieroglyphics: The Writings of Ancient Egypt.* New York: Abbeville.

Betz, Hans Dieter, Don S. Browning, Vernd Janowski, and Eberhard Jungel, eds.

2007   *Religion Past and Present: Encyclopedia of Theology and Religion.* Leiden: Brill.

Religion in Geschichte und Gegenwart is the most comprehensive and authoritative existing guide to the study of religion. The *RGG* has been the gold standard of European encyclopedias of religion and the standard of excellence in reference works in religion for almost a century.

Religion Past and Present is an extension within this tradition of German excellence. Entries on Archaeology and the Bible are edited by Hermann Michael Niemann and Guntram Koch.

Bierling, Neal

2002   *Philistines: Giving Goliath His Due.* Marco Polo Monographs 7. Warren Center, Pa.: Shangri-La.

Bierling uses archaeology, the Bible and written artifacts from Egypt, Syria-Palestine, and Mesopotamia to reconstruct Philistine culture.

Binford, Lewis R.

1962   "Archaeology as Anthropology." *American Antiquity* 28:217–25.

Binford defines the goals of processual archaeology.

2001   *Constructing Frames of Reference: An Analytical Method for Archaeological Theory Building Using Hunter-Gatherer and Environmental Data Sets.* Berkeley: University of California Press.

Binford's masterpiece on hunting and gathering cultures with charts, graphs. He develops eleven "problems," 86 "propositions," and 126 "generalizations."

Binford, Sally R., and Lewis R. Binford, eds.

1968   *New Perspectives in Archaeology.* Chicago: Aldine.

Bibliography

New or processual archaeologists explain that archaeological data has great potential for learning about past social and economic systems. Outlines the general principles of processual archaeology.

Bintliff, John
1991   "The Contribution of an *Annaliste*/Structural History Approach to Archaeology." In *The Annales School and Archaeology,*edited by John Bintliff, 1–33. London: Leicester University.

Bird, Phyllis
1974   "Images of Women in the Old Testament." In *Religion and Sexism: Images of Women in the Jewish and Christian Traditions,* edited by Rosemary Radford Ruether, 41–88. New York: Simon & Schuster.

Bird describes her hermeneutics for gendered archaeology.

Blaiklock, E. M., and R. K. Harrison, eds.
1983   *The New International Dictionary of Biblical Archaeology.* Grand Rapids: Zondervan.

Blenkinsopp, Joseph
2002   "The Bible, Archaeology and Politics or The Empty Land Revisited." *Journal for the Study of the Old Testament* 27:169–87.

Since its inception with Napoleon's invasion of Egypt in 1798, archaeology in the Middle East has always been involved in politics reflected, for example, in the mapping of Syria-Palestine and renaming settlements and physical features taken over from the local Arabs. The myth of the empty land is a common assumption in the politics of archaeology. Blenkinsopp examines publications on the archaeology of the Neo-Babylonian period in Syria-Palestine to demonstrate that the myth of the empty land still influences scholarship.

Bloch-Smith, Elizabeth
1992   *Judahite Burial Practices and Beliefs about the Dead.* Journal for the Study of the Old Testament Supplement Series 123. Sheffield: JSOT Press.

2002a   "Death in the Life of Ancient Israel." In *Sacred Time, Sacred Space: Archaeology and the Religion of Israel,* edited by Barry M. Gittlen, 139–43. Winona Lake, Ind.: Eisenbrauns.

2002b   "Life in Judah from the Perspective of the Dead." *Near Eastern Archaeology* 65:120–30.

2003a   "Bronze and Iron Age Burials and Funerary Customs in the Southern Levant" *Near Eastern Archaeology* 66:105–15.

2003b   "Israelite Ethnicity in Iron I: Archaeology Preserves What Is Remembered and What Is Forgotten in Israel's History." *Journal of Biblical Literature* 122:401–25.

Bloch-Smith, Elizabeth, and Beth Alpert Nakhai
1999   "A Landscape Comes to Life: The Iron Age I." *Near Eastern Archaeology* 62:62–92, 100–127.

Bogdanos, Matthew
2005   *Thieves of Baghdad: One Marine's Passion for Ancient Civilizations and the Journey to Recover the World's Greatest Stolen Treasures.* New York: Bloomsbury.

Bolen, Todd
        Survey of Western Palestine: The Maps. http://www.bibleplaces.com/surveywestern palestinemaps.htm

Bolen has produced an electronic edition of H. H. Kitchener and C. R. Conder's maps. The surveyors distinguished between vineyards, orchards, gardens, woods, scrubs, palms, and fir trees. Locations were designated for winepresses, milestones, tombs, wells, cisterns, and caves. The survey covered all of the territory west of the Jordan River between Tyre in the north and Beersheba in the south.

Boling, Robert G., and G. Ernest Wright
1982   *Joshua: A New Translation with Notes and Commentary.* Anchor Bible 6. Garden City, N.Y.: Doubleday.

Borghouts, J. F.

1994   "Magical Practices among the Villagers." In *Pharaoh's Workers: The Villagers of Deir el Medina,* edited by Leonard H. Lesko, 119–30, 182–85. Ithaca, N.Y.: Cornell University Press.

Borowski, Oded

1982   "Sherds, Sherds, Sherds." *Biblical Archaeology Review* 8:67–68.

Borowski briefly describes how to excavate, record, and interpret pottery.

1988   "Ceramic Dating." In *Benchmarks in Time and Culture: An Introduction to Palestinian Archaeology,* edited by Joel F. Drinkard, Jr., Gerald L. Mattingly, and J. Maxwell Miller, 223–33. Atlanta: Scholars Press.

2003   *Daily Life in Biblical Times.* Archaeology and Biblical Studies 5. Leiden/Boston: Brill.

Borowski uses archaeology and the Bible to describe Syria-Palestine, the peoples who lived there, their households, the economies of their cities and villages, farming, herding, trade, government, military, worship, art, music, and writing.

2006   "Ecological Principles in the Bible: Surviving in the Hill Country." In *"I Will Speak the Riddles of Ancient Times": Archaeological and Historical Studies in Honor of Amihai Mazar on the Occasion of His Sixtieth Birthday,* edited by Aren M. Maeir and Pierre de Miroschedji, 1:401–6. 2 vols. Winona Lake, Ind.: Eisenbrauns.

Bourdieu, Pierre

1984   *Distinction: A Social Critique of the Judgement of Taste.* Translated by R. Nice. Cambridge, Mass.: Harvard University Press.

Bow, Beverly

2003   "Sisterhood? Stories of Eligibility and Encounter in Ancient Israel." In *Life and Culture in the Ancient Near East,* edited by Richard E. Averbeck, Mark W. Chavalas, and

David B. Weisberg, 205–16. Bethesda, Md.: CDL.

Bradley, Richard

2000   *An Archaeology of Natural Places.* London: Routledge.

Braudel, Fernand

1980   "The Situation of History in 1950." In idem, *On History,* 6–22. Translated by Sarah Matthews. Chicago: University of Chicago Press.

1992   *The Mediterranean and the Mediterranean World in the Age of Philip II.* Translated by Siân Reynolds. San Francisco: HarperCollins.

Bremmer, Jan N., ed.

2007   *The Strange World of Human Sacrifice.* Studies in the History and Anthropology of Religion 1. Leuven: Peeters.

Bremmer edits studies on human sacrifice among the Aztecs and on the literary motif of human sacrifice in medieval Irish literature. Three cases of human sacrifice in Greece are analyzed: a ritual example, a mythical case, and one in which myth and ritual are interrelated. Early Christians were accused of practicing human sacrifice, and Christians themselves accused Christian heretics of practicing human sacrifice, just as the Hebrews of ancient Israel accused their neighbors of practicing human sacrifice. At the beginning of the Old Kingdom, the Egyptians buried the pharaoh's slaves to serve the pharaoh in the afterlife. In India, the Godmother Kali was worshiped with human sacrifice. In Japan, human sacrifice took the form of self-sacrifice, and there may well be a line from these early sacrifices to the ritual of the "kamikaze."

Brewer, Douglas J., and Emily Teeter

2007   *Egypt and the Egyptians.* 2nd ed. New York: Cambridge University Press.

Brichto, Herbert C.

1973   "Kin, Cult, Land and Afterlife—A Biblical Complex." *Hebrew Union College Annual* 44:27–33.

Bibliography

Members of a household were expected to honor the father and mother of the household by seeing that they were properly buried in the tomb of the household and by celebrating thanksgiving meals at which the dead were remembered.

Bright, John

1953   *The Kingdon of God: The Biblical Concept and Its Meaning for the Church*. Nashville: Abingdon-Cokesbury.

1976   *Covenant and Promise: The Prophetic Understanding of the Future in Pre-exilic Israel*. Philadelphia: Westminster.

2000   *A History of Israel*. Philadelphia: Westminster.

Brody, Aaron J.

2008   "The Specialized Religions of Ancient Mediterranean Seafarers." *Religion Compass* 2:444–54.

Ancient seafarers faced dangers and fears posed by the sea and sailing. Specialized religious beliefs and practices developed accordingly. Sailors honored deities whose attributes could benefit or devastate a voyage. Divine patrons were worshiped in harbors and at promontory shrines. Ships were considered imbued with a protective spirit and contained sacred spaces. Mariners performed religious ceremonies on land and at sea to protect their voyages. Specialized features are found in funerary practices and mortuary rituals of seafarers. Maritime religions were subsets of ancient religions, generated by unique uncertainties and perils at sea.

Bronner, Leila Leah

1993   "Valorized or Vilified? The Women of Judges in Midrashic Sources." In *Feminist Companion to Judges,* edited by Athalya Brenner, 91. Sheffield: Sheffield University.

Broshi, Magen

1986   "Religion, Ideology and Politics and Their Impact on Palestinian Archaeology." *Israel Museum Journal* 6:17–32.

Broshi, Magen, and Hanan Eshel

2000   "Daily Life at Qumran." *Near Eastern Archaeology* 63:136–37.

During their 1996–1997 excavations, Broshi and Eshel concluded that Qumran housed an ascetic community of some 150 to 200 people who lived in caves, huts, or tents around Qumran.

2003a   "Excavations at Qumran, Summer of 2001." *Israel Exploration Journal* 53:61–73.

2003b   "Whose Bones? New Qumran Excavation, New Debates." *Biblical Archaeology Review* 29:26–33, 71.

2004   "Three Seasons of Excavations at Qumran." *Journal of Roman Archaeology* 17:321–32

In 2001–2002, Eshel (Bar-Ilan University) and Broshi (Israel Museum) led excavations focused on finding where the members of the Qumran community lived. They concluded that there were heavily traveled paths between Qumran and the surrounding caves. They found three artificial caves used as dwellings and a circle of stones used as a tent site. The trails between these caves and Qumran were littered with first-century C.E. coins and sandal nails.

Brown, William P.

2000a   "Introduction to John Bright's *A History of Israel*." In John Bright, *A History of Israel,* 1–22. Louisville: Westminster John Knox.

2000b   "Appendix: An Update in the Search of Israel's History." In John Bright, *A History of Israel,* 465–85. Louisville: Westminster John Knox.

Bryant, Victor

2001   "The Origins of the Potter's Wheel." http://www.ceramicstoday.com/articles/potters_wheel2.htm.

Bryce, Trevor

2004   *Life and Society in the Hittite World*. New York: Oxford University Press.

Buckley, Thomas, and Alma Gottlieb, eds.

1988 *Blood Magic: The Anthropology of Menstruation.* Berkeley: University of California Press.

Budge, E. A. Wallis

1978/ *Egyptian Language: Easy Lessons in Egyptian*
1889 *Hieroglyphics with Sign List.* London: Routledge.

Buchholz, Hans-Günter, and Vassos Karageorghis

1973 *Prehistoric Greece and Cyprus: An Archaeological Handbook.* New York: Phaidon.

This standard work on prehistoric Greece and Cyprus by Buchholz and Karageorghis begins with the Stone Age and ends with the Mycenaean period with an emphasis on architecture and other technologies including wall painting, sarcophagi and stelae, metal vessels, sculpture, ivories, jewelry, pottery, seals, and tools.

Bullis, Douglas

2000 "The Longest Hajj: The Journeys of Ibn Battuta." Part 1, "From Pilgrim to Traveler, Tangier to Makkah"; part 2, "From Riches to Rags, Makkah to India"; part 3, "From Traveler to Memorist, China, Mali and Home." *Saudi Aramco World* 51

Bunimovitz, Shlomo

2007 "Children of Three Paradigms: My Generation in Israeli Archaeology." *Biblical Archaeology Review* 33: 30, 80.

Three schools of archaeology continue to influence Israeli excavators: cultural history, processual archaeology, and post-processual archaeology. All three of these disciplinary revolutions influence the research agendas of archaeologists such as Shlomo Bunimovitz and Zvi Lederman working at sites like Tel Beth-Shemesh.

Bunimovitz, Shlomo, and A. Faust

2003 "Building Identity: The Four-Room House and the Israelite Mind." In *Symbiosis, Symbolism, and the Power of the Past: Canaan, Ancient Israel, and Their Neighbors from the Late Bronze Age through Roman Palaestina.*

Proceedings of the Centennial Symposium, W. F. Albright Institute of Archaeological Research and American Schools of Oriental Research, Jerusalem, May 29–31, 2000, edited by William G. Dever and Seymour Gittin, 411–23. Winona Lake, Ind.: Eisenbrauns.

Bunyan, John

1998/ *The Pilgrim's Progress.* New York: Oxford
1678 University Press.

Burgh, Theodore W.

2006 *Listening to the Artifacts: Music Culture in Ancient Palestine.* New York: T&T Clark.

Iconography, figurines, and other artifacts recovered by archaeologists and musical traditions in the Bible underline the importance of music in ancient Israel. Burgh identifies the musical instruments that the Hebrews played and indicates what instruments were gender specific and in what settings music was performed.

Burkert, Walter

1972 *Homo Necans: The Anthropology of Ancient Greek Sacrificial Ritual and Myth.* Translated by Peter Bing. Berkeley: University of California Press.

Building on the work of Konrad Lorenz—*On Aggression* (1963)—Burkert studies human sacrifice in Hellenistic or western Mediterranean cultures. He argues that it is connected with the evolution of humans as hunters. Sacrifice processes the guilt that humans experience in killing fellow animals. It allows humans to deify their victims as an act of reconciliation for killing them and to reaffirm their common bond as fellow animals.

Burleigh, Nina

2007 *Mirage: Napoleon's Scientists and the Unveiling of Egypt.* San Francisco: HarperCollins.

Burleigh profiles the ten most prominent members of the scholars Napoleon drafted to introduce Europe to the culture of ancient Egypt—including the artist Dominique-Vivant Denon, the mathematician Gaspard Monge, and the inventor Nicolas-Jacques Conté.

Bibliography

Burton, Richard F.

1961 *The Lake Regions of Central Africa, a Picture of Exploration.* 2 vols. New York: Horizon.

1964 *Personal Narrative of a Pilgrimage to Al-Madinah & Meccah.* Edited by Isabel Burton. New York: Dover.

Cahill, Jane M., and James A. Passamano

2007 "Full Disclosure Matters." *Near Eastern Archaeology* 70:194–96.

Cahill and Passamano discuss copyright and fair use, the need to provide incentives for archaeologists to share their data, and the best methods for achieving uniformity in data archiving.

Callaway, Joseph A.

1979 "Dame Kathleen Kenyon 1906–1978." *Biblical Archaeologist* 42:122–25.

Campana, D. V., and P. J. Crabtree

1990 "Communal Hunting in the Natufian of the Southern Levant: The Social and Economic Implications." *Journal of Mediterranean Archaeology* 3:233–43.

Cargill, Robert R.

2008 "Virtual Qumran" http://virtualqumran .blogspot.com/

"Ancient Qumran: A Virtual Reality Tour (the movie)" is based on the UCLA Qumran Visualization Project's digital model of Qumran. It takes the viewer on a tour of the reconstructed settlement of Khirbet Qumran. It offers a history of the archaeological excavation of the site and the surrounding caves, and discusses the different theories concerning the nature and expansion of Qumran. This film is an updated and expanded version of the live-narration movie playing at the San Diego Natural History Museum as a part of their exhibition of the Dead Sea Scrolls.

Carrasco, David

1991 "The Sacrifice of Tezcatipoca: To Change Place." In *To Change Place: Aztec Ceremonial Landscapes,* edited by David Carrasco, 31–57. Niwot, Colo.: University of Colorado Press.

Carrasco applies the work of Jonathan Z. Smith, *To Take Place: Toward Theory in Ritual* (1987), and Claude Lévi-Strauss, *The Savage Mind* (1966), to Aztec culture.

Carter, Howard

1954 *The Tomb of Tutankhamen.* New York: E. P. Dutton.

Carter narrates and illustrates the discovery and interpretation of the tomb of Tutankhamen.

Casson, Lionel

1974 "The World's First Museums." In *Journal of the Ancient Near Eastern Society of Columbia University,* vol. 5, special issue: *The Gaster Festschrift,* 53–57.

2001 *Libraries in the Ancient World.* New Haven: Yale University Press.

Champollion, Jean-François

1811 *Introduction to Egypt under the Pharaohs.*

1814 *Egyptian before the Invasion of Cambyses.*

Chaney, Marvin L.

1983 "Ancient Palestinian Peasant Movements and the Formation of Premonarchic Israel." In *Palestine in Transition: The Emergence of Ancient Israel,* edited by David Noel Freedman and David Frank Graf. Social World of Biblical Antiquity 2. Sheffield: Almond.

Chapman, Rupert L.

1990 "Pioneers of Biblical Archaeology." In *Archaeology and the Bible,* edited by Rupert L. Chapman, Peter G. Dorrell, and Jonathan N. Tubb, 9–36. London: British Museum.

1990 *Archaeology and the Bible.* London: British Museum, edited by Rupert L. Chapman, Peter G. Dorrell, and Jonathan N. Tubb.

Chapman, Dorrell, and Tubb survey the contribution of the Palestine Exploration Fund to the development of biblical archaeology.

Charlesworth, James H., and Walter P. Weaver, eds.

1992   *What Has Archaeology to Do with Faith?* Faith and Scholarship Colloquies. Philadelphia: Trinity Press International.

Chavalas, Mark W.

2003   "Pusurum, a Homeowner from Khana-Period Terqa." In *Life and Culture in the Ancient Near East,* edited by Richard E. Averbeck, Mark W. Chavalas, and David B. Weisberg, 153–70. Bethesda, Md.: CDL.

Chavalas, Mark W., and K. Lawson Younger, eds.

2002   *Mesopotamia and the Bible.* Grand Rapids: Baker.

Cheng, Jack, and Marian Feldman, eds.

2007   *Ancient Near Eastern Art in Context: Studies in Honor of Irene J. Winter by Her Students.* Culture and History of the Ancient Near East 26. Leiden/Boston: Brill.

Chicago Assyrian Dictionary Project
      http://oi.uchicago.edu/research/projects/cad/

The *Chicago Assyrian Dictionary* (*CAD*), initiated in 1921 by James H. Breasted, is compiling a comprehensive dictionary of the various dialects of Akkadian, the earliest known Semitic language, which was recorded on cuneiform texts that date from 2400 B.C.E. to 100 recovered from excavations at ancient Near Eastern sites. The *Assyrian Dictionary* is a joint undertaking of resident and nonresident scholars from around the world who have contributed their time and labor over a period of seventy years to the collection of the source materials and to the publication of the Dictionary.

Chiera, Edward

1938   *They Wrote on Clay: The Babylonia Tablets Speak Today.* Edited by George G. Cameron. Chicago: University of Chicago Press.

Chilton, Bruce

2008   *Abraham's Cure: The Roots of Violence in Judaism, Christianity, and Islam.* New York: Doubleday.

Chilton investigates child sacrifice in the Bible, particularly the sacrifice of Isaac. He studies the ritual of human sacrifice in the world of the Bible and in the Bible itself; the sacrifice of Jesus and of the early martyrs; and Ibrahim's sacrifical vision in Islam. He concludes with a study of the violence of the Crusaders against Muslims, the theology of jihad, and the sobering question: "When is martyrdom heroic?"

Clark, Douglas R., and Victor H. Matthews, eds.

2003   *One Hundred Years of American Archaeology in the Middle East: Proceedings of the American Schools of Oriental Research Centennial Celebration, Washington DC, April 2000.* Boston: American Schools of Oriental Research

Clark and Matthews edit an anthology of papers by leading archaeologists working in the ancient Near East organized by the major historical archaeological periods, covering geographical areas and larger arenas of concern, including technology, religion, and economic and political realities. Papers not only review results from a century of North American archaeological endeavor in the Middle East, but are also concerned with a prospective view, seeking to address how archaeologists should proceed with their work at the beginning of the twenty-first century.

Clayton, Peter A.

1994   *Chronicle of the Pharaohs: The Reign-by-Reign Record of the Rulers and Dynasties of Ancient Egypt.* New York: Thames & Hudson.

Clayton reconstructs a history of ancient Egypt from the biographies of each pharaoh creating a history of ancient Egypt. From Narmer to Cleopatra, their cartouches are drawn, their names are translated, and the contributions of each pharaoh to the culture of Egypt are outlined.

Cline, Eric H.

2007   *From Eden to Exile: Unraveling Mysteries of*

Bibliography

the Bible. Washington, D.C.: National Geographic.

This is a print companion to the National Geographic television series *Science of the Bible.* Jesus is the focus of *Science of the Bible*; the focus of *From Eden to Exile* is ancient Israel. Hot topics create the book's outline: the Garden of Eden, Noah's ark, Sodom and Gomorrah, Moses and the exodus, Joshua and the battle of Jericho, the ark of the covenant and the Ten Lost Tribes of Israel.

Each chapter is also outlined by the hot topics. "Moses and the Exodus," for example, asks: *Did the exodus take place? When did the exodus take place? Was the exodus a single event or a gradual process? Who was the pharaoh of the exodus? How many Hebrews made the exodus? What kinds of disasters were the plagues? What caused the plagues? How was the Red Sea divided? What were the Ten Commandments?*

The book is Cline's effort to insert archaeologists and biblical scholars into the media market. He argues that ignoring notorious claims made by a growing number of unqualified individuals gives these pundits unchallenged influence over the public understanding of the relationship of archaeology and the Bible.

Clines, David J. A., J. Cheryl Exum, and Keith Whitelam, eds.
2006   *Orientalism, Assyriology and the Bible.* Sheffield: Sheffield Phoenix.

Orientalism refers both to the academic study of the Orient and to Western scholarship that clings to caricatures of the East. This is a four-part collection by art historians, Assyriologists, and biblical scholars. (1) "Intellectual and Disciplinary Histories" deals with the rise of Assyriology in the United States, shifting images of Assyria, the Smithsonian Institution exhibits of *biblical antiquities* at the 1893, 1895 world's fairs, the rise of Egyptology in the nineteenth century, the impact of the Mari excavations on biblical studies, and the genre of ancient Near Eastern anthologies by Foster, Frahm, Holloway Reid and Younger. (2) "Visual Perspectives" is a corrective to images of the ancient Near East reconstructed only from texts using the Assyrianizing engravings in the Dalziels' Bible Gallery, the reception of ancient Assyria in nineteenth-century England versus France, and artwork for twentieth-century American histories of Israel by Bohrer, Esposito, and Long. (3) "Of Harems and Heroines"

studies gender issues focusing on Semiramis and the harem in the Bible and Assyriology by Asher-Greve and Solvang. (4) "Assyriology and the Bible" studies figures (Josiah), texts (Gen 28:10-22 and the Uruk Prophecy), periods (Persian period by Grabbe, Handy, Hurowitz, and Scurlock).

Cobb, Charles
1991   "Social Reproduction and the *Longue Durée* in the Prehistory of the Midcontinental United States." In *Processual and Postprocessual Archaeologies: Multiple Ways of Knowing the Past,* edited by Robert W. Preucel, 168–82. Carbondale: Southern Illinois University.

Cohen, Getzel M., and Martha Sharp Joukowsky, eds.
        Breaking Ground: Pioneering Women Archaeologists. Ann Arbor: University of Michigan Press.

Cohen and Joukowsky edited biographies of twelve pioneering women archaeologists: Jane Dieulafoy (1851–1916), Esther B. Van Deman (1862–1937), Margaret Alice Murray (1863–1963), Gertrude L. Bell (1868–1926), Harriet Boyd Hawes (1871–1945), Edith Hayward Hall Dohan (1879–1943), Hetty Goldman (1881–1972), Gertrude Caton-Thompson (1888–1985), Dorothy Annie Elizabeth Garrod (1892–1968), Winifred Lamb (1894–1963), Theresa B. Goell (1901–1985), and Kathleen Kenyon (1906–1978).

Cole, Juan
2007   *Napoleon's Egypt: Invading the Middle East.* New York: Palgrave Macmillan.

Cole describes Napoleon's invasion of Egypt as a brutal disaster— comparable to the invasion of Iraq by the U.S.-led coalition forces in 2003—using quotations from Egyptian memoirs and diaries contemporary with Napoleon's invasion.

Coleman, Simon
2006   "Pilgrimage." In *Blackwell Companion to the Study of Religion,* 385–96. Oxford: Blackwell.

Coleman, Simon, and John Elsner
1994a   *Pilgrimage: Past and Present in the World Religions.* Cambridge, Mass.: Harvard University Press.

1994b   "The Pilgrim's Progress: Art, Architecture and Ritual Movement at Sinai." *World Archaeology* 26:73–89.

Anthropological theories of pilgrimage often neglect the cultural significance of images and architecture. Coleman and Elsner study the material culture of St. Catherine's Monastery at Mount Sinai from 500 to 600 in order to restore archaeological evidence to the anthropology of pilgrimage. The arts, architecture, and inscriptions at the monastery initiate pilgrims from around the world into a biblical spirituality.

Collingwood, R. G.
1946   *The Idea of History.* Oxford: Clarendon.

The Idea of History was not actually published by Collingwood but was put together after his death from lecture notes, short published articles, and parts of an unpublished manuscript: *The Principles of History.* That manuscript then vanished, was discovered only in 1995, and was subsequently published (see Michael Stack, review of *The Principles of History and Other Writings in Philosophy of History,* edited by W. H. Dray and W. J. van der Dussen, *University of Toronto Quarterly* 71 (2002).

Collins, Billie Jean
2007   *The Hittites and Their World.* Archaeology and Biblical Studies 7. Atlanta: Society of Biblical Literature.

Collins reviews how archaeology and language studies have reconstructed the Hittite culture, which began in 1900 B.C.E. with trade colonies and ended in 800 B.C.E. with the destruction of their great cities. She places special emphasis on how Hittite culture contributes to the understanding of the world of the Bible.

Collins, Billie Jean, ed.
2001   *A History of the Animal World in the Ancient Near East.* Handbook of Oriental Studies 64. Leiden/Boston: Brill.

Collins's zoology of the Near East concentrates on the depiction and use of animals in the art, literature, and cultures in Anatolia, Egypt, Iran, Mesopotamia, and Syria-Palestine. The seventeen chapters cover native fauna, animals in art, animals in literature, animals in religion, and the cultural use of animals.

Comaroff, John, and Jean Comaroff
1992   *Ethnography and Historical Imagination.* Boulder, Colo.: Westview.

Conder, Claude R., and Horatio H. Kitchener
1881   *The Survey of Western Palestine.* 6 vols. London: Palestine Exploration Fund.

Conkey, Margaret W., and Joan M. Gero, eds.
1991   *Engendering Archaeology: Women and Prehistory.* Social Archaeology. Cambridge, Mass.: Blackwell.

Conkey and Gero edit fourteen essays on women in ancient cultures and gender in archaeology. Conkey is professor of anthropology and director of the Archaeological Research Facility at the University of California, Berkeley.

Conkey, Margaret W., and Janet D. Spector
1984   "Archaeology and the Study of Gender." *Archaeological Method and Theory* 7:1–38.

Archaeologists often reconstruct past cultures to justify their own cultures, especially in describing the roles of women. They assume that the meaning of masculine and feminine, the capabilities of men and women, their power relations, and their appropriate roles in society were the same in ancient cultures as in their own culture. Archaeologists are neither objective nor inclusive on the subject of gender. Because archaeologists never developed a method for determining how gender operated in a culture, they simply applied the way gender operated in their own culture to the cultures they were reconstructing. Conkey especially has continued to work on the archaeological study of gender.

Coogan, Michael D., J. Cheryl Exum, and Lawrence E. Stager, eds.
1994   *Scripture and Other Artifacts: Essays on the Bible and Archaeology in Honor of Philip J. King.* Louisville: Westminster John Knox.

Bibliography

Cook, Stephen L., and S. C. Winter
1999   "Introduction: Contemporary Methods and the Place of Philology and Archaeology in Biblical Studies Today." In *On the Way to Nineveh: Studies in Honor of George M. Landes,* edited by Stephen L. Cook and S. C. Winter, 7–17. ASOR Books 4. Atlanta: Scholars Press.

Cook, Stephen L., and S. C. Winter, eds.
1999   *On the Way to Nineveh: Studies in Honor of George M. Landes.* ASOR Books 4. Atlanta: Scholars Press.

Cornfeld, Gaalyah, and David Noel Freedman
1976   *Archaeology of the Bible: Book by Book.* San Francisco: Harper & Row.

Craiger, Stephen L.
1935   *Bible and Spade: An Introduction to Biblical Archaeology.* London: Oxford University Press.

Crook, Zeba A.
2005   "Reflections on Culture and Social-Scientific Models." *Journal of Biblical Literature* 124:515–32.

Cross, Frank Moore
1973   "W. F. Albright's View of Biblical Archaeology and Its Methodology." *Biblical Archaeologist* 36:2–5.

    For Albright, Syro-Palestinian archaeology was a subdiscipline of biblical archaeology, which studied "all biblical lands from India to Spain and from southern Russia to south Arabia, and the whole history of those lands from about 10,000 B.C., or even earlier, to the present time" (Albright 1966,13). Only by using historical studies of both the Bible and other ancient Near Eastern cultures was it possible to understand a site. Although he referred to himself as an Orientalist or historian of religion, he brought virtually all the humanities to bear on his work as a biblical archaeologist. Consequently, many of his colleagues and students considered him a genius. He studied religion the way he studied pottery—by using typology. Every type of pottery has ancestors; every type inspires successors. So do religious traditions. The goal of biblical archaeology is to reconstruct the typology or evolution of religion from the Stone Age to the Byzantine period of Christianity.

Currid, John D.
1999   *Doing Archaeology in the Land of the Bible: A Basic Guide.* Grand Rapids: Baker.

    Currid writes a handbook for student volunteers explaining the dynamics of the Wheeler-Kenyon Method.

Currie, Robin, and Stephen Hyslop
2009   *The Letter and the Scroll: What Modern Archaeology Tells Us about the Bible.* Washington, D.C: National Geographic.

Curtis, J. E.
1995a   "Assyrian Civilization." In *Art and Empire: Treasures from Assyria in the British Museum,* edited by J. E. Curtis and J. E. Reade, 32–37. New York: Metropolitan Museum of Art.

1995b   "The Discovery of Assyria." In *Art and Empire: Treasures from Assyria in the British Museum,* edited by J. E. Curtis and J. E. Reade, 9–16. New York: Metropolitan Museum of Art.

Curtis, J. E., and J. E. Reade, eds.
1995   *Art and Empire: Treasures from Assyria in the British Museum.* New York: Metropolitan Museum of Art.

Dahari, Uzi
2000   *Monastic Settlements in South Sinai in the Byzantine Period: The Archaeological Remains.* IAA Reports 9. Jerusalem: Israel Antiquities Authority.

Dahood, Mitchell J.
1986   "The Moabite Stone and Northwest Semitic Philology." In *Archaeology of Jordan and Other Studies Presented to S. H. Horn,* edited by L. T. Geraty and L. G. Herr, 429–41. Berrien Spring, Mich.: Andrews University Press.

Daniels, Peter T.
1996a   "Methods of Decipherment." In *The World's*

Writing Systems, edited by Peter T. Daniels and William Bright, 141–59. New York: Oxford University Press.

1996b "The Study of Writing Systems." In *The World's Writing Systems,* edited by Peter T. Daniels and William Bright, 3–17. New York: Oxford University Press.

Daniels, Peter T., and William Bright, eds.

1996 *The World's Writing Systems.* New York: Oxford University Press.

"Humankind is defined by language; but civilization is defined by writing" (p. 1). Linguistics studies the structure of spoken languages. Grammatology (Gelb 1952) studies writing systems, the signs that record languages.

Darvill, Timothy

2002 *The Concise Oxford Dictionary of Archaeology.* Oxford: Oxford University Press.

Darvill writes over four thousand entries covering the essential vocabulary for everyday archaeology. He focuses especially on Europe, the Old World, and the Americas, and covers legislation related to the United Kingdom and the United States.

Daviau, P. M. Michèle

1993 *Houses and Their Furnishings in Bronze Age Palestine: Domestic Activity Areas and Artefact Distribution in the Middle and Late Bronze Ages.* JSOT/ASOR Monograph Series 8. Sheffield: JSOT Press.

2001 "Assyrian Influence and Changing Technologies at Tall Jawa, Jordan." In *The Land That I Will Show You: Essays in History and Archaeology of the Ancient Near East in Honor of J. Maxwell Miller,* 214–38. Journal for the Study of the Old Testament Supplement Series 343. Sheffield: Sheffield Academic Press.

Daviau describes the impact of Assyria on the site of Tell Jawa in rural Ammon.

Daviau, P. M. Michèle, and Paul-Eugene Dion

2002 "Economy-Related Finds from Khirbat al-Mudayna (Wadi ath-Thamad, Jordan)." *Bulletin of the American Schools of Oriental Research* 328:31–48.

Steiner (2002) suggests that Iron Age Moab had both a state economy and a village economy. The village economy served fortified villages, unfortified villages, and herders living on the land. Agriculture was the backbone of this village economy, but crafts, pottery, metalworking, and textiles were also produced for local markets. Steiner's description of a small state's economic organization can now be tested against the archaeological record. Finds from a pillared industrial building in the fortified village of Khirbat al-Mudayna on the Wadi ath-Thamad include two inscribed scale weights and one uninscribed weight, and seven Iron Age seals and three seal impressions (Latin: *bullae*). This small corpus is directly related to the village economy and includes the first occurrence of inscribed weights in Moab. This paper presents those weights, seals, and seal impressions in their archaeological context and studies their implications.

David, Nicholas, and Carol Kramer

2001 *Ethnoarchaeology in Action.* Cambridge World Archaeology. New York: Cambridge University.

David and Kramer study the ethnographic material culture from archaeological perspectives embracing both processual archaeology and post-processual archaeology during the 1980s and '90s. Three introductory chapters introduce the subject and its history, survey the broad range of theory required, and discuss field methods and ethics. It concludes with an appreciation of ethnoarchaeology's contributions, actual and potential, and of its place within anthropology.

Davies, Dave (Philadelphia Daily News)

2006 "Interview with Neil Asher Silberman" NPR *Fresh Air*, May 15. http://www.npr.org/tem plates/story/story.php?storyId=5401536.

Davies, Nina M.

1958 *Picture Writing in Ancient Egypt.* New York: Oxford University Press.

Bibliography

Davies, Norman de Garis
1930   *The Tomb of Ken-Amun at Thebes.* New York: Metropolitan Museum of Art.

Davies, Philip R.
1992   *In Search of "Ancient Israel."* Journal for the Study of the Old Testament Supplement Series 148. Sheffield: JSOT Press.

2000   "Minimalism, 'Ancient Israel,' and Anti-Semitism." http://www.bibleinterp.com/articles/Minimalism.htm.

2005   "Crypto-Minimalism." *Journal of Semitic Studies* 50:117–36.

Davies, Philip R., and John Rogerson
2005   *The Old Testament World.* Louisville: Westminster John Knox.

Part 1 describes the geography, the social organization, and the cultures in the world of the Bible. Part 2 reconstructs the history of Israel. Part 3 catalogues the genres in the Bible, emphasizing the importance of creation stories in the world of the Bible. Part 4 describes the development of the canon.

Davis, Thomas W.
2004   *Shifting Sands: The Rise and Fall of Biblical Archaeology.* New York: Oxford University Press.

Davis published his 1987 dissertation, directed by William G. Dever, tracing the interaction of biblical studies and archaeology in Syria-Palestine and describing the theories and methods of William Foxwell Albright and other biblical archaeologists.

Dearman, J. Andrew, ed.
1989   *Studies in the Mesha Inscription and Moab.* Archaeology and Biblical Studies 2. Atlanta: Scholars Press.

Dearman edits an anthology of eight essays on the Annals of Mesha including an introduction to the study of the annals by J. Maxwell Miller; a description of the political and social history of the period by M. Patrick Graham; and a reconstruction of the text by Kent P. Jackson.

Dearman, J. Andrew, and M. Patrick Graham, eds.
2001   *The Land That I Will Show You: Essays in History and Archaeology of the Ancient Near East in Honor of J. Maxwell Miller.* Journal for the Study of the Old Testament Supplement Series 343. Sheffield: Sheffield Academic Press.

Colleagues and students of J. Maxwell Miller (Candler School of Theology at Emory University) offer him their articles dealing with the history, chronology, geography, archaeology, and epigraphy in the world of the Bible. They range from broad methodological discussions of historiography to focused analyses of individual texts or historical issues. A review of Miller's career and a selected bibliography of his publications are included.

Dearman, J. Andrew, and Gerald L. Mattingly
1992   "Mesha Stela." In *The Anchor Bible Dictionary,* edited by David Noel Freedman, 4:708–9. 6 vols. New York: Doubleday.

De Capoa, Chiara
2003   *Old Testament Figures in Art.* Translated by Thomas Michael Hartmann. Edited by Stefano Zuffi. Los Angeles: J. Paul Getty Museum.

Deem, Ariella
1978   "And the Stone Sank into His Forehead": A Note on 1 Samuel XVII 49." *Vetus Testamentum* 28:349–51.

Deesel, J. P.
2003   "In Search of the Good Book: A Critical Survey of Handbooks on Biblical Archaeology." In *Between Text and Artifact: Integrating Archaeology in Biblical Studies Teaching,* edited by Milton C. Moreland, 67–98. Atlanta: Society of Biblical Literature.

Delaney, Carol
1988   *The Seed and the Soil: Gender and Cosmology in Turkish Village Society.* Comparative Stud-

ies on Muslim Societies 11. Berkeley: University of California Press.

Delitzsch, Friedrich

1902   *Babel and Bible: A Lecture on the Significance of Assyriological Research for Religion.* Translated by Thomas J. McCormack. Chicago: Open Court.

Demsky, Aaron

1997   "The Name of the Goddess of Ekron: A New Reading." *Journal of the Ancient Near Eastern Society of Columbia University* 25:1–5.

Dersin, Denise, ed.

1996   *What Life Was Like on the Banks of the Nile: Egypt 3050–30 B.C.* Alexandria, Va.: Time-Life Books.

> Dersin tells the history of Egypt through the daily lives of ordinary Egyptians: a tomb foreman, an independent woman, a scolding wife. Glossary.

de Vaux, Roland

1973   *Archaeology and the Dead Sea Scrolls.* Rev. ed. New York: Oxford University Press.

> The first excavations at Qumran (1951–1958) were directed by de Vaux (1903–1971). He published his preliminary reports in the *Revue biblique* (1951–1958). *Archaeology and the Dead Sea Scrolls* is his only synthesis, although only half of the book deals with Qumran. The English translation, published after de Vaux's death, expands the French original (1961). Two important conclusions guided his interpretation of the site. First, he concluded that the scrolls recovered from eleven caves around the ruins were stored there by the Qumran community. Second, he concluded that the Qumran community was a Jewish monastic order much like the Essenes described by Philo, Pliny, and Josephus.

Dever, William G.

1973   *Archaeology and Biblical Studies: Retrospects and Prospects.* Evanston: Seabury-Western Theological Seminary.

1982   "Retrospects and Prospects in Biblical and Syro-Palestinian Archeology." *Biblical Archaeologist* 45:103–7.

> Dever calls for archaeologists working in Syria-Palestine to develop (1) a theory clearly defining *Syro-Palestinian archeology* as a professional academic discipline in contrast to *biblical archaeology*—the part-time and amateur dialogue between biblical scholars, archaeologists, and archaeology lovers; (2) a common method for conducting excavations; (3) a curriculum for training graduate students; (4) solid moral and monetary support from established academic foundations; (5) strong centers for research overseas; (6) a reputation for the prompt publication of its excavations and textbooks for the discipline.

1985   "Syro-Palestinian and Biblical Archaeology." In *The Hebrew Bible and Its Modern Interpreters,* edited by Douglas A. Knight and Gene M. Tucker, 31–74. Philadelphia: Fortress Press.

1988   "Impact of the 'New Archaeology.'" In *Benchmarks in Time and Culture: An Introduction to Palestinian Archaeology,* edited by Joel F. Drinkard, Jr., Gerald L. Mattingly, and J. Maxwell Miller, 337–52. Atlanta: Scholars Press.

> Dever discusses the shifting of the paradigms of archaeological research. Before 1970 archaeologists emphasized technique; after 1970 their emphasis has been on cultural evolution using a multidisciplinary and holistic approach.

1989   *Recent Archaeological Discoveries and Biblical Research.* Seattle: University of Washington Press.

1990   "Biblical Archaeology: Death and Rebirth?" In *Biblical Archaeology Today, 1990: Proceedings of the Second International Congress on Biblical Archaeology, Jerusalem,* edited by Avraham Biran and Joseph Aviram, 706–22. Jerusalem: Israel Exploration Society.

> Dever describes the external factors that led to the demise of "biblical archaeology."

1992a   "Gezer." In *The Anchor Bible Dictionary,* edited by David Noel Freedman, 2:998–1003. 6 vols. New York: Doubleday.

Bibliography

1992b   "Archaeology, Syro-Palestinian and Biblical." In *The Anchor Bible Dictionary,* edited by David Noel Freedman, 1:354–67. 6 vols. New York: Doubleday.

Dever divides the history of archaeology into four phases: (1) the exploratory phase (1838–1914); (2) the beginning of large-scale fieldwork and the evolution of a basic chronological cultural framework (1918–1940); (3) the introduction of modern stratigraphic methods (1948–1970); (4) an incipient revolution caused by the rise of the "new archaeology" (1970–).

1993   "Gezer." In *The New Encyclopedia of Archaeological Excavations in the Holy Land,* edited by Ephraim Stern, 2:496–506. New York: Simon & Schuster.

1997   "Gezer." In *The Oxford Encyclopedia of Archaeology in the Near East,* edited by Eric M. Meyers, 2:396–400. New York: Oxford University Press.

1999   "Can 'Biblical Archaeology' Be an Academic and Professional Discipline." In *Archaeology, History and Culture in Palestine and the Near East: Essays in Memory of Albert E. Glock,* edited by Tomis Kapitan, 11–22. ASOR Books 3. Atlanta: Scholars Press.

2000   "Nelson Glueck and the Other Half of the Holy Land." In *Archaeology of Jordan and Beyond: Essays in Honor of James A. Sauer,* edited by Lawrence E. Stager, Joseph A. Greene, and Michael D. Coogan, 114–21. Winona Lake, Ind.: Eisenbrauns.

2001a   "Excavating the Hebrew Bible or Burying It Again?" *Bulletin of the American Schools of Oriental Research* 322:67–77.

2001b   *What Did the Biblical Writers Know and When Did They Know It? What Archaeology Can Tell Us about the Reality of Ancient Israel.* Grand Rapids: Eerdmans.

Dever surveys the history of archaeology and the Bible and the contributions that he has made to the field during his thirty-five years of work. He also examines the minimalist, postmodern philosophical worldview and interpretation of the Bible, and the coalition supporting those who hold the minimalist view. The chapter titles are as follows: (1) The Bible as History, Literature, and Theology; (2) Revisionists and Their Non-histories; (3) What Archaeology Is and What It Can Contribute to Biblical Studies; (4) Getting at the "History behind the History": Convergences between Texts and Artifacts—Israelite Origins and the Rise of the State; (5) Daily Life in Israel in the Time of the Divided Monarchy; (6) What Is Left of the History of Ancient Israel and Why Should It Matter to Anyone?

2004   "Kathleen Kenyon, 1905–1978." In *Breaking Ground: Pioneering Women Archaeologists,* edited by Getzel M. Cohen and Martha Sharp Joukowsky, 525–53. Ann Arbor: University of Michigan Press.

To place an archaeologist of Kenyon's stature in critical perspective is somewhat presumptuous. Yet Dever notes that Kenyon's Arab sympathies almost prevented her from directing the British School of Archaeology in Jerusalem after the 1967 war. Colleagues felt that her strategy of digging deep, narrow, unconnected trenches, which only she could draw or interpret, failed to provide an accurate overview of a site. Once she had read pottery, she discarded it, so no one could check her work. As a scholar, she was isolated; she did not read enough, and she did not publish enough. The teamwork concept that came to characterize American excavations in Jordan and Israel that adopted Kenyon's methods was inconceivable to her. She worked alone.

2005   *Did God Have a Wife? Archaeology and Folk Religion in Ancient Israel.* Grand Rapids: William B. Eerdmans.

Dever reconstructs the folk religion of ordinary people in ancient Israel and their everyday religious lives reflected in excavations reveal numerous local and household shrines where sacrifices and other rituals were carried out. He reconsiders the presence and influence of women's cults in early Israel and their implications for understanding of official religion in the Bible. Dever also pays particular attention to the goddess Asherah, reviled in official religion, but popular in the folk religion of the women of ancient Israel as Yahweh's wife.

Dever, William G., and Seymour Gitin, eds.
1984   *Symbiosis, Symbolism, and the Power of the Past: Canaan, Ancient Israel and Their Neighbors from the Late Bronze Age through Roman Palaestina: Proceedings of the Centennial Symposium, W. F. Albright Institute of Archaeological Research and the American Schools of Oriental Research, Jerusalem, May 29–31, 2000.* Winona Lake, Ind.: Eisenbrauns.

Dietz, Maribel
2005   *Wandering Monks, Virgins, and Pilgrims: Ascetic Travel in the Mediterranean World, A.D. 300–800.* University Park: Pennsylvania State University Press.

Donceel, Robert
1997   "Qumran." In *The Oxford Encyclopedia of Archaeology in the Near East,* edited by Eric M. Meyers, 4:392–96. New York: Oxford University Press.

Donceel, Robert, and Pauline Donceel-Voute
1994   "The Archaeology of Khirbet Qumran." In *Methods of Investigation of the Dead Sea Scrolls,* edited by Michael O. Wise, 1–38. Annals of the New York Academy of Sciences 722. New York. New York Academy of Sciences.

Donceel and Donceel-Voute describe their interpretation of the material remains from Qumran and the plans of the Ecole Biblique and the Catholic University of Louvain for publishing Roland de Vaux's final report. They focused their research on small finds from Qumran—glassware, metal wares, and coins, and concluded that Qumran was not a monastery but a plantation (Latin: *villa rustica*) built by a wealthy household from Jerusalem during the reign of Herod the Great (73–4 B.C.E.).

Donegan, J. B.
1978   *Women and Men Midwives: Medicine, Morality and Misogyny in Early America.* Westport, Conn.: Greenwood.

Dothan, Trude
1982   *The Philistines and Their Material Culture.* New Haven: Yale University Press.

1990   "Ekron of the Philistines, Part I: Where They Came From, How They Settled Down and the Place They Worshiped In." *Biblical Archaeology Review* 16:20–36.

Dothan describes Ekron during the early Iron Age (1200–1000 B.C.E.) when it was a large city with a rich material culture founded by the Sea Peoples and developed into an important member of the Philistine urban league. Ekron has industrial areas, unique cultic installations, and a distinctive material culture, all reflecting strong Aegean ties. The city reached its peak of development between 1100 and1000 B.C.E. However, this progress went hand in hand with a loss of distinctiveness of the Philistines' material culture. The quality of the Philistine bichrome pottery degenerated as Egyptian and Phoenician influences had their effects on Philistine material culture. Pharaoh Siamun (978–959 B.C.E.) may have destroyed Ekron during his campaign against Gezer (1 Kgs 3:1; 9:16).

Dothan, Trude, and Moshe Dothan
1992   *People of the Sea: The Search for the Philistines.* New York: Macmillan.

Dothan, Trude, and Seymour Gitin
1992   "Ekron." In *The Anchor Bible Dictionary,* edited by David Noel Freedman, 2:416–22. 6 vols. New York: Doubleday.

1997   "Miqne, Tel." In *The Oxford Encyclopedia of Archaeology in the Near East,* edited by Eric M. Meyers, 4:30–35. New York: Oxford University Press.

Doughty, Charles M.
1979/   *Travels in Arabia Deserta.* New York: Dover.
1888

Douglas, Mary
2001/   *Purity and Danger: An Analysis of Concepts of Pollution and Taboo.* London: Routledge & Kegan Paul.
1966

Bibliography

Downing, Frederick L.
2006   "The Biblical Archaeology Movement: Building and Re-building the Albright House." *Perspectives in Religious Studies* 33:495–506.

Drinkard, Joel F., Jr., Gerald L. Mattingly, and J. Maxwell Miller, eds.
1988   *Benchmarks in Time and Culture: An Introduction to Palestinian Archaeology.* Atlanta: Scholars Press.

This anthology of twenty-three essays is dedicated to Joseph A. Callaway. Part 1 presents histories of the major national schools of archaeology in Syria-Palestine. Part 2 outlines the methods and techniques used in archaeology today. Part 3 discusses selected areas where archaeology has been integrated in order to bring about historical-cultural syntheses.

Duke, Philip
1996   "Braudel and North American Archaeology: An Example from the Northern Plains." In *Archaeology, Annales and Ethnohistory,* edited by Alan Bernard Knapp, 99–111. New Directions in Archaeology. Cambridge/New York: Cambridge University.

Durkheim, Emile
1895   *Rules of the Sociological Method.* Translated by W. D. Halls. New York: Free Press.

Eakins, J. Kenneth
1988   "Future of 'Biblical Archaeology.'" In *Benchmarks in Time and Culture: An Introduction to Palestinian Archaeology,* edited by Joel F. Drinkard, Jr., Gerald L. Mattingly, and J. Maxwell Miller, 441–54. Atlanta: Scholars Press.

Earle, Timothy K., and Robert W. Preucel
1987   "Processual Archaeology and the Radical Critique." *Current Anthropology* 28:501–38.

Ebeling, Jennie R.
2000   "Recent Archaeological Discoveries at Hazor." http://www.bibleinter.com/articles/Hazor_Ebeling.htm

Edelman, Diana
1988   "Tel Masos, Geshur, and David." *Journal of Near Eastern Studies* 47:253–58.
1992   "Who or What Was Israel?" *Biblical Archaeology Review* 18:72–73.

Edwards, Douglas R., and C. Thomas McCollough, eds.
2007   *The Archaeology of Difference: Gender, Ethnicity, Class and the "Other" in Antiquity. Studies in Honor of Eric M. Meyers.* ASOR Annual Volume 60–61. Boston: American Schools of Oriental Research.

Edwards and McCollough edit an anthology of studies of the archaeology of difference based on gender, ethnicity, and social status as reflected in both traditions and material remains. Clothing, hairstyle, and housing are only a few of the signals that distinguish insiders from outsiders.

Ehrman, Bart D., Rodolphe Kasser, Marvin Meyer, and Gregor Wurst, eds.
2006   *The Gospel of Judas.* Washington, D.C.: National Geographic Society.

Eickelman, Dale F., and Piscatori, James, eds.
1990   *Muslim Travellers: Pilgrimage, Migration, and the Religious Imagination.* Comparative Studies on Muslim Societies 9. Berkeley: University of California Press.

Eilberg-Schwartz, Howard
1990   *The Savage in Judaism: An Anthropology of Israelite Religion and Ancient Judaism.* Bloomington: Indiana University Press.

Eliade, Mircea
1959   *The Sacred and the Profane: The Nature of Religion.* New York: Harcourt.

Elitsur, Yoel
2004   *Ancient Place Names in the Holy Land:
         Preservation and History*. Winona Lake, Ind.:
         Eisenbrauns.

Elliott, Mark
        *Biblical Interpretation Using Archeological
         Evidence 1900–1930*. Studies in the Bible and
         Early Christianity 51. Lewiston: Mellen.

n.d.   Bible and Interpretation. http://www.bible
         interp.com/

        Bible and Interpretation, edited by Mark W. Elliott,
        is dedicated to delivering the latest news, features,
        editorials, commentary, archaeological interpreta-
        tion and excavations relevant to the study of the
        Bible for the public and biblical scholars.

Elm, Susanna
1989   "Perceptions of Jerusalem Pilgrimage as
         Reflected in Two Early Sources on Female
         Pilgrimage (3rd and 4th Centuries AD)."
         Studia Patristica 20:219–23.

Emberling, G.
1997   "Ethnicity in Complex Society: Archaeologi-
         cal Perspectives." *Journal of Archaeological
         Research* 5:294–344.

Engelstad, Ericka
1991   "Images of Power and Contradiction: Femi-
         nist Theory and Post-processual Archaeol-
         ogy." *Antiquity* 65:502–14.

        Engelstad argues that archaeology, like many of
        the sciences, uses only masculine metaphors. The
        male archaeologist as hero explores and tames the
        mysteries of his female subject. Feminist theory has
        made important criticisms of positivist science on
        these grounds, drawing on much the same post-
        modern theory as post-processual archaeology.

Eusebius of Caesarea
1999   *Life of Constantine*. Introduction, translation,
         and commentary by A. Cameron and S. G.
         Hall. Oxford: Clarendon.

2003   *The Onomasticon by Eusebius of Caesarea:
         Palestine in the Fourth Century A.D.* Trans-
         lated by G. S. P. Freeman-Grenville. Edited
         by Rupert L. Chapman and Joan E. Taylor.
         Jerusalem: Carta.

Fagan, Brian
1975   *The Rape of the Nile: Tomb Robbers, Tour-
         ists and Archaeologists in Egypt*. New York:
         Charles Scribner's Sons.

Falconer, Steven F.
1995   "Rural Responses to Early Urbanism: Bronze
         Age Household and Village Economy at Tell
         el-Hayyat, Jordan." *Journal of Field Archaeol-
         ogy* 22:399–419.

        Temporal and spatial patterns of faunal, floral, and
        ceramic artifacts reveal several aspects of house-
        hold and village economy at Tell el-Hayyat ("Ruin
        of Snakes"). This modest village of some fifty acres
        and 100–150 inhabitants had six major settlement
        layers between 2100 and 1500 B.C.E.—the Middle
        Bronze period of intense urban development in
        southern Syria-Palestine. Existing ethnographic
        and historical data argue that village farmland dur-
        ing the period was owned by urban states, temples,
        or households. Artifacts from levels 3, 4, 5 (MB
        IIA–IIB) at Tell el-Hayyat (Jordan), however, suggest
        that farmland was owned by village households,
        and that independent villages like Tell el-Hayyat
        continued to thrive even during MB.

Falk, A.
1985   *Moshe Dayan, the Man and the Myth: A
         Psychoanalytic Biography*. Jerusalem: Cana.

        Falk understood that Dayan's claim of saving antiq-
        uities is paradoxical, and that "the fact that Israeli
        society was not able to limit the narcissistic great-
        ness complex of Moshe Dayan, and put an end to
        the attitude that he can do whatever he wants, is
        sad evidence to its lack of maturity at that time."

Faust, Avraham
2003   "Abandonment, Urbanization, Resettlement
         and the Formations of the Israelite State."
         Near Eastern Archaeology 66:147–61.

Bibliography

For Faust, none of the Iron I sites excavated to date continue to exist in the Iron II period. He proposed that the state established by David resettled villagers to larger villages or cities. The purpose of the program according to Faust is to socialize villagers to state life.

2006   *Israel's Ethnogenesis: Settlement, Interaction, Expansion and Resistance.* London: Equinox.

Faust, Avraham, and Shlomo Bunimovitz
2003   "The Four Room House: Embodying Iron Age Israelite Society." *Near Eastern Archaeology* 66: 22-31

Fazzini, Richard A., James F. Romano, and Madeleine E. Cody
1999   *Art for Eternity: Masterworks from Ancient Egypt.* Brooklyn: Brooklyn Museum of Art.

Feder, Kenneth L.
1990   *Frauds, Myths, and Mysteries: Science and Pseudoscience in Archaeology.* Mountain View, Calif.: Mayfield.

Feiler, Bruce
2001   *Walking the Bible: A Journey by Land through the Five Books of Moses.* New York: Morrow.

Journalist Bruce Feiler used a geographical outline to chart his reverse pilgrimage through the world of the Bible. This work was inspired not by his faith but rather by a search for his faith. With archaeologist Avner Goren, Feiler traveled Israel, Jordan, Turkey, Egypt, and the Palestinian territories, retracing the steps of Abraham, Moses, Aaron, and Jacob in the Torah. Goren was a reliable guide not only across the land but also through the biblical scholarship that he shares with Feiler. Feiler's interviews with archaeologists and ordinary people are fascinating.

His trek through the land clearly matures his understanding of how the land and its traditions developed. Near the end of his journal Feiler writes: "... this trip, this route, this dirt ... animates me. If that spirit is God, then I found God in the course of my journey. If that spirit is life, then I found life. If that spirit is awe, then I found awe.... I had gone to the land, I had encountered a spirit, and in so doing

I had become more human. That equation drew me back to one of the defining moments of the Pentateuch, Jacob's wrestling with the messenger of God in the valley of Jabbok.... At first Jacob doesn't know who the messenger is. They wrestle, they struggle, one seems to be winning, then the other, until finally Jacob is scarred. The scar, significantly, does not end up on Jacob's hand, nor on his head, his heart, or his eyes. Humans experience God ... not by touching him, imagining him, feeling him, or seeing him. Jacob is scarred on his leg, for the essential way humans experience God ... is by walking with him (Feiler 2001, 422).

Feinman, Peter Douglas
2004   *William Foxwell Albright and the Origins of Biblical Archaeology.* Berrien Springs, Mich.: Andrews University Press.

A dissertation and very detailed biography that mined published and unpublished papers, official records, stories, and anecdotes about W. F. Albright's childhood influences, from his birth in 1891 to his journey to Johns Hopkins in 1913. Feinman begins by introducing Albright in the context of biblical archaeology, then critically engages Albright's anecdotes about his childhood, studying the three that Albright claims put him on his life path: a book on archaeology that he purchased in Chile as a young boy, a collection of archaeology books that he purchased in Iowa, and his decision to apply to Johns Hopkins University.

Fellman, Jack
n.d.   "Eliezer Ben-Yehuda and the Revival of Hebrew (1858-1922)." http://www.jewish virtuallibrary.org/jsource/biography/ben_ yehuda.html.

Feulner, Mark A., and J. Barto Arnold III
2005   "Maritime Archaeology." In *Handbook of Archaeological Methods,* edited by Herbert D. G. Maschner and Christopher Chippindale, 1:270-305. 2 vols. Lanham, Md.: Rowman & Littlefield.

Finegan, Jack
1959   *Light from the Ancient Past: The Archeologi-*

cal Background of Judaism and Christianity. Princeton, N.J.: Princeton University Press.

Finkelstein, Israel

1996   "The Archaeology of the United Monarchy: An Alternate View." *Levant* 28:177–87.

1998   "Bible Archaeology or Archaeology of Palestine in the Iron Age? A Rejoinder." *Levant* 30:167–74.

2002   "The Philistines in the Bible: A Late-Monarchic Perspective." *Journal for the Study of the Old Testament* 27:131–67.

> Biblical traditions about the Philistines reflect little, if any, geography, culture, and history from the Iron I period (1200–1000 B.C.E.). The stories of the ark of the covenant may be an exception. The accounts of the *seranim* leaders, the five-city urban league, Goliath's armor, and the Cherethites and Pelethites in the Bible reflect the geography, culture, and history from the Twenty-Sixth Dynasty (664–525 B.C.E.) when pharaohs stationed in Philistia Greek and Syrian hoplites or infantry armed with spears who fought in phalanx formations from Caria, Ionia, Lydia, and Crete.

Finkelstein, Israel, and Amihai Mazar

2007   *The Quest for the Historical Israel: Debating Archaeology and the History of Early Israel.* Edited by Brian B. Schmidt. Society of Biblical Literature Archaeology and Biblical Studies 17. Atlanta: Society of Biblical Literature.

Finkelstein, Israel, and Neil Asher Silberman

2001   *The Bible Unearthed: Archaeology's New Vision of Ancient Israel and the Origin of Its Sacred Texts.* New York: Free Press.

> The Bible is an important artifact for understanding the ancient world, but it is not the decisive criterion by which other artifacts must be interpreted. Evidence for Abraham and Sarah, Isaac and Rebekah, Jacob, Leah, and Rachel; for the exodus from Egypt; for the conquest of Syria-Palestine, and for a state ruled by the household of David and Solomon is biblical but not archaeological. In fact, the archaeology, sociology, and history of the world of the Bible date these traditions to the days of Hezekiah

(715–687 B.C.E.) and Josiah (640–609 B.C.E.), not to 1000–925 B.C.E.

2006   *David and Solomon: In Search of the Bible's Sacred Kings and the Roots of the Western Tradition.* New York: Free Press.

> In the Bible, David is a shepherd, a warrior, and a divinely protected ruler. Solomon is a great builder, a wise judge, and a serene ruler of a vast empire. In archaeology, however, the world of David and Solomon is a modest hilltop village of farmers and herders. Finkelstein and Silberman describe how the stories of David and Solomon developed from such humble beginnings into the great traditions that shaped Western cultures in important ways

Firmage, Edwin

1992   "Zoology (Animal Profiles): Gazelle." In *The Anchor Bible Dictionary*, edited by David Noel Freedman, 6:1141–42. 6 vols. New York: Doubleday.

Firth, Susan

2003   "Spreading Word." *Pennsylvania Gazette*, January 5.

> Firth interviews Steve Tinney profiling the Pennsylvania Sumerian Dictionary Project and the University of Pennsylvania Museum of Archaeology and Anthropology.

Flam, Faye

2002   "Sumerian Dictionary to Decipher Ancient Texts." http://news.nationalgeographic.com/news/2002/07/0723_020724_cuneiform.html.

Fowler, Don D., Edward A. Jolie, and Marion W. Salter

2008   "Archaeological Ethics in Context and Practice." In *Handbook of Archaeological Theories*, edited by R. Alexander Bentley, Herbert D. G. Maschner, and Christopher Chippindale, 409–22. Lanham, Md.: Rowman & Littlefield.

Bibliography

Frahm, Eckart

2006   "Images of Assyria in Nineteenth- and
        Twentieth-Century Western Scholarship." In
        Orientalism, Assyriology and the Bible, edited
        by Steven W. Holloway, 74–94. Sheffield:
        Sheffield Phoenix.

        Frahm describes Assyria as a port of trade
        during the Old Assyrian period (2000–1500
        B.C.E.), a warrior state in the Late Bronze period
        (1500–1200 B.C.E.), and an empire during the Iron
        Age (1000–600 B.C.E.). Assyria was a culture that
        successfully reinvented itself again and again.
        Assyrian art is impressive and aesthetic. Assyrian
        politics created stability and prosperity. None-
        theless, to achieve the beauty of its art and the
        sophistication of political administration Assyria
        was obsessed with unparalleled violence in deeds,
        words, and images.

Franken, Hendricus Jacobus

1956   *The Birth of Civilization in the Near East.*
        Bloomington: Indiana University Press.

1988   *The Art and Architecture of the Ancient Ori-
        ent.* New York: Penguin.

1992   "Pottery." In *The Anchor Bible Dictionary,*
        edited by David Noel Freedman, 5:428–33. 6
        vols. New York: Doubleday.

Fraser, Michael

1994   "Egeria and the Fourth Century Liturgy of
        Jerusalem: A Select Bibliography." http://
        users.ox.ac.uk/~mikef/durham/egeria.html.

Frazer, James George

1906   *Adonis, Attis, Osiris: Studies in the History of
        Oriental Religion.* London: Macmillan.

1922   *The Golden Bough: A Study in Magic and
        Religion.* New York: Macmillan. http://www
        .bartleby.com/196/

        Frazer produced this monumental study in compar-
        ative folklore, magic, and religion to draw parallels
        between the rituals and myths of early cultures and
        those of Christianity. His work had a great impact
        on psychology and literature and remains an early
        classic in anthropology.

Freedman, David Noel, ed.

1992   *The Anchor Bible Dictionary.* 6 vols. New
        York: Doubleday.

Freedman, David Noel, and Jonas C. Greenfield

1969   *New Directions in Biblical Archaeology.* Gar-
        den City, N.Y.: Doubleday.

Freedman, David Noel, Robert B. MacDonald, and
        Daniel L. Mattson.

1975   *The Published Works of William Foxwell
        Albright: A Comprehensive Bibliography.*
        Cambridge, Mass.: American Schools of
        Oriental Research.

French, Elizabeth

2005   "Archaeologists's Wives as Travel Writers." In
        Women Travellers in the Near East, edited by
        Sarah Searight, 103–9. Oxford: Oxbow.

Frick, Frank S.

1992   "Palestine, Climate of." In *The Anchor Bible
        Dictionary,* edited by David Noel Freedman,
        5:119–26. 6 vols. New York: Doubleday.

Friedan, Betty

1963   *The Feminine Mystique.* New York: W. W.
        Norton.

Fritz, Volkmar

2006   "The Complex of Traditions in Judges 4 and
        5 and the Religion of Pre-state Israel." In *"I
        Will Speak the Riddles of Ancient Times":
        Archaeological and Historical Studies in
        Honor of Amihai Mazar on the Occasion of
        His Sixtieth Birthday,* edited by Aren M.
        Maeir and Pierre de Miroschedji, 1:689–98.
        2 vols. Winona Lake, Ind.: Eisenbrauns.

Fritz, Volkmar, and Philip R. Davies, eds.

1996   *The Origins of the Ancient Israelite States.*
        Journal for the Study of the Old Testament
        Supplement Series 228. Sheffield: JSOT Press.

Fritz and Davies offer an anthology of minimalist studies arguing that there is no hard evidence for a united monarchy ruled by David and Solomon in Israel between 1000 and 900 B.C.E.

Gadd, Cyril John, and Leon Legrain et al.

1928   *Ur Excavations: Texts, I Royal Inscriptions,* 5:256. London: British Museum and the Museum of the University of Pennsylvania.

Gallagher, Jan

2003   "An Extraordinary Everyday for Emar's Diviner." In *Life and Culture in the Ancient Near East,* edited by Richard E. Averbeck, Mark W. Chavalas, and David B. Weisberg, 171–84. Bethesda, Md.: CDL.

Galor, Katharina, Jean-Baptiste Humbert, and Jürgen Zangenberg, eds.

2006   *Qumran, The Site of the Dead Sea Scrolls: Archaeological Interpretations and Debates (Proceedings of a Conference Held at Brown University, November 17–19, 2002).* Studies on the Text of the Desert of Judah, 57. Leiden: Brill.

Fifteen papers presented in 2002 at Brown University provide the necessary data to break new ground in the recent debate about the character of Qumran. Part 1 discusses material from old and new excavations that help assess the validity of the traditional Qumran-Essene hypothesis. Part 2 discusses various aspects of the main settlement such as division of space, the character of period III, the date of the cave scroll deposits, and the use of food. Part 3 deals with the Qumran cemetery and a similar graveyard at Khirbet Qazone. Part 4 places Qumran into a wider regional context, concentrating on local agriculture and ceramic production. The articles strongly call for a new awareness of archaeological detail and, in their various ways, instigate a renewed debate about how to bring texts and material culture into a meaningful dialogue.

Gambino, Megan

2007   "Underwater World: New Evidence Reveals a City Beneath Ancient Alexandria."

http://www.smithsonianmag.com/history-archaeology/rhakotis.html.

Historians have generally agreed that Rhakotis—a fishing village or a walled city—existed at Alexandria before Alexander. Daniel Stanley of the Smithsonian Institution's National Museum of Natural History now has found artifacts of that forgotten city that existed seven hundred years before Alexander the Great founded Alexandria as part of his efforts to conquer the known world.

Gardiner, Alan H.

1957   *Egyptian Grammar: Being an Introduction to the Study of Heiroglyphs.* London: Oxford University Press.

Garr, W. Randall

1985   *Dialect Geography of Syria-Palestine, 1000–586 B.C.E.* Philadelphia: University of Pennsylvania Press.

Garr discusses the unusual ways in which the letters in the Annals of Mesha are written, and argues that the Moabite language and the Hebrew language are closely related.

Garrod, Dorothy Anne

1957   *The Natufian Culture: The Life and Economy of a Mesolithic People in the Near East.* London: British Academy.

Gelb, Ignace J.

1952   *A Study of Writing.* Chicago: University of Chicago Press.

Although writing systems have been studied for centuries by linguists, Gelb is widely regarded as the first scientific practitioner of the study of scripts; he coined the term "grammatology" to refer to the study of writing systems. In *A Study of Writing* he suggests that scripts evolve in a single direction, from words to syllables to letters. This historical typology has been criticized as overly simplistic, forcing the data to fit the model and ignoring exceptional cases. Yet, despite the refinements of Daniels (1996) and others, Gelb's rigorous study of the properties of different kinds of writing system was pioneering and innovative.

Bibliography

Gennep, Arnold van

1909/ *Rites of Passage.* Chicago: University of
1960   Chicago.

1974   "Arnold Van Gennep on the Rites of Passage."
        In *Frontiers of Anthropology,* edited by A.
        Monatu, 315–19. New York: G. P. Putnam's
        Sons.

Germond, Philippe

2005   *The Symbolic World of Egyptian Amulets from
        the Jacques-Edouard Berger Collection.* Milan:
        5 Continents.

Geus, C. H. J. De

1975   "The Importance of Archaeological Research
        into the Palestinian Agricultural Terraces,
        with an Excursus on the Hebrew Word *gbi.*"
        Palestine Exploration Quarterly 107:65–74.

Giddens, Anthony

1986   *The Constitution of Society: Outline of the
        Theory of Structuration.* Berkeley: University
        of California Press.

Gilchrist, R.

1999   *Gender and Archaeology: Contesting the Past.*
        New York: Routledge.

Gillispie, Charles Coulston, and Michel Dewachter,
    eds.

1987   *Monuments of Egypt, the Napoleonic Edi-
        tion: The Complete Archaeological Plates from
        la Description de l'Egypte.* Princeton, N.J.:
        Princeton Architectural Press in Association
        with the Architectural League of New York,
        the J. Paul Getty Trust.

Girard, René

1972   *Violence and the Sacred.* Baltimore: Johns
        Hopkins University Press.

        Girard studies human sacrifice in western Mediter-
        ranean cultures, and argues that sacrifice is a
        strategy for controlling aggression or competition,
        which consistently threatens to destroy human
        communities. Human sacrifice focuses this aggres-
        sion on a single member of the community. By
        sacrificing one human being, the community vents
        its hostility, thereby protecting other members.
        Once the victims are dead, they are often deified,
        as an act of restitution. The portion served to each
        household during the meal following the sacrifice
        reestablishes the social structure that was threat-
        ened by the violence neutralized by the sacrifice.

Gitin, Seymour

1990   "Ekron of the Philistines: Part II, Olive-Oil
        Suppliers to the World." *Biblical Archaeology
        Review* 16:32–42, 59.

        For Gitin, Tel Miqne was settled before the found-
        ing of Philistine Ekron at the beginning of the Iron
        Age. The urban center of Ekron evolved through
        a four-stage process of growth, contraction,
        regeneration and partial abandonment, reflecting
        its changing role as a border city on the frontier
        separating Philistia and Judah. The material culture
        of the Philistine coastal tradition was maintained
        throughout Ekron's six-hundred-year tradition.

2004   "The Philistines: Neighbors of the Canaan-
        ites, Phoenicians and Israelites." In *One
        Hundred Years of American Archaeology in
        the Middle East: Proceedings of the Ameri-
        can Schools of Oriental Research Centennial
        Celebration, Washington, DC, April 2000,*
        edited by Douglas R. Clark and Victor H.
        Matthews, 57–85. Boston: American Schools
        of Oriental Research.

Gittlen, Barry M., ed.

2002   *Sacred Time, Sacred Place: Archaeology and
        the Religion of Israel.* Winona Lake, Ind.:
        Eisenbrauns.

Glassner, Jean-Jacques

2003   *The Invention of Cuneiform: Writing in
        Sumer.* Baltimore: Johns Hopkins University
        Press.

        For Glassner, cuneiform writing was invented not
        as a recording device or to link symbols with the
        objects they represent but as a tool for recording
        spoken Sumerian.

Glock, Albert E.

1999a "Archaeology as Cultural Survival: The Future of the Palestinian Past." In *Archaeology, History and Culture in Palestine and the Near East: Essays in Memory of Albert E. Glock,* edited by Tomis Kapitan, 302–23. ASOR Books 3. Atlanta: Scholars Press.

1999b "Cultural Bias in Archaeology." In *Archaeology, History and Culture in Palestine and the Near East: Essays in Memory of Albert E. Glock,* edited by Tomis Kapitan, 324–42. ASOR Books 3. Atlanta: Scholars Press.

Godlewska, Anne

1999 *Geography Unbound: French Geographic Science from Cassini to Humboldt.* Chicago: University of Chicago Press.

At the end of the eighteenth century, French geographers faced a crisis. Though they had previously been ranked among the most highly regarded scientists in Europe, they suddenly found themselves directionless and disrespected because they were unable to adapt their descriptive focus easily to the new emphasis on theory and explanation that was sweeping through other disciplines. Godlewska examines this crisis, the often conservative reactions of geographers to it, and the work of researchers at the margins of the field who helped chart its future course. She tells her story partly through the lives and careers of individuals, from the deposed cabinet geographer Cassini IV to Volney, von Humboldt, and Letronne, who were innovators in human, physical, and historical geography, and partly through the institutions with which they were associated such as the *Encyclopédie de Geographie* (1995) and the Jesuit and military colleges. She presents an insightful portrait of a crucial period in the development of modern geography, whose unstable disciplinary status is still very much an issue today.

Golb, Norman

1980 "The Problem of Origin and Identification of the Dead Sea Scrolls." *Proceedings of the American Philosophical Society* 124:1-24.

Golb proposes an alternative to the Qumran-Essene hypothesis of Roland de Vaux, who concluded that the Dead Sea Scrolls were copied and stored by the Essene community that lived at Khirbet Qumran. Golb argues that the scrolls are from the libraries of various communities in Jerusalem, who hid them in the caves around Qumran when war between Judah and Rome was imminent, but that the Qumran community had nothing directly to do with the Dead Sea Scrolls.

1985 "Who Hid the Dead Sea Scrolls?" *Biblical Archaeologist* 48:68–82.

1995 *Who Wrote the Dead Sea Scrolls: The Search for the Secret of Qumran?* New York: Scribner.

Gong, Y., J. Hodgson, M. G. Lambert, and I. L. Gordon

1996 "Short-term Ingestive Behaviour of Sheep and Goats Grazing Grasses and Legumes." *New Zealand Journal of Agricultural Research* 39:63–73.

Goodman, Susan

1985 *Gertrude Bell.* Berg Women's Series. Dover, N.H.: Berg.

Gottwald, Norman K.

1979 *The Tribes of Yahweh: A Sociology of the Religion of Liberated Israel 1250–1050 B.C.E.* Maryknoll, N.Y.: Orbis Books.

Gould, Richard A.

2000 *Archaeology and the Social History of Ships.* Cambridge/New York: Cambridge University Press.

Gould writes a comprehensive treatment of underwater archaeology that examines the impact of new undersea technologies and the destructive effects of treasure hunting. Maritime archaeology deals with shipwrecks and is carried out by divers rather than diggers. Marine archaeologists study maritime history, changes in shipbuilding, navigation, the infrastructure of waterborne commerce, and offer fresh perspectives on the cultures and societies that produced the ships and sailors.

Grabbe, Lester L.

2001 "Sup-urbs or Only Hup-urbs? Prophets and

Bibliography

Populations in Ancient Israel and Socio-historical Method." In *"Every City Shall Be Forsaken": Urbanism and Prophecy in Ancient Israel and the Near East,* edited by Lester L. Grabbe and Robert D. Haak. Journal for the Study of the Old Testament Supplement Series 330. Sheffield: Sheffield Academic Press.

2003, ed. *"Like a Bird in a Cage": The Invasion of Sennacherib in 701 B.C.E.* Journal for the Study of the Old Testament Supplement Series 363. London/New York: Sheffield Academic Press.

> The European Seminar on Methodology in Israel's history has spent a number of years debating historical method. *"Like a Bird in a Cage"* is a case study on the history of Sennacherib's invasion of Judah in 701 B.C.E. Using archaeology, biblical studies, Assyriology, and Egyptology, the contributors describe various methods for reconstructing an accurate history of ancient Israel.

2007 *Ancient Israel: What Do We Know and How Do We Know It?* London/New York: T&T Clark.

> Grabbe surveys methods of reconstructing the history of Israel and reviews the archaeological and written artifacts sources from, provides an analysis of the issues in, and outlines a synthesis for Middle–Late Bronze periods (2000–1300 B.C.E.); Late Bronze II–Iron IIA periods (1300–900 B.C.E.); Iron IIB period (900–720 B.C.E.); and the Iron IIC period (720–539 B.C.E.). He also offers syntheses and analyses on the place of the social sciences, the use of archaeology, the *longue durée*, ethnicity, ideology and neo-fundamentalism, maximalists–minimalists and the ad hominem argument, and describes the six principles of his own historical method.

Granqvist, Hilma Natalia
1947 *Birth and Childhood among the Arabs: Studies in a Muhammadan Village in Palestine.* Helsinki: Söderström.

Green, Thomas J.
2008 "Cultural Resource Management." In *Handbook of Archaeological Theories,* edited by R. Alexander Bentley, Herbert D. G. Maschner, and Christopher Chippindale, 375–94. Lanham, Md.: Rowman & Littlefield.

Greenberg, Raphael
2006 "What's Cooking in Early Bronze Age II?" In *"I Will Speak the Riddles of Ancient Times": Archaeological and Historical Studies in Honor of Amihai Mazar on the Occasion of His Sixtieth Birthday,* edited by Aren M. Maeir and Pierre de Miroschedji, 1:39–48. Winona Lake, Ind.: Eisenbrauns.

Gruber, Mayer I.
1989 "Breast-Feeding Practices in Biblical Israel and in Old Babylonian Mesopotamia." *Journal of the Ancient Near Eastern Society* 19:61–83.

> Gruber explains how breast-feeding may delay the return of ovulation after birth. If Hebrew women nursed for three years, they would have carried only four children to term. Of these four only two lived to become adults.

Haarlem, Willem M. van
1992 "A Functional Analysis of Ancient Egyptian Amulets." *Sesto Congresso Internazionale di egittologia* 1:237–40.

Habricht, J. P., J. Davanzo, W. P. Butz, and L. Meyers
1985 "The Contraceptive Role of Breast Feeding." *Population Studies* 39:213–32.

Hallo, William W.
1964 "The Slandered Bride." In *Studies from the Workshop of the Chicago Assyrian Dictionary Presented to A. Leo Oppenheim, June 7, 1964,* 95–105. Chicago: Oriental Institute of the University of Chicago.

> A study of a cuneiform tablet that preserves the transcript of the trial of The Slandered Bride (UET 5:256) (*Babylonian Expedition of the University of Pennsylvania, Series A: Cunieform Texts* [BE], edited by H. V. Hilprecht 1893-1914, 6/2:58; C. J. Gadd, L. Legrain et al., *Ur Excavations, Texts: I Royal Inscriptions* [UET] 1928, 5:256; Hallo and Younger 2003,

3:199). This trial is significant for the understanding of both ancient Near Eastern legal systems in general, and legal systems in ancient Israel in particular.

Hallo, William W., and K. Lawson Younger, eds.
2003   *The Context of Scripture.* 3 vols. Leiden: Brill.

Hallo and Younger edit three volumes of canonical, monumental, and archival traditions from the world of the Bible set in their original geographical, historical, religious, political, and literary contexts with introductions and bibliographies.

Hallote, Rachel
2006   *Bible, Map and Spade: The American Palestine Exploration Society, Frederick Jones Bliss and the Forgotten Story of Early American Biblical Archaeology.* Piscataway, N.J.: Gorgias.

Rachel Hallote combines both politics and biography to study the American Palestine Exploration Society sponsored by Syrian Protestant College, now the American University of Beirut, and the work of Frederick J. Bliss (1859–1937) and other pioneering American archaeologists and their political agendas during the years 1850–1900. Because Bliss worked for the British Palestine Exploration Fund for a decade, many scholars downplayed his American nationality and sensibilities, as well as his achievements as an archaeologist.

Halpern, Baruch
1978   "The Rise of Abimelek ben-Jerubaal." *Hebrew Annual Review* 2:79–100.

Hanson, K. C.
       HomePage, http://www.kchanson.com.

Hardin, James W.
2004   "Understanding Domestic Space: An Example from Iron Age Tel Halif." *Near Eastern Archaeology* 67:71–83.

Harmanoah, Omor
2007   "Upright Stones and Building Narratives: Formation of a Shared Architectural Practice in the Ancient Near East." In *Ancient Near Eastern Art in Context: Studies in Honor of Irene J. Winter by Her Students,* edited by Jack Cheng and Marian Feldman, 67–98. *Culture and History of the Ancient Near East* 26. Leiden: Brill.

Hasel, Michael G.
1994   "Israel in the Merneptah Stela." *Bulletin of the American Schools of Oriental Research* 296:45–61.

Hasel is an Egyptologist who completed his dissertation ("Domination and Resistance: Egyptian Military Activity in the Southern Levant, 1300–1185 BC") in 1996 at the University of Arizona with William G. Dever and Richard H. Wilkinson. He studies Late Bronze Age interaction of Syria-Palestine and Egypt with the eastern Mediterranean and has excavated at Idalion (Cyprus); Ashkelon, Dor, Gezer, Masada, Hazor (Israel); and at Jalul (Jordan). He is currently Director of the Institute of Archaeology, Curator of the Lynn H. Wood Archaeological Museum, and Professor of Near Eastern Studies and Archaeology at Southern Adventist University.

2003   "Merenptah's Inscription and Reliefs and the Origin of Israel." In *The Near East in the Southwest: Essays in Honor of William G. Dever,* edited by Beth Alpert Nakhai, 19–44. Annual of the American Schools of Oriental Research 58. Boston: American Schools of Oriental Research.

Hasel argues against the interpretation of the Merenptah Inscription by Anson F. Rainey (Rainey 2001). Rainey says that the word "seed" refers to the "people" of Israel; Hasel says it refers to their "crops." Rainey considers Israel to be a city; Hasel considers Israel to be villages of farmers and herders.

Hattem, Willem C. van
1981   "Once Again: Sodom and Gomorrah." *Biblical Archaeologist* 44:87–92.

Hays-Gilpin, Kelley
2000   "Feminist Scholarship in Archaeology."

Bibliography

Annals of the American Academy of Political and Social Science 571:89–106.

Hays-Gilpin explores the history of women and feminism in archaeology, examines a few of the central issues addressed by feminist and gender-oriented archaeologists, briefly addresses equity issues for women archaeologists, and identifies some future directions.

2008   "Gender." In *Handbook of Archaeological Theories:* edited by R. Alexander Bentley, Herbert D. G. Maschner, and Christopher Chippindale, 335–50. Lanham, Md.: Rowman & Littlefield.

Hays-Gilpin, Kelley, and David S. Whitley, eds.
1998   *Reader in Gender Archaeology.* New York: Routledge.

Heider, George C.
1985   *The Cult of Molek: A Reassessment.* Journal for the Study of the Old Testament Supplement Series 43. Sheffield: JSOT Press.

Heider does a comparative study on child sacrifice.

Helms, Svend W., and A. Betts
1987   "The Desert 'Kites' of the Badiyat esh-Sham and Northern Arabia." *Paleorient* 13:41–67.

Helms and Betts analyze the relationship between kite corrals and hunting on the vast treeless plains of the basalt rich region of Badiyat esh-Sham (Jordan) during the Neolithic and later periods. Before this study these extensive stone structures were reported only in the journals of travelers.

Henige, David
2006   "A War of Pots and Kettles: The Dubious Discourse of W. G. Dever." *Scandinavian Journal of the Old Testament* 20:77–95.

Hernandez, Miguel
"Stature Estimation in Extinct Aonikenk and the Myth of Patagonian Gigantism." http://www3.interscience.wiley.com/cgi-bin/abstract/28170/.

Herodotus
1987   *The History.* Translated by David Grene. Chicago : University of Chicago Press.

Herr, Larry G., and Douglas R. Clark
2001   "Excavating the Tribe of Reuben." *Biblical Archaeology Review* 27:36–47, 64, 66.

Herscher, Ellen
1999   "International Control Efforts: Are There Any Good Solutions?" In *The Ethics of Collecting Cultural Property: Whose Culture? Whose Property?* edited by Phyllis Mauch Messenger, 117–28. Albuquerque: University of New Mexico Press.

Hess, Richard S.
2007   *Israelite Religions: An Archaeological and Biblical Survey.* Grand Rapids: Baker.

Hess reviews archaeological evidence from Syria-Palestine and Egypt to argue that archaeology has no universal principles for understanding the meaning of religion and the way it functions in cultures. Consequently, contemporary worldviews unduly influence how archaeologists understand the religion of ancient Israel.

Hilprecht, H. V.
1893   *Babylonian Expedition of the University of Pennsylvania, Series A: Cunieform Texts* [BE], *1893–1914* 6/2:58.

Hirschfeld, Yizhar
2004   *Qumran in Context: Reassessing the Archaeological Evidence.* Peabody: Hendrickson.

Hirschfeld challenges the Qumran-Essene hypothesis of Roland de Vaux and Jodi Magness and interprets Khirbet Qumran as a country house of a wealthy Herodian household. For him, the Dead Sea Scrolls were not copied and stored by a Jewish monastic community but removed from Jerusalem to the caves around Qumran for safekeeping during the first war between Judah and Rome.

Hobson, Christine

1987   *The World of the Pharaohs: A Complete Guide to Ancient Egypt.* London: Thames & Hudson.

Hobson introduces the men and women connected with origins of archaeology in Egypt. Anecdotes about these pioneers appear throughout the book. The most famous—Belzoni, Lepsius, and Flinders Petrie—are profiled, but also the less famous—Hans Sloan, James Bruce, Lady Lucie Duff-Gordon, and Amice Calverly. There is no description of the contributions of North American scholars like James H. Breasted and his successors at the Oriental Institute (University of Chicago).

Hodder, Ian

1985   *Symbols in Action: Ethnoarchaeological Studies of Material Culture.* New York: Cambridge University Press.

1991   "Postprocessual Archaeology and the Current Debate." In *Processual and Postprocessual Archaeologies: Multiple Ways of Knowing the Past,* edited by Robert Preucel, 30–41. Occasional Paper 10. Carbondale, Ill.: Center for Archaeological Investigations, Southern Illinois University.

1995,   *Interpreting Archaeology: Finding Meaning in*
ed.   *the Past.* New York: Routledge.

2001,   *Archaeological Theory Today.* Oxford: Polity.
ed.

Hodder, Ian, and Scott Hutson

2003   *Reading the Past: Current Approaches to Interpretation in Archaeology.* 3rd ed. Cambridge: Cambridge University Press.

In their classic introduction to archaeological theory and method, Hodder and Hutson argue that archaeologists must bring to bear a variety of perspectives in the complex and uncertain task of constructing meaning from the past. While remaining centered on the importance of hermeneutics, agency, and history, they explore cutting-edge developments in areas such as post-structuralism, neo-evolutionary theory, and new branches of theory such as phenomenology, feminist archaeology, cultural history, and theories of discourse and signs.

Hodges, Henry

1970   *Technology in the Ancient World.* New York: Barnes & Noble.

Hodgson, William Brown

"Biographical Sketch of Mohammed Ali, Pasha of Egypt, Syria, and Arabia. http://www.sunnah.org/history/mhdalip.htm.

Hoerth, Alfred J.

2009   *Archaeology and the Old Testament.* Grand Rapids: Baker.

Hoffmeier, James K.

1997   *Israel in Egypt: The Evidence for the Authenticity of the Exodus Tradition.* New York: Oxford University Press.

The full argument for the summary article in *Biblical Archaeology Review* 33 (2006):10–41, 77. Dedicated to Kenneth A. Kitchen (*On the Reliability of the Old Testament* [2003]) and with cover praise from Anson F. Rainey, Hoffmeier shares Kitchen's and Rainey's conviction that biblical traditions are historically reliable.

2003   "Everyday Life in Ancient Egypt." In *Life and Culture in the Ancient Near East,* edited by Richard E. Averbeck, Mark W. Chavalas, and David B. Weisberg, 327–54. Bethesda, Md.: CDL.

2004   "The North Sinai Archaeological Project's Excavations at Tell el-Borg (Sinai): An Example of the 'New' Biblical Archaeology?" In *The Future of Biblical Archaeology: Reassessing Methodologies and Assumptions. The Proceedings of a Symposium, August 12–14, 2001, at Trinity International University,* edited by James K. Hoffmeier and Alan Millard, 53–66. Grand Rapids: Eerdmans.

2005   *Ancient Israel in Sinai: The Evidence for the Authenticity of the Wilderness Tradition.* New York: Oxford University Press.

Bibliography

2007a "Rameses of the Exodus Narratives Is the 13th Century B.C. Royal Ramesside Residence." *Trinity Journal* 28 n.s.:281–89.

2007b "What Is the Biblical Date for the Exodus? A Response to Bryant Wood." *Journal of the Evangelical Theological Society* 50:225–47.

2007c "Out of Egypt: The Archaeological Context of the Exodus." *Biblical Archaeology Review* 33:30–41, 77.

> Hoffmeier argues for the identification of the El Ballah Lakes as the Sea of Reeds and proposes a route for the exodus south from Avaris (Tell el-Daba) to Succoth (Tell el-Maskhuta), then north along the east coast of El Ballah Lakes crossing just south of the Way of Horus and the forts at Tell el Borg, Tel Hebua, and Migdol.

2008 *The Archaeology of the Bible.* Oxford: Lion Hudson.

> Beginning with Genesis and the origins of the world Hoffmeier follows the Bible narrative through to the early churches of the book of Revelation. His book is divided into three sections—two of which cover the Old Testament and one covers the New Testament—and is interspersed with stories from his own experience as an archaeologist.

Hoffmeier, James K., and Alan Millard, eds.

2004 *The Future of Biblical Archaeology: Reassessing Methodologies and Assumptions. The Proceedings of a Symposium, August 12–14, 2001, at Trinity International University.* Grand Rapids: Eerdmans.

> Hoffmeier and Millard edit an anthology of papers by archaeologists from the North Sinai Archaeological Project who want to redefine biblical archaeology in the aftermath of the minimalist–maximalist debate and the schism between Assyriology and biblical studies.

Hoffner, H. A.

2003 "Daily Life among the Hittites." In *Life and Culture in the Ancient Near East,* edited by Richard E. Averbeck, Mark W. Chavalas, and David B. Weisberg, 95–120. Bethesda, Md.: CDL.

Hole, Frank Arnold

1995 "Assessing the Past through Anthropological Archaeology." In *Civilizations of the Ancient Near East,* edited by Jack M. Sasson, 4:2715–27. New York: Charles Scribner's Sons.

Holladay, John S.

1990 "Red Slip, Burnish, and the Solomonic Gateway at Gezer." *Bulletin of the American Schools of Oriental Research* 277–278:23–70.

> For Holladay, polishing or burnishing red slips on pottery is a signature of a cultural change during the Iron Age in Syria-Palestine. Just when this technological change took place and what kind of cultural evolution it represents is a matter of dispute. The excavation of the gate at Gezer, however, clearly suggests that burnished red slip pottery is the signature of state culture in Iron II Syria-Palestine.

1998 "The Kingdoms of Israel and Judah: Political and Economic Centralization in the Iron IIA-B." In *The Archaeology of Society in the Holy Land,* edited by Thomas Evan Levy, 369–98. London: Leicester University.

> Holladay offers a maximalist analysis of archaeological data for the state of Israel between 1000 and 900 B.C.E.

Holloway, Steven W.

2002 *Assur Is King! Assur Is King! Religion in the Exercise of Power in the Neo-Assyrian Empire.* Culture and History of the Ancient Near East 10. Leiden/Boston: Brill.

Holum, Kenneth G.

1990 "Hadrian and St. Helena: Imperial Travel and the Origins of Christian Holy Land Pilgrimage." In *The Blessings of Pilgrimage,* edited by R. Ousterhout. Urbana: University of Illinois Press.

2004 "Caesarea's Temple Hill: The Archaeology of Sacred Space in an Ancient Mediterranean City." *Near Eastern Archaeology* 67:184–99.

Archaeological history of the Temple Platform at Caesarea Maritima: (1) Temple to Augustus and Roma (22 B.C.E.–350 C.E.); (2) vacant (400–470); (3) intermediate commercial or residential building (470–490; (4) octagonal martyr church dedicated to St. Cornelius the Centurion (470–640); (5) mosque (640–1101); (6) Church of St. Peter and great vaulted Crusader Halls (1101–1264); (7) villas of wealthy Bosnian refugees (1884–1948).

Homan, Michael M.
2004   "Beer, Barley, and *sekar* in the Hebrew Bible." In *Le-David Maskil: A Birthday Tribute for David Noel Freedman,* edited by Richard Elliott Friedman and William H. C. Propp, 25–38. Biblical and Judaic Studies from the University of California, San Diego, 9. Winona Lake, Ind.: Eisenbrauns.

Hoover, Marleen
        "Art History Survey I." www.accd.edu/.../arts1303/Neolith1.htm.

Hopkins, David C.
1985   *The Highlands of Canaan: Agricultural Life in the Early Iron Age.* Sheffield: Almond.

Hoppe, Leslie J.
2007   "Taking a Second Look: New Excavations at Hazor." *The Bible Today* November/December:378–83.

Horn, Siegfried H.
1986   "Why the Moabite Stone Was Blown to Pieces: Ninth-century B.C. Inscription Adds New Dimension to Biblical Account of Mesha's Rebellion." *Biblical Archaeology Review* (May-June): 50-61.

Hornung, Erik, and Betsy M. Bryan, eds.
2002   *The Quest for Immortality: Treasures of Ancient Egypt.* Washington, D.C.: National Gallery of Art.

Horowitz, W.
2000   "Two Late Bronze Age Tablets from Hazor." *Israel Exploration Journal* 50:16–28.

Horowitz, W., and T. Oshima
2000   "Two More Cuneiform Finds from Hazor." *Israel Exploration Journal* 52:179–86.

Howard, Calvin D.
1999   "Amorphous Silica, Soil Solutions, and Archaeological Flint Gloss." *North American Archaeologist* 20:209–15.

        Natural chemical processes in soils produce glossy conditions on artifacts of flint and chert that mimic, modify, or destroy ancient use-wear traces, thus making affected artifacts difficult or unacceptable for microwear studies. These glosses include general gloss patina or soil sheen, and intensely brilliant specular spots. The information presented suggests that this enigmatic "bright spot" phenomenon is the result of deposition and solidification of silica gel precipitated from soil colloids in the artifacts in situ environment and should not be confused with ancient use-wear evidence.

Howard, Kathleen, ed.
1986   *Treasures of the Holy Land: Ancient Art from the Israel Museum.* New York: Metropolitan Museum.

Howell, Georgina
2006   *Daughter of the Desert.* New York: Macmillan.

Hunt, Alice Wells
2005   "Bringing Dialogue from Cacophony: Can Bakhtin Speak to Biblical Historiography?" *Perspectives in Religious Studies* 32:325–37.

Hunt, E. D.
1982   *Holy Land Pilgrimage in the Later Roman Empire A.D. 312–460.* Oxford: Clarendon.

Ibn Batuta
1986   *Travels in Asia and Africa, 1325–1354.*

Bibliography

Translated by H. A. R. Gibb. New Delhi: Manshiram Manoharlal.

Institute of Nautical Archaeology
Bronze Age Shipwreck Excavation at Cape Gelidonya, 1960 http://ina.tamu.edu/capegelidonya.htm.

Bronze Age Shipwreck Excavation at Uluburun, 1984-1994 http://ina.tamu.edu/ub_main.htm.

Isbouts, Jean-Pierre
2007   *The Biblical World: An Illustrated Atlas.* Washington D.C.: National Geographic.

Isbouts creates a popular, illustrated reconstruction of the world of the Bible including maps and timelines. Chapters summarize the Bible, place the tradition in a particular historical period and include finds from geography, archaeology, and literary criticism. Sidebars highlight daily life, such as marriage, childbirth, food supply, dress, trade, language, art, and burial practices.

Ishida, Hideto
2002   "Insight into Ancient Egyptian Beer Brewing Using Current Folkloristic Methods." *Master Brewers Association of the Americas Tech Quarterly* 39:81–88.

Isserlin, B. S. J.
2001   *The Israelites.* Minneapolis: Fortress.

Jackson, Kent P.
1989   "The Language of the Mesha Inscription." In *Studies in the Mesha Inscription and Moab,* edited by J. Andrew Dearman, 96–130. Archaeology and Biblical Studies 2; Atlanta: Scholars Press.

Jackson argues that Moabite and Hebrew are more closely related to Hebrew than Garr (1985) proposed. He also offers a basic grammar of Moabite and a brief survey of other Moabite inscriptions.

Jacobs, Paul, and Christopher Holland
2007   "Sharing Archaeological Data: The Distributed Archive Method." *Near Eastern Archaeology* 70:197–201.

Jacobs and Holland discuss copyright and fair use, the need to provide incentives for archaeologists to share their data, and the best methods for achieving uniformity in data archiving.

Jakobson, Roman, and Morris Halle
1980   *Fundamentals of Language.* New York: Mouton.

Jamieson-Drake, David W.
1991   *Scribes and Schools in Monarchic Judah: A Socio-archeological Approach.* Journal for the Study of the Old Testament Supplement Series 109. Sheffield: Almond.

1997   "Historical Archaeology." In *Oxford Encyclopedia of Archaeology in the Near East,* edited by Eric M. Meyers, 3:28–30. New York: Oxford University Press.

Historical Archaeology is a partnership between archaeology and history, rather than history and anthropology, and places a priority on the role of writings in the interpretation of material remains.

Janzen, J. Gerald
1987   "A Certain Women in the Rhetoric of Judges 9." *Journal for the Study of the Old Testament* 38:35.

Jensen, M. D., R. C. Benson, and I. M. Bobak
1977   *Maternity Care, the Nurse and the Family.* St Louis. C. V. Mosby.

Joffe, Alexander H.
2006   "The Rise of Secondary States in the Iron Age Levant: Archeological and Historical Considerations." In *Excavating Asian History: Interdisciplinary Studies in Archaeology and History,* edited by Norman Yoffee and Bradley L. Crowell, 67–112. Tucson: University of Arizona Press.

Johnson, Amber L., ed.

2004   *Processual Archaeology: Exploring Analytical Strategies, Frames of Reference and Culture Process.* Westport, Conn.: Praeger.

Johnson, Matthew

1999   *Archaeological Theory: An Introduction.* Oxford: Blackwell.

Johnson introduces each of the contemporary theories of archaeology, and describes the historical context where each developed.

Johnston, R. H.

1974   "The Biblical Potter." *Biblical Archaeologist* 37:86–106.

Building on the work of Matson (1965), Johnston uses ethnoarchaeology—studying the techniques used by the potters of Cyprus and other sites in the Middle East today—to better understand the mechanics of pottery making in the world of the Bible. He worked for four seasons with G. Ernest Wright at Idalion, Bab-edh-Dhra, and Shechem.

Jordan, Brigitte

1983   *Birth in Four Cultures: A Cross-cultural Investigation of Childbirth in Yucatan, Holland, Sweden, and the United States.* Montreal: Eden.

Josephus, Flavius

2000   *Flavius Josephus: Translation and Commentary.* Edited by Steve Mason and Louis H. Feldman. Leiden: Brill. http://members.aol .com/FLJOSEPHUS/home.htm

Kahane, P. P.

1965   *The Bible in Archaeology.* Jerusalem: Israel Museum.

Kansa, Sarah Whitcher, Eric C. Kansa, and Jason M. Schultz

2007   "Open Context, Data Sharing, and Archaeology." *Near Eastern Archaeology* 70:188–94.

Kansa, Kansa, and Schultz discuss the benefits and challenges of data sharing in archaeology. Open Context is a free, open-access resource for the electronic publication of primary field research from archaeology and related disciplines.

Kapitan, Tomis, ed.

1999   *Archaeology, History and Culture in Palestine and the Near East: Essays in Memory of Albert E. Glock.* ASOR Books 3. Atlanta: Scholars Press.

Karmon, Y.

1960   "An Analysis of Jacotin's Map of Palestine." *Israel Exploration Journal* 10:155–73, 244–53.

Keefe, Alice A.

2001   *Woman's Body and the Social Body of Hosea.* Journal for the Study of the Old Testament Supplement Series 338; Gender, Culture, History 10; New York: Sheffield Academic Press.

Keller, Werner

1955   *The Bible as History: A Confirmation of the Book of Books.* Translated by William Neil. New York: William Morrow.

Kemp, Barry J.

1989   *Ancient Egypt: Anatomy of a Civilization.* London: Routledge.

Kemp includes a discussion of the administration of baking and bread as rations.

Kenyon, Kathleen M.

1952   *Beginning in Archaeology.* New York: Praeger.

1957   *Samaria Sebaste III: The Objects.* London: Palestine Exploration Fund.

1960   *Archaeology in the Holy Land. Nashville:* Thomas Nelson.

1971   *Royal Cities of the Old Testament.* New York: Shocken.

Bibliography

Kenyon, Kathleen M., and P. R. S. Moorey
1987   *The Bible and Recent Archaeology.* Atlanta: John Knox.

> Kathleen M. Kenyon (1906–1978) published *The Bible and Recent Archaeology* (1978) shortly before her death. P. Roger Moorey (1937–2004) issued a revised edition of these short essays in 1987. The book follows the archaeological calendar for the Bronze Age to Roman period. Moore accepts the arguments of Frank Yurco (Field Museum of Natural History, Chicago) that a battle scene on the walls of a Karnak temple depicts the campaign described in the Annals of Merneptah, rather than the Annals of Ramses II (*Journal of the American Research Center in Egypt* 23[1986]:189–215).

Killebrew, Ann E.
2005   *Biblical Peoples and Ethnicity: An Archaeological Study of Egyptians, Canaanites, Philistines, and Early Israel, 1300–1100 B.C.E.* Archaeology and Biblical Studies 9. Atlanta: Society of Biblical Literature.

2006   "The Emergence of Ancient Israel: The Social Boundaries of a 'Mixed Multitude' in Canaan." In *"I Will Speak the Riddles of Ancient Times": Archaeological and Historical Studies in Honor of Amihai Mazar on the Occasion of His Sixtieth Birthday,* edited by Aren M. Maeir and Pierre de Miroschedji, 1:555–72. Winona Lake, Ind.: Eisenbrauns.

Killebrew, Ann E., and Daniel Mack
2001   Sea Peoples and the Philistines on the Web. http://www.courses.psu.edu/cams/cams400w_aek11/www/index.htm.

> A project of CAMS 400W (Fall Semester 2001), under the direction of Ann Killebrew, Professor of Classics and Ancient Mediterranean Studies, in collaboration with Daniel Mack, humanities librarian at University Libraries.

King, Jaime Litvak
1987   "Cultural Property and National Sovereignty." In *The Ethics of Collecting Cultural Property: Whose Culture? Whose Property?* edited by Phyllis Mauch Messenger, 199–208. Albuquerque: University of New Mexico Press.

King, Noel Quinton
1986   "Egeria, Fa Hsien and Ibn Battuta: Search for Identity through Pilgrimage?" In *Identity Issues and World Religions,* 42–46. Bedford Park: Australian Association for Study of Religions.

King, Philip J.
1983   *American Archaeology in the Mideast: A History of the American Schools of Oriental Research.* Winona Lake, Ind.: American Schools of Oriental Research.

> King anchors his story of the American Schools of Oriental Research on the biographies of Edward Robinson (1794–1863), Charles Clermont-Ganneau (1846–1923), William Foxwell Albright, James H. Breasted (1865–1935), Nelson Glueck (1900–1971), G. Ernest Wright, Millar Burrows (1889–1980), G. Lankester Harding, Roland de Vaux (1903–1971), Carl H. Kraeling (1897–1966), Kathleen Kenyon, Yigael Yadin (1917–1984), A. Henry Detweiler (1906–1970), James B. Pritchard (1909–1997), Joseph A. Callaway, Paul W. Lapp (1930–1970), William G. Dever, H. Dunscombe Colt, Frank Moore Cross and other notable excavators who worked in the world of the Bible before 1980.

1988   *Amos, Hosea, Micah—An Archaeological Commentary.* Philadelphia: Westminster.

> Philip J. King published two volumes using a canonical outline: *Amos, Hosea, Micah: An Archaeological Commentary* (1988) and *Jeremiah: An Archaeological Companion* (1993). The chapters of both volumes, however, are arranged thematically. After an introductory essay on the relationship of archaeology and biblical studies, for example, King provides a biography of Jeremiah and an outline of the contents of the book of Jeremiah. Then there are chapters demonstrating what archaeologists have learned about the history and the geography of the period, the political relationship of Edom and Judah, writing, worship, burials, farming, and crafts. Both works use archaeology to better understand the social world of the Bible. For example, a trial in the book of Jeremiah (Jer 47:1-7) sentences not only the Philistine cities of Ashkelon and Gaza but also the Phoenician cities of Tyre and Sidon to be

destroyed by Babylon. The relationship between the Philistines and the Phoenicians was unclear until Phoenician artifacts were recovered from the 604 B.C.E. destruction layers during the 1992 season at Ashkelon indicating the Philistines and the Phoenicians were covenant partners. Similarly, another trial of Jerusalem indicts its people for burning incense on "all the houses upon whose roofs offerings have been made" (Jer 19:13). The use of roofs as sacred space was unknown until incense stands that had been on the roofs of houses were recovered at Ashkelon (King 1993, xxv).

1993   *Jeremiah: An Archaeological Companion.* Louisville: Westminster/John Knox.

King, Philip J., and Lawrence E. Stager
2001   *Life in Biblical Israel.* Louisville: Westminster John Knox.

King and Lawrence E. Stager use the kind of thematic outline of the social world of ancient Israel that King used in his archaeological commentaries. After introducing the archaeology of daily life, they discuss the household, farming, herding, the state, clothing, music, writing and worship. The book is a careful description of daily life based on the post-processual archaeology of the family done by Stager (Stager 1985, 1–35).

Kitchen, K. A.
1996   *The Third Intermediate Period in Egypt 1100–650 B.C.E.* Warminster: Aris & Phillips.

1999   *Poetry of Ancient Egypt.* Gothenburg: Åström.

2000   *Ramesside Inscriptions: Historical and Biographical.* Oxford: Blackwell.

2003   *On the Reliability of the Old Testament.* Grand Rapids: Eerdmans.

Kletter, Raz
2002   "A Very General Archaeologist: Moshe Dayan and Israeli Archaeology." *Journal of Hebrew Scriptures* vol. 4, article 5. http://www.arts.ualberta.ca/JHS/Articles/article_27.pdf.

Kletter (Israel Antiquities Authority) studies written sources whose authors bore no known grudge against Dayan to explain how Dayan could have collected antiquities illegally for some thirty years from more than thirty-five sites.

2005   *Just Past? The Making of Israeli Archaeology.* London: Equinox.

History of Israeli archaeology in the 1950s and early 1960s: intrigues, budgets, dreams and failures. Documentary material in English and Hebrew as well as original documents never before published.

2006   "Can a Proto-Israelite Please Stand Up?" In *"I Will Speak the Riddles of Ancient Times": Archaeological and Historical Studies in Honor of Amihai Mazar on the Occasion of His Sixtieth Birthday,* edited by Aren M. Maeir and Pierre de Miroschedji, 1:573–86. Winona Lake, Ind.: Eisenbrauns.

Knapp, A. Bernard, ed.
1992   *Archaeology, Annales, and Ethnohistory.* Cambridge: Cambridge University Press.

Koczka, Charles S.
1987   "The Need for Enforcing Regulations on the International Art Trade." In *The Ethics of Collecting Cultural Property: Whose Culture? Whose Property?* edited by Phyllis Mauch Messenger, 185–98. Albuquerque: University of New Mexico Press.

Köhler, Ludwig
1953   *Hebrew Man.* Translated by Peter R. Ackroyd. New York: Abingdon.

Kollek, Teddy, and Moshe Pearlman
1970   *Pilgrims to the Holy Land: The Story of Pilgrimages through the Ages.* London: Weidenfeld & Nicolson.

Kramer, Samuel Noah
1956   *History Begins at Sumer: Thirty-nine Firsts in Recorded History.* Philadelphia: University of Pennsylvania Press.

Bibliography

For Kramer, the Sumerians created civilization in the world of the Bible. This ingenius and amazing people in Iraq were the first to develop written language, law codes, schools, philosophy, ethics, farms, healthcare, taxes, and love songs.

1978a   *Cradle of Civilization*. Alexandria: Time-Life.

1978b   "The Literate Man." In idem, *Cradle of Civilization*, 118–37. Alexandria: Time-Life.

Kuhn, Thomas S.

1970   *The Structure of Scientific Revolutions*. Chicago: University of Chicago Press.

Kuhn argues that academic disciplines are paradigms based on research that solves problems, raises new problems, and proposes new theories. Paradigms are not theories but a consensus about what works among those in any discipline. When paradigms no longer evaluate evidence accurately nor produce effective solutions, they shift.

Lampl, Paul

1968   *Cities and Planning in the Ancient Near East*. New York: George Braziller.

Lance, H. Darrell

1981   *The Old Testament and the Archaeologist*. Philadelphia: Fortress.

Lane, Edward William

1836   *An Account of the Manners and Customs of the Modern Egyptians*. New York: Cosimo.

1863   *Arabic-English Lexicon*. http://www.studyquran.co.uk/LLhome.htm.

2000   *Description of Egypt: Notes and Views in Egypt and Nubia Made during the Years 1825–1828*. Edited by Jason Thompson. Cairo: American University in Cairo.

Lapp, Paul W.

1961   *Palestinian Ceramic Chronology 200 B.C.–A.D. 70*. Boston: American Schools of Oriental Research.

Lapp published this still widely used study as his dissertation under G. Ernest Wright at Harvard University.

1975   *The Tale of the Tell: Archaeological Studies by Paul W. Lapp*. Edited by Nancy L. Lapp. Pittsburgh Theological Monograph Series 5. Pittsburgh: Pickwick.

Larson, Mogens Trolle

1997   "Hincks versus Rawlinson: The Decipherment of the Cuneiform System of Writing." In *Ultra Terminum Vagari: Scritti in onore di Carl Nylander*, edited by Borje Magnusson, 339–56. Rome: Quasar.

Laughlin, John C. H.

2000   *Archaeology and the Bible*. New York: Routledge.

Laughlin describes the development of archaeology in the Near East including the rise and fall of biblical archaeology and how recent discoveries and theories challenge established interpretations of the exodus and conquest traditions. He also explains fieldwork methods and the broad cultural horizon of the Bible.

Lawler, Andrew

2007   "Raising Alexandria." *Smithsonian* April. http://www.smithsonianmag.com/science-nature/alexandria.html.

More than two thousand years after Alexander the Great founded the city, archaeologists are discovering the remains of the Pharaohs' lighthouse, which was one of the seven wonders of the ancient world, and the remains of Cleopatra's palace.

Lekson, Stephen

2001   "The Legacy of Lewis Binford." *American Scientist* (Nov.-Dec). http://www.americanscientist.org/template/BookReviewTypeDetail/assetid/14411.

Lemche, Niels Peter

n.d.   "Conservative Scholarship –Critical Scholarship of How Did We Get Caught by This

Bogus Discussion?" http://www.bibleinterp.com/articles/Conservative_Scholarship.htm).

1985   *Early Israel: Anthropological and Historical Studies on the Israelite Society before the Monarchy.* Vetus Testamentum Supplements 37. Leiden: Brill.

1997   "On Doing Sociology with 'Solomon.'" In *The Age of Solomon: Scholarship at the Turn of the Millennium,* edited by Lowell K. Handy, 321–25. Studies in the History and Culture of the Ancient Near East 11. Leiden: Brill.

Lemche offers a minimalist response to the maximalist analysis by John S. Holladay ("The Kingdoms of Israel and Judah: Political and Economic Centralization in the Iron IIA-B," in *The Archaeology of Society in the Holy Land,* edited by Thomas Evan Levy [London: Leicester University] 369–98) of archaeological data for the state of Israel between 1000 and 900 B.C.E. He concludes that Holladay's work is an example of biblical archaeology's "contaminated method."

2003   "On the Problems of Reconstructing Pre-Hellenistic Israelite (Palestinian) History." In *"Like a Bird in a Cage": The Invasion of Sennacherib in 701 B.C.E.,* edited by Lester L. Grabbe, 150–67. Journal for the Study of the Old Testament Supplement Series 363. London/New York: Sheffield Academic Press.

Le Roy Ladurie, Emmauel

1974   *The Peasants of Languedoc.* Translated by John Day. Edited by George Huppert. Urbana: University of Illinois Press.

Letter of Aristeas

http://www.earlyjewishwritings.com/letteraristeas.html.

The Letter of Aristeas describes how Pharaoh Ptolemy Philadelphus (285-247 B.C.E.) commissioned a translation of the Bible into Greek for the library of Alexandria. The high priest Eleazar in Jerusalem chose seventy-two translators, who worked on the Island of Pharos (Egypt) and completed the translation in seventy-two days.

Levenson, Jon D.

1993   *The Death and Resurrection of the Beloved Son.* New Haven: Yale University Press.

Levenson studies human sacrifice in ancient Israel and early Christianity. He argues that the firstborn belongs to Yahweh. "You shall give me the firstborn among your sons" (Exod 22:28). Yahweh can ask for the firstborn to be sacrificed, or for an animal to be substituted, or for a vow of celibacy to be substituted. The fathers of most households did not have to sacrifice their firstborn, but some—Abraham, Jephthah and Moab—did.

Levi-Strauss, Claude

1966   *The Savage Mind.* Chicago: University of Chicago Press.

Levy, Thomas E., ed.

1998   *The Archaeology of Society in the Holy Land.* London: Leicester University.

This work combines themes with the archaeological calendar as an outline for this anthology from thirty contributors all of whom follow some form of the Annales school of archaeology. For example, Stager describes "The Impact of the Sea Peoples (1185-1050 B.C.E.)"; Israel Finkelstein, "The Great Transformation: The 'Conquest' of the Highlands Frontiers and the Rise of the Territorial States"; Ostein S. LaBianca and Randall W. Younker, "The Kingdoms of Ammon, Moab and Edom: The Archaeology of Society in Late Bronze/Iron Age Transjordan (ca 1400–500 B.C.E.)."

2009   *The New Biblical Archaeology: From Text to Turf.* London: Equinox.

Levy edits essays reflecting recent major changes in the historical archaeology of Syria-Palestine. They represent a fundamental paradigm shift brought about by the application of objective, science-based dating methods, Geographic Information Systems, anthropological models, and an array of computer-based and digital technology tools to the study of ancient texts and the archaeological record. Examples include the Vedas, the *Iliad* and the *Odyssey* of Homer, Icelandic sagas, and Umayyad, Abbasid, Ayyubid Islamic traditions.

Bibliography

1998   *The Archaeology of Society in the Holy Land.* London: Leicester University.

     The Archaeology of Society in the Holy Land (1995-1998) edited by Thomas E. Levy combines themes with the archaeological calendar as an outline for this anthology from thirty contributors all of whom follow some form of the Annales School of Archaeology. For example Stager describes *The Impact of the Sea Peoples (1185-1050 B.C.E.)*; Israel Finkelstein, *The Great Transformation: The 'Conquest' of the Highlands Frontiers and the Rise of the Territorial States*; Ostein S. LaBianca and Randall W. Younker, *The Kingdoms of Ammon, Moab and Edom: The Archaeology of Society in Late Bronze/Iron Age Transjordan (ca 1400-500 B.C.E.)*.

Levy, Thomas E., and Augustin F. C. Hall
1998   "Social Change and the Archaeology of the Holy Land." In *The Archaeology of Society in the Holy Land,* edited by Thomas E. Levy, 2–8. London: Leicester University.

Levy, Thomas E., Russell B. Adams, and Adolfo Muniz
2004   "Archaeology and the Shasu Nomads: Recent Excavations in the Jabal Hamarat Fidan, Jordan." In *Le-David Maskil: A Birthday Tribute for David Noel Freedman,* edited by Richard Elliott Friedman and William H. C. Propp, 63–90. Biblical and Judaic Studies from the University of California, San Diego, 9. Winona Lake, Ind.: Eisenbrauns.

Lloyd, S.
1984   *The Archaeology of Mesopotamia: From the Old Stone Age to the Persian Conquest.* London: Thames & Hudson.

     Systematic survey of the archaeology of Mesopotamia.

Lorenz, Konrad
1966   *On Aggression.* Translated by Marjorie Kerr Wilson. New York: Harcourt, Brace & World.

Louvre
1989   *The Louvre: Seven Faces of a Museum.* Paris: Editions de la Reunion des musées nationaux.

     Catalogue for the Louvre.

Machinist, Peter
1996   "William Foxwell Albright: The Man and His Work." In *The Study of the Ancient Near East in the Twenty-first Century: The William Foxwell Albright Centennial Conference,* edited by J. S. Cooper and G. M. Schwartz, 385–403. Winona Lake, Ind.: Eisenbrauns.

     For Machinist, Albright brought his formidable understanding of the traditions, languages, world views, archaeology, chronology, and history of virtually every culture in the ancient Near East to bear on his interpretation of ancient Israel and the Bible. Albright's work was interdisciplinary but individual; today work continues to be interdisciplinary but collaborative. Machinist (Harvard University) evaluates the role of the Bible, orientalism, archaeology, and science in Albright's work. The *Bible* was always the point of departure and the ultimate point of return in Albright's work across many different fields. *Orientalism,* or ancient Near Eastern studies, placed the Bible in the larger context of the languages and cultures in the world of the Bible. *Archaeology* also grounded Albright's understanding of the Bible in a context outside of itself. Finally, Albright used a scientific rather than a theological approach to the Bible. He rationally and empirically collected data that would ground his interpretations on a tangible body of verifiable facts. As an *archaeologist,* Albright collected and interpreted specific material remains; as a *linguist* he clarified vocabulary and usage; and as a *historian* he described the evolution of Western civilization from the culture in ancient Israel and the Bible. Albright used diagnostic details—the investigation of words and other concrete objects reflecting daily life—to establish his chronologies or typologies, patterns of evolution or development for pottery, language, and worldviews such as monotheism.

Magen, Yitzhak, and Yuval Peleg
2006   "Back to Qumran: Ten Years of Excavation and Research, 1993–2004." In *Qumran, the*

Site of the Dead Sea Scrolls: Archaeological Interpretations and Debates. Proceedings of a Conference Held at Brown University, November 17–19, 2002, edited by Katharina Galor, Jean-Baptiste Humbert, and Jürgen Zangenberg, 55–113. Studies on the Texts of the Desert of Judah 57. Leiden: Brill.

In 1993–2004 Magen and Peleg directed excavations at Qumran and concluded that the water system at Qumran was part of a pottery factory. The cisterns were used to wash the clay before it was used to make pots.

2007   *The Qumran Excavations 1993–2004: Preliminary Report.* Jerusalem: Israel Antiquities Authority.

Magen and Peleg propose that Qumran was originally a military post responsible for the security of the Dead Sea shore. From the Roman conquest of Judah (63 B.C.E.) to the earthquake of 31 B.C.E., the site became a pottery factory, and date and date honey plantation. It retained the same function during the Herodian period, when more kilns were constructed and production increased. Its occupants even added a synagogue to serve its workers. The authors suggest that the scrolls are unconnected with the site but were brought there from Judean synagogues and hidden there at the time of the First Revolt.

Magness, Jodi
n.d.   Review of Yizhar Hirschfeld, *Qumran in Context: Reassessing the Archaeological Evidence.*" Greater Atlanta Biblical Archaeology Association. http://www.gabaa.net/newsfeed/br_hirsch.htm.

1995   "The Chronology of the Settlement at Qumran in the Herodian Period." *Dead Sea Discoveries* 2:58–65.

Magness makes her argument for redating Qumran. She argues that the Qumran community developed the site no earlier than 100–50 B.C.E. and stayed until 9 B.C.E., when Qumran was abandoned until 4 B.C.E.

2002   *The Archaeology of Qumran and the Dead Sea Scrolls.* Grand Rapids: Eerdmans.

"I find myself—an American Jewish woman—in the curious position of defending the interpretation proposed by de Vaux who was a French Dominican priest! But this book is not about my personal beliefs and background or about de Vaux's. It is about the archaeological evidence. Obviously, de Vaux's interpretation of Qumran was influenced by his background (who isn't?). De Vaux's bias is evident in his use of monastic terms to describe some of the rooms and installations at Qumran (such as "refectory" and "scriptorium"). But the objections that have been raised by de Vaux's critics have obscured the fact that his interpretation of the site is basically correct" (pp. 15-16).

Maeir, Aren M., and Pierre de Miroschedji, eds.
2006   *"I Will Speak the Riddles of Ancient Times": Archaeological and Historical Studies in Honor of Amihai Mazar on the Occasion of His Sixtieth Birthday.* 2 vols. Winona Lake, Ind.: Eisenbrauns.

Marx, Karl
1848   *Communist Manifesto.* New York: New York Labor News.

Marzahn, Joachim
n.d.   *The Ishtar Gate: The Processional Way, The New Year Festival of Babylon.* Berlin: Vorderasiatisches Museum.

Maschner, Herbert D. G., and Christopher Chippindale, eds.
2005   *Handbook of Archaeological Methods.* 2 vols. Walnut Creek, Calif.: Altamira.

Matson, Frederick R.
1965   *Ceramics and Man.* Viking Fund Publications in Anthropology 41. Chicago: Aldine.

Matson shows how to use pottery to better understand the cultural context where pottery was produced. The ecology of pottery is one aspect of ceramic ecology, which may be considered as one facet of cultural ecology, which attempts to relate the raw materials and ethnologies that the local potter has available to the function in the culture of the products fashioned.

Bibliography

Matthews, Charles D.

1932   "Palestine, Holy Land of Islam." *Journal of Biblical Literature* 51:171–78.

Matthews, Victor H.

2007a   "Historical Geography." In *Studying the Ancient Israelites: A Guide to Sources and Methods,* 19–58. Grand Rapids: Baker Academic.

2007b   "Archaeology." In *Studying the Ancient Israelites: A Guide to Sources and Methods,* 59–90. Grand Rapids: Baker Academic.

Matthews, Victor H., and Don C. Benjamin

1991,   *Old Testament Parallels: Laws and Stories*
2006   *from the Ancient Near East.* Mahwah, N.J.: Paulist. 3rd rev. and enl. ed., 2006.

1993   *Social World of Ancient Israel 1250–587 B.C.E.* Peabody, Mass.: Hendrickson.

Mattingly, Gerald L.

1992   "Mesha." In *The Anchor Bible Dictionary,* edited by David Noel Freedman, 4:707. 6 vols. New York: Doubleday.

Mayes, Stanley

2003   *The Great Belzoni: The Circus Strongman Who Discovered Egypt's Ancient Treasures.* New York: L. B. Tauris.

Mazar, Amihai

1990a   "The First Agricultural Cities: The Neolithic Period (ca. 8500–4300 B.C.E." In idem, *Archaeology of the Land of the Bible, 10,000–586 B.C.E.,* 35–58. New York: Doubleday.

1990b   *Archaeology of the Land of the Bible 10,000–586 B.C.E.* New York: Doubleday.

Archaeology of the Land of the Bible, 10,000–586 B.C.E. (1990) by Amihai Mazar and *Archaeology of the Land of the Bible: The Assyrian, Babylonian, and Persian Periods, 732–332 B.C.E.* (2001) by Ephraim Stern use the archaeological calendar as an outline. In his book, which is part of the Anchor Bible Reference Library, Mazar chooses one or more sites to describe the cultures of each archaeological period. The Carmel caves and the city of Jericho, for example, are exhibits for the Neolithic period (10,000–4,000 B.C.E.). Chapter outlines, however, are thematic. Mazar summarizes what material remains reveal about settlement planning, domestic and monumental architecture, farming and herding, trade, pottery, tools and weapons, liturgical art, and burials. Anthropology plays little role in his reconstruction of the world of the Bible (Shanks 2001). Explanations of artifacts to better understand the Bible appear only as asides. The index of citations from the Bible for this book of 576 pages is only one and one-half pages in length.

2001,   *Studies in the Archaeology of the Iron Age in*
ed.   *Israel and Jordan.* Journal for the Study of the Old Testament Supplement Series 331. Sheffield: Sheffield Academic.

Mazar, Amihai, ed.

2006   "Jerusalem in the 10th Century B.C.E.: The Glass Half Full." In *Essays on Ancient Israel in Its Near Eastern Context,* ed. Yairah Amit, 255–72. Winona Lake, Ind.: Eisenbrauns.

McCarter, Susan Foster

2007   *Neolithic.* New York: Routledge.

McCarter explains the evolution of the domestication of plants and animals, and the impact of farming and herding on population, social organization, nutrition, disease, architecture, exchange systems, technology, and religion.

McGeough, Kevin M.

2006   "Birth Bricks, Potter's Wheels, and Exodus 1,16." *Biblica* 87:305–18.

McIntosh, Roderick, Susan Keech McIntosh, and Tereba Togola

1995   "The Good Collector and the Premise of Mutual Respect among Nations." *African Arts* 28:60–69, 110–12.

Alpha Oumar Konare, president of Mali (1992–2002), said that Mali (Africa) regards good collectors and public trust museums as natural partners in its goal of sharing Mali's antiquities with the world. Here three archaeologists describe good collectors and the role they can play in eliminating illegal collecting and trafficking in antiquities.

McIntosh, Susan Keech
2000 "The 'Good Collector': Fabulous Beast or Endangered Species?" *Public Archaeology* 1:73–76.

Good collectors use their artifacts to open the eyes of others to the nobility of the maker cultures; their pride comes not from possessing artifacts but from using them for education; aesthetics are important to collectors, but not at the expense of the archaeological context of their artifacts.

McKenzie, D.
1907 "Children and Wells." *Folklore* 18:253–82.

McNutt, Paula
1990 *The Forging of Israel: Iron Technology, Symbolism and Tradition in Ancient Society.* Social World of Biblical Antiquity 8. Sheffield: Almond.

Mellaart, James
1965 *Earliest Civilizations of the Near East.* New York: McGraw Hill.

Merton, Robert K.
1949 *Social Theory and Social Structure.* New York: Free Press.

This work continues to be of central importance in the social sciences because it provides the most systematic outline of the theoretical foundations of functional sociology. Among the enduring concepts that Merton proposed is *middle range theory,* which is a balanced application of both theory and method in conducting studies.

Meskell, Lynn
2002 *Private Life in New Kingdom Egypt.* Princeton, N.J.: Princeton University Press.

Messinger, Phyllis Mauch, ed.
1989 *The Ethics of Collecting Cultural Property: Whose Culture? Whose Property?* Albuquerque: University of New Mexico Press.

Meyers, Carol L.
1988 *Discovering Eve: Ancient Israelite Women in Context.* New York: Oxford University Press.

1991 "Of Drums and Damsels: Women's Performance in Ancient Israel." *Biblical Archaeologist* 54:16–27.

1997 "The Family in Ancient Israel." In *Families in Ancient Israel,* edited by Leo G. Perdue, Joseph Blenkinsopp, John J. Collins, and Carol L. Meyers, 1–47. Louisville: Westminster John Knox.

2002 "Having Their Space and Eating There Too: Bread Production and Female Power in Ancient Israelite Households." *Nashim: A Journal of Jewish Women's Studies and Gender Issues* 5:14–44.

2003a "Engendering Syro-Palestinian Archaeology: Reasons and Resources." *Near Eastern Archaeology* 66:185–97.

2003b "Where the Girls Are: Archaeology and Women's Lives in Ancient Israel." In *Between Text and Artifact: Integrating Archaeology in Biblical Studies Teaching,* edited by Milton C. Moreland, 31–51. Archaeology and Biblical Studies 8. Atlanta: Society of Biblical Literature.

2003c "Material Remains and Social Relations: Women's Culture in Agrarian Households of the Iron Age." In *Symbiosis, Symbolism, and the Power of the Past: Canaan, Ancient Israel, and Their Neighbors from the Late Bronze Age through Roman Palaestina,* 425–44. Winona Lake, Ind.: Eisenbrauns.

2003d "Everyday Life in Biblical Israel." In *Life and Culture in the Ancient Near East,* edited by Richard E. Averbeck, Mark W. Chavalas, and

Bibliography

David B. Weisberg, 185–204. Bethesda, Md.: CDL.

2005   *Households and Holiness: The Religious Culture of Israelite Women.* Minneapolis: Fortress.

Meyers, Carol L., and Eric M. Meyers

1987   *Haggai, Zechariah 1–8: A New Translation with Introduction and Commentary.* Anchor Bible 25B. Garden City. N.Y.: Doubleday.

Meyers, Eric M.

1985   "The Shelomith Seal and the Judean Restoration: Some Additional Considerations." *Eretz Israel* 18:33–38.

1994   "Second Temple Studies in the Light of Recent Archaeology: Part 1, The Persian and Hellenistic periods." In *Currents in Research: Biblical Studies:* 25-42. Edited by Alan J. Hauser and Philip Sellew. Sheffield: Sheffield Academic.

Through the lens of his own interpretation of the Second Temple period Meyers summarizes the archaeological highlights of the Persian (Iron III) and Hellenistic periods in Judah.

1997, ed.   *The Oxford Encyclopedia of Archaeology in the Near East.* New York: Oxford University Press.

Originally, the five-volume *Oxford Encyclopedia of Archaeology in the Near East* (1997), edited by Eric M. Meyers, with 560 contributors, was to be a one-volume introduction to archaeology and the Bible modeled on the *Biblisches Reallexikon* (1937–1977) by Kurt Galling. Four-hundred fifty of the 1,125 entries are site reports from Syria-Palestine to Iran, Anatolia, to Arabia, including Egypt, Ethiopia, Cyprus, North Africa, Morocco, Malta, and Sardinia. These reports are the basis for an additional 650 articles on geography—Ethiopia, Nubia, North Africa, and everyday life—farming, herding, household, medicine, clothing, and diet. There are also entries on the environment, the economies of the peoples of the world of the Bible—glass making, shipbuilding, and metalworking. Finally, there are entries on archaeological theory, methods, and practice—new archaeology, underwater archae-ology, survey archaeology, salvage archaeology, development and archaeology, museums, ethics and archaeology, ideology and archaeology, nationalism and archaeology, tourism and archae-ology. Biblical archaeology is described within the larger context of archaeology in the Near East.

Miller, J. Maxwell

1974   "The Moabite Stone as a Memorial Stele." *Palestine Exploration Quarterly* 106:9–18.

1982   *Introducing the Holy Land: A Guidebook for First-time Visitors.* Macon, Ga.: Mercer University Press.

1988   "Antecedents to Modern Archaeology." In *Benchmarks in Time and Culture: Essays in Honor of Joseph A. Callaway,* edited by Joel F. Drinkard, Jr., Gerald L. Mattingly, and J. Maxwell Miller, 3–14. Atlanta: American Schools of Oriental Research.

1989   "Moab and the Moabites." In *Studies in the Mesha Inscription and Moab,* edited by J. Andrew Dearman, 1–40. Archaeology and Biblical Studies 2. Atlanta: Scholars Press.

Miller provides a survey of the primary and secondary sources for the Annals of Mesha, especially the history of exploration of Moab and the identification of sites mentioned in the Bible.

Miller, J. Maxwell, and John H. Hayes

2006   *A History of Ancient Israel and Judah.* 2nd ed. Louisville: Westminster John Knox.

This survey uses the archaeological calendar. Hayes and Miller make careful use of archaeology to assess and revise the history that William F. Albright (1891–1971) proposed and that is reflected in works such as *A History of Israel* (1959, 2000) by John Bright (1908–1995). Albright's and Bright's histories of Israel used archaeology to demonstrate the historical reliability of the Bible. Hayes and Miller, in contrast, use archaeology to evaluate and to interpret the biblical traditions.

Miller, Patrick D.

1969   "A Note on the Mesha Inscription." *Orientalia* 38:461–64.

Miller, Robert D.
2005   *Chieftains of the Highland Clans: A History of Israel in the Twelfth and Eleventh Centuries B.C.* Grand Rapids: Eerdmans.

Mitchell, Stephen
2004   *Gilgamesh: A New English Version.* New York: Free Press.

Mitchell, T. C.
1988   *The Bible in the British Museum: Interpreting the Evidence.* London: British Museum.

Mitchell translates sixty Near Eastern and western Mediterranean traditions from 2000 B.C.E. to 100 and discusses the contribution they make to the understanding of the world of the Bible.

Mithen, Steven J.
1989   "Evolutionary Theory and Post-Processual Archaeology." *Antiquity* 63:483–94.

Mollenkott, Virginia Ramey
1983   *The Divine Feminine: Biblical Imagery of God as Female.* New York: Crossroad.

Molnár, Zs.
Neutron Activation Analysis. http://www .reak.bme.hu/nti/Education/Wigner_ Course/WignerManuals/Budapest/NEU TRON_ACTIVATION_ANALYSIS.htm.

Archaeologists use Neutron Activation Analysis (NAA) as a quantitative and qualitative method of high efficiency for the precise determination of a number of main components and trace elements in pottery. NAA, based on the nuclear reaction between neutrons and target nuclei, is a useful method for the simultaneous determination of about twenty-five to thirty major, minor, and trace elements of geological, environmental, and biological samples.

Moorey, Roger
1969   *Archaeology, Artefacts and the Bible.* Oxford: Ashmolean Museum.

1981   *Excavation in Palestine.* Grand Rapids: Eerdmans.

1991   *A Century of Biblical Archaeology.* Louisville: Westminster John Knox.

1994   *Ancient Mesopotamian Materials and Industries: The Archaeological Evidence.* Oxford: Clarendon.

Moorey, Roger, and Peter Parr, eds.
1978   *Archaeology in the Levant: Essays for Kathleen Kenyon.* Warminster: Aris & Phillips.

Moreland, Milton C., ed.
2003   *Between Text and Artifact: Integrating Archaeology in Biblical Studies Teaching.* Archaeology and Biblical Studies 8. Atlanta: Society of Biblical Literature.

Moreland edits thirteen essays from archaeologists and biblical scholars who teach in undergraduate, graduate, and seminary settings. The essays give practical advice about how to integrate archaeology and the Bible into the classroom and about the best available literature and audio-visual material in the field of archaeology related to the Bible, the New Testament, early Judaism, women in the ancient world, and the Dead Sea Scrolls. The essays illustrate how archaeological data can visualize the items, environments, and landscapes from the world of the Bible.

Morton, William H.
1985   "The 1954, 55 and 65 Excavation at Dhiban in Jordan." In *Studies in the Mesha Inscription and Moab,* edited by J. Andrew Dearman, 239–46. Archaeology and Biblical Studies 2. Atlanta: Scholars Press.

Morton reports on three brief seasons of digging at Dhibon, which is mentioned in the Annals of Mesha. Morton identifies some of the building projects described by Mesha, for example, the large building on the top of the tell.

Mosca, Paul
1975   "Child Sacrifice in Canaanite and Israelite

Bibliography

Religion: A Study in *Mulk* and *Mlk.*" Ph.D. diss., Harvard University.

Muckelroy, Keith

1978   *Maritime Archaeology.* New York: Cambridge University Press.

   The first attempt to develop a theory of underwater archaeology for the specialist.

1980,   *Archaeology under Water: An Atlas of the*
   ed.   *World's Submerged Sites.* New York: McGraw Hill.

   Muckelroy edits a solid introduction to the field of underwater archaeology.

Muhly, James D.

1977   "The Cape Gelidonya Shipwreck and the Bronze Age Metals Trade in the Eastern Mediterranean." *Journal of Field Archaeology* 4:353–62.

Murphy-O'Connor, Jerome

1986   *The Holy Land: An Archaeological Guide from Earliest Times to 1700.* New York: Oxford University Press.

   In this work, Murphy-O'Connor follows a geographical outline. He begins with a description of sites related to the Bible in Jerusalem and then continues alphabetically for sites throughout Israel. In his discussion of Megiddo, for example, Murphy-O'Connor indexes the appearance of the city in the Annals of Tutmosis III (Matthews and Benjamin 2006, 142–45); in the El-Amarna Letters (Matthews and Benjamin 2006, 146–50); in the inventory of cities that the Hebrews did not conquer in the book of Judges (Judg 1:27); in the Annals of Sheshonq (945–924 B.C.E.); and in the Annals of Omri and Ahab in the books of Samuel–Kings.

Nadel, Dani, Ehud Weiss, Orit Simchoni, Alexander Tsatskin, Avinoam Danin, and Mordechai Kislev

2004   "Stone Age Hut in Israel Yields World's Oldest Evidence of Bedding." *Proceedings of the National Academy of Sciences* [PNAS] 101 (April 27): 6821–26. http://www.pnas.org/cgi/content/full/101/17/6821.

   Paleolithic houses built by humans have been excavated in Europe, but none showed designated zones for work, for food preparation, and for sleeping. Now, however, archaeologists have recovered houses in a Paleolithic (25,000–10,000 B.C.E.) fishing, hunting, and gathering camp of Ohalo II on the shore of the Sea of Galilee. The grass bedding consists of bunches of partially charred *Puccinellia confer convoluta* stems and leaves, covered by a thin compact layer of clay. The bedding is arranged on the floor around a central hearth clearly identifying the three zones—a hearth for food preparation and workspace and beds along the walls.

Nakhai, Beth Alpert

2001   *Archaeology and the Religions of Canaan and Israel.* ASOR Books 7. Boston: American Schools of Oriental Research.

2003,   *The Near East in the Southwest: Essays in*
   ed.   *Honor of William G. Dever.* Annual of the American Schools of Oriental Research 58. Boston: American Schools of Oriental Research.

2005   "Daily Life in the Ancient Near East: New Thoughts on an Old Topic." *Religious Studies Review* 31:147–53.

Negev, Avraham, ed.

1986   *The New Archaeological Encyclopedia of the Holy Land.* Rev. ed. Nashville: Thomas Nelson.

Nelson, Robert S.

2006   "Where God Walked and Monks Pray." In *Holy Image, Hallowed Ground: Icons from Sinai,* edited by Robert S. Nelson and Kristen M. Collins, 1–37. Los Angeles: J. Paul Getty Museum.

Nelson, S. M.

1997   *Gender in Archaeology: Analyzing Power and Prestige.* Walnut Creek, Calif.: AltaMira.

Nelson, S. M., and M. Rosen-Ayalon, eds.

2001   *In Pursuit of Gender: Worldwide Archaeological Approaches.* Walnut Creek, Calif.: AltaMira.

Nemet-Nejat, Karen Rhea

2002   *Daily Life in Ancient Mesopotamia.* Peabody, Mass.: Hendrickson.

Netzer, Ehud

2008   *The Architecture of Herod the Great Builder.* Grand Rapids: Baker.

Neusner, Jacob

1973   *The Idea of Purity in Ancient Judaism.* Studies in Judaism in Late Antiquity 1. Leiden: Brill.

1994   *Purity in Rabbinic Judaism, a Systematic Account: The Sources, Media, Effects, and Removal of Uncleanness.* South Florida Studies in the History of Judaism 95. Atlanta: Scholars Press.

Newman, John Philip

1875   *Thrones and Palaces of Babylon and Nineveh: From Sea to Sea—A Thousand Miles on Horseback.* New York: Harper & Brothers.

Noort, Ed

2007   "Child Sacrifice in Ancient Israel: The Status Quaestionis." In *The Strange World of Human Sacrifice,* edited by J. N. Bremmer, 103–25. Studies in the History and Anthropology of Religion 1. Leuven: Peeters.

For Noort, prophetic indictments of the rulers of Israel and Judah for human sacrifice suggest that at certain times and under certain circumstances the Hebrews did offer human sacrifices to Yahweh. He argues that if human sacrifices were ever offered to Yahweh by the Hebrews, they most likely offered these sacrifices in Judah after 700 B.C.E. when traditions such as Yahweh giving Israel "statutes that were not good and ordinances by which they could not live" (Ezek 20:25)—referring to human sacrifice—developed. The household of David in Jerusalem

associated Yahweh with the stars, which were worshiped with human sacrifice in other Mediterranean cultures.

Noth, Martin

1972   *A History of the Pentateuchal Traditions.* Translated by Bernhard W. Anderson. Englewood Cliffs, N.J.: Prentice-Hall.

Anderson translates *Uberlieferungsgeschichtliche Studien,* which is arguably the most influential work of Martin Noth.

1983   *A History of Israel.* London: A. & C. Black.

Noy, Tamar.

1986a   "The Natufian Culture." In *Treasures of the Holy Land: Ancient Art from the Israel Museum,* 31–40. New York: Metropolitan Museum of Art.

1986b   "Neolithic Period: ca. 8500–ca. 4500 B.C." In *Treasures of the Holy Land: Ancient Art from the Israel Museum,* 41–56. New York: Metropolitan Museum of Art.

Nur, Amos

1994   *"The Walls Came Tumbling Down: Earthquakes in the Holy Land."* Stanford: ESI Productions. http://srb.stanford.edu/nur/.

Amos Nur (Stanford University) is Loel Professor of Geophysics, director of the Rock Physics and Borehole Geophysics Project. A native of Israel, Nur earned his B.S. in geology at Hebrew University, Jerusalem, and his Ph.D. in geophysics at MIT in 1969. He was a research associate at MIT until 1970, when he joined Stanford's geophysics faculty. He was chair of the Geophysics Department from 1986 to 1991 and from 1997 to 2000. Nur was the SEG Distinguished Lecturer in 1997, and the AAPG Distinguished Lecturer in 1998. Nur's research interests are in wave propagation, fluid flow, permeability, fractures, and electrostatic properties of sedimentary rocks and how these apply to geophysical exploration, reservoir evaluation, and geothermal resources. In the area of tectonophysics, Nur is pursuing research on the mechanics of faults and accretion tectonics.

Bibliography

O'Brien, Michael J.

2005　*Archaeology as a Process: Processualism and Its Progeny.* Salt Lake City: University of Utah.

O'Brien traces the intellectual history of American archaeology in terms of the research groups that were at the forefront of these various approaches, concentrating as much on the archaeologists as on method and theory. This work contains rare photographs of well-known archaeologists; documents the swirl and excitement of archaeological controversy for the past forty years; examines how archaeology is conducted—the ins and outs of how various groups work to promote themselves—and how personal ambition and animosities can function to further rather than to retard the development of the discipline.

O'Brien, Michael J., and R. Lee Lyman

2004　"History and Explanation in Archaeology." *Anthropological Theory* 4:173–97.

Historical Processualism (Pauketat 2001, 73–98) explains culture change without human behavior or universal laws. The method uses Darwin's principles of evolution to identify causes of cultural change that are scientifically verifiable to argue that humans continually develop new ways of doing things.

O'Keefe, Patrick J.

1998　"Codes of Ethics: Form and Function in Cultural Heritage Management." *International Journal of Cultural Property* 7:32–51.

2000　"Archaeology and Human Rights." *Public Archaeology* 1:181–94.

Oppenheim, A. Leo

1977　*Ancient Mesopotamia: Portrait of a Dead Civilization.* Revised by Erica Reiner. 2nd ed. Chicago: University of Chicago Press.

Origen

1857　"In Joannem." In *Patrologiae Cursus Completus, Series Graeca,* edited by J. P. Migne, vol. 14. Paris.

Ornit, Sebbane, and Ruth Amiran

2006　"Arad." In *The Oxford Encyclopedia of Archaeology in the Near East,* edited by Eric M. Meyers, 1:169–74. New York: Oxford University.

Ortiz, Steven M.

2004　"Deconstructing and Reconstructing the United Monarchy: House of David or Tent of David (Current Trends in Iron Age Chronology)." In *The Future of Biblical Archaeology: Reassessing Methodologies and Assumptions. The Proceedings of a Symposium, August 12–14, 2001, at Trinity International University,* edited by James K. Hoffmeier and Alan Millard, 121–47. Grand Rapids: Eerdmans.

Palestine Pilgrims' Text Society

1971　*The Library of the Palestine Pilgrims' Text Society.* New York: AMS Publishing.

Between 1887 and 1897 the Society collected, translated, and edited the journals of early pilgrims in the world of the Bible.

Panitz-Cohen, Nava, and Amihai Mazar, eds.

2006　*Timnah (Tel Batash) III: The Finds from the Second Millennium B.C.E.* Qedem 45. Jerusalem: Hebrew University of Jerusalem.

Pardee, Dennis

1979　"Literary Sources for the History of Palestine and Syria II: Hebrew, Moabite, Ammonite and Edomite Inscriptions." *Andrews University Seminary Studies* 17:47–70.

Parsons, Marie

　　　"Giovanni Belzoni: Circus Giant and Collector of Egyptian Antiquities." http://www.touregypt.net/featurestories/belzoni.htm.

Patai, Raphael

1959　*Sex and the Family in the Bible and the Middle East.* Garden City, N.Y.: Doubleday.

1973　*The Arab Mind.* New York: Charles Scribner's Sons.

Patterson, Thomas C.
1990   "Some Theoretical Tensions Within and Between the Processual and Postprocessual Archaeologies." *Journal of Anthropological Archaeology* 9:189–200.

Pearlman, Moshe
1980   *Digging up the Bible: The Stories behind the Great Archaeological Discoveries in the Holy Land.* New York: William Morrow.

This book uses the hot-topics outline. Its strategy is kiss and tell. Sometimes, in almost tabloid fashion, Pearlman tells the stories behind the stories of Roland de Vaux, Edward Robinson, William Matthew Flinders Petrie, Jean-François Champollion, Henry Creswicke Rawlinson, Paul E. Botta, and Austen H. Layard, ending eventually with Kathleen Kenyon in Jerusalem and Yigael Yadin at Masada.

Perdue, Leo G., Joseph Blenkinsopp, John J. Collins, Carol L. Meyers, eds.
1997   *Families in Ancient Israel: The Family, Religion and Culture.* Louisville: Westminster John Knox.

Perdue, Leo G., Lawrence E. Toombs, and Gary L. Johnson, eds.
1987   *Archaeology and Biblical Interpretation: Essays in Memory of D. Glenn Rose.* Atlanta: John Knox.

Petit Larousse illustré
1959   Paris: Librairie Larousse.

Phillips, Philip
1955   "American Archaeology and General Anthropological Theory." *Southwestern Journal of Anthropology* 11:246–50.

Phillips pioneered processual archaeology with the argument that "New World archaeology is anthropology or it is nothing."

Philo
1941   *Every Good Man Is Free. On the Contemplative Life. On the Eternity of the World. Against Flaccus. Apology for the Jews. On Providence.* Translated by F. H. Colson. Loeb Classical Library. Cambridge, Mass.: Harvard University Press.

Phipps, William E.
1992   *Assertive Biblical Women.* Contributions in Women's Studies 128. Westport, Conn.: Greenwood.

Pigafetta, Antonio
1969   *The Voyage of Magellan.* Translated by Paula Spurlin Paige. Englewood Cliffs, N.J.: Prentice-Hall.

Pilch, John J.
1999   *The Cultural Dictionary of the Bible.* Collegeville, Minn.: Liturgical Press.

Pliny the Elder (*Gaius Plinius Secundus*)
1938   *Natural History.* Translated by D. E. Eichholz, W. H. S. Jones, and H. Rackham. Loeb Classical Library: Cambridge, Mass.: Harvard University Press.

Pluciennik, Mark, and Marek Zvelebil
2008   "The Origins and Spread of Agriculture." In *Handbook of Archaeological Theories,* edited by R. Alexander Bentley, Herbert D. G. Maschner, and Christopher Chippindale, 467–86. Lanham, Md.: Rowman & Littlefield.

Pollock, Susan M.
1991   "Women in a Men's World: Images of Sumerian Women." In *Engendering Archaeology: Women and Prehistory,* edited by Joan M. Gero and Margaret W. Conkey, 366–87. Oxford: Basil Blackwell.

1999   *Ancient Mesopotamia: The Eden That Never Was.* Cambridge: Cambridge University Press.

Bibliography

Pollock, Susan M., and Reinhard Bernbeck, eds.

2000   "'And They Said, Let Us Make Gods in Our Image': Gendered Ideologies in Ancient Mesopotamia." In *Reading the Body: Representations and Remains in the Archaeological Record,* ed. Alison E. Rautman, 150–64. Philadelphia: University of Pennsylvania Press.

2003, eds.   *Archaeologies of the Middle East.* Oxford: Blackwell.

Preucel, Robert W.

1995   "The Postprocessual Condition." *Journal of Archaeological Research* 2:147–75.

Price, Megan

2005   "Three Travelers in Nineteenth Century Egypt: Sarah Belzoni, Amelia Edwards and Margaret Benson." In *Women Travellers in the Near East,* edited by Sara Searight, 40–51. Oxford: Oxbow.

Quirke, Stephen, and Jeffrey Spencer, eds.

1992   *British Museum Book of Ancient Egypt.* London: Thames & Hudson.

Rainey, Anson F.

1988   "Historical Geography." In *Benchmarks in Time and Culture: An Introduction to Palestinian Archaeology,* edited by Joel F. Drinkard, Jr., Gerald L. Mattingly, and J. Maxwell Miller, 355–68. Atlanta: Scholars Press.

2001   "Israel in Merenptah's Inscription and Reliefs." *Israel Exploration Journal* 51:57–75.

Rainey studies the Merenptah Stela and the newly identified Merenptah reliefs at Karnak using the work of Evelyn van der Steen (1999). He concludes that "Israel" in the Merenptah Stela is part of the migration of the *Shashu* farmers and herders from east of the Jordan River into the hills west of the river, and that "seed" refers to the people of Israel, and not to their crops.

2006   "Sinuhe's World." In *"I Will Speak the Riddles of Ancient Times": Archaeological and Historical Studies in Honor of Amihai Mazar on the Occasion of His Sixtieth Birthday,* edited by Aren M. Maeir and Pierre de Miroschedji, 1:277–302. 2 vols. Winona Lake, Ind.: Eisenbrauns.

Rainey, Anson F., and R. Steven Notley

2006   *The Sacred Bridge: Carta's Atlas of the Biblical World.* Jerusalem: Carta.

A historical geography based on archaeology and ancient traditions.

Ramsay, W. M., and Gertrude L. Bell

1910   "The Thousand and One Churches." *Journal of Hellenic Studies* 30:173–74.

Rast, Walter

1992   *Through the Ages in Palestinian Archaeology: An Introductory Handbook.* Philadelphia: Trinity Press International.

2003   "Bible and Archaeology." In *Near Eastern Archaeology,* edited by Suzanne Richard, 48–53. Winona Lake, Ind.: Eisenbrauns.

Rawlinson, Henry C.

1852   *Outlines of Assyrian History from the Inscriptions of Nineveh: The Twenty-ninth Annual Report of the Royal Asiatic Society of Great Britain.* London: John W. Parker & Son.

Reade, Julian

1983   *Assyrian Sculpture.* London: British Museum.

Reeves, Nicholas

2000   *Ancient Egypt: The Great Discoveries.* London: Thames & Hudson.

Regev, Eyal

2007   "The Archaeology of Sectarianism: A Socio-anthropological Analysis of Kh. Qumran." Paper presented at the Annual Meeting of

American Schools of Oriental Research. San Diego.

Regev argues that the archaeology of space at Qumran reflects a cloister that segregated outsiders from insiders, and classes of insiders from one another.

Reed, Stephanie

2007 "Blurring the Edges: A Reconsideration of the Treatment of Enemies in Ashurbanipal's Reliefs." In *Ancient Near Eastern Art in Context: Studies in Honor of Irene J. Winter by Her Students,* edited by Jack Cheng and Marian Feldman, 99–128. *Culture and History of the Ancient Near East* 26. Leiden: Brill.

Reid, Barbara E.

1996 "Soul: Spirit of God/Holy Spirit." In *The Collegeville Pastoral Dictionary of the Biblical Theology,* edited by Carroll Stuhlmueller et al., 945–47. Collegeville, Minn.: Liturgical Press.

Reid, Donald Malcolm

2002 *Whose Pharaohs? Archaeology, Museums, and Egyptian National Identity from Napoleon to World War I.* Berkeley: University of California Press.

Reid examines how Egyptian nationalists and European imperialists used archaeology between 1798 (the French Expedition) and 1914 (World War I). Imperialism and nationalism were both partners with archaeology.

Renfrew, Colin

2000 "The Fallacy of the 'Good Collector' of Looted Antiquities." *Public Archaeology* 1:76–78.

The only "good collector" (*pace* McIntosh, McIntosh, and Togola 1995; and S. K. McIntosh 2000) of illegally stolen artifacts from ancient cultures is an ex-collector. The end of using stolen artifacts for appreciation and education does not justify the stealing and trafficking in illegal antiquities.

Renfrew, Colin, and Paul G. Bahn

1996 *Archaeology: Theories, Methods and Practice.* London: Thames & Hudson. http://www.thamesandhudsonusa.com/web/archaeology/.

2007 *Archaeology Essentials: Theories, Methods, and Practice.* London: Thames & Hudson.

An abridged version of their textbook (1996) on what archaeologists do and how they do it

Rhodes, Matthew

2006 "History of the Diocese of Egypt and North Africa." http://www.geocities.com/dioceseofegypt/history1.html.

Richard, Suzanne, ed.

2003 *Near Eastern Archaeology: A Reader.* Winona Lake, Ind.: Eisenbrauns.

Ricoeur, Paul

1980 *The Contribution of French Historiography to the Theory of History: The Zaharoff Lecture for 1978–1979.* Oxford: Clarendon.

In the spirit of the Annales school, Ricoeur cautions historians not to succumb to the methodological illusion whereby the historical fact is held to exist in a latent state in documents and the historian to be the parasite of the historical equation. To counter this methodological illusion, one must assert that in history the initiative does not belong to the document but to the question posed by the historian. The latter has logical precedence in the historical inquiry (p. 17).

Ringgren, Helmer, David Noel Freedman, Michael P. O'Connor

1986 "YHWH." In *Theological Dictionary of the Old Testament,* edited by G. J. Botterweck and Helmer Ringgren, translated by J. T. Willis, G. W. Bromiley, and D. E. Green, 5:500–521. 8 vols. Grand Rapids: Eerdmans, 1974–.

Bibliography

Ritner, Robert K.
1984   "A Uterine Amulet in the Oriental Institute Collection." *Journal of Near Eastern Studies* 43:209–21.

Roaf, Michael
1990a   *Cultural Atlas of Mesopotamia and the Ancient Near East.* New York: Facts on File.

    Well-illustrated and detailed atlas-like work on ancient Mesopotamia.

1990b   "Toward Civilization." In *Cultural Atlas of Mesopotamia and the Ancient Near East,* 42–56. New York: Facts on File.

Roberts, David
1849   *The Holy Land, Syria, Idumea, Arabia, Egypt, and Nubia.* London: E. G. Moon.

Roberts, J., and D. Van Lier
1984   "Which Positions for the Second Stage?" *Childbirth Educator* 3:33–41.

Robinson, Edward
1841   *Biblical Researches in Palestine.* London: John Murray.

    Robinson kept a three-volume, detailed journal describing the flora and fauna, social customs, and geography of the world of the Bible.

Rofé, Alexander
1987   "The Battle of David and Goliath: Folklore, Theology, Eschatology." In *Judaic Perspectives on Ancient Israel,* edited by Jacob Neusner, Baruch A. Levine, and Ernest S. Frerichs, 117–51. Philadelphia: Fortress Press.

Rogers, Everett M. Rogers
1962/   *Diffusion of Innovations.* 5th ed. New York:
2003   Free Press.

    For Rogers, diffusion is the process in which an innovation is communicated through certain channels over time among the members of a social system. It is a special type of communication, in that the messages are concerned with new ideas.

Rogers, Robert William
1915   *A History of Babylonia and Assyria.* 6th ed. New York: Abingdon.

Rohl, David M.
1995   *Pharaohs and Kings: A Biblical Quest.* New York: Crown.

    Rohl proposes a radically revised chronology for relating biblical events to the history of Egypt. For example, Shishak (1 Kgs 14:25-28; 2 Chr 12:1-12) is not Shoshenq I (945–924 B.C.E.) but Sysa, a nickname or hypocoristicon of Ramses II (1290–1225 B.C.E.), is the only pharaoh to have recorded a defeat of (Jeru-) Shalem.

Rouse, Irving
1953   "The Strategy of Culture History." In *Anthropology Today,* edited by Sol Tax, 84–103. Chicago: University of Chicago Press.

    Irving reviews the research planning of cultural historians excavating between 1900 and 1960.

Routledge, Bruce
2004   *Moab in the Iron Age: Hegemony, Polity, Archaeology.* Philadelphia: University of Pennsylvania Press.

    Routledge (University of Liverpool) studies Bronze and Iron Age cultures of Syria-Palestine, especially Iron Age cultures in south-central Jordan—the land of Moab. In Jordan he directs ongoing research projects at the sites of Khirbat al-Mudayna al-'Aliya and Dhiban. Routledge follows the cultural theories of state-formation of Antonio Gramsci, and the theories of political economy of settlement in arid and semi-arid regions, material culture studies, and exchange theory of Marcel Mauss.

Roux, Georges
1992   *Ancient Iraq.* Harmondsworth: Penguin.

    General and systematic survey of the history of Mesopotamia.

Running, Leona Glidden, and David Noel Freedman
1975   *William Foxwell Albright: A Twentieth Century Genius.* New York: Morgan.

A flattering intellectual biography of William Foxwell Albright based on his own correspondence. Freedman was Albright's last student and later his editorial assistant. He describes this biography as "a labor of love undertaken in grateful homage by a devoted disciple toward a revered teacher—yet at the same time a genuine attempt to present objectively the man as he really was, letting him speak for himself" (ix).

Saggs, H. W. F.

1965   *Everyday Life in Babylonia and Assyria.* New York: Dorset.

Said, Edward W.

1978/   *Orientalism: Western Conceptions of the*
2003   *Orient.* London: Routledge & Kegan Paul.

Saleh, Mohamed, and Hourig Sourouzian

1987   *Official Catalogue. The Egyptian Museum Cairo.* Munich: Prestel.

Sales, R. H.

1957   "Human Sacrifice in Biblical Thought." *Journal of the American Academy of Religion* 25:112–17.

Sales identifies the most commonly discussed biblical traditions dealing with human sacrifice (Gen 22:1-19; Exod 13:2; 22:29; 34:20; Lev 18:21; 20:1-5; Num 3:11-13; 18:15-16; Judg 11; 1 Kgs 3; 18:40; 2 Kgs 10:25-27; 16:2-4; 21:5-16; 2 Chr 28:3-4; 33:6; Isa 40-55).

Samuel, Delwen

1996   "Investigation of Ancient Egyptian Baking and Brewing Methods by Correlative Microscopy." *Science* 273:488–90.

Samuel presents the microscopy analysis of loaves and their interpretation and discusses the relationship of bread and beer.

2001   "Bread." In *The Oxford Encyclopedia of Ancient Egypt,* edited by Donald Redford, 1:196–98. Oxford: Oxford University Press.

Preferred grain for Egyptian bread was bread wheat (Latin: *triticum aestivum*); most common

was emmer wheat (Latin: *triticum dioccum*). From the Neolithic period to the Old Kingdom period saddle querns or mills were placed on the floor making grinding flour a laborious process. During the Middle and New Kingdoms mills were placed on platforms, called "querns emplacements" which made grinding flour easier, more comfortable, and quicker. No grit was used to grind flour in Egypt; flour textures could be precisely controlled by the miller.

Saoud, Rabah

2002   "Muslim Architecture under the Abbassid Patronage (750-892AD)." http://www .muslimheritage.com/includes/viewResource .cfm?resourceID=183.

Sasson, Jack M., ed.

1995   *Civilizations of the Ancient Near East.* 4 vols. New York: Charles Scribner's Sons.

These four volumes follow a thematic outline using anthropology. The first volume begins with an essay on the discipline of Near Eastern studies as well as essays on the environment and population in the world of the Bible. Sasson groups the essays around ten themes. There are sections, for example, reconstructing social institutions such as the economy, trade, technology, art, science, and writing. Among the concluding essays is "Assessing the Past through Anthropological Archaeology" by Frank Hole.

Schloen, J. David, ed.

2009   *Exploring the Longue Durée: Essays in Honor of Lawrence E. Stager.* Winona Lake, Ind.: Eisenbrauns.

The contents of this volume are as follows: 1. "Lawrence Stager and Biblical Archaeology," by J. David Schloen; 2. "Solomon's Patrimonial Kingdom: A View from the Land of Gilead," by Tristan J. Barako; 3. "The Dolphin Jug: A Typological and Chronological Assessment," by Manfred Bietak and Karin Kopetzky; 4. "Assyrians Abet Israelite Cultic Reforms: Sennacherib and the Centralization of the Israelite Cult," by Elizabeth Bloch-Smith; 5. "'Those Who Add House to House': Household Archaeology and the Use of Domestic Space in an Iron II Residential Compound at Tell en-Nasbeh," by Aaron J. Brody; 6. "More Light on Old Reliefs: New Kingdom

Bibliography

Egyptian Siege Tactics and Asiatic Resistance," by Aaron A. Burke; 7. "Cores, Peripheries, and Ports of Power: Theories of Canaanite Development in the Early Second Millennium B.C.E.," by Susan L. Cohen; 8. "The Social Worlds of the Book of Job," by Michael D. Coogan; 9. "Telltale Remnants of Oral Epic in the Older Sources of the Tetrateuch: Double and Triple Proper Names in Early Hebrew Sources and in Homeric and Ugaritic Epic Poetry," by Frank Moore Cross; 10. "Merenptah's 'Israel,' the Bible's, and Ours," by William G. Dever;11. "Linchpins Revisited," by Trude Dothan and Alexandra S. Drenka; 12. "Cities, Villages, and Farmsteads: The Landscape of Leviticus 25:29-31," by Avraham Faust; 13. "Destructions: Megiddo as a Case Study," by Israel Finkelstein; 14. "The Late Iron Age II Incense Altars from Ashkelon," by Seymour Gitin; 15. "Palmachim–Giv'at Ha'esev: A Navigational Landmark for Ancient Mariners?" by Ram Gophna and Shmuel Liphschitz; 16. "Wine for the Elite, Oil for the Masses: Some Aspects of Early Agricultural Technology in Cyprus," by Sophocles Hadjisavvas; 17. "The Dawn of an Age: Megiddo in the Iron Age I," by Baruch Halpern; 18. "Compositional Techniques in the Book of Haggai," by Paul D. Hanson; 19. "Lifting the Veil on a 'Dark Age': Tayinat and the North Orontes Valley during the Early Iron Age," by Timothy P. Harrison; 20. "Other Edens," by Ronald Hendel; 21. "The House of the Father at Iron I Tall al-'Umayri, Jordan," by Larry G. Herr; 22. "Israel's Ancestors Were Not Nomads," by Theodore Hiebert; 23. "How Much Is That in . . . ? Monetization, Money, Royal States, and Empires," by John S. Holladay; 24. "The Levitical Diaspora (I): A Sociological Comparison with Morocco's Ahansal," by Jeremy M. Hutton; 25. "A Cypriot Workshop of Middle Bronze Age Askoi," by Vassos Karageorghis; 26. "Slavery in Antiquity," by Philip J. King; 27. "Ethnic Identity in Biblical Edom, Israel, and Midian: Some Insights from Mortuary Contexts in the Lowlands of Edom," by Thomas E. Levy; 28. "A Reconstruction of Achaemenid-Period Ashkelon Based on the Faunal Evidence," by David Lipovitch; 29. "Hazael, Birhadad, and the .r.," by Aren M. Maeir; 30. "Divination at Ebla during the Old Syrian Period: The Archaeological Evidence," by Nicol Marchetti; 31. "Egyptian Fingerprints at Late Bronze Age Ashkelon: Egyptian-Style Beer Jars," by Mario A. S. Martin 32. "From the Buqê'ah to Ashkelon," by Daniel M. Master; 33. "The Iron Age Dwellings at Tell Qasile," by Amihai Mazar; 34. "The Armor of Goliath," by Alan Millard; 35. "Facts or Factoids? Some Historical Observations on the Trophy Inscription from Kition (KAI 288)," by Paul G. Mosca; 36. "Ashkelon under the Assyrian Empire," by Nadav Na'aman; 37. "The Built Tombs on the Spring Hill and the Palace of the Lords of Jericho (`dmr r.`) in the Middle Bronze Age," by Lorenzo Nigro; 38. "A New Join of Fragments of the Baal Cycle," by Dennis Pardee; 39. "L'inscription phénicienne du pithos d'Amathonte et son contexte," by Émile Puech; 40. "A Fragmentary Tablet from Tel Aphek with Unknown Script," by Itamar Singer; 41. "Camels in Ur III Babylonia?" by Piotr Steinkeller; 42. "A Persian-period Hoard of Bullae from Samaria," by Ephraim Stern; 43. "Trade and Power in Late Bronze Age Canaan," by Michael Sugerman; 44. "East of Ashkelon: The Setting and Settling of the Judean Lowlands in the Iron Age IIA," by Ron E. Tappy; 45. "The Books of the Hebrew Bible as Material Artifacts," by Karel van der Toorn; 46. "The Temple Mount in Jerusalem during the First Temple Period: An Archaeologist's View," by David Ussishkin; 47. "The Israelite mi.p..â, the Priestly Writings, and Changing Valences in Israel's Kinship Terminology," by David S. Vanderhooft; 48. "Two New Hellenistic Lead Weights of the Tanit Series," by Samuel R. Wolff and Gerald Finkielsztejn; 49. "Behavioral Patterns in Transition: Eleventh-Century B.C.E. Innovation in Domestic Textile Production," by Assaf Yasur-Landau; 50. "Bedhat esh-Sha'ab: An Iron Age I Enclosure in the Jordan Valley," by Adam Zertal and Dror Ben-Yosef.

Schmidt, Peter R., and Roderick J. McIntosh
1996   *Plundering Africa's Past.* Bloomington: Indiana University Press.

Schroer, Silvia, and Thomas Staubli
2001   *Body Symbolism in the Bible.* Collegeville, Minn.: Liturgical Press.

Schwappach-Shirrif, Lisa
2004   *Treasures of the Rosicrucian Egyptian Museum: A Catalogue.* San Jose: Grand Lodge of the English Language Jurisdiction, AMORC.

Schwimmer, Brian
1995   "Segmentary Lineages." http://umanitoba.ca/faculties/arts/anthropology/tutor/descent/unilineal/segments.html.

Scolnic, Benjamin Edidin

2004 "A New Working Hypothesis for the Identification of Migdol." In *The Future of Biblical Archaeology: Reassessing Methodologies and Assumptions. The Proceedings of a Symposium, August 12–14, 2001, at Trinity International University,* edited by James K. Hoffmeier and Alan Millard, 91–120. Grand Rapids: Eerdmans.

Scrolls from the Dead Sea: The Ancient Library of Qumran and Modern Scholarship. http://www.ibiblio.org/expo/deadsea.scrolls.exhibit/intro.html.

Illustrated cyber-exhibit posted by the Library of Congress.

Searight, Sarah, ed.

2005 *Women Travellers in the Near East.* Oxford: Oxbow.

Women travelers in world of the Bible during the nineteenth century were educated, enlightened, and sometimes romantic. Some traveled alone, a few with companions. Some had private incomes that facilitated their travels. They were not much concerned with public opinion back home that was critical of their independence. They were physically and mentally resilient. Above all, they were inquisitive. Some wrote fascinating journals and letters of their exotic travels.

Sertillanges, A. C.

1923 *The Intellectual Life: Its Spirit, Conditions, and Methods.* Washington, D.C.: Catholic University of America Press.

Severin, T.

1973 *Vanishing Primitive Man.* New York: Oxford University Press.

Shai, Itzhaq

2006 "The Political Organization of the Philistines." In *"I Will Speak the Riddles of Ancient Times": Archaeological and Historical Studies in Honor of Amihai Mazar on the Occasion of His Sixtieth Birthday,* edited by Aren M. Maeir and Pierre de Miroschedji, 1:347–60. 2 vols. Winona Lake, Ind.: Eisenbrauns.

Shanks, Hershel

1983 "The Sad Case of Tel Gezer." *Biblical Archaeology Review* 9:30–42.

1988, *Ancient Israel: A Short History from*
ed. *Abraham to the Roman Destruction of the Temple.* Englewood Cliffs, N.J.: Prentice-Hall.

1996 "Magnificent Obsession: The Private World of the Antiquities Collector." *Biblical Archaeology Review* 22:22–35.

1997 "Leading Archaeologist Chastised for Publishing Artifacts in Private Collections: Debate Over Antiquities Market Continues." *Biblical Archaeology Review* 23:33.

1999a "Don't Buy Forgeries (In Other Words, Don't Collect)." *Biblical Archaeology Review* 25:6.

1999b "Bringing Collectors and Their Collections Out of Hiding." *Biblical Archaeology Review* 25:40.

2000 "Sacrilegious Neglect." *Biblical Archaeology Review* 26:41.

2001 "The Age of BAR: Scholars Talk about How the Field Has Changed." *Biblical Archaeology Review* 27:21–35.

Shanks discusses with leading archaeologists how biblical archaeology has changed since 1976 when the first issue of *Biblical Archaeology Review* was published.

2005 "Should the Israel Museum Take the Dayan Collection off Display?" *Biblical Archaeology Review* 31:53–57.

2007 *The Copper Scroll and the Search for the Temple Treasure.* Washington, D.C.: Biblical Archaeology Society.

Shanks tells the story of the discovery, unfolding, translation, and the interpretation of the Copper Scroll found near Khirbet Qumran. The scroll itself is an enigma. It is the only Dead Sea Scroll ham-

Bibliography

mered in copper and only one of four or five scrolls that has survived complete.

Shanks, Michael

2008 "Post Processual Archaeology and After." In *Handbook of Archaeological Theories,* edited by R. Alexander Bentley, Herbert D. G. Maschner, and Christopher Chippindale, 133–46. Lanham, Md.: Rowman & Littlefield.

Shaw, Ian, and Paul Nicholson

2003 *The British Museum Dictionary of Ancient Egypt.* London: British Museum.

Shestack, Alan

1987 "The Museum and Cultural Property: The Transformation of Institutional Ethics." In *The Ethics of Collecting Cultural Property: Whose Culture? Whose Property?,* edited by Phyllis Mauch Messenger, 93–101. Albuquerque: University of New Mexico Press.

Siebert, I.

1974 *Women in the Ancient Near East.* New York: Abner Schram.

Silberman, Neil Asher

1982 *Digging for God and Country: Exploration, Archeology, and the Secret Struggle for the Holy Land—1799–1917.* New York: Doubleday.

Silberman uses a political outline in reporting on how archaeology became a tool for empire building. Napoleon used archaeology in Egypt to define his empire as the direct descendant of the empire of Alexander and the empires of the pharaohs (Silberman 1982, 10–17). Similarly, Wilhelm II (1888–1918) challenged British supremacy in the Middle East by offering the Ottoman Empire of Abdul Hamid (1842–1918) technical and financial support to build a railway from Constantinople to Palestine, to build a German Lutheran Church of the Redeemer adjacent to Holy Sepulchre, and a German Catholic Monastery and Church of the Dormition of Mary. In return, the Deutscher Palaestina Verein was given permission to conduct inaugu-

ral excavations at the coveted sites of Megiddo, Jericho, Jerusalem, the Roman Baalbek in Lebanon, and Galilean synagogues from the first century of the Common Era and to finish mapping the land east of the Jordan River. Consequently, archaeological, and therefore political, supremacy in the world of the Bible passed from Britain to Germany (Silberman 1982, 161–70).

1989 *Between Past and Present: Archaeology, Ideology and Nationalism in the Modern Middle East.* New York: H. Holt.

Time and again, states and individuals have called on archaeology to define borders, legitimize ideologies, investigate issues of contemporary concern, and establish genealogies for a leader or a whole people. Silberman explores the interaction between archaeological research and political and social trends.

2001 *Archaeology and Society in the 21st Century: The Dead Sea Scrolls and Other Case Studies,* edited by Neil Asher Silberman and Ernest S. Frerichs. Jerusalem: Israel Exploration Society.

This anniversary volume celebrates the fiftieth anniversary (1948–1998) of the discovery of the Dead Sea Scrolls. The collection contains eighteen chapters in five sections; an introduction (E. S. Frerichs and N. A. Silberman) and a conclusion, "Many Battles of the Scrolls" (L. Schiffman). Each section has a chapter on the scrolls and comparative case studies: (1) politics and the past (N. A. Silberman, L. Silverblatt, and M. Hall); (2) presenting the past to the public (A. Roitman, G. Bisheh, and C. Doumas); (3) deciphering ancient writing (B. Fagan, E. Tov, D. Redford, and G. E. Stuart); (4) antiquities looting and law (Gerstenblith, H. Shanks, E. Herscher, and H. A. Davis); (5) the power of the past in the twenty-first century (L. Schiffman. P. E. Hyman, and D. Lowenthal).

2003 "A Century of American Archaeology in the Middle East: Looking Back and Looking Ahead." In *One Hundred Years of American Archaeology in the Middle East: Proceedings of the American Schools of Oriental Research Centennial Celebration, Washington DC, April 2000,* edited by Douglas R. Clark and Victor H. Matthews, 7–17. Boston: American Schools of Oriental Research.

Simmons, Alan H.

2007   *The Neolithic Revolution in the Near East: Transforming the Human Landscape.* Tucson: University of Arizona Press.

Simmons traces the evolution of Neolithic technologies, for example, sea trade with Cyprus, and their impact on the sensitive relationship between humans and their environment, and how quickly events such as climate change can alter the landscape.

Singer, Itamar

2006   "The Hittites and the Bible Revisited." In *"I Will Speak the Riddles of Ancient Times": Archaeological and Historical Studies in Honor of Amihai Mazar on the Occasion of His Sixtieth Birthday,* edited by Aren M. Maeir and Pierre de Miroschedji, 1:723–56. Winona Lake, Ind.: Eisenbrauns.

Sivan, Hagith

1988a   "Holy Land Pilgrimage and Western Audiences: Some Reflections on Egeria and Her Circle." *Classical Quarterly* 38:528–35.

1988b   "Who Was Egeria? Piety and Pilgrimage in the Age of Gratian." *Harvard Theological Review* 81:59–72.

Skeen, Judy Lynn

1993   "A Comparative Study of the Wandering People of Hebrews and the Pilgrimage of Egeria." Ph.D., dissertation. Southern Baptist Theological Seminary.

Slater, Robert

1992   *Warrior Statesman: The Life of Moshe Dayan.* London: Robson.

Smelik, Klass A. D.

1990   "The Literary Structure of King Mesha's Inscription." *Journal for the Study of the Old Testament* 46:21–30.

1992   "King Mesha's Inscription." In idem, *Converting the Past: Studies in Ancient Israelite and Moabite Historiography,* 59–92. Oudtestamentische studiën 28. Leiden: Brill.

Smelik provides a historical reconstruction for the Annals of Mesha and the Annals of Jehoram.

2003   "The Inscription of King Mesha." In *The Context of Scripture,* edited by William W. Hallo and K. Lawson Younger, Jr., 2:137–38. Leiden: Brill.

Smith, George

1872a   "The Chaldean History of the Deluge." *The London Times* (December 4, 1872): 27551.

1872b   "The Chaldean Story of the Deluge." *The London Times* (December 5, 1872): 27552.

Smith, Jonathan Z.

1987   *To Take Place: Toward Theory in Ritual.* Chicago: University of Chicago Press.

Smith, Laurajane

1994   "Heritage Management as Postprocessual Archaeology?" *Antiquity* 68:300–309.

Smith explores the relationship between explicitly political postmodern or post-processual archaeology and heritage management where archaeology most directly engages politics. He investigates (1) the political and cultural role played by archaeologists as intellectuals; (2) the degree to which archaeological knowledge and ideology have been both institutionalized and constrained within state institutions and discourses; (3) the role heritage plays in the politically fraught process of the construction of cultural identity.

Smith, Mahlon H.

"The Dead Sea Scrolls."

Virtual Religion Network: resources for research and reflection
http://virtualreligion.net/iho/qumran.html

Smith reconstructs a helpful, and remarkably detailed, timetable for the discovery and debate of the Dead Sea Scrolls.

Bibliography

Smith, Mark S.

1990   *The Early History of God: Yahweh and the Other Deities in Ancient Israel.* San Francisco: Harper & Row.

2001   *The Origins of Biblical Monotheism: Israel's Polytheistic Background and the Ugaritic Texts.* Oxford: Oxford University Press.

Snell, Daniel C.

1997   *Life in the Ancient Near East, 3100–332 B.C.E.* New Haven: Yale University Press.

Sorensen, M. L. S.

2000   *Gender Archaeology.* Cambridge: Polity.

Stack, Michael

2002   "A Review of *The Principles of History and Other Writings in Philosophy of History.* Edited by W. H. Dray and W. J. van der Dussen." *University of Toronto Quarterly* 71.

Stager, Lawrence E.

1985   "The Archaeology of the Family in Ancient Israel." *Bulletin of the American Schools of Oriental Research* 260:1–35.

> Stager conducts a study of long-term trends (French: *longue durée*) among people of ancient Israel, who, after 1200 B.C.E., built villages on the hilltops north of Jerusalem and who built terraces on the slopes of the valleys below for their crops. A pivotal institution in this culture was the household, whose political and economic structure can be reconstructed using the remains of their pillared houses. He uses archaeological, textual, and ethnographic data to recreate the social structure of early Israel.

Stager, Lawrence E., and Samuel R. Wolff

1984   "Child Sacrifice at Carthage: Religious Rite or Population Control—Archaeological Evidence Provides Basis for a New Analysis." *Biblical Archaeology Review* 10:31–51.

Stanford Encyclopedia of Philosophy, *s.v.* "Critical Theory." http://plato.stanford.edu/.

Steen, Eveline van der

1999   "Survival and Adaptation: Life East of the Jordan in the Transition from the Late Bronze Age to the Early Iron Age." *Palestine Exploration Quarterly* 131:176–92.

Steinberg, Naomi

1999   "The Problem of Human Sacrifice in War: An Analysis of Judges 11." In *On the Way to Nineveh: Studies in Honor of George M. Landes,* edited by Stephen L. Cook and S. C. Winter,114–35. ASOR Books 4. Atlanta: Scholars Press.

Steiner, Margarete Laura

2002   "Mesha versus Solomon: Two Models of Economic Organization in Iron Age II." *Svensk Exegetisk Årsbok* 67:37–45.

Stern, Ephraim

1982   *Material Culture of the Land of the Bible in the Persian Period, 538–332 B.C.E.* Arminster: Aris & Phillips.

1993, ed.   *The New Encyclopedia of Archaeological Excavations in the Holy Land.* New York: Simon & Schuster.

> Encyclopedias like this one are site specific. They describe a single site, stratum by stratum, using material remains to reconstruct the cultures of each archaeological period. The profile of *Bab edh-Dhra* by R. Thomas Shaub, for example, identifies the site geographically on the eastern shore of the Dead Sea in Jordan today (http://www.nd.edu/~edsp/personnel.html) and a brief history of excavations there. He then describes the material remains from the Paleolithic period, the Neolithic period, the Chalcolithic period, the Early Bronze Age IA, Early Bronze Age IB, Early Bronze Age IC, Early Bronze Age II, Early Bronze Age III, and Late Early Bronze Age II or Early Bronze Age IV (Stern 1993, 1:130–36). Schaub introduces the exclusively archaeological survey by indexing the work that he and Walter E. Rast and subsequently Willem C. van Hattem published elsewhere (Rast 1974; Van Hattem 1981). Both articles suggest that the ruins of magnificent Bronze Age cities like Bab edh Dhra may have

inspired the stories of Lot and his daughters in the book of Genesis (Gen 19:1-38).

2001 *Archaeology of the Land of the Bible: The Assyrian, Babylonian, and Persian Periods 732–332 B.C.E.* New York: Doubleday.

Stiebing, William H., Jr.

1989 *Out of the Desert? Archaeology and the Exodus/ Conquest Narratives.* Buffalo: Prometheus.

Stiebing argues that the plagues were a literary description of economic disasters caused by natural disasters in Egypt.

Stierlin, Henri

1995 *The Pharaohs: Master Builders.* Paris: Pierre Terrail.

From 3000 B.C.E. to the Common Era, pharaohs built pyramids at Giza, sanctuaries at Luxor, Karnak, and Philae; tombs in the Valley of the Pharaohs. Each building was not only an architectural masterpiece but a sacrament reflecting the worldview of this ancient people.

Strathern, Paul

2007 *Napoleon in Egypt: A Clash of Cultures.* New York: Random House.

Napoleon is a historical figure whose character is so complex, and whose exploits are spread across such a broad canvas, that it is almost impossible to do them justice. Strathern has written a narrative of the Egyptian adventure, which simultaneously demonstrates how Napoleon's invasion of Egypt foreshadowed many aspects of his later rule in France. Here in embryo are many of the later preoccupations of Napoleon's peculiar brand of megalomania.

Strawn, Brett A.

2005 *What Is Stronger than a Lion? Leonine Image and Metaphor in the Hebrew Bible and the Ancient Near East.* Orbis Biblicus et Orientalis 212. Fribourg: Academic Press.

Strawn classifies more than two hundred biblical uses of lions as metaphors for the righteous, for the wicked, for rulers, and for divine patrons. Seals and onomastica from Israel (1500–332 B.C.E.) represent rulers and divine patrons acting in their official capacity as lions. Lions are also metaphors for Yahweh, especially in the book of Psalms. These images develop from female divine patrons like Sekhmet or Ishtar rather than from male patrons like Baal or Seth. Lions in other ancient Near Eastern parallels are also metaphors for power, both protecting and threatening. One appendix discusses the Hebrew words for "lion"; another provides 483 line drawings of lions.

Stuart, George E.

1987 "Working Together to Preserve Our Past." In *The Ethics of Collecting Cultural Property: Whose Culture? Whose Property?,* edited by Phyllis Mauch Messenger, 243–52. Albuquerque: University of New Mexico.

Sullivan, Thelma D.

1972 "Tlaloc: A New Etymological Interpretation of the God's Name and What It Reveals of His Essence and Nature." *Proceedings of the 40ᵗʰ International Congress of Americanists* 2:103. Genoa.

The Aztecs sacrificed their children at significant places in nature—water sources, fertile fields— where Tlaloc sacrificed her children for the Aztecs. Wherever there were openings or *mouths* in the body of Tlaloc, the Aztecs offered sacrifice. The creation stories of the Aztecs explain that for Tlaloc to be able to release life-giving power, she had to be dismembered. In order to give birth, she had to be split in two. A parallel tradition appears in the *Enuma Elish* stories, where Marduk kills Tiamat and then cuts her body in two to create the heavens and the earth.

Sumption, Jonathan

1976 *Pilgrimage: An Image of Medieval Religion.* Totowa, N.J.: Rowman & Littlefield.

Sweeney, Marvin A.

2000 *The Twelve Prophets.* Berit Olam: Studies in Hebrew Narrative and Poetry. Collegeville, Minn.: Liturgical Press.

Bibliography

Thomas, Nancy

1995   *The American Discovery of Ancient Egypt.* Los Angeles: Los Angeles County Museum of Art.

Thomas edits an exhibition catalogue that describes the contributions of American Egyptologists to the understanding of Egypt and Nubia. In contrast to the well-known efforts of European Egyptologists like Jean-François Champollion and Howard Carter, American achievements have often gone unnoticed. For example, George A. Reisner (1867–1942) reconstructed the culture of the Nile Valley of the Fourth Dynasty pharaohs who built the pyramids and of the rulers of Nubia and Kush; and he revolutionized archaeological field techniques. The essays clarify various perceptions of ancient Egypt in the writings of American travelers, collectors, and archaeologists between 1899 and 1960. A list of excavations directed by Americans appears in the appendix.

Thompson, Henry O.

1987   *Biblical Archaeology: The World, the Mediterranean, the Bible.* New York: Paragon House.

Thompson uses historical and thematic outlines in his introduction to archaeology and the Bible: Archaeology Itself; The History of Archaeology; Archaeology and Science; Daily Life in Biblical Times; Archaeology Illuminates the Bible; and Archaeology and Religion.

1992   "Yahweh." In *The Anchor Bible Dictionary,* edited by David Noel Freedman, 6:1001–12. 6 vols. New York: Doubleday.

Thompson, J. A.

1962   *The Bible and Archaeology.* Grand Rapids: Eerdmans.

1986   *Handbook of Life in Bible Times.* Downers Grove, Ill.: InterVarsity.

Thompson, Jason

1992   *Sir Gardner Wilkinson and His Circle.* Austin: University of Texas Press.

2008a   *Edward William Lane: A Biography.* Oxford: Oxbow.

2008b   "An Account of the Journeys and Writings of the Indefatigable Mr. Lane." *Saudi Aramco World,* March/April: 30–39.

Lane became Britain's more renowned scholar of the culture of Egypt. He wrote a fascinating study of Egyptian society—*An Account of the Manners and Customs of the Modern Egyptians* (1836)—a classic study that is still in print. His Arabic-English dictionary is still a basic, irreplaceable reference work.

Thompson, Thomas L.

1996   "Historiography of Ancient Palestine and Early Jewish Historiography: W. G. Dever and the Not So New Biblical Archaeology." In *The Origins of the Ancient Israelite States,* edited by Volkmar Fritz and Philip R. Davies, 26–43. Journal for the Study of the Old Testament Supplement Series 228. Sheffield: JSOT Press.

Thompson offers a minimalist assessment of how biblical archaeology continues to fail to answer its own research questions and of archaeological standards in general.

2006   "Archaeology and the Bible Revisited." *Scandinavian Journal of the Old Testament* 20:286–13.

Throckmorton, Peter

1960   "Thirty-three Centuries under the Sea." *National Geographic* 117:682–703.

1962   "Oldest Known Shipwreck Yields Bronze Age Cargo." *National Geographic* 121:696–711.

Throckmorton provides a popular account of the excavation.

1964   *The Lost Ships: An Adventure in Underwater Archaeology.* Boston: Little, Brown.

1987,   *The Sea Remembers: Shipwrecks and Archaeology from Homer's Greece to the Rediscovery of the Titanic.* New York: Weidenfeld & Nicolson.
ed.

Throckmorton edits the most comprehensive overview of underwater archaeology from its beginnings.

Toivari-Vitala, J.
2001   *Women at Deir el-Medina: A Study of the Status and Roles of the Female Inhabitants in the Workmen's Community during the Ramesside Period.* Leiden: Nederlands Instituut voor het Nabije Oosten.

Toorn, Karel van der
2007   *Scribal Culture and the Making of the Hebrew Bible.* Cambridge, Mass.: Harvard University Press.

Towler, J., and J. Bramall
1986   *Midwives in History and Society.* London: Croom Helm.

Trible, Phyllis
1973   "Depatriarchalizing in Biblical Interpretation." *Journal of the American Academy of Religion* 41:30–38.
        A seminal study.

Trigger, Bruce
2006   *A History of Archaeological Thought.* 2nd ed. New York: Cambridge University Press.
        Trigger examines the history of archaeology from medieval times to the present in worldwide perspective. He places the development of archaeological thought and theory within a broad social and intellectual framework and seeks to determine the extent to which these trends were a reflection of the personal and collective interests of archaeologists as these relate to the fluctuating middle-class fortunes. Subjective influences have been powerful; nonetheless, the accumulation of archaeological data has exercised a growing constraint on interpretation. Consequently, objectivity of archaeological research has steadily increased and enhanced its value for understanding human history.

Trope, Betsy Teasley, Stephen Quirke, and Peter Lacovara
2005   *Excavating Egypt: Great Discoveries from the Petrie Museum of Egyptian Archaeology.* Atlanta: Emory University Press.

Tubb, Jonathan N., and Rupert L. Chapman.
1990   *Archaeology and the Bible.* London: British Museum

Tyldesley, Joyce
2005   *Egypt: How a Lost Civilization Was Rediscovered.* Berkeley: University of California Press.

Ullmann-Margalit, Edna
2008   "Dissecting the Qumran-Essene Hypothesis." *Biblical Archaeology Review* 34:63–67, 86.
        Ullmann-Margalit evaluates the competing interpretations of Qumran and the Dead Sea Scrolls as a philosopher of science. She concludes: "All in all the Qumran-Essene theory has found ingenious ways to co-opt some of its challengers. Subtly adapted and re-described, it endures as the reigning consensus in Qumran studies. Barring dramatic new evidence that might yet come to light and cause a sea-change, this status of the Qumran-Essene theory, as far as I can judge, is just about right" (2008, 67).

Van Beek, Gus W.
1988   "Excavation of Tells." In *Benchmarks in Time and Culture: An Introduction to Palestinian Archaeology,* edited by Joel F. Drinkard, Jr., Gerald L. Mattingly, and J. Maxwell Miller, 131–67. Atlanta: Scholars Press.
        Van Beek describes the excavation process step by step: the nature of a tell, site selection, selection of areas to be excavated, staff selection, funding, tell stratification, contour plans, test pits and trenches, excavating layers, excating walls, balk removal, recording the information and the task of interpretation.

1989, ed.   *The Scholarship of William Foxwell Albright: An Appraisal.* Harvard Semitic Studies 33. Atlanta: Scholars Press.
        On the 350th anniversary of the founding of Maryland, Van Beek appraises the legacy of William Foxwell Albright at a symposium by Albright's students for Albright—a son of the state for most of his professional career at Johns Hopkins University.

Bibliography

Vaughn, Andrew G.

2003   "Is Biblical Archaeology Theologically Useful Today? Yes, a Programmatic Proposal." In *Jerusalem in Bible and Archaeology: The First Temple Period,* edited by Andrew Vaughn and Ann E. Killebrew, 407–30. Society of Biblical Literature Symposium Series 18. Atlanta: Society of Biblical Literature.

Vaughn, Andrew G., and Ann E. Killebrew, eds.

2003   *Jerusalem in Bible and Archaeology: The First Temple Period.* Society of Biblical Symposium Series 18. Atlanta: Society of Biblical Literature.

Vieweger, Dieter, and Jutta Haser

2007   "Tall Zira'a: Five Thousand Years of Palestinian History on a Single-settlement Mound." *Near Eastern Archaeology* 70:147–67.

Wachsmann, Shelley

1994   *Seagoing Ships and Seamanship in the Late Bronze Age.* College Station: Texas A&M University Press.

Wallach, Janet

1999   *Desert Queen: The Extraordinary Life of Gertrude Bell, Adventurer, Adviser to Kings, Ally of Lawrence of Arabia.* New York: Doubleday.

In the wake of the first Gulf War (1990–1991) Wallach writes a biography of Gertrude Bell, the English woman who almost single-handedly created the state of Iraq.

Walton, John H.

2006   *Ancient Near Eastern Thought and the Old Testament: Introducing the Conceptual World of the Hebrew Bible.* Grand Rapids: Baker Academic.

Walton writes a comprehensive and comparative study of the cultural worlds of ancient Israel and its neighbors in the world of the Bible. The introduction explains the importance and the methods of comparative study. The comparisons explain how these ancient peoples thought about religion, the cosmos, and themselves.

Warren, Karen J.

1987   "A Philosophical Perspective on the Ethics and Resolution of Cultural Properties Issues." In *The Ethics of Collecting Cultural Property: Whose Culture? Whose Property?,* edited by Phyllis Mauch Messenger, 1–25. Albuquerque: University of New Mexico Press.

Warzeski, Jeanne-Marie

2005   "'Women's Work for Women': American Presbyterian Missionary Women in Egypt, 1854–1914." In *Women Travellers in the Near East,* edited by Sara Searight, 79–91. Oxford: Oxbow.

Watson, Patty Jo

1999   "Ethnographic Analogy and Ethnoarchaeology." In *Archaeology, History and Culture in Palestine and the Near East: Essays in Memory of Albert E. Glock,* edited by Tomis Kapitan, 47–65. ASOR Books 3. Atlanta: Scholars Press.

2008   "Processualism and After." In *Handbook of Archaeological Theories,* edited by R. Alexander Bentley, Herbert D. G. Maschner, and Christopher Chippindale, 29–38. Lanham, Md.: Rowman & Littlefield.

Watson, Patty Jo, Steven LaBlanc, and Charles Redman

1984   *Archaeological Explanation: The Scientific Method in Archaeology.* New York: Columbia University Press.

The authors promoted the use of processual archaeology and called for archaeologists to use the same scientific method as other scientists. Any archaeological hypothesis should be rigorously tested in the field before it is used to interpret a culture or to reconstruct its structure.

Watson, Wilfred G. E.
2003   "Daily Life in Ancient Ugarit (Syria)." In *Life and Culture in the Ancient Near East,* edited by Richard E. Averbeck, Mark W. Chavalas, and David B. Weisberg, 121–52. Bethesda, Md.: CDL.

Waxman, Sharon
2008   "Loot: The Battle over the Stolen Treasures of the Ancient World." *New York: Times.* http://sharonwaxman.typepad.com/loot/.

Waxman, a former *New York Times* correspondent, interviews smugglers, government officials, dealers, and curators about whether artifacts should be moved to countries where they are safe, well cared for, and accessible to the greatest number of visitors, or should remain in their countries of origin. Her suggestion is a collaborative middle way.

Webster, Gary S.
2008   "Culture History: A Culture-historical Approach." In *Handbook of Archaeological Theories,* edited by R. Alexander Bentley, Herbert D. G. Maschner, and Christopher Chippindale, 11–28. Lanham, Md.: Rowman & Littlefield.

Wegner, J.
2002   "A Decorated Birth-Brick from South Abydos." *Egyptian Archaeology* 20:3–4.

Weisberg, David B.
2003   "Everyday Life in the Neo-Babylonia Period: The Integration of Material and Non-material Culture." In *Life and Culture in the Ancient Near East,* edited by Richard E. Averbeck, Mark W. Chavalas, and David B. Weisberg, 83–94. Bethesda, Md.: CDL.

Wells, Bruce
2005   "Sex, Lies, and Virginal Rape: The Slandered Bride and False Accusation in Deuteronomy." *Journal of Biblical Literature* 124:41–72.

Wertz, R. W., and D. C. Wertz
1977   *Lying-In: A History of Childbirth in America.* New York: Free Press.

West, John Anthony
1989/   *The Traveler's Key to Ancient Egypt: A Guide*
1995   *to the Sacred Places of Ancient Egypt.*

Geography is the outline for introductions to archaeology and the Bible such as West's *Traveler's Key* (rev. ed., 1995). West begins with a discussion of the history of ancient Egypt and the history of archaeology in Egypt, and then moves from north to south along the Nile River describing, for example, the antiquities on the Giza Plain, at Saqqara, Memphis, Beni Hassan, Luxor, Abydos, Dendera, Edfu, Aswan, and Abu Simbel. The final chapter is about Alexandria on the Mediterranean Coast, presumably because it was, until recently, thought to have been an exclusively Hellenistic site (http://www.smithsonianmagazine.com/issues/2007/april/alexandria.php). West does not refer to the book of Judges in his discussion of the Amarna Letters, but he does note the similarity of the Hymn to the Aten and Psalm 104.

Westbrook, Raymond
1985   "Biblical and Cuneiform Law Codes." *Revue biblique* 92:247–64.

Westbrook demonstrates that the legal systems of ancient Israel and Judah, as reflected in the Bible, were similar to those of other Near Eastern cultures. One legal system was not directly dependent on another, but the similarity across systems in the world of the Bible strongly favors the conclusion that most Near Eastern cultures, including ancient Israel, appear to have operated by many of the same legal rules and customs. Understanding how law worked in one society can aid in understanding how law may have worked in another.

1988   *Studies in Biblical and Cuneiform Law.* Paris: Gabalda.

1994   "What Is the Covenant Code?" In *Theory and Method in Biblical and Cuneiform Law: Revision, Interpolation, and Development,* edited by Bernard M. Levinson, 15–36. Journal for the Study of the Old Testament Supplement Series 181. Sheffield: Sheffield Academic Press.

Bibliography

Wevers, J. W., and D. B. Redford, eds.

1972 *Studies on the Ancient Palestinian World: Presented to Professor F. V. Winnett on the Occasion of His Retirement, 1 July 1971.* Toronto: University of Toronto Press.

Wheeler, Mortimer

1954 *Archaeology from the Earth.* Harmondsworth: Penguin.

1955 *Still Digging.* London: Michael Joseph.

1959 *Early India and Pakistan to Ashoka.* New York: Frederick A. Praeger.

1966a *Civilizations of the Indus Valley and Beyond.* London: Thames & Hudson.

1966b *Alms for Oblivion: An Antiquarian's Scrapbook.* London: Weidenfeld & Nicolson.

Whitelam, Keith W.

1996 *The Invention of Ancient Israel: The Silencing of Palestinian History.* New York: Routledge.

Wildung, Dietrich

1998 *Egyptian Art in Berlin: Masterpieces in the Bodemuseum and in Charlottenburg.* Berlin: Ägyptisches Museum und Papyrussammlung.

Wilkinson, John

1977/ *Jerusalem Pilgrims before the Crusades.*
2002 Warminster: Aris & Phillips.

1999 *Egeria's Travels to the Holy Land: Newly Translated, with Supporting Documents and Notes.* Warminster: Aris & Phillips.

Wilkinson, John Gardiner

1837 *Manners and Customs of the Ancient Egyptians.* London: John Murray.

Wilkinson, Tony J.

2003 *Archaeological Landscapes of the Near East.* Tucson: University of Arizona Press.

Using the principles that underlie the preservation and recovery of landscape features, as well as how the cultural landscape was managed through time, Wilkinson provides an overview of Asia Minor to the Arabian Peninsula and from the east coast of the Mediterranean Sea to Persia beginning in the Neolithic period to describe the dynamic character of the Near Eastern landscape. Landscape archaeology is a framework for other studies requiring an understanding of the economic and physical infrastructure of the world of the Bible.

Willey, Gordon R., and Phillip Phillips

1958 *Method and Theory in American Archaeology.* Chicago: University of Chicago Press.

Wilson, Charles William, ed.

1971 *Itinerary from Bordeaux to Jerusalem (333).* Translated by Aubrey Stewart. New York: AMS.

Wilson, Edmund

1969 *The Dead Sea Scrolls, 1947–1969.* London: Collins Fontana.

Wilson publishes a revised and expanded edition of W. A. Allen, *The Scrolls from the Dead Sea* (1955). The influence of his series of articles in the *New Yorker* magazine on which the book is based captured public attention for Qumran and the Dead Sea Scrolls.

Wilson, Kevin A.

2004 "The Campaign of Pharaoh Shoshenq I in Palestine." http://www.bibleinterp.com/articles/Wilson-Campaign_of_Shoshenq_I_1.htm.

Wilson argues that Shoshenq's campaign was not as widespread as previously thought. Instead, it focused only on Jerusalem, and Jerusalem itself was not destroyed. This means that archaeologists will need to find another method for determining the date of tenth-century strata. It also means that they will need to find other suspects for the destruction layers previously assigned to Shoshenq.

Winstone, H. V. F.

2004 *Gertrude Bell: A Biography.* New York: Quartet.

Wood, Bryant G.

1992 "Potter's Wheel." In *The Anchor Bible Dictionary,* edited by David Noel Freedman, 5:427–28. 6 vols. New York: Doubleday.

Wright, G. Ernest

1952 *God Who Acts: Biblical Theology as Recital.* Studies in Biblical Theology 8. London: SCM.

1955 "Israelite Daily life." *Biblical Archaeologist* 18:50–79.

1957 *Biblical Archaeology.* Philadelphia: Westminster.

1962 *The Pottery of Palestine from the Earliest Times to the End of the Early Bronze Age.* New Haven: American Schools of Oriental Research.

1963 *Shechem: Biography of a Biblical City.* New York: McGraw Hill.

1965, ed. *The Bible and the Ancient Near East: Essays in Honor of William Foxwell Albright.* New York: Doubleday.

1969a "Biblical Archaeology Today." In *New Directions in Biblical Archaeology,* edited by David Noel Freedman and Jonas C. Greenfield, 149–65. Garden City, N.Y.: Doubleday.

Biblical archaeology is a subdiscipline of both anthropology, which studies cultures, and of history, which studies events. Biblical archaeologists give the Bible the benefit of the doubt unless there is contrary evidence in the material remains. Their goal is to read the Bible in the setting of its time, its people, and its land. Archaeology has had a profound impact on the understanding of Northwest Semitic languages and their genres. Archaeology has also had a profound impact on the understanding of the theology and anthropology of ancient Israel. The Hebrews did not describe their divine patron with timeless philosophical terms; they told stories about what Yahweh had done. This event-centered thinking cannot be systematized; it includes the confessional recital of past events together with the deductions drawn from them by a worshiping community as a means of renewal in various historical situations. Likewise, the Hebrews described humans by describing their relationships and commitments. In the Bible, humans are historical creatures. Human nature changes and has repeatedly changed. It is impossible for the Bible to understand what it means to be human apart from the actions of those humans in a particular point in time.

1969b *The Old Testament and Theology.* New York: Harper & Row.

Wright, J. Edward

2002 "W. F. Albright's Vision of Israelite Religion." *Near Eastern Archaeology* 65:63–68.

Albright was not so much a twentieth-century genius (Running and Freedman 1975) as a twentiety-century *American Protestant* genius; not the scholar of all time but a scholar of his time. He was an accomplished excavator, pottery expert, language specialist, and historian of the cultures in the world of the Bible. His technical studies in any of these areas are classics. He was also, however, a devout Christian from the Reformation tradition in the United States. Therefore, when Albright used his archaeological work to illuminate the Bible, he allowed his theology to guide his archaeology. His goal was to demonstrate that the way in which American Protestant pastors preached the Bible was historically reliable, and that the Reformation tradition of Christianity in the United States—in contrast to the faith traditions of Catholics and Jews—was biblically faithful. Therefore, Abraham, Isaac, and Jacob were real people whose stories in the book of Genesis accurately reflected daily life in the Middle Bronze Period. The faith of Abraham and, later, of Moses, was uniquely monotheistic and moral in contrast to the polytheistic and explicitly sexual rituals of the indigenous peoples of Syria-Palestine. Joshua led a military crusade that conquered the militarily superior, but culturally inferior, Canaanites.

Yadin, Azzan

1955 "Goliath's Javelin and the *menor 'orgin.*" *Palestine Exploration Quarterly* 8:58–69.

1958 "Solomon's City Wall and Gate at Gezer." *Israel Exploration Journal* 8:80–86.

For Yadin, the excavation of nearly identical tenth-century city walls and gates at three of the four sites listed in the books of Samuel–Kings (1 Kgs 9:15-17)

Bibliography

implies that the defenses could only have been constructed by a highly centralized state of Israel.

1963   *The Art of Warfare in Biblical Land in Light
        of Archaeological Study.* New York: McGraw
        Hill.

1993   "Hazor." In *New Encyclopedia of Archaeological
        Excavations in the Holy Land,* edited by Ephraim
        Stern et al., 2:594–603. Jerusalem: Israel
        Exploration Society.

2004   "Goliath's Armor and Israelite Collective
        Memory." *Vetus Testamentum* 14:374–95.

        Yadin argues that the style of Goliath's armor and
        the institution of one-on-one combat in the story
        of how David delivered Israel from Goliath identify
        it as a biblical parallel to the *Iliad* of Homer, in which
        Menelaus and Paris duel in fine armor. The bibli-
        cal hero story is a response to burgeoning Greek
        national identity in Syria-Palestine and maintains a
        literary dialogue with the Greek epic tradition.

Yamauchi, Edwin M.

1983   "Magic in the Biblical World." *Tyndale Bul-
        letin* 34:169–200.

2003   "Athletics in the Ancient Near East." In *Life
        and Culture in the Ancient Near East,* edited
        by Richard E. Averbeck, Mark W. Chavalas,
        and David B. Weisberg, 491–500. Bethesda,
        Md.: CDL.

Yardeni, Ada

2007   "A Note on a Qumran Scribe." In *New Seals
        and Inscriptions, Hebrew, Idumean and
        Cuneiform,* edited by Meir Lubetski, 287–98.
        Sheffield: Sheffield Phoenix.

        Yardeni argues that, between 100 B.C.E. and 70, a
        scribe with a unique way of writing the letter *lamed*
        copied more than fifty biblical and nonbiblical
        scrolls recovered from Caves 1, 2, 3, 4, 6, and 11 at
        Qumran and also scrolls at Masada.

Yoffee, Norman, and Bradley L. Crowell

2006   "Historical Archaeology in Asia: An
        Introduction." In *Excavating Asian History:
        Interdisciplinary Studies in Archaeology and
        History,* edited by Norman Yoffee and Brad-
        ley L. Crowell, 3–14. Tucson: University of
        Arizona Press.

Yon, Marguerite

2006   *The City of Ugarit at Tell Ras Shamra.* Winona
        Lake, Ind.: Eisenbrauns.

        An updated translation from a 1994 French intro-
        duction to the excavations at the port of Ugarit
        on the northern Mediterranean coast of Syria, as
        well as the nearby port of Mahadu (Arabic: Minet
        el-Beida) and the village at Ras Ibn Hani. Yon con-
        centrates on the thirteenth- and twelfth-century
        strata, before Ugarit's destruction by the Sea
        Peoples. Architectural plans demonstrate the use of
        space at Ugarit. Tablets, seals, stelae, ceramics, and
        handiwork in gold, ivory, and faience reflect the
        city's cosmopolitan character.

Younger, K. Lawson, Jr.

1990   *Ancient Conquest Accounts: A Study of Ancient
        Near Eastern and Biblical History Writing.*
        Journal for the Study of the Old Testament
        Supplement Series 19. Sheffield: JSOT Press.

2003   "'Give Us Our Daily Bread': Everyday Life for
        the Israelite Deportees." In *Life and Culture
        in the Ancient Near East,* edited by Richard E.
        Averbeck, Mark W. Chavalas, and David B.
        Weisberg, 269–88. Bethesda, Md.: CDL.

Younker, Randall W.

2004   "Integrating Faith, the Bible, and Archaeol-
        ogy: A Review of the 'Andrews University
        Way' of doing Archaeology." In *The Future
        of Biblical Archaeology: Reassessing Method-
        ologies and Assumptions,* edited by James K.
        Hoffmeier and Alan Millard, 43–52. Grand
        Rapids: Eerdmans.

Yurco, Frank J.

1986   "Merenptah's Canaanite Campaign." *Journal
        of the American Research Center in Egypt*
        23:189–215.

        For Yurco, a battle scene on the walls of a Karnak
        temple depicts the campaign described in the
        Annals of Merenptah, rather than the Annals of

Ramesses II. Therefore, Yurco considers the figures on the bottom of the drawing to be the first pictures found in Egypt of the biblical Hebrews.

Zevit, Ziony
2001   *The Religions of Ancient Israel: A Synthesis of Parallactic Approaches.* London: Continuum.

This is an anthology of essays using archaeology to reconstruct Hebrew faith practice. The outline of the book is thematic. Essays reconstruct places of worship and liturgical furniture. They also describe the significance of inscriptions at sanctuaries, how the Hebrews describe their own worship, how outsiders describe Hebrew worship, and the names used by Hebrews for their divine patron.

2002   "Three Debates about Bible and Archaeology." *Biblica* 83:1–27.

Ziffer, Irit
2007   "A Note on the Nahal Mishmar 'Crowns.'" In *Ancient Near Eastern Art in Context: Studies in Honor of Irene J. Winter by Her Students,* edited by Jack Cheng and Marian Feldman, 45–66. *Culture and History of the Ancient Near East* 26. Leiden: Brill.

Zohary, M.
1982   *Plants of the Bible.* Cambridge: Cambridge University Press.

Zuckerman, S.
2006   "Where Is the Hazor Archive Buried?" *Biblical Archaeology Review* 32:28–37.

INTERNET SOURCES

Abzu: A Guide to Information Related to the Study of the Ancient Near East on the Web
http://www.etana.org/abzu/abzu-search.pl

Abzu is a guide to networked open-access data relevant to the study and public presentation of the ancient Near East and the ancient Mediterranean world.

"The Amazing Worlds of Archaeology, Anthropology & Ancient Civilizations—History, Social Studies and More"
http://www.archaeolink.com/index.htm

Resources for homework, lesson plans, and other research projects.

Ancient Egypt
http://www.teachers.ash.org.au/jmresources/Egypt/links.html

Extensive list of Internet resources.

Ancient Near East
http://www.ancientneareast.net/israel.html

A gateway site for archaeological sites in the ancient Near East.

Archaeology in the Levant
http://anthro.ucsd.edu/~tlevy/

The University of California, San Diego, Levantine Archaeology Laboratory focuses on archaeological investigations of the evolution of societies in the southern Levant from the Neolithic period to the Iron Age. Most of the data come from UCSD-sponsored excavations in Jordan and Israel. Parallels are also drawn from ongoing ethnoarchaeological work in India to help build models for the past.

Archaeology: What Is It?
http://imnh.isu.edu/digitalatlas/arch/ArchDef/main.htm

ArchNet Digital Library, Massachusetts Institute of Technology
http://archnet.org

ArchNet is a project being developed at the MIT School of Architecture and Planning in close cooperation with, and with the full support of The Aga Khan Trust for Culture, an agency of the Aga Khan Development Network. The Aga Khan Trust for Culture is a private, non-denominational, international development agency with programs dedicated to the improvement of built environments in societies where Muslims have a significant presence.

Bibliography

Art Resource

http://www.artres.com/c/htm/Home.aspx

Art Resource is an art stock photo archive licensing images to all media.

Ashmolean Museum of Art and Archaeology

http://www.ashmolean.org

The Ashmolean Museum of Art and Archaeology at Oxford University is one of a few research collections of ancient Near Eastern artifacts at university and national museums around the world. Together with library resources, teaching, and research in ancient Near Eastern archaeology and languages, its historic collection has laid so many of the foundations of the present knowledge of the world of the Bible.

Atkinson, Kenneth

2008 Review of Katharina Galor, Jean-Baptiste Humbert, and Jürgen Zangenberg, eds., *Qumran, The Site of the Dead Sea Scrolls: Archaeological Interpretations and Debates. Proceedings of a Conference Held at Brown University, November 17–19, 2002.* Leiden: Brill, 2006. *Review of Biblical Literature* http://www.bookreviews.org

BBC Online Network

"First farmers discovered" (October 28, 1999) http://news.bbc.co.uk/hi/english/sci/tech/ newsid_489000/489449.stm

Bell, Gertrude: Gertrude Bell Archive

http://www.gerty.ncl.ac.uk/

The Gertrude Bell papers consist of about sixteen hundred detailed and lively letters to her parents; her sixteen diaries, which she kept while she was traveling; and some forty packets of miscellaneous items. There are also about seven thousand photographs, taken by her from 1900 to 1918. Those of Middle Eastern archaeological sites are of great value because they record structures that have since eroded or, in some cases, have disappeared altogether. Photographs of the desert tribes are of considerable anthropological and ethnographical interest.

Bible and Interpretation

http://www.bibleinterp.com/

Bible and Interpretation, edited by Mark W. Elliott, is dedicated to delivering the latest news, features, editorials, commentary, archaeological interpretation and excavations relevant to the study of the Bible for the public and biblical scholars.

Bible and Women Pilgrims

http://www.umilta.net/egeria.html

Bolen, Todd

Survey of Western Palestine: The Maps. http://www.bibleplaces.com/surveywestern palestinemaps.htm

Bolen has produced an electronic edition of H. H. Kitchener and C. R. Conder's maps. The surveyors distinguished between vineyards, orchards, gardens, woods, scrubs, palms, and fir trees. Locations were designated for winepresses, milestones, tombs, wells, cisterns, and caves. The survey covered all of the territory west of the Jordan River between Tyre in the north and Beersheba in the south.

Bryant, Victor

2001 "The Origins of the Potter's Wheel." http:// www.ceramicstoday.com/articles/potters_ wheel2.htm

Byzantine Studies Page

http://www.fordham.edu/halsall/byzan tium/

Canaan and Ancient Israel, University of Pennsylvania Museum

http://www.museum.upenn.edu/Canaan/ Bibliography.html

While many are familiar with the ancient Canaanites and Israelite peoples through stories from the Bible, this exhibit explores the identities of these peoples in prehistoric times through the material remains that they left behind.

Cargill, Robert R.

2008   "Virtual Qumran" http://virtualqumran. blogspot.com/

"Ancient Qumran: A Virtual Reality Tour (the movie)" is based on the UCLA Qumran Visualization Project's digital model of Qumran. It takes the viewer on a tour of the reconstructed settlement of Khirbet Qumran. It offers a history of the archaeological excavation of the site and the surrounding caves, and discusses the different theories concerning the nature and expansion of Qumran. This film is an updated and expanded version of the live-narration movie playing at the San Diego Natural History Museum as a part of their exhibition of the Dead Sea Scrolls.

Chicago Assyrian Dictionary Project

http://oi.uchicago.edu/research/projects/cad/

The *Chicago Assyrian Dictionary (CAD)*, initiated in 1921 by James H. Breasted, is compiling a comprehensive dictionary of the various dialects of Akkadian, the earliest known Semitic language, which was recorded on cuneiform texts that date from 2400 B.C.E. to 100 recovered from excavations at ancient Near Eastern sites. The *Assyrian Dictionary* is a joint undertaking of resident and nonresident scholars from around the world who have contributed their time and labor over a period of seventy years to the collection of the source materials and to the publication of the *Dictionary*.

Coptic Museum, Cairo

http://www.copticmuseum.gov.eg/english/default.htm

Morcos Smeika Pasha, the Ottoman governor of Egypt, founded the Coptic Museum in 1910. The museum was built on land at the Fort of Babylon donated by Coptic popes Kerolos V and Abba Yuanis XIX. It houses some sixteen thousand artifacts reflecting the history of Christianity in Egypt.

Council for British Research in the Levant

http://www.cbrl.org.uk/

The Council for British Research in the Levant (CBRL)—formerly the British School of Archaeology in Jerusalem and the British Institute at Amman for Archaeology and History—is the British Academy sponsored institute for research into the humanities and social sciences with research centers in Amman and Jerusalem and field bases in Homs and Wadi Faynan. The CBRL promotes research in the modern countries of Cyprus, Israel, Jordan, Lebanon, the Palestinian Territories, and Syria, closely related to the former Bilad el-Sham.

Cyberpursuits: Archaeology

http://www.cyberpursuits.com/archeo

Cyberpursuits: Archaeology is an archive of links to archaeological sites and projects of specific geographic regions and specific disciplines such as underwater and marine archaeology. There are pages that lead to reference material, academic departments, libraries, museums, publications, and organizations.

Digmaster (Cobb Institute, Mississippi State University)

http://www.cobb.msstate.edu/dig/

A database of artifacts from the Near East (Lahav, Maresha, Peirides).

Dinur Center Archaeology Project (Hebrew University of Jerusalem)

http://jewish history.huji.ac.il/links/Archaeology.htm

Links to home pages of archaeological excavations.

Ebeling, Jennie R.

2000   "Recent Archaeological Discoveries at Hazor." http://www.bibleinter.com/articles/Hazor_Ebeling.htm

Franciscan Cyperspot: Christian Pilgrimage to the Holy Land

http://www.christusrex.org/www1/ofm/pilgr/00PilgrHome.html

Thousands of pilgrims visited the Holy Land in the first centuries of Christianity to follow in the "footsteps of Christ, of the Prophets and of the Apostles" (Origen). Some wrote journals that were famous; other diaries were left neglected for centuries in archives and libraries. All of them are of some interest, not only to scholars but to all those who love the holy places. The "Christian Pilgrimage to the Holy Land" project offers the best of these early pilgrims' accounts in a simple, interactive interface on the Internet.

Bibliography

Glossarist: archaeology glossaries and archaeology
    dictionaries
    http://www.glossarist.com

Hanson, K. C.
    HomePage, http://www.kchanson.com

Hazor Excavations in Memory of Yigael Yadin
    http://unixware.mscc.huji.ac.il/~hatsor/
    hazor.html

Hernandez, Miguel
    "Stature Estimation in Extinct Aonikenk and
    the Myth of Patagonian Gigantism."

    http://www3.interscience.wiley.com/cgi-bin/
    abstract/28170/

History of the Ancient Near East Electronic Com-
    pendium: Ancient Israel, Iraq, Egypt, Turkey,
    Iran, Syria, Lebanon, Jordan, Arabia, Cyprus,
    and Bahrain.
    http://ancientneareast.com/index.html

    Initially promises to be a significant resource for
    information and images on the Web. The site, how-
    ever, is top-heavy with marketing pop-ups, and
    usable information is very limited.

Hodgson, William Brown
    "Biographical Sketch of Mohammed Ali,
    Pasha of Egypt, Syria, and Arabia."
    http://www.sunnah.org/history/mhdalip.
    htm

Human Relations Area Files
    http://www.yale.edu/hraf/
    The Human Relations Area Files, Inc. (HRAF) is an
    internationally recognized organization in the field
    of cultural anthropology. The mission of HRAF is to
    encourage and facilitate worldwide comparative
    studies of human behavior, society, and culture.
    Founded in 1949 at Yale University, HRAF is a finan-
    cially autonomous research agency of Yale. HRAF
    produces two major collections (the HRAF Collec-
    tion of Ethnography and the HRAF Collection of
    Archaeology), encyclopedias, and other resources
    for teaching and research.

Institute of Nautical Archaeology
    Bronze Age Shipwreck Excavation at Cape
    Gelidonya, 1960
    http://ina.tamu.edu/capegelidonya.htm

    Bronze Age Shipwreck Excavation at Ulubu-
    run, 1984–1994
    http://ina.tamu.edu/ub_main.htm

Kadesh Barnea (Tell el Qudeirat)
    http://www.deltasinai.com/sinai-01.htm

Killebrew, Ann E., and Daniel Mack
2001   Sea Peoples and the Philistines on the Web
        http://www.courses.psu.edu/cams/
        cams400w_aek11/www/index.htm

Kletter, Raz
2002   "A Very General Archaeologist: Moshe Dayan
        and Israeli Archaeology." *Journal of Hebrew
        Scriptures* vol. 4, article 5. http://www.arts.
        ualberta.ca/JHS/Articles/article_27.pdf

Lane, Edward William
1863   *Arabic-English Lexicon.*
        http://www.studyquran.co.uk/LLhome.htm

Language of Ancient Egypt
        http://www.ancient-egypt.org/index.html

Lawler, Andrew
2007   "Raising Alexandria." *Smithsonian* April.
        http://www.smithsonianmag.com/science-
        nature/alexandria.html

        More than two thousand years after Alexander the
        Great founded the city, archaeologists are discover-
        ing the remains of the Pharaohs' lighthouse, which
        was one of the seven wonders of the ancient world,
        and the remains of Cleopatra's palace.

Lekson, Stephen
2001   "The Legacy of Lewis Binford." *American
        Scientist* (Nov.-Dec).
        http://www.american scientist.org/template/
        BookReviewType Detail/assetid/14411

Lemche, Niels Peter
"Conservative Scholarship—Critical Scholarship of How Did We Get Caught by This Bogus Discussion?" http://www.bibleinterp.com/articles/Conservative_Scholarship.htm.

Lemelek Research Web site
http://www.lmlk.com/research/index.html

Information about, and images of the *lmlk* ("belonging to the king") seal impressions found in and around Jerusalem on fragmented jar handles, which are interpreted as royal stamps referring to rulers of Judah.

Letter of Aristeas
http://www.earlyjewishwritings.com/letteraristeas.html

The Letter of Aristeas describes how Pharaoh Ptolemy Philadelphus (285-247 B.C.E.) commissioned a translation of the Bible into Greek for the library of Alexandria. The high priest Eleazar in Jerusalem chose seventy-two translators, who worked on the Island of Pharos (Egypt) and completed the translation in seventy-two days.

Levant
http://www.art.man.ac.uk/ARTHIST/levant.htm

Levant is the annual of the Council for British Research in the Levant (formerly the British School of Archaeology in Jerusalem and the British Institute at Amman for Archaeology and History). It is a fully refereed journal, devoted primarily to the archaeology of Palestine, Transjordan, Syria, and Lebanon, but the range of cognate disciplines and the geographical coverage are interpreted more widely.

Madaba Map
http://www.christusrex.org/www1/ofm/mad/index.html

Magness, Jodi
Review of Yizhar Hirschfeld, *Qumran in Context: Reassessing the Archaeological Evidence.*" Greater Atlanta Biblical Archaeology Association. http://www.gabaa.net/newsfeed/br_hirsch.htm

Megiddo Expedition
http://megiddo.tau.ac.il/

Microliths
http://www.hf.uio.no/iakh/forskning/sarc/iakh/lithic/microliths.html

Molnár, Zs.
Neutron Activation Analysis http://www.reak.bme.hu/nti/Education/Wigner_Course/WignerManuals/Budapest/NEUTRON_ACTIVATION_ANALYSIS.htm

Archaeologists use Neutron Activation Analysis (NAA) as a quantitative and qualitative method of high efficiency for the precise determination of a number of main-components and trace elements in pottery. NAA, based on the nuclear reaction between neutrons and target nuclei, is a useful method for the simultaneous determination of about 25-30 major, minor, and trace elements of geological, environmental, biological samples.

"Mysteries of the Bible" History Channel
http://www.history.com

The on-going *Mysteries of the Bible* series on the History Channel uses a hot-topics outline. This what-you-always-wanted-to-know-about-archaeology-and-the-Bible-but-were-afraid-to-ask approach starts with the inquiring minds of the television watching public and uses archaeology to both answer and intrigue. The producers promise to reveal to the audience the secrets that the guardians of religious traditions do not want their followers to know.

Nadel, Dani, Ehud Weiss, Orit Simchoni, Alexander Tsatskin, Avinoam Danin, and Mordechai Kislev
2004   "Stone Age Hut in Israel Yields World's Oldest Evidence of Bedding." *Proceedings of the National Academy of Sciences* [PNAS] 101

Bibliography

(April 27): 6821–26. http://www.pnas.org/
cgi/content/full/101/17/6821

Paleolithic houses built by humans have been
excavated in Europe, but none showed designated zones for work, for food preparation, and
for sleeping. Now, however, archaeologists have
recovered houses in a Paleolithic (25,000–10,000
B.C.E.) fishing, hunting, and gathering camp of
Ohalo II on the shore of the Sea of Galilee. The
grass bedding consists of bunches of partially
charred *Puccinellia confer convoluta* stems and
leaves, covered by a thin compact layer of clay. The
bedding is arranged on the floor around a central
hearth clearly identifying the three zones—a
hearth for food preparation and workspace and
beds along the walls.

Near East and Middle East Archaeology
http://www.cyberpursuits.com/archeo/
ne-arch.asp

Near East and Middle East Archaeology is a gateway site for archaeological sites in the ancient Near
East. Beverly Freed, a private Internet contractor,
has assembled Web pages to sites and projects of
specific geographic regions and specific disciplines
such as underwater archaeology. There are pages
that can lead to reference material, academic
departments, libraries, museums, publications,
organizations, and other endeavors. Archaeology grows as a science and continues to add new
disciplines to its roster, such as urban archaeology
and geo-archaeology.

Ohio 5 Foreign Language Technology Project
http://go.owu.edu/%7E05medww/egeria/

Omniglot: Writing Systems & Languages of the
World
2006   http://www.omniglot.com/writing/egyp
tian_demotic.htm

Parsons, Marie
"Giovanni Belzoni: Circus Giant and Collector of Egyptian Antiquities."
http://www.touregypt.net/featurestories/
belzoni.htm

Past: The Newsletter of the Prehistoric Society.
www.ucl.ac.uk/prehistoric/past/past30.html

Petrie Museum
Institute of Archaeology, University College
London.

http://www.petrie.ucl.ac.uk/museum/petrie
.html

The Petrie Museum houses artifacts from Petrie's
excavations in Egypt and Sudan.

Phoenix Data Systems
http://www.phoenixdatasystems.com/

An picture resource for Syria-Palestine, and especially Petra, containing individual images and series
that can be manipulated.

Oriental Institute, University of Chicago, The
Research Archives
http://oilib.uchicago.edu/cgi-bin/opac/o_
search.html

The computer catalogue of the Oriental Institute
Research Archives contains entries for materials
catalogued in the library since 1987 and complete
analytics (essays, articles, and book reviews) for
materials catalogued since 1990. The catalogue
also includes earlier materials, and retrospective
cataloguing of the entire collection will ultimately
make all Research Archives materials accessible. At
present, the Research Archives on-line catalogue
contains well over two hundred thousand entries,
searchable through a library database program.

Renfrew, Colin, and Paul G. Bahn
1996   *Archaeology: Theories, Methods and Practice.*
London: Thames & Hudson. http://www
.thamesandhudsonusa.com/web/archaeology/

Rhodes, Matthew
2006   "History of the Diocese of Egypt and North
Africa." http://www.geocities.com/diocese
ofegypt/history1.html

Saoud, Rabah
2002   "Muslim Architecture under the Abbassid
Patronage (750-892AD)." http://www
.muslimheritage.com/includes/viewResource
.cfm?resourceID=183

Schwimmer, Brian
1995   "Segmentary Lineages." http://umanitoba.ca/
        faculties/arts/anthropology/tutor/descent/
        unilineal/segments.html

Scrolls from the Dead Sea: The Ancient Library of
        Qumran and Modern Scholarship.
        http://www.ibiblio.org/expo/deadsea.scrolls
        .exhibit/intro.html
        Illustrated cyber-exhibit posted by the Library of
        Congress.

Smith, Mahlon H.
        "The Dead Sea Scrolls." Virtual Religion Net-
        work: resources for research and reflection.
        http://virtualreligion.net/iho/qumran.html
        Smith reconstructs a helpful, and remarkably
        detailed, timetable for the discovery and debate of
        the Dead Sea Scrolls.

"Sphinx and the Pyramids: 100 years of American
        Archaeology at Giza."
        http://www.fas.harvard.edu/~semitic/hsm/
        GizaBuiltEgypt.htm

Stanford Encyclopedia of Philosophy, s.v. "Critical
        Theory."
        http://plato.stanford.edu/

Tel El Borg Excavations
        http://tellelborg.org/

Tel Gezer Excavation and Publication Project
        http://www.gezerproject.org/

Tell Arad: Early Bronze Canaanite City and Iron Age
        Israelite Fortress
        http://ebibletools.com/israel/arad/index.html

Texas Beyond History: The Virtual Museum of Texas
        Cultural Heritage.
        The University of Texas at Austin. College of
        Liberal Arts.
        www.texasbeyondhistory.net/.../ gallery.html

Travelers in Egypt
2006   "Entering Inside the Second Pyramid."
        http://www.travellersinegypt.org/
        archives/2006/01/entering_inside_the_
        second_pyr.html

Tutankhamen's Tomb
        http://www.crystalinks.com/tutstomb.html

Underwater Archaeology Glossary
        http://www.abc.se/~pa/uwa/glossary.htm

University of Texas, Department of Anthropology
        http://www.utexas.edu/courses/wilson/
        ant304/projects/projects97/gebhardp/
        gebhardp.html
        Notes on Renfrew and Bahn 1996, 36–39.

Waxman, Sharon
2008   "Loot: The Battle over the Stolen Treasures of
        the Ancient World." New York: Times.
        http://sharonwaxman.typepad.com/loot/
        Waxman, a former New York Times correspondent,
        interviews smugglers, government officials, deal-
        ers, and curators about whether artifacts should be
        moved to countries where they are safe, well cared
        for, and accessible to the greatest number of visi-
        tors, or should remain in their countries of origin.
        Her suggestion is a collaborative middle way.

Wilson, Kevin A.
2004   "The Campaign of Pharaoh Shoshenq I in
        Palestine." http://www.bibleinterp.com/
        articles/Wilson-Campaign_of_Shoshenq
        _I_1.htm
        Wilson argues that Shoshenq's campaign was not
        as widespread as previously thought. Instead, it
        focused only on Jerusalem, and Jerusalem itself
        was not destroyed. This means that archaeologists
        will need to find another method for determin-
        ing the date of tenth-century strata. It also means
        that they will need to find other suspects for
        the destruction layers previously assigned to
        Shoshenq.

Index

Index

Index

Index

Index

Index

Index

Index

Index